TALES FROM THE GIBBET POST: 100 YEARS OF MURDER, RIOT AND EXECUTION IN 18TH CENTURY BRITAIN

Part I (1700-1760)

DANIEL COl

GW00382044

This work was first published as a Kindle e-book in Great Britain in 2013 by Daniel Codd (3rd edition August 2017).

This version was first published by Kindle Direct Publishing in August 2017.

ISBN: 9781549527814

CONTENTS

Chapter 3: THE REIGN OF KING GEORGE I (d.11 June 1727)

ACKNOWLEDGEMENTS

General:

Nicola Stone, for her continual support; Lizzie Myers of Huntstile Organic Farm, North Petherton, Somerset, for her information on Susannah Bruford, the West Monkton murderess; John Harrison, of Speedwell Cavern, Winnats Pass, Peak District, for allowing me to see Clara's saddle; Bob Burn-Murdoch, curator of Norris Museum, St Ives, Cambridgeshire, for helping me with information on Gervase Matcham (part of his gibbet irons are retained by the museum: index no.X.2392, see www.norrismuseum.org.uk); Marilyn Williamson of Leicestershire County Council, for her help with the story of Papillon Hall and the 'Spanish Lady's shoes; Richard Farhall, Rye Town Clerk, Rye Town Council, for helping me with John Breeds' gibbet and skull; Milly Farrell, Acting Curator (Museums & Archives) at the Royal College of Surgeons in Lincoln's Inn Fields, for her assistance re: Jonathan Wild's skeleton. Thanks also to Kevin Moore, CEO, Jamaica Inn: the photo of a 'wrecker' (or shipwreck looter) in farmer's smock and of the Abbey Burn Foot murder victim's skull are used with the kind permission of the Jamaica Inn Daphne du Maurier/Smuggler's Museum, Bodmin Moor (www.Jamaicainn.co.uk/museum).

Photos and illustrations:

Many thanks must go to Natalie Costaras of Wellcome Images, 183 Euston Road, London NW1 2BE for her helpful information regarding the illustrating of this work. (Please see their website Images.wellcome.ac.uk for more information on this collection of images on all themes.) Many thanks also to Jeremy Smith, Assistant Librarian, City of London, London Metropolitan Archives (www.cityoflondon.gov.uk/lma) for allowing me to use the image entitled, 'The attack on Newgate Prison'. This image is catalogue no. q8038812 and can be found along with many other images of the time on the Collage website (collage@cityoflondon.gov.uk). Photo of Epping Forest is copyright of Malc McDonald/www.Geograph.co.uk. The help of Bob Embleton is greatly appreciated, in allowing me to use his photo to illustrate the Berrow murders; also Colin Smith, for kindly providing the Inkpen gibbet photo; Ron Strutt for his help with the Battle of Goudhurst (photo of Goudhurst is copyright Ron Strutt/Geograph). Thanks also to Adelaide (Maria) Hill of Shutterstock Inc, 60 Broad Street, 30th Floor, New York 10004 for answering my questions concerning use of images in this work. Photograph of Arthur's Seat, Edinburgh, and Culloden Battlefield are courtesy of Brendan Howard/shutterstock.com; St Mary's Church, Rye, is courtesy of Jorisvo/shutterstock.com; Old Bailey, London, is courtesy of Anibal Trejo/shutterstock.com; Dover Castle is courtesy of Filip Fuxa/shutterstock.com (www.shutterstock.com). Photograph of Hounslow Heath is copyright of Ian Yarham (many thanks for your help).

Photograph of Maidstone is used courtesy of Danny Robinson. Photograph of Fishguard is the copyright of Ceridwen, and used with her kind permission. Photo of the Sailor's Stone, Hindhead, is copyright of Peter Trimming (many thanks). Early depictions of College Green, Bristol, and Clifton Down are used courtesy of Mr Philip S Evans of www.oldukphotos.com. Photograph of Inchdrewer Castle is used courtesy of copyright owner Richard Paxman/Geograph. Photo of Bishopsgate is reproduced courtesy of John Winfield/Geograph. Both photos of the New Drop gallows in Rutland County Museum, Oakham, are used with the kind permission of Rutland County Council (www.rutland.gov.uk/museum). Thanks to Robert Clayton for arranging this. Early depiction of Preston used with the kind permission of Lancashire Record Office, LCC, Preston PR1 2RE (Dorothy MacLeod). Photograph of Execution Dock at Wapping is copyright of Fin Fahay and used under the Wikipedia Creative Commons License: http://creativecommons.org/licenses/by-sa/2.5/deed.en. Photo of Thames/Wapping ('Battleground London') used courtesy of O Teather. All other photographs are copyright Daniel Codd unless stated otherwise. The original sources of all pictorial images (which are public domain illustrations reproduced from various archive works in this author's collection) are noted in the text, with the exception of (1) Sarah Malcolm and (2) 'A duel won and lost', which are copyright of Daniel Codd.
Sources:
    Many thanks also must go to Liam Kelly at The British Newspaper Archive Support Team for his assistance in answering my queries regarding permission to use the archive website. Although the content of this book is fully drawn from a vast amalgamation of contemporary periodicals, journals, diaries, pamphlets, news-sheets, trial records, works on law and legal oddities, archive history books and archive works on local history and folklore, the British Newspaper Archive can and does provide an excellent field for starting one's research, and their website can be found at www.britishnewspaperarchive.co.uk. In particular I would also like to thank the Lancashire Record Office, Lancashire Central Library, Northampton Central Library, Lincoln Archives and Lincoln Central Library for allowing me access to archive material during the course of my research throughout the years.

    The authors of this work thought long and hard about the best way of sourcing *Tales from the Gibbet Post* and came to the conclusion that to reference every quote and detail might end up doubling the size of the work. The question also becomes one of 'which source to quote', since the more one delves the more it becomes something of a redundant exercise: it is clear that the London and provincial newspapers, and the periodicals of the day, swapped and reported each other's stories among themselves as a matter of routine. This is not to mention the endless array of later literature – including the *Newgate Calendar* in its various guises – that also drew on these earlier reports. Therefore some sources are incorporated into the text, but the reader must also take any un-sourced quotes as being verbatim from the news literature of the day. In short, this book is the culmination of many years' worth of research, gratefully aided and fleshed out with the assistance of those mentioned above, plus many others. With this last in mind I would also like to thank the kindness and generosity the authors have been shown at scores of libraries, museums and tourist attractions, large and small, across Britain throughout this journey of exploration; for within such places lie the half-hidden origins of books like this.

FOREWORD

This work is a catalogue of, and reflection on, the early 18th century's worst murderers and their horrific crimes: a 60-year story chronicling the most appalling excesses of violence, cruelty, massacre and riot to stain Britain's reputation throughout the reigns of four monarchs.

Fundamentally, this work is born out of three observations. The first is that a great number of works concentrating on real-life crime largely tend to ignore (or so it appears) examples concerning the 18th century, for the most part focussing on Jack the Ripper and beyond; this is quite natural, since the Victorian, Edwardian and second Elizabethan eras are the ones with which we can more familiarly identify. And of course, the more recent the crime, the more fascinating it can be in the context of one's own generation.

However, with the exception of a few classic cases from the 1700s – Richard Turpin, Sarah Malcolm, Catherine Hayes, Elizabeth Brownrigg –the 18th century for the most part is an era almost *too* far back for us to identify with on *any* level, in terms of society, punishment and politics…although of course there will always be a fascination with the activities of highwaymen, pirates and smugglers. The era is, in fact, of more interest to *historians* than to criminologists: for it harks back to a time when the police force as we understand it was non-existent, gibbeting the corpses of executed criminals was normal, and duelling to preserve one's honour was an occurrence so frequent it was barely noteworthy. These concepts are things of a time past, that have very little relevance to the Britain of today, other than to excite the interest of social historians; the era can be – to some – difficult to identify with. It is also clear that, besides a handful of exceptions, criminologists might feel that the 18th century produced very little to offer by way of interest: for the vast majority of murder cases during the era were born out of the motives of robbery or rage. It is extraordinary to observe (contradictorily) the remarkably commonplace nature of the circumstances that led to so many murders throughout the 18th century.

Tempering this, however, a second observation might be made: that these murder cases, complete with their primitive police mechanics and inadequate reporting, form the backdrop to the society that we have gradually developed into over the last couple of centuries. Not exclusively, of course; but they do provide interesting pointers to the direction Britain was heading in. And if one *did* so wish to understand what life was like in a previous era, in order to see how we came about our present lot, one can do little better than study the sensational crimes of that time. These often provide the best understanding of the day-to-day social, economic, religious and political circumstances that the people of the time lived in, and as such anyone wishing to understand *any* era ought to study the great murder trials of the time. In the case of the 18th century, its murder cases and trials highlight the squalid, precarious and violence-driven lives that many people lived. And despite the commonplace *motives* behind some of the cases recounted in this work, many of the murders herein provide incidental details of real-life soap opera that almost beggar belief. Added to this, even the casual researcher will very quickly observe the runaway murder rates during this period, and the frighteningly high levels of infanticide, housebreaking and lethal street robbery. Put simply, looking at the great crimes of the 18th century might illustrate to some how far we have come in our approach to law and order.

The grounding for this work is also in no small part born out of a third (personal) observation by this author, concerning a time when I was researching a number of books on the supernatural in places as diverse as the English East Midlands, Cambridgeshire, Somerset, Bristol, Lancashire and Devon. I found that many 'ghost stories' were woven around 18th century murders that had imprinted themselves on the collective memory of a local community; but in time I came to understand that the actual *details* of the crime concerned were in many ways more fascinating than the attendant folklore, painting as they did a picture of a time long past when our grandfather's grandfathers were still several generations from being born.

However, it is with folklore in mind that we begin our study of murder in the 1700s; for first of all we consider the following cases - if only to understand how oral tradition saw in the 18th century an era of casual violence and roadside executions suitable for weaving stories of the supernatural around. Many a ghostly tale was built on the foundation of a *real life* 18th century murder case, either in contemporary print or some years afterwards; but many a well-known ghostly anecdote appears to be born out of a largely *fictional* murder too. It is almost as if the 18th century crime rate *lent* itself to ghost stories that had a foundation in an act of impulsive violence. Some typical examples of this are as follows, with possible origins of the crime concerned suggested where applicable.

One well-known story concerns Longleat House, the famous Elizabethan country house west of Warminster in Wiltshire. This historic stately home, enshrouded by woodland and famous for its park, was (supposedly) the scene of murder some time in the early 18th century when inhabited by Thomas Thynne, 2nd Viscount Weymouth, and his second wife, Louisa, the daughter of Earl John Carteret of Granville. Apparently, Lady Louisa took a lover, who disguised himself as a footman, until at length their liaison was discovered by Lord Weymouth; both men fought a duel for her hand, which Weymouth won when he killed the young man stone dead in front of Lady Louisa. *Life* (28 December 1953) was one of scores of publications that repeated this legend down the decades: 'But you remember that (Louisa's) husband suddenly left Longleat, giving no reason for his departure, and went to live in a small house in the village. And many years after her husband's death, a body was found buried beneath the paving-stones of the cellar: the body of an unknown youth wearing the same sort of boots as were worn at the time that the second Viscount Weymouth lived at Longleat.' Weymouth died in 1741, meaning that the duel – if it ever actually happened – must have occurred at some point during the previous 12 years, for 1729 was the year his *first* wife passed away. Suffice to say that Lady Louisa's 'ghost' is believed to have haunted Longleat for many a year now.

Any in-depth look at murder in the 18th century needs to get past folkloric tales like this, but for our purposes they are useful; for these yarns are the ones most likely to be commonly repeated, with the ghost story just as often likely added as a dramatic 'punch line'. It might even be entertained that stories of this nature bear the *stamp* of possibility; for (as we shall come to find out) many *genuine* cases of the era can be seen to have occurred under similar circumstances.

Before we move on, a number of other folkloric cases might be interesting to consider, in view of their details - since they illustrate how future generations came to behold the 18th century and its criminality problem.

In the East Anglian county of Norfolk, it was probably the notorious enmity between Britain's first 'prime minister' Sir Robert Walpole and his brother-in-law (and fellow Whig statesman) Charles, Viscount Townshend, that bred the rumour that Dorothy Walpole was done away with.

Dorothy was Sir Robert's sister, and the siblings were raised at Houghton Hall, Norfolk. According to the story, their father (also a Member of Parliament, and also called Robert) became guardian to the young Charles Townshend of Raynham Hall when the boy was 13. As Charles and Dorothy grew up together they fell in love but were denied permission to marry by Dorothy's father, who believed their relationship was unsuitable; he also did not wish to be thought of as seeking the Townshend family fortune.

In 1713, however, the pair *did* marry, upon the death of Charles' first wife, and for a while the childhood sweethearts were very happy. Unfortunately their situation degenerated when Dorothy's clandestine past in Paris caught up with her, and Charles – enraged and heartbroken – allegedly took to confining Dorothy in her chambers at Raynham Hall, near Fakenham in Norfolk. This unhappy domestic situation was not helped by Sir Robert's Walpole's burgeoning hatred of Charles, who - although his brother-in-law and a cabinet minister - could not bear the man at times.

The relationship between the two men worsened following Dorothy's death aged 40 on 29 March 1726. Officially, the cause was smallpox, but local gossip claimed that she was *pushed* from atop Raynham's grand staircase by her husband, and that this act contributed to her death. According to some, she was found at the foot of the stair with a broken neck. It is unclear how much of this was common parlance at the time; the story may have developed in the first part of the 19th century as an explanation for the allegations of a 'ghost' that allegedly inhabited Raynham Hall (see *Country Life*, December 1936). The earliest folklore, such as that outlined in the *Reading Mercury* (19 September 1885), simply states: 'Lady Dorothy Walpole, who married Charles, Lord *Townsend*…after an unhappy life died *rather mysteriously.*'

The driveway to Raynham Hall: there is an (unsubstantiated) story that the prime minister's sister met with foul play here.

However, although the folklore of Dorothy's demise at least had a basis in *fact* – insomuch that she died relatively young and the Walpole/Townshend relationship was acrimonious at times – some 18th century crimes appear to be outright fabrication. One of Kent's most famous sea yarns tells of a three-masted schooner destined to reappear every 50 years following its original destruction on the treacherous Goodwin Sands, a ten-mile long sand bank five miles off the coast of Deal. The schooner, according to a plausible-sounding legend, was deliberately driven onto the Sands by the first mate, John Rivers, on 13 February 1724. Rivers had become insane with jealousy upon the wedding of his captain, Simon Reed (or Peel), to a woman called Annette, with whom he was also in love. According to the famous tale, Rivers first fatally shot his captain and then deliberately drove the schooner onto the Goodwins, where it disintegrated with the loss of life of all on board, including Rivers, Annette and the entire wedding party. The schooner was called the *Lady Lovibund* (although there are various spellings), and although the story is endlessly recycled in books on 'true' ghost stories, it appears to date no earlier than 1924: the first references to the story are in *Notes & Queries Volume 157* (1929), citing the *Daily Chronicle* (14 February 1924). From the point of view of the researcher, this is a little disappointing: for if the story were true, it would have presented a crime of a type unique in British history. However, the more one thinks about it, the more unlikely the incident becomes: how, for example, could the sequence of events be known if the schooner was destroyed and all the actors in the drama killed? Even as far back as 1929 *Notes & Queries* was questioning this story, yet nonetheless it refuses to go away. At best it appears that the story of the *Lady Lovibund* might be founded on an old folk tale; more likely, the story is a total invention based on nothing more than the observation that some fourteen ships per annum were being wrecked on the Goodwins by the mid-1800s. The nearest this author can find to an *actual* event of this nature concerns reports in May 1721 that several of Lord Polwarth's servants, coming from Copenhagen, were lost (together with his lordship's expensive baggage) upon the Goodwin Sands. Some news-sheets, citing a Mr King's letter in the *St James's Evening Post* (01 June 1721), reported: 'Some give out, that the Lord Polwarth's servants were murdered by the seamen, who would have run the ship *ashoar*, but striking on the Goodwin Sands, they all perished.' Later reports, drawing upon *Stanley's Newsletter* (13 June 1721) suggested that the ship had in fact struck the *Gunfleet* Sands, off Clacton-on-Sea, however; either way, it appeared a serious crime had occurred. The reports make it clear Lord Polwarth's ship carried valuable plate and linen, and it was believed the crew had steered the vessel onto the Sands deliberately. Other persons who came in boats under the pretence of giving assistance turned out to be smugglers, or pirates, and they proceeded to slaughter all of Lord Polwarth's servants, as well as three Danish passengers. For good measure they also sacrificed one of their own comrades and then escaped; and when Lord Polwarth got wind of this outrage he offered a £100 reward for the capture of the criminals. Although it is not clear, it seems the massacre might have come to light only because *one* dead crewmember was found in the scuttled vessel, suggesting the others were part of a conspiracy.

Two killings that allegedly occurred at Carshalton House are also dubious as history. Standing in wooded grounds at the west end of the old village, Carshalton House was the parish's principal mansion and seat of a residence built by the celebrated Dr John Radcliffe in Surrey. Radcliffe was in his time a remarkable man: a politician, a physician to royalty and the founder of the Radcliffe Library in Oxford. His notoriously blunt personality and eccentricities are perhaps the basis for the following story, the first part of which, at least, appears to be true.

Some accounts suggest Radcliffe was sent for by order of council during the time of Queen Anne's final illness and decline, but he refused to journey to the capital to assist her: as an explanation he 'said he had taken physic'. Because of this, Radcliffe apparently became the focus of much popular resentment, and professed to having received letters that he would be 'pulled to pieces' if he ever came to London. Radcliffe died aged 64 on 1 November 1714 through, it was said, his dread of being murdered and for want of company in his countryside retreat. Folklore insists that when the envoy from Queen Anne arrived at Carshalton with the order that Dr Radcliffe must travel to court, Radcliffe flatly refused. An unseemly scuffle between the doctor and the messenger was the result, with the envoy crashing down the staircase and breaking his neck. In all probability Radcliffe would have been too ill himself with the gout (the same complaint that tortured her majesty) to battle the messenger.

Carshalton was afterwards purchased by Sir John Fellowes, sub-governor of the South Sea Company, on whose instructions it was rebuilt. Folklore tells us that a few years after his purchase Fellowes supposedly had a fight with a tax collector on the mansion's first floor landing, knocking the man over the balustrade with fatal results. Sir John died at the house on 26 July 1724 at the age of 54. Again, there is nothing in the contemporary literature to suggest this event *actually* ever happened; but these fatalities at Carshalton are nowadays suggested as the likely explanation for 'ghosts' reportedly seen at the grand old house.

Perhaps the most intriguing observation of this place is that made in *A Topographical History of Surrey* by E W Brayley (1841). During Fellowes' time, 'In levelling the ground to make an avenue, many bones, supposed to be human, were found.' Little more are we told of this, and although it is likely the workmen unearthed some prehistoric deposit, perhaps in the common mind the find indicated something a little more sinister – especially given Radcliffe's position as a foremost doctor in an era when body-snatching for anatomy and dissection was a widespread problem.

This observation is made on the basis that recent investigations suggest two of the era's pioneering apothecaries were not merely engaged in body-snatching, but also in wholesale serial killing to obtain corpses for anatomical experiments and studies on pregnancy. As reported in the *Observer* (7 February 2010) and elsewhere, citing recent research published by the *Journal of the Royal Society of Medicine*, William Hunter and William Smellie, the founding fathers of obstetrics, might have been responsible for the murders of dozens of pregnant women in and around London between 1749 and 1755. Utilizing henchmen, it has been speculated the killings were born out of a professional rivalry between the two men, who each wished to be dignified with the title of the foremost childbirth doctor of the age. The claims were reinforced by the fact that *natural* deaths of heavily pregnant women were comparatively rare in the capital, and London was a city at times in such a state of near-anarchy that it was entirely possible for people to be forcibly 'disappeared'. According to the article, by 1755 questions were being asked as to where the constant supply of bodies was coming from that fed their research, and at this point the supply slackened off, the two men perhaps being shielded from further investigation by their eminent positions and an official unwillingness to delve further. Whether this is what was happening can never be proved *absolutely*, but without question the era we are about to consider could easily have provided the backdrop for such an outrage. That people might be murdered for the purposes of dissection and anatomical research is clear from a letter to the *Newcastle Courant* (13 March 1742) which reported that 'last Tuesday' a corpse was found in the residence of a surgeon near the Netherbow, Edinburgh. The mob formed the opinion the man had been deliberately murdered – an observation apparently based upon the state of the clothes he wore. The mob began attacking the 'Surgeons shops', growing in number and drunkenness, and threatening a pitched battle with the 'Magistrates, Officers, Town and Canongate Guards'.

One of the most notorious criminals of the age – Sweeney Todd, the 'Demon Barber of Fleet Street' – can also be considered mythical, although there are some scholars and folklorists that like to propagate the legend as being *based* on fact. Long a feature of morbid Victorian 'penny dreadfuls' (and later a musical), the original story called '*Sweeney Todd; or, the String of Pearls*' (1843) related how a certain barber in Fleet Street, London, had cut the throats of his customers and then sunk them down a trap into a kitchen. Here they were made into - and sold as - mutton pies by one Mrs Lovett, a neighbouring acquaintance of Todd's. This supposedly happened in the later years of George III's reign, with Todd meeting his end on the gallows at Tyburn in 1802. The story was apparently well known by Dickens' time, for in *The Life and Adventures of Martin Chuzzlewit* (1844) one character remarks: 'He'll begin to be afraid I have strayed into one of those streets where the countrymen are murdered; and that I have been made *meat pies*, or some such horrible thing…'

By 1878, when *Sweeny* Todd's case was discussed in *Notes and Queries* in articles entitled 'An old Cockney Tradition', it was clear the infamous barber was part of London folklore. One contributor asserted that: '…the lower classes of London believe in the substantial truth of this story. I can trace this credulity back (by report, of course) for at least seventy years. It is never recounted without the addition that the shaver was at last detected, convicted and suffered at Tyburn.' However, the contributor made it clear that he could find nothing in the literature of the period that confirmed the case, and the same is still true today: we have no *conclusive* proof that Sweeney Todd ever existed, although this author is always open to arguments that Todd was a real, historical figure. According to a recent, realistic retelling of the gruesome tale, the lack of trial or execution records is accounted for by the supposition that Todd – being a barber – asked for a razor so that he might shave himself before his execution, and so slit his own throat in his cell at Newgate. This plausible scenario is depicted in the 2006 film *Sweeney Todd*, where the demonic barber is portrayed by actor Ray Winstone; but until proof is forthcoming then Sweeney Todd must be classed as a bogeyman figure, an urban legend, or at best a composite of other criminals. Perhaps the genesis of the tale is in an event reported in October 1753 in the *Gentleman's Magazine* concerning the arrest of an apprentice baker called Holmes in London. Holmes' disappearance from his apprenticeship in Lincolnshire had caused his employer to be accused of murdering the missing lad and baking him in the oven. The rumours had caused the baker to lose much business, and he was threatened with a prosecution for murder. There is also an *actual* account of a killer barber in *Dodsley's Annual Register*: this tells us how, in December 1784, a journeyman barber killed a drunken young customer at his establishment near Hyde Park Corner, cutting the man's throat after surmising he had taken liberties with his wife. The (unnamed) murderer immediately fled. Another similar incident was reported in the *Gentleman's Magazine*, concerning the case of a master barber, Thomas Wise; being frustrated in his advances towards a Worcester servant girl, he went to her master's house on 15 November 1758 and cut her throat from ear to ear with a razor, before doing the same to himself. A coroner's jury brought in a verdict of wilful murder against Wise, and his corpse was 'buried under the gallows in a most ignominious manner'.

From Reading, Berkshire, there is a strange legend of a kind of Bluebeard. In 1857 one Henry T Riley contacted *Notes & Queries* with this snippet of local lore: '*Query relative to Mr Herby*.- About the middle of the last century (i.e. mid-1700s), a person of this name resided in the vicinity of Reading. There was considerable mystery attached to him; and it was generally said that he had a plurality of wives. He suddenly disappeared, and his wives were found murdered. Can any of your readers say if the mystery was solved? And if it was ever discovered who he really was?'

This author cannot find any more on this intriguing anecdote, and it appears to be folklore; for where the story stems from is wholly unclear. But perhaps the most outrageous tale of these times is the immense scale of mass murder suggested in a 1789 pamphlet to have been perpetrated by John Gregg and his family in coastal Devonshire. This reported that Gregg's gang 'took up their abode in a cave near to the sea-side, in Chovaley (Clovelly), in Devonshire, where they liv'd twenty-five years without so much as once going to visit any city, or town; they robbed above one thousand persons, and murdered and *eat* all whom they robbed: at last they were happily discover'd by a pack of blood-hounds, and John Gregg, his wife, eight sons, six daughters, eighteen grandsons, and fourteen grand-daughters, were all seized and executed by being cast alive into three fires, and were burnt.' This supposedly occurred *c.*1740, and that such atrocity could continue on such a scale undiscovered for so long is, to put it mildly, unlikely; it is now speculated that the case is either a massively misremembered report of a real incident or, more likely, a story that began with smuggling gangs desirous of keeping nosey locals away from the cliffs and caves for fear of meeting Gregg's 'ghost'.

Clovelly Bay, Devon: reputedly the haunt of an inbred tribe of cannibals called Gregg in the 18th century. The story is fanciful in the extreme, but the legend lingers on.

Such stories as these do make it a little difficult for the researcher, for there is often much legend and lore to wade through. The point of referring to these kind of folkloric crimes in this foreword is to illustrate that, although there is nothing to substantiate them other than local storytelling and probable invention, the fact remains that these crimes could *easily* have occurred in the way we are led to believe, in the era we are now about to consider. Dismissing certain crimes from the 18th century as folklore may seem like a curious starting point, but the very *real* and documented murder cases from this period display dimensions of cruelty, calculation, barbarism, degeneracy and randomness worthy of any folk tale; and the whole is made all the more disturbing when taken into account with the brutal punishments inflicted, and the shocking, detached behaviour of the mob.

For this was a time when pity and sympathy were strange and valuable emotions, ones that huge sections of society simply had no comprehension of; although occasionally a certain human drama might stir the consciences of some deep thinkers. Such a case occurred on 18 April 1732, when 'the necessity of my affairs' led Mr Richard Smith *and* his wife Bridget to commit suicide by hanging themselves in their chamber. Smith was a book binder 'and prisoner for debt within the liberties of the King's Bench': when he and his wife were found they were both stretched by their necks two yards apart from each other. A curtain was drawn between them, indicating they had not wished to see each other die. Mrs Smith was some eight months pregnant: but worse than this, their appalling circumstances had first led Smith to put a pistol to his 2-year-old child's head and fire while it lay in the cradle, killing it instantly. Smith left numerous final notes to his relatives and acquaintances, one of which speaks to the family's pathetic and harrowing situation: 'I have a suit of black clothes at the Cock, in Mint-street, which lies for 7 shillings and sixpence. If you can find any chap for my dog and *antient* cat, it would be kind. I have here sent a shilling for the porter.' Mr Smith was clearly a sensitive man – his concern for the welfare of his pet dog and cat illustrates this. Nor was he a *natural* murderer: his environment in the capital appears to have driven him to desperation.

This tragic murder was reported in the *Gentleman's Magazine* at the time, and elsewhere. But cases like this – with their humanitarian element – do not seem to have cropped up very often though, and when they did they swept under the radar of the vast majority of the hardened and illiterate London populace. Contradictorily, *genuine* remorse among convicted felons was a frequent detail of many scaffold confessions. However, such remorse was more an attempt to avoid the gibbet and earn a Christian burial; many criminals were certainly not God-fearing enough to have prevented them from committing the act in the first place. And although poverty and desperation were undoubtedly the factors behind many murders, it may be observed equally that many were also born out of drunkenness, bravado, an almost ridiculous blindness to punishment when in a state of rage, and, in some cases, a Mafia-like existence in organised crime that for some was a way of life.

This was also a time when every murder was 'cruel and barbarous', or 'inhuman' and 'shocking'…although the flowery language of the fledgling newspapers, periodicals and pamphlets (littered with their inconsistent use of punctuation and capital lettering) existed only to lure the attention of the reader. It is unlikely that most crimes of violence 'shocked' the public at large, particularly so in the capital where stomachs were strong and death was everywhere. Although crime was a societal problem, it was perhaps seen *only* in the faceless context of such, like the threat of a foreign invasion or rumours of a Jacobite plot. In most cases, particularly in the first half of the 18th century, the individual robbery, or death of a newly born child found slain by the roadside, prompted little excitement. It was merely another 'incident', symptomatic of the times in a world where many knew no better. Some of the contemporary periodicals certainly present the most brutal of murders and crimes in this manner at any rate, being casually light on their detail as they are.

In this work, which by and large draws upon original archive sources, certain crimes – such as the robberies that frequently ended in murder, or the tavern brawls that ended in a drunken duel – are only illustrated by occasional examples: for some crimes were simply so endemic in nature that it is impossible in a work of this size to include more than a few representative cases. There are many instances where nameless victims were found dead - perhaps floating in the muddy water on the edge of a river for example, or laid on a patch of open heath - which feature little reported detail other than that the body displayed injuries consistent with a murderous attack. The *North Country Journal* (6 March 1736), for instance, told its readers that the 'celebrated' Mrs Anne Dalton was found drowned in the river at Bath, with the coroner bringing in a verdict of 'Wilful Murder' based on the fact that 'her head was cut in a most terrible manner'. This is all we learn; it is not even reported what the nature of Mrs Dalton's celebrity was. But at least this victim's identity was ascertained: so many murder victims appear to have remained unidentified, and their killers never caught.

For the era we are to consider it is clear that each major population centre entertained its own villains, whose deeds have been remembered *locally* down the centuries; for example, it is impossible to pick up and thumb through a book on Oxfordshire history without chancing upon the name of Mary Blandy. Hopefully this work, quite apart from recounting these locally infamous crimes, will also depict for the reader's benefit names and events long forgotten to history.

In terms of sources, it is also perhaps worth pointing out that this work is drawn from a fantastic variety of archive material, much of it contemporary; this includes, of course, the *Newgate Calendar* in its many guises down the years – although it is also worth mentioning that the *Calendar* ignored many of the provincial murder cases and unsolved homicides noted in this particular work. Many of these accounts are drawn from an amalgamation of reports in the *Gentleman's Magazine, Annual Register, London Magazine, Gentleman's*

Monthly Intelligencer, Scots Magazine etc. as well from a variety of contemporary newspapers and later historical literature.

The reader should also remember that much source material from this era can be unreliable, misreported, frustratingly brief or confusingly worded; in some cases certain events even appear to be missing altogether from the media of the time, perhaps accounting for a certain number of crimes that were only referenced many decades later in works by local historians that drew upon the foggy memories of elderly people. That said, the reader can to be assured that each and every story in this compilation has been researched as thoroughly as possible, and as such ought to represent the truest and most accurate picture of what is said to have occurred in each case; that is to say, nothing has been 'invented' and no detail is *assumed*. This is, of course, notwithstanding the author's own observations and conclusions about certain aspects of the subject matter. It is also the authors' hope that they will be forgiven for any slight historical inaccuracy that might have slipped through the net: all that can be said is that each source utilised was considered the most reliable available, and it is hoped this work will serve as a good starting point for anyone wishing to delve further.

A warning also needs to be given concerning dates: until 1752, the Julian calendar was used to record events, but this gradually moved out of phase with the solar year; thus on 3 September the British calendar leapt forward by 11 days so that the following day became 14 September. This brought Britain in line with Europe and the Gregorian calendar, but as usual drunken crowds resenting any kind of authority took to roaming the streets, stoning carriages and allegedly demanding, 'Give us back our 11 days!' (Or more importantly the 11 days wages they felt they had lost.) For the sake of ease, pre-1752 dates within this compilation are those that were recorded in the original source.

Following the English Civil War, the Commonwealth, the Protectorate, the Restoration, the Monmouth Rebellion and the Glorious Revolution, England's internal conflicts appeared to be subsiding by the late 17th century, with her position on the world stage becoming clearer. However, although England, Scotland and Wales, forged into the United Kingdom of Great Britain on 1 May 1707, still had many conflicts to overcome, this is the chronology of a war fought daily in the streets, towns and villages, on the coastlines and along the highways, and in houses and taverns up and down the kingdom: the war on crime, an 'invisible' conflict that defined society in the 18th century and which the government at times almost came close to being overwhelmed by.

These are the stories of the most infamous murders committed across the land during Britain's century-long crime wave.

CHAPTER 1

THE REIGN OF KING WILLIAM III (d.8 March 1702)

INTRODUCTION

The last memory of thousands in the 18th century: the hangman's noose. (This one belongs to Oakham's New Drop gallows, now in Rutland County Museum.)

By the end of the 17th century, these islands were in the grip of a crime wave. Despite the best efforts of Anglican moral puritan organizations, such as the Society for Promoting Christian Knowledge founded by Dr Thomas Bray,

England was a land where rates of robbery and murder were soaring. In the last years of William and Mary, crime had risen to such alarming proportions that the authorities had reacted by imposing ruthless punishments for offences other than treason, murder and highway robbery. For example, a statute enacted as of May 1699 made burglary, housebreaking, and the theft of goods worth more than five shillings from shops, warehouses, coach houses or stables a capital offence. Lethal punishment was also directed at those who ordered such felonies or assisted in them.

Although not representative of the whole nation, to understand what life was like in the capital during the first part of the 18th century forces the historian to step into an alien world: familiar to us now through numerous landmarks such as Westminster, the Thames, St Paul's Cathedral and certain street names, but at the same time entirely different socially. Many of London's districts at the time can realistically be described as dangerous, dirty, disturbing and sometimes semi-anarchic places.

Here, even the higher levels of society wagered in rowdy pits on the outcome of endless boxing bouts, bull baiting, cock fights and dog fights. Adequate lighting and sewerage were non-existent for the vast multitude. The paving was so uneven that each stone wrenched the unwary step aside, while heaps of refuse rendered the crowded roadway an even worse scene of confusion. Upon the advent of a royal procession, faggots had to be thrown into the ruts that criss-crossed the road in order to make their majesty's unpleasant journey marginally more comfortable. For all of London's greatness, all the social pictures of the days of King William III, Queen Anne and the first two Georges illustrate a state of police worse than the days of Elizabeth I, a century and a half earlier. The old salutary terror of the Tudor Star-chamber had been lost, and many common people of the time despised the ordinary administration of justice, or else in their passion paid little heed to any consequence their violent actions might bring upon themselves. London was a prey to daring thieves, hired assassins and loutish young rakes who went about armed and looking for trouble. Quite frequently, a passing jest, a warmly expressed difference of opinion or an accidental push could only be atoned for by drawn swords or pistol shot. Ladies of rank and fortune were sometimes literally abducted and borne forcibly to a wedding ceremony against their will that tied them to a stranger. People walked past bodies lying in the gutter with as little comment as if they were passing a dead animal, preferring not to concern themselves with the question of whether the person was dead drunk, or actually dead.

The capital's watchmen do not appear to have been equipped to deal with serious disorder or violence, and because their vigilance on behalf of the authorities was their prize asset they were treated with no respect by parts of London society. (This illustration originally featured in the historical works of Charles Knight in the 1860s.)

Policing was primitive. The watchmen, who appear to have been called beadles until the accession of Queen Anne, William III's successor, were the regular guardians of order in London and other cities. With their long, many-caped coats, their rattles, and their hourly announcements of the weather and the time of night, they today present a picturesque feature of the past. They stood sentry in watch-boxes too, tiny, primitive police stations: but for the most part the watchmen of the capital had a reputation among the drunken louts as timid, infirm and elderly men, who would shut themselves in their boxes when brawls erupted in the dark streets. Parish constables did their bit, but they were more akin to a civilian defence force, being neither paid nor working full time. Professional thief takers were employed by the government in want of a *true* police force as we would understand the term. However, these were often (by necessity) of a criminal background themselves, sometimes corrupt and driven by the bounties and rewards promised by either the government or crime victims, rather than by their principles. Civil disturbances were quelled by the military, and it was often found needful to employ dragoons to patrol the heaths and common land outside London as a safeguard against highwaymen and footpads – who were simply scared away somewhere else by the institution of these mounted patrols.

The capital boasted two of the most notorious landmarks in the country, highly visible places that struck terror and loathing into the hearts of the common people. Newgate Prison, a monstrous fortification of a place that loomed on (what is now) the corner of Newgate Street and Old Bailey, was a gaol for felons and debtors appertaining to the City of London and wider county of Middlesex. Medieval in its origins, it appears to have at first been sufficiently large for the necessities of the city and the shire; certainly no attempt was made to enlarge it in 1672 when the gate was rebuilt. However, by the 18th century it is clear that this grim fortress had become wholly unfit for purpose: badly ventilated, ill supplied with water and crowded throughout the year, it was seldom free from disease, and a mere spell within its walls could be a death sentence in itself. Nor was it escape-proof, as the celebrated career criminal Jack Sheppard proved more than once. This structure would not be pulled down until 1904. Other places of incarceration became known as 'bridewells' on account of Bridewell Palace - a former residence of King Henry VIII on the banks of the Fleet – which had fallen from such heights that it was by the 1700s a poorhouse and gaol.

Part of the present Old Bailey (Central Criminal Court) stands on the site of the medieval Newgate gaol.

Tyburn (variously known as Tyburn Gallows, Tyburn Tree, or Deadly Never Green) was the principal place of public execution for criminals convicted in Middlesex, the ancient county containing the metropolitan City of London. Tyburn had existed since at least the reign of King Henry VI, and derived its name from Tyburn Brook, which rose near Hampstead. Tyburn, originally *Teyborne*, appears to have been so named because of the nearby *bornes* and springs, and the tying up of men there; however, others believed that *Tieburne* derived from the Lollards, for whom this instrument of death was originally set up. Lollards, according to popular belief, had their necks *tied* to the beam and their lower parts *burnt* in the fire.

The structure was horizontally triangular in plan, standing on three truly immense sturdy legs, allowing it to accommodate numerous dangling victims at once; thus it provided a grim and obvious reminder to the frequently restive and sometimes rebellious population of the capital. The occasion of an execution generally mirrored a public festival; if a criminal or traitor was particularly notorious, thousands might turn out to watch them dance the 'Tyburn jig'. A brave exit might be boisterously applauded by the mob; a display of cowardice or weakness ensured the felon a poor place in the folk memory of Londoners. The structure appears to have been a permanent landmark, and Peter Cunningham's *Handbook of London; Past and Present Volume 1* (1850) tells us: 'It stood, as I believe, on the site of Connaught-place, though No.49, Connaught-square is said to be the spot.'

Site of Tyburn Tree, at the junction of Edgware Road, Marble Arch and Oxford Street.

However, although Tyburn was the most notorious place of common execution in the metropolis, every assize town across the land had a comparative location, often just outside the town walls, where the dangling bodies of convicted felons greeted any traveller arriving at the city gates. These too might often be referred to as 'Tyburn' by the populace of that locale.

By the dawn of the new century many a country view across the nation in general was already spoiled by the grim and sinister sight of a rotting human carcass encased in a metal cage that hung from a wooden beam, or sturdy oak. This was a practice followed throughout the 18th century, occurring post-execution and known as 'gibbeting', the gibbet frequently being situated as near as possible to the location of the encased subject's crime. Gibbeting was described in the *Gentleman's Magazine* in 1789 as still teaching criminals a valuable lesson, even as the century we are about to explore was drawing to a close; for a contributor describes the practice as: '...the hanging of a notorious criminal in irons, as a public and lasting spectacle, after he has suffered death *in* the gallows, for the purpose of example, and deterring of others from the commission of the like heinous offence. A design truly benevolent and laudable.' Despite the gibbet's 'laudability' it does not, however, seem to have had quite the desired effect, even despite its greater threat of denying the condemned criminal a Christian burial. For when this gruesome *post mortem* fate was combined with that of a sure execution, it frequently only encouraged the criminal to slay his victim in order to avoid being identified in the future. This ghoulish punishment was also known as 'hanging in chains', and afterwards the corpse of the offender might be seen suspended by the roadside for years, or even decades - sometimes until the body presented nothing more than a wind-bleached skeleton and the original circumstances of the crime had been long forgotten. Occasionally the gibbet post bore its grisly burden until the beam collapsed in strong winds, or the contraption simply fell apart through the ravages of time.

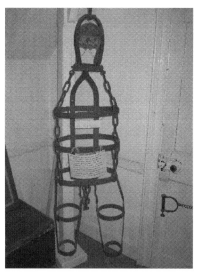

A gibbet cage in Rye Town Hall, the final suit of assassin John Breeds.

Although King William III saw but three years of the new century, two crimes that occurred during these early days serve as an indicator of the times, but for different reasons.

The first concerns a stark reminder of the superstition that still gripped parts of the kingdom.

THE MURDER OF A 'WITCH'

An incident of *c*.8 January 1700 indicates just how frighteningly quickly things could get out of control when a community was inflamed and agitated.

The crowd had taken to 'learnedly debating' a prolonged argument between a young watchmaker's apprentice and an old woman, Amey Townsend, in St Albans, Hertfordshire, and many had come to the conclusion she had bewitched him. This controversy had followed a violent altercation between Amey and the boy during which he had physically attacked her in an attempt to 'blood her', accusing Amey of being a witch. (Scratching, or 'blooding', a witch was held to deprive them of their power.) It was while the injured woman sought assistance for these vicious scratches that the rabble began to close in around her. Their fear inflamed, they proceeded to drag the poor old woman through a river near the town a number of times before losing interest and dumping her at her home, drenched and half-dead from hypothermia.

However, driven by rumours that some had seen her bob like a cork and not sink, the crowd subsequently reassembled, dragged the old woman out of her convalescent bed and hoisted her above their heads in a chair, whence they proceeded to parade her around St Albans shouting, 'A Townsend! A Townsend!'

Finally the mob thrust her before a Justice of the Peace. In order to placate them he had her imprisoned in the town-house, where she shortly thereafter died of her mistreatment some two hours later.

It was reported at the time in the *Post Boy*: 'And we hear that several are taken up to answer for it at the next assizes for Hertfordshire, where (there is) no question but that some of them will decently swing for it.'

'KNOCK'D OUT HIS BRAINS'

A second example of mob behaviour concerns a remarkable sequence of events reported from Denbigh, south of Prestatyn, in September 1701. A young woman had been hanged following her conviction for murdering her bastard child. But as she was being carried away to be interred, she put her head out of the coffin and all present realised she was still alive.

At this, the hangman ordered the whole cortege to turn around, back to the place of execution, so as to string her up again; but the mob attacked him, 'knock'd out his brains, and rescu'd the woman'. This is a curious example of the mob defending a member of their own community at the expense of the fatally injured executioner, who, it must be remembered, was a representative of the authorities. Thus, such an act was in open defiance of the rule of law, and is an illustration of how certain situations could be entirely unpredictable in the way that they played out.

The story was reported in a monthly periodical, the *Post Angel*.

MURDER AT THE DUTCHMAN'S INN

One of the century's first murder cases to cause a stir concerned Michael van Berghen and his wife Catherine. The van Berghens had come to Britain from the Netherlands; by 1700 they were keeping a public house in East Smithfield, London, together with one Geraldius Dromelius, who acted as their servant.

By chance, a country gentleman named Oliver Norris, who lodged at an inn near Aldgate, ended up in their tavern at around 8 o'clock one night and proceeded to drink for three hours. By 11 o'clock he was too intoxicated to walk and so ordered the maidservant to call a coach to take him home.

Mrs van Berghen had already observed that the man appeared particularly well-to-do, and was desirous of keeping Norris at her establishment. To this end, she told the maid to inform Norris that a coach could not be procured. This was done, and so Norris opted to try and walk home by himself. However, he had not got far before he realised he was missing a purse containing a significant sum of money, and in a rage he returned to the van Berghen's inn where he accused them of stealing from him.

The crime occurred under the following circumstances, it was later judged. Van Berghen and his wife threatened to throw Norris out but he stoutly refused to budge, placing himself in an apartment where the tablecloth was laid for supper. Dromelius, the servant, suddenly entered the room: he began arguing with the gentlemen and insults were hurled from both sides. As the quarrel grew more heated, van Berghen grabbed a poker and forcefully dashed Mr Norris on the head with it, striking him so violently that it fractured his skull. Dromelius then proceeded to cut the victim's throat - and with Norris still warm on the floor he was quickly stripped entirely naked by the two men. The servant then knifed the incapacitated Norris several more times in different parts of his body. Mrs van Berghen was by this point also present in the room.

Van Berghen and Dromelius dragged their victim's body through the dismal, unlit back alleys to a ditch that communicated with the River Thames, and there threw it in, while back at the inn Mrs van Berghen vigorously scrubbed the floor to remove all traces of the blood that had spattered everywhere. Norris's clothes were put in a hamper and placed in the care of Dromelius, who carried them across the Thames to Rotherhithe, where he employed the waterman to carry the hamper to lodgings he retained: here he proposed to remain until he could find a favourable opportunity to return to Holland. (Whether the van Berghens knew this is what he proposed is unclear.)

Norris's body was swept onto the banks of the Thames in the vicinity of (where is now) Tower Bridge, which crosses the river by East Smithfield.

The following morning, Mr Norris's naked corpse was found at low water. Many people in the neighbourhood went to take a view of it, hoping that they would be able to identify it, while others began looking for bloodstains which might indicate the route the body had been brought from. This proved unsuccessful; but a number of people who had been up and about at a very early hour recalled seeing van Berghen and Dromelius (who were naturally quite well known in East Smithfield) in the vicinity of the place where the murder victim was found. Others reported that despite the unsociable hour a light had been visible within the van Berghen's tavern, being carried backwards and forwards for quite some time.

It naturally followed that the inn was searched. A little spot of blood was found behind the door of a room, and the place presented the appearance of having been freshly mopped; Geraldius Dromelius's absence was also viewed suspiciously – and the van Berghens could present no account of him other than that he had departed their service some time ago. Both husband and wife were arrested.

Also arrested was the serving maid, who either through fear for her neck or unsubtle persuasion became the chief evidence against the couple. The waterman who took Dromelius to Rotherhithe also came forward, and led the authorities to his client's lodgings. The Dutchman was still there, and was similarly taken into custody alongside his employers.

The three prisoners were tried at the Old Bailey on 24 June 1700. According to their status, the jury was comprised of six Britons and six foreign nationals – all of whom unanimously pronounced the van Berghens and Dromelius guilty of murder. While he was in Newgate prison, Dromelius attempted to divert suspicion away from his employers, for it appeared he was deeply in love with Catherine van Berghen. However, it only reinforced the guilt of all of them - for his story was of such a nonsensical nature that it trapped him by its errors. For instance, he claimed that Norris had been stabbed not at the inn but in a 'broken building' nearby (this to suggest Catherine was not present) and had died when his own sword was wrestled from him. This was patently false, for there were no bloodstains at the building indicated and, more tellingly, Norris's clothes bore no holes from sword thrusts – proving he had been stabbed *after* death while naked.

On 10 July 1700 the van Berghens and Dromelius were taken to be executed near the Hartshorn brew house, this being the nearest convenient site in East Smithfield to where the murder was committed. Dromelius persisted with his tale, while desiring the prayers of the multitudes who turned out to see him die. Mrs van Berghen also denied that the crime had occurred within her establishment, claiming the first she knew of it was after the fact from her husband; she also declared that she was only guilty of allowing Dromelius to escape unhindered – a crime for which she would not have been hanged in the Netherlands, she continued. Van Berghen also claimed that Dromelius was the sole murderer, and like his wife stated the first he knew of it was when his servant came to him in the middle of the night and begged his master to help him escape. Van Berghen also claimed that after Dromelius had fled to Rotherhithe he had offered some persons money to go there and apprehend his servant; however, this had not been proved at all during the trial.

A Smithfield execution, as originally depicted in William Jackson's New & Complete Newgate Calendar Volume 4 *(1795).*

There is some confusion regarding just exactly how the events of that night *did* play out. Nonetheless, the sentences were carried out and the van Berghens were attended at the place of their execution by an English clergyman, as well as some divines from the Netherlands. The husband could barely speak the English tongue and so conversed in Latin – a circumstance that led many to believe that his status in his home country had been one of some standing, and thus his end was as squalid a downfall as one might imagine.

Following their execution by hanging, the bodies of the men were suspended from gibbet posts, bound with metal straps – or 'hung in chains' – between Bow and Mile End. The body of Mrs van Berghen was buried.

THE DOCTOR'S DECISION

Richard Caddell was a native of Bromsgrove in Worcestershire, who bore a very promising future. He had been apprenticed to an apothecary in his home town, and next travelled to London to obtain first-hand experience of life in the capital's developing hospitals. In time he returned to Worcestershire, taking a position in Worcester itself as a widely-respected apothecary under the guidance of a Mr Randall, the town's foremost surgeon. He also lived under Randall's roof and subsequently married his daughter.

Caddell's life could not have looked rosier, but there next followed a development which he never really recovered from. His wife died while giving birth to their first child, and Caddell subsequently took himself to Lichfield in Staffordshire. Here, he took a position under the roof of Mr Dean, a surgeon of that place, and began to court Mr Dean's daughter.

Caddell might very well have ended up marrying the young woman. However, nearby there lived another young woman named Elizabeth Price, who supported herself by needlework. Miss Price was single, her reputation unfortunately somewhat sullied (such were the times) by her being seduced by an army officer who had then deserted her. Caddell is said to have possessed an amiable temper, and no doubt listened sympathetically to the woman's woes; this, coupled with the fact that Miss Price appears to have been rather more eager to move their relationship forward than Miss Dean, led to her and Caddell embarking on an affair.

Predictably, Miss Price fell pregnant. Caddell, however, continued to romance Miss Dean: and when poor Elizabeth learned she had once again been seduced and abandoned, she threatened Caddell by saying she would reveal her pregnant state publicly and thus destroy his hopes with Miss Dean.

What happened next is an example of a type of crime that happened so often throughout the 18th century that it almost seems like a kind of cliché. Elizabeth Price's plan was to blackmail Caddell into marrying her, but this he had no intention of allowing to happen. So he called at her house on a Saturday evening and asked if she might walk with him on Sunday afternoon in some quiet fields, where they might there have some peace to discuss the wedding arrangements.

The next day Elizabeth Price met Caddell at the Nag's Head on the outskirts of Lichfield, on the road leading to Burton upon Trent. They walked and talked in the fields till evening, whereupon they sat down under a hedge. Following a little conversation, Caddell quickly pulled out a knife and drew it across Elizabeth's throat, watching her until he was convinced that her convulsions had stopped and she was deceased. He then ran off as quickly as he could, leaving behind not only the knife but 'a case of instruments' – by which we suppose this means his medical instruments, something that would infallibly identify him.

Lichfield's doctor commits murder. (This illustration originally appeared in Knapp and Baldwin's Newgate Calendar Volume 1 *in 1824.)*

When Caddell arrived home at Mr Dean's house, he appeared incredibly confused and highly excitable. Elizabeth Price's slain body was found in the field the following morning, along with the incriminating instruments. Furthermore, when the victim's body was laid out, many people came to view her – including her landlady, who confirmed that Elizabeth had told her she would be walking with Richard Caddell on the Sunday afternoon just gone.

Caddell was immediately arrested, and soon afterwards tried at Stafford where he was convicted of murder and executed on 21 July 1700. His crime, by any standards, was hardly unique, as we shall see: although Caddell's educated position and line of work made his fall that much greater than others living in the British countryside who fell into the same set of circumstances and resorted to the ultimate means of escaping it.

THE MURDER OF SIR ANDREW SLANNING, BART

The era was one where men of rank, position and title could die in the most common manner: for example, consider Sir George Humble, who was killed in a quarrel at the Blue Posts Tavern in the metropolis in March 1702. Far away in the north of England, Ferdinando Forster, Esq, one of Northumberland's parliamentary representatives, was fatally stabbed in the back on 22 August 1701. This had followed an altercation between himself and one John Fenwick of Rock, during dinner at the Black Horse Inn in Newcastle. Fenwick had challenged the politician to a duel, and then stabbed him as they walked out into Newgate Street. Fenwick was hanged on 25 September at the White Cross, the town gates being shut to thwart a rescue attempt: after all, the name of Fenwick was in itself held in great esteem by the people of the north.

In Suffolk, Sir John Hanmer, 3rd Baronet, died suddenly and his body was carried home to Hanmer, Wrexham, where he was interred on 12 August 1701. One history of Hanmer observes: 'It is to be feared he fell in a duel.'

A murderous fate had also befallen Sir Andrew Slanning. The baronet had made the acquaintance of an orange-seller in the pit at Drury Lane playhouse in Covent Garden, London, and left with the woman at the end of the performance. As they departed they were followed by a goldsmith's apprentice named John Cowland, who for some reason had taken offence at this union; perhaps it was because he knew Slanning to be married, and some kind of puritanical jealousy had been inflamed. Walking behind the pair, and accompanied by some friends, Cowland grabbed the woman's neck; after a brief argument both the baronet and Cowland drew their swords, but – company coming up – both backed off.

The whole group made for the Rose Tavern, where, thanks to the endeavours of one Captain Wagget, it appeared the matter had ended. However, as the baronet went up some stairs for some wine, Cowland appeared from nowhere; he drew his sword and without warning plunged it into Sir Andrew's stomach. Mortally wounded, the baronet cried 'Murder!' upon which three persons rushed up the stairs and wrestled Cowland's sword from him. It was found to be wet with blood to a depth of five inches. The apprehended man attempted to flee into the street, but was easily caught and conducted before a Justice of the Peace.

Cowland was tried at the Old Bailey on 5 December 1700. It was established that Sir Andrew had been worth 20'000 pounds a year, and his murder had made the family line extinct. Cowland was convicted, and (despite 'great interest' being made to secure his pardon) he was hanged at Tyburn on 20 December, apparently sincerely penitent for his crime.

'GO HOME AND KILL YOUR FAMILY'

In the parish of Milverton, Somerset, there lived a 28-year-old man of good estate called Sir William Watts. He was married to a very beautiful woman from the neighbourhood, who bore him three children.

Watts seems, however, to have been jealous to the point of insanity. He regularly accused his wife of infidelity, claiming the children were not his, and frequently beat and abused her.

The catalyst seems to have been an encounter Watts had with a nobleman he bumped into while walking in some fields. The two began talking, and the gentleman told Watts that it sounded like his wife was a whore, and should he go home and find her not there then this would prove it. The nobleman then persuaded Watts that, should that be the case, he should kill his entire household and leave England immediately on a ship.

Watts returned home and found his wife to be missing, and the children in the care of a serving maid. He ordered the maid to go and find his wife, and bring her to him; and after she had gone he took a long knife and went upstairs to the children's bedroom. Without any ado, he grabbed his youngest child, a boy, by the hair and cut his throat from ear to ear. Then he murdered his youngest daughter in the same manner.

The eldest child, a girl, begged her father to allow her to say her prayers before he killed her, and Watts consented to this. As she was thus engaged, his wife returned home, however, and Watts turned his attention to her, sparing his eldest daughter and attacking his wife instead. She was stabbed three times in the chest and then had her throat cut by the madman.

The screaming brought neighbours running to the property, and they wrestled the knife out of Watts's hands before holding on to him until he could be transported to Taunton Gaol. At the next assizes, he was tried and found guilty of the murders, and swiftly hanged afterwards.

The exact date this tragedy occurred is unclear, although the details were published around 1700, and suggest Watts's trial took place at the last assizes. There was naturally much speculation that the nobleman Watts had encountered in the field shortly before the massacre was the Devil himself.

TIMOTHY BUCKLEY'S LIFE OF CRIME

Timothy Buckley was born in Stamford, Lincolnshire, and his downfall provides an early example of the spiral into criminality that forced many out onto the highway, armed and ready to kill.

When a young man, he was apprenticed to a shoemaker in Stamford, but after three years of learning this trade he opted to run away from his master and seek his fortune in the capital. When in London, he fell in easily with a group of street criminals, and was initiated in the art of pickpocketing and all sorts of street plundering. By the time he had arrived at adulthood, he had fallen in with a notorious and prolific gang of housebreakers and graduated to highway robbery.

Despite his ways, it is said that Buckley retained an element of decency – by criminal standards – in that he would only attack pawnbrokers, publicans, bakers and doctors, declaring that he felt entitled to some portion of the gain these had made by cheating their customers. In the end, Buckley was apprehended by a constable (who also carried on the business of a baker) in the parish of St Giles in the Fields. This person took him into custody for some misdemeanour and saw to it he was sent to join the army in Flanders.

Buckley deserted, however, and returned to his old haunts in England. Shortly after his return he ambushed the baker's wife as she travelled alone from Hampstead, raping the woman and robbing her of rings and money to a considerable amount. This, of course, was to be revenged upon his captor, and after this wicked act Buckley became a career criminal, operating fully outside of the law.

He appears to have been a prolific robber, although his success met with some check on occasion; Old Bailey records indicate he was condemned to die at one point - and yet afterwards he received a pardon for some reason or another. Several times he appeared at the bar of justice, and just as often escaped; until at last his time came.

Buckley had removed himself to the Midlands, and here he committed a burglary at Ashby-de-la-Zouch, near Coalville in Leicestershire. This netted him £80, and he used this money to purchase a good horse at a fair in Derby. His downfall occurred when he shortly thereafter attempted to hold-up a coach on the Derby road, about two miles out of Nottingham. The coach carried three gentlemen and was attended by two footmen, all of whom appear to have been armed; and when Buckley called upon them to deliver their goods, one of the gentlemen discharged a blunderbuss at Buckley which killed his horse beneath him. There then followed a bloody gunfight in which Buckley discharged eight pistols at his opponents, fatally wounding one of the gentlemen and one of the footmen. Having received no less than eleven wounds to his person during the shooting melee, Buckley eventually sagged and fainted through loss of blood, allowing himself to be seized and taken to Nottingham Gaol.

Remarkably, Buckley did not die of his injuries, and underwent the sentence of the law in 1701, afterwards being hung in chains near the site of the battle following his execution. He was 29 years of age at the time of his death; it might be observed that, for many of the bandits who terrorised the country throughout the century, this could be considered 'old age'.

BUSBY'S STOOP

In Yorkshire, at the point where the road from Ripon to Thirsk crosses that from Topcliffe to Northallerton, stands a public house called 'Busby Stoop', which derives its name from a gibbet post, or stoop, that once stood at this crossroads.

The circumstances behind this are generally said to be as follows. In the first years of the 1700s there lived at Danotty Hall, by the River Swale, a man called Daniel Autie, otherwise Dan Auty, or 'Danotty'. Auty was one of the most notorious thieves and 'clippers' (a name for a forger) in this part of England, a native of Dewsbury whose entire family bore a poor reputation. Auty himself was frequently in gaol for clipping money, although he had as yet escaped unscathed from the full penalties of the law that his livelihood demanded. He was even implicated in the theft of communion plate from York Minster, and he worked through an extensive network of brother forgers, thieves, corrupt silversmiths, buyers and sellers.

York Minster, where Auty had the audacity to steal plate.

By 1702 he had established a career in forgery – clipping coins and melting the clippings into new money, while at the same time deteriorating the value of legitimate coinage. The organisation was run from Danotty Hall, where he had apartments fitted up for carrying out his business secretly; the house is said to have been a roomy one, with double walls. In his illicit trade he was assisted by his son-in-law, Thomas Busby, who had married Auty's daughter and resided at the hall. At some point a quarrel arose between the old man and his son-in-law over the running of the business, possibly in response to Busby wishing to take over the whole organisation. This he achieved directly by murdering his father-in-law one night while he was abed. Some versions claim that Busby garrotted the old man in his bedchamber, while others claim he took a hammer to his victim's head and beat his skull in; at any rate, Busby was very quickly arrested, tried and sentenced to death.

Following his execution in 1702, Busby's corpse was suspended in the vicinity of Sandhutton; and the antiquary Ralph Thoresby saw this spectacle for himself, recording in his dairy on 17 May 1703: 'Along the banks of Swale are the very pleasant gardens of William Robinson, lately lord mayor of York, but a few miles after (is the) more doleful object of Mr. Busby hanging in chains for the murder of his father-in-law, Daniel Auty, formerly a Leeds clothier, who, having too little honesty to balance his skill in engraving etc., was generally suspected for coining, and other indirect ways of attaining that estate which was the occasion of his death, even within sight of his own house.'

Details of this crime are hard to pin down. There is a suggestion that Busby committed a second murder after that of old Auty, on a maidservant who had discovered his grim secret. This appears to be folklore, however, and it would seem that Busby was actually betrayed by his wife following the disappearance of her father – whose body had been dragged into nearby woodland. According to more folklore, Busby was taken while in a state of utter inebriation: he was covered in his victim's blood and slumped in an oaken chair at Danotty Hall – which is (at the time of writing) hung in Thirsk Museum.

'THE MOST CELEBRATED WIT AND BEAUTY OF HER AGE'

In the days when Dorchester, Dorset, was a lot smaller, about a quarter of a mile from the town could be found the amphitheatre called Mambury, or Maumbury. It was originally considered a Roman work, with Dr Stukeley calculating that it could accommodate 12'960 spectators in its ample area; today it presents a large circular grassy open space often used for open-air concerts and other large social events. In the early 18th century it was the site of a grim execution carried out before an estimated 10'000 people.

The events that led up to this are as follows. Mary, the teenage daughter of Richard Brookes of Dorchester, was married off to a well-to-do grocer called Richard Channing. The marriage was at the compulsion of Mary's parents, and was a farce from the start - for clearly Mary did not love her new husband. She kept company with her former gallants, and by her extravagance almost ruined her husband. Finally she took the decision to get rid of Channing, procuring white mercury (via a maid servant) from an apothecary, which she stirred into his rice-milk and twice after into a glass of wine. According to one account, Mary made certain that she was the one responsible for dishing out the portions; after all, she did not want to wipe out everyone sat at the breakfast table, just her husband. The poisoned bowl she presented to Channing, who ate heartily before perceiving that his pudding tasted amiss. He asked his brother to try some, but Mary refused to allow the youth to partake; Channing then ordered the maid to partake, but Mary angrily picked up the poisoned bowl and conveyed it away, thus preventing anyone else present from tasting the contents. Shortly afterwards, Channing's body and features began to swell grotesquely, and he died in contorted agony even before a physician could be brought.

There being visible proof of poisoning, and Mary being the only suspect, a Justice of the Peace committed Mary Channing to Dorchester Gaol. Evidence was procured against her from her domestics, and she languished in jail awaiting the ensuing assizes.

At the next assizes in Dorchester in 1705 Mary was tried for her husband's murder before Judge Price. She cut an impressive figure in court and made a notable defence 'full of wit and ingenuity'; nonetheless she was convicted of murder and sentenced to death. Drama followed drama, for Mary pleaded *ex necessitate legis* – that is, she revealed she was pregnant, and so far gone that to execute her would constitute the murder of her unborn child. Mary was thus remanded during her pregnancy, but following the delivery of her child she was summoned to the Lent assizes to once more have her death sentence confirmed upon her.

On 21 March 1705 Mary was taken to Maumbury Rings and tied to a stake in front of a crowd numbering in thousands. Her last act was to remove her gown and white silk hood, and present them to a maid; she was then ruthlessly garrotted by the town executioner before the woodchips around her body were set alight: and thus – hooded, limp and bound to the stake – Mary's body was enveloped by the conflagration. She was aged around 18 or 19 when she was executed, her last words reportedly being to declare her faith in Christ – while blaming her parent's behaviour as the sole cause of the unhappy tragedy.

Mary Channing persisted in her innocence to the very end, and her story is a famous one indeed in Dorchester. Confusions regarding the details of this extraordinary case were repeated in popular broadsides and other accounts through the decades; but according to *The Complete Newgate Calendar Volume 2*, a partial reason for the sensation caused by the trial was Mary Brookes herself. Some versions of her story read as though they were drawn from memory, being half-accurate, which perhaps evidences the sensation the case caused in the area. Nonetheless, the *Calendar* assured its readers she was, by the standards of her contemporaries, highly intelligent and very quick witted: 'In a word, she was generally esteemed the most celebrated wit and accomplished beauty of her age.'

CHAPTER 2

THE REIGN OF QUEEN ANNE (d.1 August 1714)

INTRODUCTION

When William died in 1702 the throne was inherited by his sister-in-law Anne, daughter of the deposed King James II.

Queen Anne's reign was noteworthy for victories on the European stage – at Blenheim on 2 August 1704 and at Malplaquet in September 1709. At home, southern England was beset by a natural catastrophe the like of which no one could remember, when in November 1703 thousands lost their lives due to the effects of a two-day storm. It has to be wondered how far the lasting aftermath of such a disaster fuelled the desperation and poverty that led to so many barbarous crimes of avarice in flooded areas where people had lost everything. However, Anne's lasting legacy is that during her reign it came to pass that the United Kingdom of Great Britain was created on 1 May 1707. A central feature of the Act of Union (which brought England and Scotland together) was that it denied a separate Scottish – and by association, Jacobite and Roman Catholic – succession upon the queen's death. In other words, it guaranteed the whole island the Protestant succession already enshrined in English legislation. This, as the new nation would find to its great cost later in the century, became the source of much division across the country; it also became an instrumental factor in much bitter political rivalry and violence in the years and decades following Anne's death.

Tumult was frequent in Anne's time, most noticeably evident in the mob rioting that threatened London upon the trial of Dr Henry Sacheverell in March 1710. The mob, in Sacheverell's support, considered the doctor half-hero, half-martyr for his verbal attacks on some members of her Majesty's Whig government during a sermon at St Paul's Cathedral. Support for him only increased upon his subsequent arrest on suspicion of being a 'concealed Jacobite'. The crowds wrecked dissenting chapels from Drury Lane to Blackfriars, these being seen as complicit in a general threat to the church that the Whigs were ignoring; pulpits were torn down, with the mob accidentally destroying an Anglican church owing to its want of a steeple. Eventually they retreated in the face of an advance by the military. But this demonstrates the powerful threat that mob violence posed, for that September Anne dissolved parliament and called an election as a direct result of the Sacheverell clashes.

St Paul's Cathedral: the doctor's sermon here produced widespread disorder in London.

London was at the time a city beset by street gangs. These were often comprised of swaggering young bullies or loutish thugs who were in many cases comparatively well off. However, bands of young rakes had been making night in the capital steadily more dangerous since the time of the Restoration, with their 'clubs' being given varying slang denominations. The first of these were the Mums and the Tityre-tus, who were then succeeded by the Hectors and the Scourers, who (it was observed) made any venture between the Rose Tavern and the Piazza a gamble with one's own life. Next came the Nickers, whose delight it was to smash windows with showers of coins upon being presented with a bill in a tavern. This alone tells us that the Nickers were comprised of troublesome men with too much money and not enough responsibility; and in many ways the shocking example set by these 'gentlemen' to the lower classes of London society is illustrative of the almost semi-anarchic state that the metropolis presented during Anne's time. The crisis reached a head during the latter years of her reign with the 'Mohock' scare, which is outlined later on.

Far away from the capital a burgeoning smuggling industry was enveloping many coastal communities, and much like piracy, highway robbery and 'wrecking', this is a type of crime that has come to symbolise and define the times…although the mythology and romanticism now associated with such lawlessness masks the bare truth that all involved were driven by one motive: avarice. During the 17th and 18th centuries, smuggling became part of a way of life in some places, being a far more profitable 'occupation' than either mining or fishing. At one stage it was estimated that more illicit spirits were coming in through Devon and Cornwall alone than were entering the country legally through London's docks. Known as 'free-traders', these gangs often battled with excise-men on cliff-tops and sank customs cutters at every opportunity.

In fact, coastal Britain was plagued by these audacious and frequently ruthless bands of seafaring rogues to such an extent that the following legend recorded in Reverend Sabine Baring-Gould's *Mehalah: A Story of the Salt Marshes* (1880) probably contains more than a grain of truth. He wrote of the Essex smugglers: 'Deeds of violence were not rare, and many a revenue officer fell victim to his zeal. On Sunken Island, off Mersea, the story went that a whole boat's crew were found with their throats cut; they were transported thence to the churchyard, there buried, and their keel turned over them. The gypsies were thought to pursue over-conscientious and successful officers over the mainland, and remove them with a bullet should they escape the smugglers on the water.' *Mehalah* is set in the latter 1700s, with the legend of the Sunken Island massacre referred to briefly as having occurred at an uncertain point in the past. Today, however, it has become part of Essex folklore, with some saying that 22 customs men were slaughtered in the atrocity, and others claiming to know that they were buried at Virley. Either way, it paints a grim picture of the barbarity coastal people were considered capable of. Exaggerated, yes, but unfortunately not so ridiculous as to be too far from the truth, as we shall see later on.

This modern sculpture (in Scarborough) depicts a smuggler and his apprentice. There is a certain romanticism about smuggling in general these days.

That the authorities and the smugglers were fighting a form of low-key warfare is clear, even from the 18th century's very earliest reports. In Sussex the wool-smugglers went by the name of 'Owlers' (supposedly from their only venturing abroad in the night). A letter from a Mr Fox dated 8 May 1718 appeared in some of the provincial news-sheets of the day, for instance, explaining that one of these 'Owlers' had lately been put on trial at the King's-Bench-Bar following an appeal for justice by the brother of a murdered customs officer. It was actually acknowledged at the man's trial that he was *not* the murderer; but because he was a man active in the company of those who committed the crime, he was convicted by Lord Parker and the court anyway. On 21 January 1720 several of the Sussex Owlers were killed in a pitched battle at Ferring with customs officers under William Goldsmith. These 'Owlers' are also reported to have infested the Kentish coast during this time.

The general threat from criminal violence during Anne's reign is perhaps best summed up in the following report, which appeared in the *Flying Post* (3-5 January 1705): 'We hear that on Tuesday night last, five housebreakers broke into Sir Charles Thorn's house near *Bedington* in Surrey, and having gagg'd his servants, got into his bed chamber. At their entrance, Sir Charles fir'd a pistol at them, which unhappily miss'd doing execution; upon this they bound and gagg'd him, and afterwards one of them attempted to insult his lady; at which Sir Charles being exasperated, with much struggling he got his hands at liberty, and flung a periwig block at the villain's head; who in revenge stabbed Sir Charles, and cut his throat from ear to ear, and left him dead on the spot. They afterwards ransack'd the house, and it is said, carried off to the value of £900 in money and plate. The Lady Thorn is so ill by this barbarous treatment, that her life is dispair'd of.'

Beddington at this time was a distinct village district, long before it was swallowed up by, and incorporated into, Greater London. Sir Charles' house was not some ill-lit back street tavern in the metropolis, but his own property away from the capital. Yet this man's distance, title and wealth did not protect him; rather, it appears to have made him a *target*. When such a terrible fate might befall a distinguished fellow in this manner, then the lot of the ordinary man may be surmised to have been even more perilous – as might the lot of those attempting to keep order in these dangerous times.

A PARISH CONSTABLE'S DEATH AT MAY FAIR

In the capital, the intervening ground between Park Lane and Devonshire House was the site of an ancient and annual festival, May Fair, which operated from 1 May onwards. This fair had been an event since the days of King Edward I, and an advertisement that appeared in London journals on 27 April 1700 gives an idea of its place in the cultural calendar: 'In Brookfield market-place, at the east corner of Hyde Park, is a fair to be kept for the space of sixteen days, beginning from the 1st of May; the first three days for live cattle and leather, with the same entertainments as at Bartholomew Fair, where there are shops to be let ready built for all manner of tradesmen that usually keep fairs, and so to continue yearly at the same place.' Even exotic animals like tame elephants and tigers were sometimes brought to the fair to be sold.

By now, however, the fair was becoming a great nuisance to the authorities, with pickpockets and other criminals mingling among the crowds. They were so active at the 1702 May Fair that the magistrates felt compelled to interfere, despite it being evident that any act of repression by the authorities risked rousing the anger of the public in general; consequently the 1702 festival became the setting for a *battle royale* between the parish constables and Londoners on 16 May, with a number of soldiers siding with the crowd. A peace officer named John Cooper was fatally injured in these violent disturbances, and later buried at St James' Church. The following year the *Observator*, a twice-weekly newspaper, commented on this event in the run-up to the fair of 1703: 'This fair is kept contrary to law, and in defiance of justice; for (at) the last fair, when the civil magistrates came to keep the Queen's peace, one constable was killed and three others wounded.'

May Fair was held near Queen Elizabeth Gate in the capital.

Cooper had been stabbed in the belly with a sword by a man named Thomas Cook, who fled to Ireland but there betrayed himself in taverns by continually boasting of his part in the riot. In front of one landlord, Cook actually declared that, 'The constables played their part with their staves, and I played mine; and when the man dropped, I wiped my sword, put it up, and went away.'

At length he was arrested and shipped to Chester, then taken to London and tried at the Old Bailey. Cook denied being the murderer, and there was some debate over whether he was the *actual* killer; but in the end - following two reprieves - he was hanged on 11 August 1703 at Tyburn. It is interesting to note the performances that convicted felons might put on as they stood with the noose around their neck, for Cook even sang a little ditty to the crowd, which no doubt pleased them; it ended, 'This I write as my last farewell; hoping my soul with Christ shall dwell. Amen.'

By 1708 the fair itself had become such a headache that the authorities had it discontinued: and for a time at least, while not being entirely suppressed, it ceased to be the event it once had been.

'THE GLOUCESTERSHIRE TRAGEDY'

A chapbook printed in 1703 provided a gruesome account of a 'true' crime that had lately occurred at Alvington, Gloucestershire, although the details are so Shakespearian in their melodrama that the tragedy is highly unlikely to have played out the way we are told.

Mary Williams led a 'wicked and lewd' life, and had taken as a lover a farmer's son, by whom she became pregnant. However, he soon deserted her for another woman, and the chapbook assures us that this was because 'her (Mary's) mother's *ghost* appear'd to them while they were in the very act' of making love.

Sometime thereafter Mary gave birth to two sons, presumably twins. The farmer's son had by this time chosen to marry his new sweetheart and so a vengeful Mary drowned one of the infants in a pond. The other she cut to pieces and baked in a pie, which she sent to him 'fill'd with blood' on the day he was due to marry. The chapbook concludes with an 'account of her Apprehension, Tryal, Conviction; (and) Confession at the place of execution'.

THE PITTENWEEM MURDER

In 1704-5, three people died and numerous others were mercilessly tortured as the result of wild accusations made by a youth named Patrick Morton. Morton was a 16-year-old blacksmith's boy living at Pittenweem, a small and secluded fishing village tucked in the corner of Fife on the eastern Scottish coast, and after a long sickness he claimed very vocally that witches were tormenting him.

Furthermore, Morton knew who his persecutors were, and this led to the arrest of a number of people on the orders of the magistrates and the minister of Pittenweem, one Patrick Cowper. One of the women who died under interrogation was the wife of a former town treasurer, Beatrix Laing, who stood accused of sending evil spirits to torture the youth; after five months alone in a pitch dark dungeon, and frequent visits to the torture chamber, she was freed – only to expire soon afterwards at St Agnes, friendless and ruined. Furthermore, Thomas Brown, another accused 'witch', starved to death during his dungeon captivity.

Nearly 100 years after the notorious Pendle witch trials, clearly some were ready to believe Satanic gatherings like this still occurred. (This illustration is a reproduction in Clitheroe Castle Museum of an original woodcut.)

Another of those accused was a woman called Janet Corphat, or Bornfoot, who found herself committed as a prisoner to the tollbooth. Here, she was well guarded by men who pinched, pricked and otherwise tormented her, preventing her from sleeping and threatening her with death unless she confessed to being a witch. In the end, Janet confessed, and while languishing in her cell she was visited by a number of learned men – the Earl of Kellie, Lord Lyon and the Laird of Randerston among them – who listened to her assert that the minister had beaten her and she only confessed 'to please the minister and the *baillies*'. Finally, Janet was taken out of gaol and – upon the order of the minister – she was locked up in the local church lest her protestations of innocence began to subvert the minds of others who had similarly confessed.

The room where Janet was secured had a very low window, and as such she was able to scramble out of her confinement during the night. The following day she was discovered in a parish eight miles from Pittenweem and sent back into the custody of Mr Cowper, the minister there.

However, for reasons that are now unclear, Cowper appeared to have lost interest in Janet Corphat somewhat, and directed her to stay in the house of a female called Nichola Lawson – one of the few who would accommodate her, given that the latter had also been incriminated in the witch scare. By this time, Pittenweem and the surrounding area were in an uproar about the escaped witch. Representatives of the mob marched to see Cowper, who told them he was no longer concerned in the matter and they could do as they pleased with Janet. This they did, and their actions were as inhumane as can be imagined.

Swept up in a puritanical fury that would not have been out of place in Cromwell's time, on 30 January 1705 the mob immediately took Janet from Lawson's house. She was punched, hit and slapped, tied with a rope and then dragged by her heels through the streets to the shoreline. No real attempts were made by anyone in authority to protect her, and the mob had the brazen audacity to tie a rope between a ship off the shore and a high point on land – from which she was suspended like a ghastly, swinging puppet. All the while the people pelted her with stones, until at last – becoming tired and bored – they loosened her and, with an almighty swing, let her drop to the ground. As she lay on the hard sands, a crowd closed around her and beat her with stones and staves, before laying a heavy door on her body. They threatened to press her to death unless she confessed to being a witch; Janet's protestations did not satisfy them, so they piled large stones upon the door and literally crushed the life out of the poor woman. For good measure, they called over a man with a horse and sledge and made him walk the animal backwards and forward over the woman's body a number of times before finally tossing her mangled corpse outside Nichola Lawson's door. Throughout the spectacle, Janet's daughter had watched from the sidelines, unable to help her mother through fear she would be killed, and we are told she was perhaps the only person present who wished the mob would desist.

There was a council to treat Ms Lawson the same, but by now the mob was weary, having tormented Janet for three hours. Astonishingly, Mr Cowper made no reference to the murder when preaching the following Sunday in Pittenweem's church. Sadly, although all the other accused witches were freed, and Patrick Morton was exposed as a liar who had come under the influence of a fanatical priest, none among the lynch mob was ever brought to justice. Patrick

Cowper, the priest in question and Pittenweem's minister, perhaps bore more responsibility for the murder than the people who actually *committed* it – for it appears his words, his actions and his encouragement were the reason behind the entire episode from start to finish.

THE RAKE'S PROGRESS

Edward Jeffries' crime is indicative of the rakish life that too many fell into during the 18th century, his end dramatically illustrating a real-life 'Rake's Progress'.

Jeffries hailed from Devizes in Wiltshire, and started out well as the clerk to an eminent attorney in London, afterwards carrying on business by himself. However, when he was a young man his father died, and Edward was left a considerable fortune; from this point on he embarked on the debaucheries of the age, drinking, whoring and gambling his inheritance away in a catastrophic downward spiral. His fortune received a boost when he married a young lady from St Albans – but being unable to forgo his former lifestyle, and frittering her money away, they separated.

Jeffries next took as a lover an immoral young woman called Elizabeth Torshell, who also courted a man named Robert Woodcock. Sharing the same woman was a frequent cause of argument between the two men, but at length they appeared to have been largely reconciled – for Jeffries and Woodcock were lately being seen dining together at the Blue Posts tavern in Pall Mall. However, after one dinner, as they walked through fields near Chelsea, the issue of Ms Torshell once more became a source of argument between them, and Jeffries drew his sword.

Woodcock, we learn, was left handed, and before he could unsheathe his own weapon Jeffries lunged at him and inflicted a stab wound so serious that the victim died almost immediately. Jeffries had the presence of mind to smear blood all over the deceased's sword, to imply he might have wounded himself, but he also could not resist rifling the dead man's pockets. He then went to Chelsea, where he had an appointment with Ms Torshell.

Some boys playing in the field at the time had heard some of the two men's discourse, and next found the dead man's body. The corpse was taken to St Martin-in-the-Fields, and the following day Ms Torshell came to the church along with crowds of others and identified the corpse as that of Mr Woodcock.

Ms Torshell was taken into custody and her lodgings searched. Here, a number of items were found that had been brought to the room by Jeffries – although Ms Torshell stated that she believed them to have belonged to Woodcock. Upon this, Edward Jeffries was also arrested and the pair were thrown into Newgate.

Both were tried for murder in September 1705, and Jeffries introduced a number of witnesses to the bar – each of whom testified that he was somewhere else at the time of the murder. However, as these could not agree on their details, it only added weight to the evidence *against* Jeffries and he was convicted. Ms Torshell was acquitted of any involvement.

While awaiting execution in Newgate the convicted man earnestly attempted to obtain a reprieve, and – remarkably – this was promised through the mediation of the Duke of Ormond. On 9 September 1705 news of this development reached Jeffries' ears even as he was being taken to Tyburn and having reached as far as St Giles's.

The reprieve, however, only turned out to be a temporary respite, for it merely deferred his execution until 21 September to allow any fresh evidence in his innocence to appear. Since none was forthcoming, Jeffries went to the gallows accordingly. Perhaps the most interesting thing about this rake's progress is his demise: he steadfastly refused to admit his guilt in the murder and seems to have ended his life in high spirits, not dejected in the least by his calamitous situation. He forgave those who had injured him and died gallantly with perfect charity towards mankind, his last words being that he desired the prayers of all good Christians.

MURDER IN THE TOWER

The Tower of London is one of the capital's most famous landmarks, an immense place drenched in history standing on the north bank of the Thames. Many are the famous names of prisoners incarcerated here, and the crimes committed, but the Tower was also the setting for an almost-forgotten murder – remarkable at the time for extinguishing the life of yet another promising young gentleman.

The victim was Lieutenant William Cope of the Queen's Guards in the Tower, the principal commanding officer there; he was also the son of Sir John Cope. On 7 June 1706 he was upon guard in the Guard-room, accompanied by several others including a woman of his acquaintance. It appears that John Mawgridge, who held the position of drum major, said something offensive to the woman and angry words were exchanged. Cope attempted to defend the woman's honour but the situation became so heated that Mawgridge demanded satisfaction by way of a duel. Lt Cope coolly said that it was not convenient to fight now but he would gladly cross swords with Mawgridge at another time and place; and in the meantime told him to shut up or leave the company. As Mawgridge left the room he threw a glass bottle full of wine at Cope, who rose and threw one back at his antagonist, which hit him on the head. Mawgridge very quickly drew his sword and simply plunged it into the left part of Lt Cope's breast, even while an attempt was being made to protect Cope by a third party named Robert Martin. The stabbed man was not holding his sword at the time, and he died of his injury.

The Tower of London, site of the murder

Mawgridge was committed to Newgate, and on 1 July 1706 indicted at a Sessions of the Peace held in the Guildhall, London. He pleaded not guilty to a charge of murdering the lieutenant, and the case is interesting from a legal point of view because there next followed a period of legal wrangling over whether Mawgridge was guilty of murder or manslaughter. On 22 November he was brought to the Queen's Bench bar, and again a few days later, whence the decision on his conviction was again deferred to the middle of December while a 'special verdict' was argued among a party of judges at Sergeant's Inn.

While all this dragged on, Mawgridge managed to break out of the Queen's Bench Prison on the night of 20 January 1707 (with the assistance of one Edward Bailey, who was later thrown into Newgate) and flee to the Continent.

Mawgridge's escape notwithstanding, a verdict of 'Guilty of murder' was finally brought in against him on 24 January 1707. The Lord Chief Justice Holt having informed Queen Anne of the judge's decision, the monarch granted the victim's father Sir John Cope a privy seal to hunt down his son's killer and bring him back if found hiding in any country friendly to Britain. Remarkably, this was accomplished, for it was reported in January 1708 that Mawgridge had been arrested in Ghent, Flanders. He was returned to Newgate at the beginning of March, and the authorities wasted little time in seeing to it he was punished; for we learn that he was hanged at Tyburn on 28 April 1708 alongside a man named Bayley (convicted of killing his own brother) and one Gregg for treasonable correspondence with France. The latter was sentenced to be quartered, and have his head stuck upon Westminster Hall as a warning to others.

THE CANNIBALIZED KITCHEN-BOY

Although James Douglas, the second Duke of Queensbury, established his position in British history by being the main instrument in carrying through the Union between Scotland and England, his Grace's eldest son, also James, was an idiot of the most unhappy sort; rabid, gluttonous and of an immense height from an early age. This young madman was kept confined in a ground apartment in the west wing of the family lodgings at Queensberry House, Edinburgh - a receptacle which had its windows boarded up to prevent him looking out or being seen.

The duke would regularly travel between his lodgings and Parliament House, notwithstanding several intimated threats against his person. On the day of Union (1 May 1707) the entire household left Holyrood in case there was trouble – for all Edinburgh had gathered in Parliament Square to mob the chief promoters of the detested Act. Among those who left the house on the day was the idiot James's keeper.

The duke's son was left alone in the building, except for a young boy who turned the roasting spit in the kitchen. Upon discerning that the burgh of Canongate was like a city of the dead, James managed to break free of his confinement and wander the house from room to room like a feral animal. His wild roaming led him to the kitchen, where the smell of lunch being cooked lured him, and here he found the little turnspit sat quietly by the fire.

The madman seized the poor kitchen boy and killed him there and then. He next removed the meat from the fire and impaled the boy's body on the spit in its place, which he then began roasting. When the duke and his domestics returned in triumph they found James in the kitchen *eating* the partially roasted corpse of his victim.

According to the common people, this horrid crime was God's judgement upon the duke for his support of the Union. However, James – being utterly incapable – was not executed, and actually outlived the duke, who died in 1711. The title passed to a younger brother, Charles, and the madman James ultimately died in England in early 1715. Although his coffin was interred in the family vault at Durisdeer, his plain coffin – of great length – was unadorned with the heraldic follies that bedecked his relatives' coffins.

Queensberry House today (2012) forms part of the Scottish Parliament complex, and the oven where the boy's body was roasted is still pointed out in a private bar for MSPs.

THE MYSTERIOUS DEATH OF THE 'FIRST JOURNALIST'

In 1707 politics was a deadly game, occasioning the death of a controversial newspaper editor.

John Tutchin was a radical Whig, born in Lymington *c*.1664. He was in many ways something of a pioneering English journalist, responsible for the *Observator*. His controversial activism earned him many a trip before the bar, and also many enemies.

The *Observator* was begun on 1 April 1702, edited by Tutchin, a fellow who had suffered much for his politics. He had sided with the cause of Monmouth during the rebellion against the House of Stuart in 1685, and for an article in which he declared his allegiances he was sentenced by Judge Jeffries to be whipped through several towns in the west of England. So brutal was this flagellation that Tutchin actually petitioned King James II to hang him instead.

When the king died in exile, Tutchin wrote 'an invective against his memory, being occasioned by some humane elegies on his death'. By this time, however, he had also aroused the wrath of the Tories for other reasons: namely his slanderous piece directed against Vice-Admiral Sir Thomas Dilkes. Tutchin was constantly promised a beating by his political opponents: and true to their word, he was in August 1707 suddenly assaulted by six ruffians armed with sticks and canes as he sat waiting upon an appointment in rooms above a public house. Tutchin had nothing to defend himself with but his hands, for his sword and cane were placed elsewhere; his assailants beat him so severely that he died in much distress on 23 September, aged 44.

Other accounts claim he was waylaid and attacked in the street, although this may have been another assault, and the circumstances, generally speaking, of the vicious beating(s) are not at all clear. There is also some field for speculation that the attack was not the *sole* cause of Tutchin's death.

After the attack he declared in the pages of the *Observator* that despite 'public assaults, private assassinations and innumerable difficulties' he would continue to publish. An edition of the *Observator*, published 20 September 1707, lamented Tutchin's current imprisonment for a small debt. In the article, he noted that ever since he had received the violent blows to his head he had been languishing, and his head was 'imposthumated'. He further wrote: 'Add to this an empty purse, sick heart, numerous family, and being neglected by my friends that I have served; and you need not wonder that my pulse beats low.' Although there is no question but that he was seriously injured in one of the assaults, Tutchin's *actual* death occurred three days after writing these words, during his confinement in the Queen's Bench Prison in the Mint district of Southwark, where he was incarcerated for debt. Although his supporters later insisted he had died from the bruises occasioned in the attack, it is likely that the *actual* cause of his death was gaol fever aggravated by injuries from a flogging that his weakened condition exacerbated. However it came about though, it is clear that Tutchin's death was – via one means or another – wholly unnatural.

An autopsy confirmed Tutchin had suffered severe wounds to one kidney and his cranium, and whether he would have ever made a full recovery from these injuries was in question; at any rate, no one was ever charged with the original murderous attack (or attacks) upon his person.

John Churchill, 1st Duke of Marlborough, was one of Tutchin's many enemies, for he railed in a letter to Robert Harley, 'If I can't have justice done me, then I must find some friend who will break his (Tutchin's) and the printer's bones.' However, there is no evidence that the duke ordered the attack…although it is possible his enmity *inspired* it.

In some verses printed upon his death, the slain editor is called 'Captain Tutchin', and it is said he was buried in the parish of 'Christ Church in Surrey'.

THE ARTISAN'S PACT

In 1707 Mr John Strahan, Writer to the Signet of Edinburgh, was the owner of Craigcrook, a romantically-situated old manor house under the lee of Corstorphine Hill, on the western skirts of Edinburgh. Strahan also had a house in the High Street of Edinburgh and was the owner of considerable wealth – the bulk of which he would later 'mortify' for the support of poor old men, women and orphans.

Strahan had a young servant, Helen Bell, who kept his town mansion, and she appears to have been left there a good deal by herself. Because of this circumstance, and perfectly naturally, she sometimes allowed gentlemen friends and suitors into her master's house to see her. On Hallowe'en 1707 she invited two young artisans, William Thomson and John Robertson, onto the premises and happened to mention that on the morning of Monday 3 November she would be going out to Craigcrook and leaving the High Street house empty.

At about five o'clock on the morning in question Helen left the town premises, locking the door and starting out west for the brief journey to her master's manor house. As she walked through Edinburgh's silent streets she was unexpectedly joined near the West Bow by Thomson and Robertson, who explained they were heading in that direction and would accompany her part of the way to Craigcrook. She was foolish enough to pass them a couple of bottles and the house-key to the High Street premises to lighten her load, although possibly she thought the two young men were trying to win her hand and so being courteous. However, upon coming to a difficult part of the route called the Three Steps, at the foot of the Castle Rock, the two men threw her to the ground and beat the poor girl's skull in with a hammer.

Of course, the whole thing had been a contrivance aimed at robbing the house in the High Street, and the two men hastened back through the still-silent streets of Edinburgh with the house-key in their possession. As they returned through the Grassmarket the two men made a pact: they swore to each other to give their souls and bodies to the Devil if either should inform on the other, even if they were caught. The two men thought of ways to make this bond 'official' as they walked, and (according to the later testimony of one of them) a man suddenly appeared between them in the middle of the West Bow and offered to write the bond – if they would but produce some of their own blood for him to use as ink. Thomson demurred, and the mysterious stranger melted away into the shadows of Edinburgh's unlit streets. (One Victorian writer, Robert Chambers, observed of this, 'It is not very wonderful that almost any sort of hallucination should have taken possession of these miserable men.' I might add that the mysterious fellow was perhaps some early-rising wag who overheard the two men talking and thought he would have a joke at their expense; or, more likely, Thomson invented this detail because he later thought it might present him as a God-fearing man when it came to his punishment.)

The two murderers, having made their way into Mr Strahan's house, broke open his study door and next forced open the chest where his money was secreted. Here they discovered £1'000 in bags of £50 each, 'all milled money' except for £100 which was in gold. All of this they stole. Robertson proposed to set fire to the house before they departed – but Thomson said there had been wickedness enough and refused to have anything more to do with their enterprise, even though Robertson apparently threatened to murder him also.

When the girl's beaten body was discovered, and thence the robbery also, Mr Strahan advertised a hefty reward for the capture of the criminals. For some weeks the perpetrators remained unidentified; we are told by Robert Chambers, however: 'At length, some suspicion lighting on Thomson, he was taken up, and, having made a voluntary confession of the murder and robbery, he expiated his offence in the Grassmarket.' Most sources suggest Robertson was executed also for the crime, having been implicated by his confederate.

As to how they were caught, a wild tale exists. It is to the effect that Lady Craigcrook, twelve months after the killing, dreamed she saw the murderer – who she recognised as an ex-servant. She 'saw' him kill the girl and hide the money in two old barrels filled with trash. Her husband made enquiries, and found the fellow to be possessed of a suspicious amount of money – so he had the man arrested and his house searched. Sure enough, a portion of the missing coin was found on the man's property. This man we may take to be William Thomson, but whether there is any truth in the yarn appears to be unknown.

William Thomson is said to have been a wright in Edinburgh, while John Robertson was a smith from Pleasance.

MARAUDING LIKE VIKINGS IN WORCESTERSHIRE

On the night of 7 November 1707, Mrs Ann Palmer of Upton Snodsbury, Worcestershire, and her maid servant Hester Loxley were both murdered and their house set afire. This was not the first time that something like this had happened; on 4 February an elderly woman named Ann Cormel had been robbed, murdered and her house set ablaze in Bretforton. However, initially Ann Cormel's death was not ruled a murder: the huge wound in her skull was judged to have occurred when a heavy beam had crashed down on her.

The identity of the latest two victims drew attention to Mrs Palmer's son John, and his brother-in-law Thomas Symonds. Both were gentlemen of the county, and worth much; Palmer, for example, was possessed of an estate worth nearly 200 pounds annually, plus 740 pounds in bonds, whereas Symonds was descended from the famous Justice Symonds of Cromwell's time. In fact, Symonds stood to inherit a fine old black-and-white timbered house within the manor of White Ladies Aston, where Oliver Cromwell himself had slept before the Battle of Worcester.

It appears these two rakes had fallen into a degenerate lifestyle of drinking and gambling, and at length they had formed a band of desperate villains. Their robberies were born out of a desire for money, and they had become marauders akin to the Vikings of old; in these outrages they were accompanied by three labourers named William Hobbins, John Allen, and Gyles Hunt.

Palmer was the only son of the old lady, and by her death stood to possess her fortune. It is an interesting fact that Hester Loxley, the murdered maidservant, had on 2 October 1703 escaped a dreadful fire in the parish that claimed the lives of one James Collins, his wife and seven children. Hester managed to survive unscathed, bar a broken limb, and soon after this accident went to live with Mrs Palmer. It is entirely possible that John Palmer torched his victim's houses in the hope that they would be passed off as similar accidents, for he would undoubtedly have known of the maid's adventure. Further to this, Palmer had sometimes been heard to make reference to killing his mother for the sake of gain.

The group were apprehended, examined, and tried at Worcester before Mr Justice Powell, where one among their number came out as a witness against the two gentlemen.

While Palmer and Symonds lay under condemnation for Mrs Palmer's murder, one Bishop Talbot of Oxford endeavoured to bring them to a confession and a just sense of their guilt. When he had accomplished this, Bishop Talbot attempted to defer their punishment, and so rode – on a rainy day and through high flooding – from Worcester to Gloucester in four hours, where he managed to secure them a reprieve for three weeks. Nevertheless, it meant little: the gentlemen were hanged on 8 May 1708 and their corpses suspended in chains; Hobbins and Allen, the two 'inferior criminals' who rode with them also suffered. Gyles Hunt, who had turned evidence against the gang, was pardoned.

Following the executions, the estate of White Ladies Aston was forfeited to Bishop Lloyd of Worcester, although he refused to accept it: for he declared himself unwilling to accept the 'price of blood' - despite having a family to feed and not much money.

DEATH OF AN ADMIRAL

Admiral Sir Cloudesley Shovell was an extremely brave and honoured man, his ascension through the ranks all the more remarkable for his humble upbringing. Born in 1650, by the time he was 53 he commanded the British fleet stationed in the Mediterranean; and, in the ensuing year, commanded the van of the combined fleet during the battle of Malaga.

Unfortunately, on his way homewards from the siege of Toulon, a most disastrous accident occurred; the admiral's vessel, the *Association*, together with two other ships of war, one carrying 70, the other 50, guns, was cast away on the rocks of the Scilly Isles off Cornwall on the evening of 22 October 1707.

The disaster was a national tragedy on an almighty scale. Some 2'000 persons lost their lives in the rough and surging waters off the Scillies, and after the admiral's corpse was found washed up on the sands of Porth Hellick Cove, St Mary's, it was conveyed to London where it was interred in Westminster Abbey with all due ceremony and at the public expense.

There was, however, a sinister postscript to this story. Many years later an aged woman, in the presence of the minister of the parish, confessed that on the night in question she had found the admiral miraculously alive on the shore, and had thence proceeded to 'treacherously and inhumanely' murder him. This act she revealed on her deathbed, claiming she could not die in peace without confessing. Plunder had been the motive for her crime, and she had yet in her possession an emerald ring that she had kept all these years lest an attempt to sell it revealed its original owner. The ring was given to the minister, and thereafter delivered to the Earl of Berkeley, an intimate friend of the admiral's, in whose possession it remained.

How the admiral supposedly met his end. This illustration originally appeared in the historical works of John Cassell in 1860.

There are a number of folkloric elements regarding this event. Some said that the sole survivor (a man who had clung to a rock in Hellweathers Neck, off St Agnes) testified that Admiral Shovell had ordered the execution of a crewmember shortly before the disaster. This crewman had claimed the flotilla was in danger of hitting the Scillies, and Shovell – outraged at the man's impudence – had him hanged by the neck from the yardarm. This poor fellow's last words were to the effect that those who saw him hang would never reach shore alive.

Some claimed that the admiral, when found deceased on the shore, was completely naked and laid out on the hatch of the ship; a circumstance which (if true) suggested he *might* have made it ashore alive but was then killed in some other manner and stripped of his clothes. Whatever the truth, the Earl of Romney, another acquaintance of the admiral, certainly believed his friend had met with foul play, for he observed, 'From the channel through which the communication was made, we have every reason to conclude that this account is most undoubtedly authentic.'

A MASS SLAUGHTER IN BEACONSFIELD

In 1708, Robert Greenway, of Beaconsfield, Buckinghamshire, utterly lost his mind. Whether he had any history of instability is unknown, but according to a pamphlet on the case, he started singing and dancing on the morning of 2 January. He encouraged his sister to join in, but when she refused he made an attempt to throttle her.

Greenway's sister managed to escape from him, and ran to some neighbours for help. When the group returned to the house they found he had hacked his wife, Jane, and four children to death with a hedge-bill.

The murderer was presented before Justice Lewis of Beaconsfield, who had him imprisoned in Aylesbury Gaol. Quite what became of him is unclear: the last we hear of the matter is from the pamphlet, which assures us 'Note the truth of this will be attested by the Beaconsfield carriers that come to the Bell in Warwick Lane.'

THE ROMANTIC HIGHWAY ROBBER

Jack Ovet was at one time a useful member of society, but like so many of his ilk he fell into a life of crime. He came from Nottingham, and was apprenticed to a shoemaker in his youth; for some time he followed this calling, until a naturally licentious and profligate disposition led him to purchase a horse and pistols and thunder off in the direction of London.

On the road to the capital he committed a robbery – it may have been his first – and deprived a gentleman of £20. This fellow stood up to Ovet, declaring that, had he not been ambushed and taken by surprise, he would have fought the robber off: to which Ovet (allegedly) handed him his money back and said, 'Here's your money again, and whoever is the better man, let him win it and wear it.' This proposal was agreed to, and both men drew their swords: Ovet fatally wounded his opponent, and carried on his way £20 the richer.

Already a thief and a killer at the very start of his career, Ovet committed murder a second time not long afterwards when he fatally wounded a man during a quarrel. However, the sword of justice had yet to overtake him, and he continued his profession on the highway, next robbing a man named Rogers of 280 guineas and a great quantity of silver cutlery that the man had strapped to his packhorse. Securing the man's horse to a tree, Ovet leisurely made his getaway carrying the spoils.

Ovet remained in the capital, and his next major robbery occurred thanks to an act of cunning simplicity. While drinking in the Star Inn in the Strand, he chanced to overhear a soap-boiler and a carrier planning how they might send £100 to a friend of the soap-maker in the countryside; at length, they decided to hide the money in a soap barrel, and accordingly the carrier loaded the barrel – with its secret contents – onto his wagon and set off the following morning. Of course, Jack pursued the man out of London and held him up that afternoon, threatening to shoot him dead before plundering the contents of the wagon until he found the hidden £100.

A crime Ovet committed after this episode displays all the elements of chivalry which future generations might come to expect from a typical 18th century highwayman story. He held up the Worcester stagecoach in the road, within which several young gentlewomen were passengers. Ovet robbed them all, but one of the women he found so charmingly attractive that (so it is said) he made this speech to her: 'Madam, cast not your eyes down, neither cover your face with those modest blushes; your charms have softened my temper, and I am no longer the man I was. What I have taken from you – through sheer necessity at present – is only borrowed, for as no object on earth ever had such an effect on me as you, assure yourself that, if you please to tell me where I may direct to you, I will, upon honour, make good your loss to the very utmost.' This young lady told him where he might send repayment to her, and after that Ovet rode off on his horse: a week later she received a letter from the highwayman, for she had, apparently, utterly conquered his heart and soul.

A highwayman finds his target full of women: an illustration from JM Rymer's Edith the Captive *(1861).*

However, the romance was destined not to play itself out. Ovet removed himself to Leicestershire, and continued his occupation on the highway until one hold-up led to an accomplice of his being fatally wounded and he himself pursued until he was run to ground. He was confined in gaol and at the next Leicester Assizes he was sentenced to death – this sentence being carried out upon the gallows on Wednesday 5 May 1708.

Jack Ovet was aged about 32 when he was hanged. The most interesting details of his story are the romantic elements, which seem almost clichéd when we think of the dashing image of the typical highwayman. Many accounts of crime and criminals in the early part of the 18th century came from pamphlets and chapbooks, rather than news-sheets and trial reporting as it would come to do later on in the century, so it is difficult to know how much of Ovet's adventures are folklore or embellishments. Still, the account does not shirk from noting the man murdered two people, so perhaps there is some truth in the entire story after all – including the 'romance' of highway robbery that later centuries would associate with these criminals.

A NATURAL BORN KILLER

The crimes of Tom Dorbel remind us that, whatever might have been the poverty and class divide that produced many felons, some were simply natural born villains.

Tom was apprenticed to a glover, but before he had served half his time he had fled his master and made his way to London – where he took up with a group of loutish young men as ignorant to the rule of law as himself. He was committing highway robbery before he was 18 years old, and of his first attempt a curious story is told. Tom apparently attempted to rob a travelling Welshman on the road, but the victim complained that it was not his money to hand over, but his master's; therefore, to prove to his master that he had been robbed the victim persuaded Tom to fire his pistols at his coat. Tom duly took the Welshman's coat off his back, hung it from a tree and emptied his pistols at it – upon which, of course, the victim now threatened Tom and told him to give him his stolen property back: Tom, having used his fire on a dangling coat, was forced to hand back the money he had taken.

He terrorised the highway for five years, until at length he was ruthless – or stupid – enough to allow himself to enter into a very dangerous arrangement with a gentleman's son. This fellow had been arrested for robbery on the highway, and he agreed to pay Tom a handsome sum of money if Tom would stand up in court, interrupt the trial and admit *he* had committed the gentleman's crime. Tom agreed to take the rap, and in doing so caused the case against the gentleman's son to collapse in confusion: the only consequence was that, naturally, Tom was himself arrested for the crime.

One assumes that this eventuality was planned for. At any rate, Tom's trial for highway robbery itself collapsed because no-one could identify him conclusively as the criminal – quite naturally, since this was one crime he *hadn't* committed. Upon his liberation he attempted to recover the money he had wasted while languishing in gaol by holding up the Duke of Norfolk near Salisbury, Wiltshire.

Salisbury Plain's most famous landmark: Dorbel terrorised the vicinity of Salisbury until his horse was shot and he was taken.

Tom's horse was shot during the incident and he himself taken. He was sentenced to death at the next assizes but (it is said) recruited a lawyer for the sum of 50 guineas to secure him a pardon. This man managed to procure a release and rode from London to Wiltshire on the day of Tom's execution to present it to the authorities; in fact, he forced his horse to run so hard that the poor animal dropped down dead when he arrived at the place where Tom was to be put to death. It is further said that the energetic lawyer produced the pardon even as Tom stood in the gallows cart about to be launched into oblivion. Tom Dorbel was released; but such was his ingratitude that he refused to pay the lawyer a penny, alleging that any obligation given by a man under sentence of death was not valid!

This escape from the jaws of death terrified Tom, and he opted to look for valid employment. For six or seven years he worked as a footman – until, while in the employ of a lady in Ormond Street, London, his natural criminal tendencies came horribly to the surface.

Up until this point, Dorbel seems to have been making quite a good name for himself. His mistress had a brother in Bristol who was a merchant, and the brother had allowed for his 16-year-old daughter to come to London to live with her aunt and perfect her education. Tom Dorbel at this time entertained the complete trust of his mistress, and so was dispatched to the West Country to bring the girl back to the capital. The journey was a long one, and as their coach neared London Tom found himself left alone with the girl. We are told that he 'shockingly abused' her (presumably this means he raped her) before robbing her of a gold watch, a diamond ring and £100 worth of jewels. He then cut and smashed his way out the back of the coach, leaving the girl inside brutally mistreated; in fact, so violent had his assault on her been that she died not long afterwards, shortly after her grief-stricken aunt had paid her a final visit and exchanged a few words with her. The girl's distraught father is said to have gone out of his mind with regret.

A manhunt was quickly launched for Dorbel, since it was obvious who was behind the murder, and riders went after him in different directions. He was apprehended shortly after robbing a gentleman of three pounds and five shillings. This time, there was no scheme that could save him: he was tried, and condemned to be executed and hung in chains. The sentence against this incorrigible villain was enforced on 23 March 1708.

THE TRIALS OF CHRISTOPHER SLAUGHTERFORD

Christopher Slaughterford was a miller's son apprenticed in Godalming, Surrey. When his apprenticeship finished, the young man took a malthouse at Shalford, between Godalming and Guildford, employing his aunt as the housekeeper and earning a moderate sum of money.

Slaughterford desired the attentions of Jane Young, and it became well known about the village that he would have taken her hand in marriage; however, the young woman completely disappeared on 5 October 1708, and it was a month before her body was found submerged in a local pond bearing several marks of violence about her person.

Slaughterford had been suspected in Jane's disappearance, since he had been seen in her company on the evening she went missing; and when people began to openly accuse him of being a murderer the young man took himself voluntarily to two Justices of the Peace. These examined him, and afterwards discharged him. However, since this failed to stem the tide of local accusations Slaughterford actually presented himself before a *third* magistrate and insisted he be tried for murder so as to prove his innocence once and for all. After being voluntarily committed to the Marshalsea Prison, he was tried for Jane Young's murder at Kingston Assizes – and acquitted.

The majority of Slaughterford's neighbours continued to insist he was a murderer, however, and so a fund was raised on behalf of Jane's parents to appeal against the verdict. And so it came to pass that the appeal was successfully granted to Henry Young, Jane's brother, upon whose continual accusations Christopher Slaughterford found himself once more on trial for murder at the court of Queen's Bench before Mr Justice Holt.

The Surrey jury heard much circumstantial evidence, such as the testimony of a man who claimed to have met a man and a woman on common ground about a quarter of a mile from where Jane's body was discovered; this was at three in the morning on 6 October, and the man had worn light-coloured clothes, such as it was proved the prisoner had on the day before Jane's disappearance. Soon after he passed them, this witness heard shrieking on the wind, like that of a woman being attacked. However, the witness did not investigate. Other witnesses perceived a latent guilt in some of the comments Slaughterford made while Jane was missing. For instance, a new mother said, 'What if Jane Young should lay you a new child such as mine is here?' to which Christopher replied, 'It is now impossible' before bursting into tears.

The evidence against the young man was in most respects no different to that presented at the first trial; yet despite his aunt and a young serving lad both declaring that Slaughterford had definitely *not* left the house on the night of 5-6 October, he was convicted of Jane's murder and sentenced to death. Unfortunately, the second jury was different to the first, and they appear to have sat with the predetermined stance that if 'Slaughterford didn't kill the girl then who did?'

From the moment of his conviction till that of his execution, Christopher Slaughterford steadfastly denied killing Jane Young, despite the visitations of a minister from Guildford who pressed him to confess. He was hanged at Guildford on 9 July 1709, throwing himself off the ladder as soon as the executioner had tied him up and put the noose round his neck. On the day of his death Slaughterford had written a last note, in which he declared his innocence and begged that his mother not suffer the stigma of his being hanged, 'as I expect salvation at the hands of almighty God'. He also forgave his enemies, including those who had apparently begun to point the finger of suspicion at his aunt as being the guilty party.

This case left an uneasy feeling among many in Surrey that Christopher Slaughterford had been an innocent man hanged.

THE MYSTERY OF SIR MICHAEL BALFOUR

Sir Michael Balfour, 5th Baronet Denmill, was a quiet country gentleman who lived with his wife Marjorie and their seven children at a semi-castellated old manor house called Denmylne, southeast of Newburgh in Fife. He appears to have had debts, but it does not appear they were serious; nothing suggests he was in any unduly complicated circumstances – which makes his disappearance all the more mysterious.

One day in March 1709 Balfour set off at an early hour from his home, which was in a pass through the Fife hills. He was attended by a servant, and explained his errand to his wife as being 'to visit some friends and for other business'.

At the end of the day, their business done, the baronet and his man returned in the direction of Newburgh. However, Sir Michael sent his servant off to Cupar on an errand, telling the latter he would be home before him and he would see him there. The two parted company, and Sir Michael rode off on his own; he was – literally - never seen again, alive or dead.

Naturally the neighbourhood was searched, then the surrounding towns. In desperation the search even extended as far as London, where advertisements were placed in the news-sheets asking for information. Next, advertisements were placed in some continental newspapers, but every avenue of enquiry utterly failed to produce any suggestion as to what might have happened to the baronet. Speculation at the time was rife: Sir Michael had taken himself off on his own accord because of melancholy, or displeasure; he had gone into hiding to avoid his creditors; it was even suggested he had been carried off by spirits. Some guessed that Sir Michael and his horse had simply fallen catastrophically into a deep coal pit on the way home, although these were searched without yielding any results.

It is reported that the courts initially stalled the baronet's creditors, partially blocking their attempt to seize Denmylne on the basis that Sir Michael might turn up alive. However, he never did, nor did any news of him ever surface; after many years had passed it became common speculation in Fife that he had been murdered.

To some extent this theory was backed up in November 1724, 15 years after Sir Michael disappeared. The public's curiosity was tantalised that year by a story published in a broadside entitled 'Murder will out', which claimed to be based on the dying words of a young woman who, when an infant, had seen her parents assassinate Sir Michael on the day he disappeared. According to the story, the baronet had been killed when he made an impromptu visit to his murderer's house: for the young woman's parents were his tenants, and he had called to collect a debt they owed him. While Sir Michael sat at the couple's fireside he was killed in cold blood with his own sword, and then buried in a grave; this fate also befell his horse, which joined its owner in the hastily-dug pit.

It was reported that the girl had given up this grim secret as her own life ebbed away, and Sir Michael's bones had been recovered; they had lately been transferred to the sepulchre belonging to his family. However, the baronet's son and heir flatly refuted the story when it appeared in the *Edinburgh Evening Courant*, and angrily forced the news-sheet to print a retraction.

The Scottish historian Robert Chambers visited the scene of the disappearance over a century later, and recorded: 'I have become satisfied that the disappearance of this gentleman from the field of visible life was never explained, and it now probably never will be. In time, the property (Denmylne) was bought by a neighbouring gentleman, who did not require to use the mansion as his residence. Denmill Castle accordingly fell out of order, and became a ruin.'

THE ESCAPE OF ROBERT, LORD BALFOUR OF BURLEIGH

The Honourable Robert Balfour was son and heir apparent to the fourth Lord Balfour of Burleigh, born in 1687 at the seat of his father, Lord Burleigh, near Kinross. He was well educated, having studied extensively at Orwell and St Andrews, and upon his return home it was intended by his father that he should join the Duke of Marlborough's army, then in Flanders.

At his father's house young Robert became enamoured of Miss Robertson, governess to his sisters, and in order to end this it was arranged by the family that he should make the tour through France and Italy as quickly as possible; the blameless Miss Robertson was subsequently dismissed by her employers. But before he left Scotland, Robert declared his intentions to the woman – and also vowed that he would kill any man she married while he was away.

Miss Robertson deemed this an empty threat, and – during Robert's absence – married a schoolmaster called Henry Stenhouse on 6 December 1705, with whom she went to live in Inverkeithing. Upon Robert's return to Scotland he learned of this union and proceeded to his enemy's house on 9 April 1707, accompanied by two attendants. Mrs Stenhouse saw her former beau approaching, and – remembering his oath – screamed in fright. Stenhouse rushed to see what the matter was, but by this time Robert had called out his enemy's name and entered the house; in the presence of some of Stenhouse's scholars he shot the man directly in the shoulder, wounding the man so critically that he died twelve days afterwards. (Other accounts suggest Stenhouse was shot in the chest, but this appears less likely.)

The offender immediately fled, but was eventually arrested near Edinburgh following a proclamation issued by Queen Anne herself for his apprehension. Robert Balfour went on trial in the High Court of Justiciary on 4 August 1709; his defence counsel attempted to convince the court that he had wielded the weapon not with the intention of murder, but 'to frighten or correct'. This story was disbelieved and on 29 November Balfour was convicted of murder; on account of his noble background he was sentenced to be beheaded on 6 January the following year.

The method of execution was to be a guillotine-like contraption called 'the maiden'. (One of the curiosities of dieing by this method was that horse thieves and cattle raiders could actually be killed by the animals they had stolen. For the string of the machine was tied to the beast, which, on being whipped, moved forward, pulling out the peg and letting the blade fall. In this manner the stolen animal actually became the 'executioner'.)

Balfour, however, was fated to cheat the maiden. On 5 January 1710, the day before his execution, he was allowed a visit by his sister, and – she being very like him in face and stature – they exchanged clothes. Balfour thus escaped both his wardens and Edinburgh Tolbooth, managing to ride out to a distant village on a horse provided by some of his friends. Here he hid until an opportunity presented itself to leave Scotland's shores. It is said that before he left the country he skulked for some time in the neighbourhood of Burleigh Castle, the family seat, where a hollow ash tree was long pointed out as his place of concealment. It earned the name Burleigh's Hole, but in 1822 it was completely blown down.

Before Balfour's father died in the year 1713, he managed to secure a pardon for his wayward son. Robert subsequently returned and became the fifth Lord Burleigh, succeeding the honours of his family and dieing in 1757, sincerely penitent for the murder he had committed.

The family title, however, became extinct upon his death, it being recalled that Robert had been present at a meeting at Lochmaben on 29 May 1714 where he had drunk the health of the Pretender at the Cross before the first Jacobite Rising; his demise in the years following the second rising ensured the eradication of the title on the grounds of Balfour being a confirmed Jacobite sympathiser.

THE FRENCH CONNECTION

On 10 August 1710 the Honourable Robert Harley was constituted one of the commissioners of the Treasury, and also Chancellor and Under-treasurer of the Exchequer.

Three days after having been 'sworn in of the privy council' he was in this capacity present at the interrogation of a French spy for high treason under a committee within a building along Whitehall. The Frenchman being interrogated on this day, 8 March 1711, was the ex-abbe de la Bourlie, commonly called the Marquis of Guiscard. While in the clerk's room awaiting his examination, Guiscard had managed to grab and secrete a penknife that he had spotted about the clerk's person. This he produced during his examination, lunging at Mr Harley and stabbing him in an attempt to kill him. However, the chancellor was only wounded; Guiscard was violently subdued and afterwards thrown into Newgate, where he died on 17 March. It was discovered that Harley had been stabbed under the breast, on his right side.

The attempted assassination of Mr Harley. This illustration originally appeared in the historical works of John Cassell in 1860.

While languishing in Newgate, the marquis explained that his original plan had in fact been to assassinate another person present at his examination, one Henry St John, later the famous Viscount Bolingbroke. St John had been active in the prosecution of one Greg, whom he had interrogated and later executed as a traitor for treasonable correspondence with France. When St John attended the marquis' own interrogation, he changed seats with Harley – so when he made his fatal lunge, Guiscard had been forced to settle for the dignitary nearest him in order to avenge the executed Greg. He had apparently consoled himself with the thought that if he could strike a mortal blow on his enemy's dearest friend, then that would be good enough.

Supporters of Harley attempted to cast blame for the assassination attempt on the rival Whig party, but there was no real proof: Guiscard was merely a 'secret common spy and agent for the French ministry'. The marquis had been stabbed a number of times in the struggle to subdue him (including once by St John), and these injuries – rather than jail fever – probably caused his death. This is suggested by a clause in a subsequent Act of Parliament designed to protect politicians against future assassination attempts, which exonerated any persons who might have inflicted a wound or bruise upon the marquis, by which violence he might have received his death.

Mr Harley, despite suffering a severe stab wound that confined him for some time away from public duty, nonetheless recovered and returned to public life.

MURDER BY THE DUKE'S SERVANT

At the junction of Grosvenor Street and Lower Bridge Street in Chester can be found the Falcon Inn, a place of great antiquity. It was outside this landmark building near the River Dee that a notable killing occurred in 1711, according to the city historian Joseph Hemingway, writing in the 19th century.

During the mayoralty of John Minshull, bookseller, the city was visited by the Lord Lieutenant of Ireland, James Butler, 2nd Duke of Ormond. The Irish statesman and his retinue stopped for refreshment at the inn, at that time run by a family named Kenna. There they stayed until 'the wind served for him to proceed on his journey' to Park-gate.

On the morning, when he and his suite were setting off, one of Mr Kenna's waiters ran after a servant of his Excellency, to demand payment for some articles which he had overlooked. The duke's servant refused to hand over any more money; and so the waiter obstinately held onto the fellow's horse's bridle while still demanding the bill be paid in full. In the end the matter was resolved when the duke's servant drew a pistol from his holsters and fired it at the waiter, killing him on the spot.

The murderer was secured and imprisoned, and in the run-up to the trial the Duke of Ormond ordered that if his man should be convicted then word was to be sent to him immediately so that he might petition the queen for a pardon. The prisoner was tried at Chester and found guilty of murder, and when the mayor, John Minshull, was reminded of the duke's request, he stated, 'I will take care to save her majesty and the lord lieutenant any further trouble in this matter.' Minshull was not messing around: he ordered the murderer's execution to be carried out the day following his conviction.

Hemingway wrote of this crime and other stories about the Falcon: '…the truth of which I think may be relied on, as they rest on an authority already quoted, namely, the *MS.* remains of the late Alderman Broster'.

A QUANTITY OF YELLOW ARSENIC

Elizabeth Mason was a native of Melton Mowbray, Leicestershire, although at the age of seven she was taken from her then-home in Sutton, near

Peterborough, to London by one Mrs Scoles, who professed to be the child's godmother.

Mrs Scoles resided in the capital with her sister, Mrs Cholwell, and as Elizabeth grew up they gainfully employed her as their personal household domestic. The sisters were well-to-do, by the standard of the times, residing first near Temple-bar and then Covent Garden – where the following tragedy was enacted.

When she reached maturity Elizabeth formed the opinion that should both her mistresses die she would be the natural benefactor of their estate and possessions. On the Thursday of Easter Week in 1712 Elizabeth accordingly took herself to a druggist's shop, where she purchased a quantity of yellow arsenic on the pretence that she wanted it to kill rats. The following morning she stirred some of the deadly substance into a cup of coffee, which she presented to Mrs Scoles. The woman became immediately ill upon drinking the contaminated coffee, and announced that her end was near; she died the very next day in intense agony.

Mrs Cholwell barely touched her own cup of coffee, which had also been poisoned, and as a consequence survived. This forced Elizabeth to return to the druggist's shop and purchase a second quantity of arsenic, which she stirred into Mrs Cholwell's water-gruel and served to the woman at breakfast the following morning. Providentially, the gruel was too hot, and while Mrs Cholwell left it to cool the arsenic sank to the bottom. When it had cooled, she drank the gruel and immediately fell sick; observing the sediment at the bottom of the basin, Mrs Cholwell sent for her apothecary – who made her drink a quantity of oil and vomit the contents of her stomach up. By this method the arsenic she had partaken of was expelled.

Elizabeth Mason was taken into custody on suspicion of murder and attempted murder, and when she was interrogated by two Justices of the Peace on 30 April she confessed her guilt and was committed to Newgate. On 6 June 1712 she was tried for the murder of Mrs Scoles and, upon admitting her guilt, she was sentenced to death. While in the condemned cell in Newgate the ordinary asked her whether she had any lover, or someone else who had tempted her into committing the crime; Elizabeth answered in the negative.

In fact, her admission of guilt was remarkably frank, and is possibly the most fascinating thing about the whole case. She also admitted that she had frequently defrauded her mistresses and then lied to cover up her thieving, until her greed became so overwhelming that she turned to murder to claim everything the women possessed. Just before her execution at Tyburn on 18 June 1712 Elizabeth even went so far as to acknowledge she ought to be made a public example of so that other young people did not fall into avarice and murder as she had done. That one so cold-blooded could platform herself as a moral lesson to the London public at large, and even acknowledge the justification of her own death, seems remarkable, to say the least. This illustrates a curious phenomenon of the times: that murderers, when caught, seem more often than not to have fully confessed very quickly upon their arrest.

'THE MOST TERRIBLE ACCIDENT THAT HATH ALMOST EVER HAPPENED'

Duelling in Anne's time was a persistent issue; one Richard Thornhill, for instance, shot dead Sir Cholmondeley Deering, of Kent, during a duel fought on 9 May 1711 at Tothill Fields, central London. It is written that they were armed with swords and pistols, and when they aimed the latter at each other they were so close that the muzzles touched. Their quarrel had arisen out of an argument they had had in Hampton Court, when Deering had beaten out some of Thornhill's teeth. The latter was indicted for murder at the Old Bailey on 18 May but subsequently acquitted; about two months later Thornhill was himself murdered on Turnham Green, Chiswick, by two men who exclaimed, 'Remember Sir Cholmondeley Deering!' as they stabbed him to death. But on 15 November 1712 there occurred a duel – 'the most terrible accident that hath almost ever happened' according to one correspondent – that put an end to the short, violent life of the rakish Whig politician Charles Mohun, 4th Baron Mohun.

The duel had its origins in a protracted dispute over property with James Douglas, 4th Duke of Hamilton. Both men had married nieces of Lord Macclesfield, and 'Mohun gave the affront, and yet sent the challenge'. The two men's differing political alliances (Hamilton was a Tory) were also a natural source of enmity between them. Thus, accompanied by seconds, the two men met at seven in the morning 'by the Ring in Hyde Park'; armed with swords, they entered into a battle where they fought like 'enraged lions'.

Baron Mohun was fatally injured during this encounter, but shortly afterwards the Duke of Hamilton himself died in unclear circumstances. Despite his victory he appears to have been wounded by Mohun, who, on the back foot against his stronger opponent, shortened his sword and 'stabbed him in at the shoulder to the heart'. However, it might be that - having honourably won the duel - Hamilton was actually assassinated after the event; because, according to certain correspondence, Baron Mohun's footman immediately stabbed Hamilton upon seeing his master die. So, most likely, Hamilton's fatal wound was dealt by Mohun's second, Captain George McCartney, who had been simultaneously fighting with Colonel John Hamilton, the duke's second, in an attempt to discourage the duke during the battle.

There was a skill and a science to duelling, making those trained in such practices more efficient killers.

While his opponent Mohun lay dead, the critically-wounded duke was gently carried to a nearby cake-house, but he died on the grass before he could be taken inside. He was brought to his home in St James's Square at eight o' clock, the duchess being woken and informed that her husband had been murdered.

Tory writers suggested the whole affair was a Whig plot to get rid of the Duke of Hamilton; he appears to have been very highly thought of. A friend writing at the time described him as a 'frank, honest, good-natured man', and his death is said to have left Queen Anne 'stupefied with grief'.

Such conspiratorial allegations were thrown about on account of another, unconnected event. On 4 November, shortly before the deadly combat in Hyde Park, a bandbox had been posted to the Earl of Oxford: when part-opened the box showed a pistol within pointing upwards. Further examination by a gentleman present (Jonathan Swift, in fact) showed that the contraption was a clever booby trap which – had the box not been so carefully opened – would have discharged two barrels in different directions. The papers made much of the 'Bandbox Plot', but whether it was a hoax, an attempt at intimidation or a genuine attempt to cleverly kill the earl is unclear. But the charged climate meant that it was only natural the Tories saw conspiracy in the Duke of Hamilton's slaying.

George McCartney fled England after the duel, but returned from Holland upon the accession of King George I. He was tried for murder in June 1716, although Colonel John Hamilton – who appeared against him – was discredited and McCartney was cleared of the capital charge. He was, however, found guilty of being an accessory and 'burnt in the hand'. Within a month he was given an appointment in the army and promoted to Lieutenant General.

Colonel Hamilton's evidence may in part have been discredited as he himself was already convicted on charges relating to the two deaths. Shortly after the duel, he had surrendered himself and gone on trial at the Old Bailey on 12 December 1712. The following day he was convicted on two counts of manslaughter and 'burnt in the hand'. After McCartney's trial collapsed, Colonel Hamilton himself died in October 1716 from 'a sudden vomiting of blood'.

As for Baron Mohun, he was aged about 37 when he died that day in Hyde Park. He had a lot of blood on his hands, being a fanatical duellist and having already twice been cleared of murder in 1693 and 1699.

THE MISSING PARSON

In the north of England, when a missing parson's niece fell seriously ill her deathbed confession solved a four-year mystery.

The name of the vanished parson was Enoch Sinclere, 'vicar of one of the sister churches' in Holderness, East Yorkshire (he was, in fact, the vicar of Owthorne, near Withernsea). He had lived with his two nieces and two domestics, one male and one female. The day before his disappearance in 1708 Sinclere had ridden his horse out on an errand, with the intention of returning – yet the horse was subsequently found wandering by itself, still bridled and saddled.

When 15-year-old Lucy Sinclere made her statement four years later, her information led not only to the discovery of the parson's remains – fully clothed and buried in a yard near his home not far from the River Humber - but also to the arrest of the main suspects in his disappearance. These were Lucy's sister Mary and her husband Adam Alvin, who had been Sinclere's servant at the time.

A few weeks following the recovery of the parson's body on 18 April 1712, Adam Alvin was arrested in Sunderland and committed to Durham Gaol (although some accounts say he was taken in London). Young Lucy, who would have been about 11 when her uncle disappeared, seems to have been privy to the whole affair, for upon her appearing before three Yorkshire Justices of the Peace, her testimony was taken by messenger to Sunderland, where its damaging content led to the arrest of Alvin's wife (and Lucy's sister) Mary, also on a charge of murder on 4 June 1712.

It was supposed at the trial that Alvin had murdered the parson for two reasons: Reverend Sinclere had disapproved of his union with Mary, and she also stood to inherit her uncle's property. Thus, Alvin was convicted of the killing at York Assizes and on 21 August sentenced to be executed at York's Tyburn (on an area to the south of the city that is now part of York Racecourse).

His execution was preceded by a remarkable event. The day before, a sermon was preached for the benefit of the condemned man by Reverend Mr Mace. Alvin loudly declared he was entirely innocent, and the shock of this caused Mr Mace to collapse at his own pulpit and expire immediately. Alvin took to declaring that the hand of God had been visibly displayed on the matter of his innocence, and the people actually began to believe that this must be the case. However, this doubt only lasted until the following morning when Alvin made a full confession before 'being launched into eternity under all the agonizing horrors of despair'. He died at the same time as a highway robber and a woman convicted of murdering her infant child.

Mary Sinclere was acquitted. Young Lucy, whose guilt had revealed the dark truth of the whole affair, died of her illness.

THE WEAPON OF SEX

The case of Mr John Sayer, Esq, is not remarkable so much for his death by murder as it is for the conduct of his wife, Mary, who – to put it mildly – appears to have been a sex-obsessed nymphomaniac.

Mr Sayer was well-to-do, being worth £1'000 a year and possessed of the manor of Biddlesden in Buckinghamshire. He married Mary, the daughter of Admiral Nevil, in 1699, but it is clear they were very different characters: she attractive and quick witted, he good natured and inoffensive – and in many ways, making the perfect cuckold. Despite bearing Sayer two children (one of which, a daughter, died in infancy), Mary Sayer's conduct towards her husband, and deliberate flouting of her marriage vows, was nothing short of disgraceful.

Her attitude towards her husband had been displayed very clearly only a few days after their wedding, when Mary had viciously kicked John and hinted that she would take a lover; John, who was utterly smitten, took it all with patience and calm, continually loading her with presents to keep her by his side. Following the death of their first child Mr and Mrs Sayer took a house in 'Lisle Street, Leicester Fields' (Leicester Square, London); and it was after the birth of their second child that Mrs Sayer's behaviour began to become more openly scandalous – encouraged as it was by her mother, who had married one Colonel Salisbury following the admiral's death.

Mary Sayer and her mother, now Mrs Salisbury, were of the same mould. The similarities between them were breath-taking, both being of good standing yet completely obsessed with sex and bearing no regard for their husbands whatsoever; in fact, by this time Mary was openly having an affair - and this situation the two women used to their advantage in a truly awesome scheme to contrive the deaths of both of their husbands. One day the colonel took it upon himself to have words with his daughter-in-law about her disgraceful behaviour. Mary effectively told him where to go in such offensive language that he launched a cup of tea over her; so Mary used this as the reason to persuade her weak-willed husband to defend her honour and challenge Colonel Salisbury to a duel. The plan was sublime: the colonel was a veteran swordsman, and the two women hoped that he would kill Mr Sayer in combat and then either be jailed or hanged for it. The colonel was a man of great intelligence and discretion, however, for he saw what was happening, and when Mr Sayer challenged him to a duel he took the opportunity to talk to his misguided son-in-law while they took a coach towards Montague House in Bloomsbury. He addressed him as follows: 'Son Sayer, let us come to a right understanding of this business. 'Tis very well known that I am a swordsman, and I should be very far from any honour by killing you. But, to come nearer to the point in hand, thou shouldst know, Jack, for all the world knows, that thy wife and mine are both what they should not be. They want to get rid of us at once. If thou shouldst drop, they'll have me hanged for it after.'

There was so much obvious truth in this that the gentlemen drove home together – much to the abject mortification of the women. Mr Sayer and his wife gradually proceeded to drift further and further apart after this, although they remained married.

It was by now about the year 1709. Mary Sayer took herself to live at the house in Buckinghamshire, embarking on an immediate affair with the curate there, with such brazen openness that her servants began to take the curate for their new master. When Mrs Sayer returned to London (and to her husband - or rather, his money) the curate followed her, but very quickly died of the smallpox.

Mrs Sayer's move to London did not mean a return to the marital state, however; the curate's place in her bed was supplanted by an officer of the guards, who was in turn replaced by 'a man of great distinction'. Throughout this time Mr Sayer found his finances severely disrupted by his wife's extravagances, and at length a friend suggested he consult an attorney at law, named Richard Noble.

All the factors were coming together that were to result in Mr Sayer's untimely demise. Richard Noble was young – not yet thirty – and the son of a reputable Bath coffee-house proprietor. He was well-educated, and following his apprenticeship to a renowned New Inn attorney he afterwards took chambers there himself and conducted his own business. Soon after his introduction to the Sayer family this bright and charming fellow struck up an affair not only with Mrs Sayer, but also her mother, Mrs Salisbury.

Later in 1709 Richard Noble was empowered to draw up a deed of separation between Mr and Mrs Sayer, and he harassed Sayer by various suits in chancery connected with his wife's separate estate. It appears that the whole process was arranged and dictated by Mrs Sayer – her husband being so weak willed as to sign deeds without having counsel of his own to examine them. Noble was soon living with Mary Sayer, who on 5 March 1711 bore him a son in Bath. In order that this last fact should not reach the ears of Mr Sayer – who might use such 'criminal intercourse' in a counter lawsuit – Mary Sayer and her mother tricked the luckless gentleman into leaving England for the Netherlands. This they did by making Noble send an official letter to Mr Sayer telling him he was to be appointed High Sheriff of Buckinghamshire, a position he did not want; and Mrs Salisbury actually paid to get Mr Sayer out of the country. Upon his departure Sayer's faithless wife was heard to comment that she wished her gullible husband would drown on the voyage to Holland.

Mr Sayer remained in Holland nearly a year, during which time Noble publicly cohabited with his client's wife. When he eventually returned to London Mary refused to have anything more to do with him, and – after stealing £2'000 worth of exchequer bills and other effects from him - she went to live on 23 May 1712 in private lodgings with Noble, where she gave birth to a second child by the attorney.

Unseemly and never-ending legalities over the ownership of the Sayer's money ensued, which there is not much point in going into too much detail over; suffice to say that during this period Mrs Sayer's insatiable appetite for sex meant that during Noble's occasional absences she managed to fill the gap, as it were, with other casual lovers.

As the legal merry-go-round continued, things began to go Mr Sayer's way: he obtained a deed of separation and took out a notice in the news-sheets to the effect that Mrs Sayer was a thief, a liar and ought not to be trusted by tradesmen. This forced Mrs Sayer, the attorney Noble, Mrs Salisbury (the mother) and the two children to take lodgings in the Mint, Southwark, to avoid being associated with the advertisement. In January 1713 Sayer procured a warrant empowering him to arrest his ex-wife 'as being gone from her husband, and living in a loose, dishonourable manner': a move which, remarkable as it may seem, he hoped might make her return to him, since they were, as yet, still technically married. Failing that, Mr Sayer hoped at the least he might recover most of his possessions from his wife's new house in George Street.

When Mr Sayer went to his wife's house he was accompanied by two parish constables and six assistants. They had a warrant from a Justice of the Peace, but had to be careful: if the populace of Southwark had thought them bailiffs then they were likely to be attacked, or even killed, and this appears to have been one of the principal reasons Mrs Sayer opted to settle there. Therefore, the group intimated they were hunting a suspected criminal; nonetheless, it must have been a very intimidating experience when the little group went into the Mint, which had earned a reputation for having one of the lowest standards of living anywhere in the capital by this era. For Mrs Sayer, this must have been the most dismal of places, coming from a privileged background as she did; the place was a refuge for persons of desperate circumstances and abandoned character, where murder was common and disease rife thanks to the tides of sewage that lapped along the place from the Thames.

On 29 January 1713 Mr Sayer and his men entered his wife's house and converged on a back room, where his wife, her mother and Mr Noble were at dinner. Upon seeing Mr Sayer, Noble immediately drew a sword and stabbed his former client in the chest: the wounded man slumped backwards into the arms of his servant, James Terry, clutching his left side and gasping, 'I am killed!' Mr Sayer died almost immediately, such was depth of the wound. Noble was immediately grappled to the floor by the dead man's assistants, who also secured the two women. It is an interesting detail that, apprehensive the mob might attack them under the misapprehension the prisoners were debtors, one of the constables was forced to carry the bloodied sword aloft before him as they retreated out of Southwark, to make it clear that a murder had been committed. This had the desired effect on the mob, who, although extremely threatening, abstained from attempting to rescue the three prisoners. It is reported that the two women did naught but bewail the fate of Mr Noble, the killer attorney whose disgrace was now so complete it is difficult to imagine a more complete fall from prominence.

It only remains to be said that the three prisoners were put to the bar at Kingston-upon-Thames, then part of Surrey, on 12 March 1713, Noble charged with murder and the two women charged with having assisted him in the fact. The following day the jury pronounced Noble guilty of murder. Mrs Sayer and her mother, Mrs Salisbury, were acquitted. Upon being brought to the bar to receive his sentence from Lord Chief Justice Parker on Monday 16 March, Noble made an incredibly educated and impassioned plea to the court that his crime was not a deliberate murder in the eyes of the law, and that mercy ought to be shown towards him; his long and emotive speech perhaps reminded everyone present just what a remarkably fine man he might have become had not his association with Mrs Sayer led him astray. In the end, he suffered execution at Gallows-hill, Kingston, on 28 March 1713 aged about 28, displaying every sign of genuine repentance.

One is only left wondering what became of Mrs Mary Sayer. It is certain that Noble saw nothing of her (or her mother) after his conviction, although they continued to try and earn him a reprieve. When it became clear this would not happen, Mrs Sayer disguised herself as a serving-maid and made earnest solicitations to gain access to his cell to see Noble one last time; Noble, receiving her letter, and perceiving she wished his body for a final sexual liaison, sent word back to her that he was 'a man still, and liable to passions' – but he had only a short time left and needed to prepare his soul.

The essayist and political pamphleteer Jonathan Swift recorded an additional piece of information about Noble's end: 'Mr Noble, who was hanged last

Saturday, was recovered by his friends, and then seized again by the sheriff, and is now in a messenger's hands at the Black Swan in Holborn.'

THE MYSTERIOUS FIRE OF INCHDREWER CASTLE

The remains of the old castle of Inchdrewer stand on the high ground of the Hill of Tipperty, about three miles SW of Banff and looking out towards the North Sea. This castle is, more properly, a baronial tower, built about the time of James IV or V, and it is still largely entire.

This is despite a mysterious event that occurred on the evening of 13 November 1713. It is said that, having embraced the Roman Catholic faith, Sir George Ogilvy, 3rd Lord Banff, had lately spent some time in Ireland, possibly engaged in some of the intrigues then playing out in support of the Pretender. Shortly after his return to Scotland, Lord Banff perished in a disastrous blaze at Inchdrewer; he was aged about 64.

It was widely believed that during his absence he had left the castle in the charge of his domestics, who pillaged some of his valuable property while he was away. When he returned, they entered into a criminal conspiracy to murder his lordship, setting his apartment on fire for the sake of concealment. Lord Banff was afterwards interred in the vaulted aisle of the old church here.

Inchdrewer Castle. (Photo courtesy of Richard Paxman.)

Many viewed Lord Banff's bizarre death as divine judgement on his religion, for he had apparently made threats to burn the Protestants in the build-up to the Pretender's rebellion. But there are conflicting theories, for in truth Ogilvy appears to have *renounced* Catholicism in 1705 and sat on the last Scottish Parliament that voted for the union with England; for this, it is believed, he might have been murdered by certain members of a family whose honour or reputation he had sullied. It is also said he may have met his end through a quarrel over the inheritance of land; or possibly the whole thing was the result of an awful accident. With such a muddle of speculation, the truth is now likely to remain a mystery: however, it certainly says a lot about the politics in Scotland at this time that murder was supposed to be the more likely explanation.

ATTACKS ON TURNKEYS

Two remarkable cases serve to illustrate the brazenness and violence employed by desperate men determined to escape punishment. In 1713, William Lowther, a Cumberland seaman, and Richard Keele, a Winchester barber, along with Charles Houghton and a man named Cullum, were sentenced at the Old Bailey to two years hard labour within the Clerkenwell Bridewell (in the modern Borough of Islington). Mr Boreman, the gaoler, insisted the four be placed in irons to restrict their movement during the journey to the prison; this treatment the prisoners rebelled against, somehow managing to overpower Boreman near their destination and break into the armoury. Boreman and an assistant were mercilessly beaten, and Lowther actually bit the nose off one of them; when a *turnkey* called William Perry cautiously approached the fracas, he was fatally stabbed by Houghton - who was himself then shot to death in the fray.

The prisoners made a victorious escape but it was shorted lived: with 'the neighbours giving their assistance' Keele and Lowther were re-arrested, along with a number of others who had taken the opportunity to escape during the confusion.

On 10 December 1713 both were tried at the Old Bailey and capitally convicted. Three days later, in the early morning, they were carried from Newgate to Clerkenwell Green and hanged on a specially erected gallows. On the scaffold, Keele asked the under-sheriff if he was to hang in chains after his death, and was told: 'Don't concern yourself about your body, but take care of your poor soul.' A day after their execution, Keele and Lowther's corpses were put in a cart drawn by four horses decorated with plumes of black feathers, and taken to hang in metal cages suspended from a gibbet post.

The phrase 'turnkey' refers to the jailers who held the prison keys. An attack on another turnkey that occurred *within* the Old Bailey court was, if anything, even more astonishing. William Johnson, formerly a Northamptonshire butcher, but lately a highway robber who had so far been extremely lucky to escape

79

conviction, entered the Old Bailey pursuant to the trial of an acquaintance, Jane Housden. She was to be tried for coining, and just as she was brought down to the bar Johnson called to her. The head turnkey of Newgate, Mr Spurling, told Johnson he would have to wait till after the trial to talk to her, and so Johnson produced a pistol and simply shot the man to death in full view of the presence of the court.

The crime was almost suicidal in its public spectacle, and when order had been restored and Johnson disarmed, the judges deemed it unnecessary for Ms Housden's coining trial to continue. Both she and Johnson were almost immediately convicted of Spurling's murder and sentenced to death, Housden having been heard to egg Johnson on. Both had the impudence to deny the killing to the last, even upon the advent of their executions on 19 September 1712. After hanging the usual time, Johnson's body was hung in chains near Holloway, between Islington and Highgate.

Johnson fatally shoots Mr Spurling in full view of the court. (As originally depicted in Knapp's 1824 Newgate Calendar Volume 1.*)*

THE MURDER OF MR RICHARD DOBELL

On 1 December 1713 Mr Richard Dobell left his home in Chichester, Sussex, to go to a place about two miles out of town called East Ashling. Dobell owned a farm there, and having collected the rent from the tenant he set off once more back in the direction of Chichester.

About a mile from the town Mr Dobell was ambushed in the road at a spot between two small hills. It was between three and four in the afternoon, and Mr Dobell was quite simply murdered in cold blood.

Around this time a woman named Elizabeth Andrew, going to milking not far from that place, heard a voice, unknown to her, at a distance utter these words: 'What mean you? Oh Christ! Pray don't!' Upon hearing this, she listened very earnestly but could discern no more.

On the morning of 2 December market traders found Mr Dobell lying quite dead, positioned with his head about a yard from the road. His own neck-cloth had been tied around his neck and knotted three times by his assailant, who had used so much force in garrotting his victim that one end of the cloth was torn by the violence of the pulling. Mr Dobell's body also displayed vicious bruising to the elbow, sides, breast and belly, suggesting he had been beaten or otherwise roughly treated. His pocket was turned inside out and his money had been stolen, although the thief had left his watch, knife and fork.

So viciously had Mr Dobell been strangled that when his corpse was laid out, and the neck-cloth untied, his body actually made considerable post-mortem noise, which those present ascribed to his last inhaled breath finally managing to find passage out of his body.

It later transpired that shortly after the crime had been committed a lad had passed the body in the road, but – thinking the man asleep – had taken no action. Numerous other people had passed the body during the night but not spotted it in the winter darkness. Mr Dobell's poor mother offered a reward of £100 for information, but it appears this ruthless murder went unsolved; which was particularly worrying, as a subsequent sermon lamented: 'We know there have been three very horrid murders committed near this city in a very short time.'

These other cases concerned: 'The Widow Turner, whose throat was cut at Lavant. (And) a maid drown'd.'

THE MOHOCKS, AND OTHER MURDEROUS 'CLUBS'

Queen Anne's reign, it is said, was beset by a peculiar type of social problem: a fraternity of bored and loutish young rakes who wandered parts of the capital inflicting pointless violence on complete strangers, merely for the sake of having done so. These shadowy gangs went by the collective name of Mohocks, naming themselves after the Mohawk tribe of North America, although there were other groups with other names.

The Annals of Queen Anne for the Year 1712 shed light on these monstrous young hooligans. Recent night time disorders had been committed by 'great numbers of persons disaffected to her Majesty's Government, who, under the name of *MOHOCKS* or *HAWKUBITES*, (have) combined together to disturb the public peace'. Although this implies a political agenda, perhaps it merely means the Mohocks had an utter disregard for the rule of law: for their violence was certainly wanton enough. They slit completely innocent people's noses in the street, or else bashed their noses flat; forced iron instruments into men's mouths; and drove pins into other people's bodies. Lists were printed out naming a number of persons who had supposedly committed these acts and who were now reported to be languishing in a number of prisons: among the suspects were several men of position and title. Whether this list concerned *real* arrests or not is unclear, but it struck such terror in the heart of Londoners that Queen Anne herself issued a royal proclamation: 'For the suppressing of riots, and the discovery of such as had been guilty of the late barbarities within the cities of London and Westminster, and parts adjacent; charging and commanding, that the said offenders should be prosecuted with the utmost severity and rigour of the law; and promising a reward of one hundred pounds for the discovery and apprehending of any person, who, since the 1st day of February last, had, without any provocation, wounded, stabbed, or maimed, or who should, before the 1st day of May, wound, stab or maim, any of her Majesty's subjects.' There is a feeling that a kind of panic swept through the city, with some claiming the Mohocks were thugs hired by the Whigs to terrorize the populace.

Although details of just who the Mohocks were, as well as specific instances of their violence, are hard to come by, the terror they occasioned was very real. Nonetheless, the *Spectator* reported ample anecdotal evidence of their existence: 'An outrageous ambition of doing all possible to hurt their fellow-creatures is the great cement of their assembly, and the only qualification required in their members. In order to exert this principle in its full strength and perfection, they take care to drink themselves to a pitch that is beyond the possibility of attending to any motions of reason or humanity, then make a general sally, and attack all that are so unfortunate as to walk the streets through which they patrol. Some are knocked down, others stabbed, others cut and *carbanadoed*.'

The president of the Mohock Club, it was reckoned, was styled the Emperor of the Mohocks; his coat of arms was a Turkish crescent which his highness had 'engraven upon his forehead'. It was also believed that members of the group were sub-divided and classed by the type of crime they specialised in. Some flattened noses and used their fingers to bore out the eyeballs of their victims. Some were called the 'dancing-masters' on account of using their swords to slice the tendons and legs of people in the street. A third set were the 'tumblers', who set women on their heads and mutilated their limbs. Another pastime of these wretches was to force women into empty barrels and send them careening down

Snow Hill. Their most disgraceful exploits occurred on the occasions when they spotted a victim in the street and surrounded him; one among their number would stab him in the buttocks, forcing him to wheel round – whereupon the others would then do the same. As the stabbed man turned at every occasion the Mohocks would yell 'A sweat, a sweat!' - on account of their only losing interest in the sport when their bloodied victim could not longer stand and collapsed sweating because of his enforced 'exercise'.

The correspondence (9 March 1712) of the well-known essayist and political pamphleteer Jonathan Swift explains that he was forced to abandon his beloved evening walks when he learned from friends that the Mohocks had a particular hatred of him: 'I walked in the Park (the Green Park) this evening, and came home early, to avoid the Mohocks.' And on 16 March he wrote: 'Lord Winchelsea told me to-day at court that two of the Mohocks caught a maid of old Lady Winchelsea's, at the door of their house in the Park, with a candle, who had just *lighted out* somebody. They cut all her face and beat her, without any provocation.'

Green Park, where this attack occurred, was the site of a grim find in the mid-1700s. Some labourers employed in cutting a drain across it from Piccadilly, east of the Ranger's Lodge, found a human skeleton. These remains appeared to have been in the ground some 30 or 40 years, and bore marks of violence upon the skull. That the Mohocks were responsible is a natural supposition; but the wooded parkland hereabouts had an unsavoury reputation in general, and the place had also occasionally been the haunt of duellists in the near past.

On 19 April a report appeared in the *London Gazette* declaring that several persons linked to 'Mohocking' were going through the legal process, although many of the more violent criminals had as yet gone unidentified. Part of the report listed details of thirteen assaults that appeared to fit the pattern by nature of their randomness, which had occurred between February and the end of March 1712. On 26 April two supposed members of the Mohocks were arraigned at the General Quarter Sessions of the Peace for stabbing and wounding in the breast, back and arms one John White and his wife without provocation. Those accused, John Goulding (alias Mackenzie) and John Bend, were, however, habitual pickpockets, and their involvement in such a secret society was questionable. The Bench fined them £100 each, they being ordered to remain in prison until it was paid.

Four people indicted at the Old Bailey on 6 June 1712 were also linked to 'Mohocking': these were Sir Mark Cole, John Reading, Robert Squibb and Hugh Jones, all of whom were convicted of a vicious assault on a watchman called John Bouch, of Essex Street, on 11 March. Bouch had been in his watch-house when a company of men appeared and entered into conversation with him; they asked him what he did, and he replied he took care of the street with his dog, whereupon one shouted, 'Damn me, I'll take care of your dog and you too!'

before lashing out at Bouch. One among their number shouted a word like 'Stout!' - whereupon some twenty men rushed out of the darkness and assaulted the watchman with sticks and jabbed swords at him. As he skirmished with them they threatened to roll him about the street and nail him to the wall of his watch-house, but Bouch defended himself bravely with a staff and the group gradually dispersed.

Bouch pursued them with the assistance of a constable and other watchmen, and took hold of the four defendants. The sequence of events is confusing, for there was an alternative version of what happened – endorsed by one Mr Salt, the 'high constable' – which claimed that those on trial were part of a group who assembled at the Bear tavern to form vigilante groups. These intended to patrol the streets and hunt down Mohocks, and as such they ought not to be in court. Salt had himself been at this vigilante meeting, and testified they had found and helped three bloodied victims of a collision between Mohocks and Lord Hinchingbrooke's party in 'Pissing Alley' near the Strand. Salt further believed the incident in Essex Street had been provoked by Bouch after one of those on trial threw a stick at his dog to stop it barking: the accused were, according to Salt, in fact trying to preserve the peace, and were *not* Mohocks. Nonetheless, the court convicted the four and fined them 3 shillings and 4 pence apiece, a relatively minor punishment; Salt was removed from his position, which implies his version of events was considered a fabrication and possibly corrupt.

The writing of Jonathan Swift provides more evidence of the panic the Mohock scare generated. He wrote: 'Young Davenant was telling us at court how he was set upon by the Mohocks, and how they ran his chair through with a sword. It is not safe being in the streets at night for them. The Bishop of Salisbury's son is said to be of the gang. They are all Whigs; and a great lady sent (for) me to speak to her father and to (the) Lord Treasurer, to have a care of them, and to be careful likewise of myself: for she heard they had malicious intentions against the ministers and their friends.' Elsewhere he notes, 'The Mohocks go on still, and cut people's faces every night, but they shan't cut mine. I like it better as it is.' Perhaps most interestingly, he hints at one of them dying, for he wrote: 'Lord Treasurer advised me not to go in a chair, because the Mohocks insult chairs more than they do those on foot. Several of them, Lord Treasurer told me, are actually taken up. I heard, at dinner, that *one of them was killed last night*. We shall know more in a little time. I do not like(n) them as to men.'

Before long the phenomenon of 'Mohocking' was also being reported from Dublin in Ireland. It is unclear if the secret society of Mohocks ever existed in the way that history has supposed it did: that is to say, an *organised* delinquent criminal fraternity comprised of the upper middle classes, which struck from the shadows and killed at random only to vanish back into the gloom…remaining unidentified and at liberty to attack again. However, they are the very personification of the barbarism and insecurity that bedevilled London at this time. The very thought that such a society existed seems to have terrified the capital for a while, and there do appear to have been numerous wanton acts of criminal violence that occurred. All that can be said is that perhaps the notion of the Mohocks was a half-truth in its day.

In 1712 John Gay published a humorous treatise on the scare, entitled '*A Wonderful Prophecy*', that in part read:

From Mohock, and from Hawkubite,
Good Lord, deliver me,
Who wander through the streets by night,
Committing cruelty.
They slash our sons with bloody knives,
And on our daughters fall;
And, if they ravish not our wives,
We have good luck withal.
Coaches and chairs they overturn,
Nay carts, most easily:
Therefore from Gog, and eke Magog,
Good Lord, deliver me!

The treatise makes reference to a recent killing blamed on the Mohocks: that of a porter slain in Fleet Street who had a hook rammed in his mouth and his nostrils cut. Although Gay's work is semi-serious (quoted in the person of the victim's prophesying ghost), it is likely that it drew on an *actual* murder, however.

The word *Mohocking* continued to be used as a euphemism for pointless gang violence by bored young rakes long after the reign of Anne. A report from Edinburgh dated 28 November 1738 told how a 'journeyman weaver' had been surrounded by a company of young gentlemen in the early hours of the morning. One had struck at his head with a cutlass, and in doing so wounded the victim severely in the arm. The others stabbed him in the buttocks with their swords before allowing him to pass, and this treatment they also meted out to numerous others. The *Newcastle Courant* reported: 'The *Spectator* long since laugh'd the London rakes out of this practice: and we believe it has not been heard of since in any town in Great Britain, till these squires have thought fit to attempt its revival.'

In the end, the last word on the excesses of the Mohocks and the Hawkubites needs to go the *Gentleman's Magazine* of 1791: 'The stories of the *Mohawks* appear to have been enormously exaggerated by the usual effects of popular *panicks*; and perhaps even then it was as doubtful as it is now, how far these disorders exceeded those so usual and even fashionable formerly in the streets of midnight London, under the name of drunken frolicks.'

CHAPTER 3

THE REIGN OF KING GEORGE I (d.11 June 1727)

INTRODUCTION

King George I inherited a land riddled with social problems and in parts ripe for rebellion. The year following George's accession on 1 August 1714 saw furious anti-Hanoverian rioting in Manchester and other parts of the kingdom; with the advent of the Jacobite Rising, some hundreds died during the Siege of Preston - which itself occurred simultaneously alongside the crushing of the Stuart Pretender's rebellion at Sheriffmuir, near Stirling, on 13 November 1715. However, although the royal army halted the insurrection that day the threat continued to exist and there were a number of bloody skirmishes throughout the next few years.

Not surprisingly, the early years of the new king's reign were marked by a constant fear that Jacobite supporters of James Stuart lurked on every corner to assassinate the first Protestant Hanoverian monarch; Robert Walpole, the First Lord of the Treasury and Chancellor of the Exchequer – Britain's 'prime minister' – was particularly concerned by the threat. In 1718, one James Shepherd was executed for a design to kill the king, as was a certain John Matthews, for printing and publishing a treasonable libel. A resurgent Jacobite rebellion in support of 'King James III', led by exiled Highland chieftains and Spanish mercenaries, was crushed in another battle at Glen Shiel on 10 June 1719. Lethal firefights at Loch Affaric in October 1721 and the Choille Van (White Wood) in August 1722 were symptomatic of the legacy of the rebellion. The threat of trouble was envisaged everywhere.

In 1722 the king took a summer tour round the west of England and thence to Portsmouth; upon his return to the capital there was uncovered a dangerous conspiracy against the government. The plot – that appeared to involve assassinating the king as he travelled to Hanover later that summer, then capturing the Royal Exchange, the Bank of England, the Tower and St James's Palace – led to several lords being committed to the Tower. London was within two weeks flooded with thousands of troops, and a large military camp was set up in Hyde Park in the event that the plot developed into an actual rebellion.

St James's Palace in the time of Queen Anne: one of the strategic points in London that was to be assaulted as part of the insurrection. This illustration originally appeared in the historical works of John Cassell in 1860.

The plot came to light when the king's German mistress, Melusine von der Schulenberg, the Duchess of Kendal, claimed to have received an anonymous warning that an attempt would be made to assassinate the king and proclaim James Stuart, the 34-year-old son of James II, as King James III. The king was to be killed shortly after he left London for Hanover, according to the information, whereupon arms were to be distributed among the plotter's supporters, who would take over key points in the city in a grand *coup d'etat*.

Francis Atterbury, the Bishop of Rochester, was closely linked to the conspiracy. Atterbury had been a Minister of the Crown under the brief premiership of Bolingbroke during the final days of Queen Anne – upon whose death he alone had been bold enough to suggest that they should proclaim the son of James II as her successor. In truth many - including James - had closer blood ties than the Hanoverian, but George was Anne's nearest *Protestant* relative. Ever since, Atterbury had been noted for his disaffection with the Hanoverian government, and by the time the plot came to light he had –

apparently – rashly embraced the hope that a few troops under the Duke of Ormond, landed on the southern coast, would be enough to overthrow the regime.

By the end of May 1722 several inferior, but active, conspirators had been taken into custody. These were a non-juring clergyman named Kelly (Atterbury's secretary), an Irish Catholic priest called Neynoe, Christopher Layer (a young barrister of the Temple), and an Irish Jesuit named Plunket. Their examinations led to the arrest of Bishop Atterbury; he was also a Tory adversary of the Whig government, and was committed a close prisoner to the Tower on 24 August 1722.

The High-Church Party were furious at what they considered the sacrilegious imprisonment of a clergyman, and the Tories vocally declared the plot to be fiction: they argued that the Pretender had not quitted Rome in preparation for heading to Britain, and had no designs on the government. This was soon contradicted by the Pretender's own declaration; and documents subsequently came to light (after the fact) that destroyed any doubt as to the guilt of Bishop Atterbury in the conspiracy.

At the beginning of 1723 Christopher Layer was brought to trial and convicted of having enlisted men for the Pretender's service, in order to raise a new rebellion; he was executed at Tyburn on 17 May, the only one of the conspirators to receive the death penalty. In May, Atterbury was brought before the House of Lords and banished; on 18 June 1723 he boarded a ship to France, leaving Britain's shores and immediately entering into the service of the Stuart Pretender. That the rebellion came so close to London must have worried the government tremendously; from the point of view of this book, it illustrates that no one was immune from the spectre of murder – not even the king himself.

That the threat of disorder was an ever-present feature of life is clear. For instance, Glasgow saw violent scenes during George's reign that typify the era, when protests against the imposition of new taxes on malt, ale and beer led to a bloody collision between the mob and the military under Captain Bushel. The outbreaks of violence took a deadly turn on 25 June 1725 when the soldiery at the Guard House on the southwest corner of Candleriggs Street fired volley after volley into a stone-throwing crowd of Glaswegians. The mob, enraged by the shootings, turned its attention to the Town-house, where – in the presence of the terrified provost – they raided the magazine for arms and rang the fire bell to alarm the whole city. Bushel was forced to retreat with his company to Dumbarton, and during the mob offensive (they now being armed) he was forced yet again to order his troops to fire into the crowd to secure his own escape. Nine people were killed that day, and 17 wounded, a number of them men and women drawn to Candleriggs Street out of curiosity. The randomness of such encounters is well-illustrated by historian James Pagan's observation (1847) that, 'A party of gentlemen, who were amusing themselves in a neighbouring bowling green, were alarmed at the firing, and hastily rushing into Candleriggs Street to inquire the cause, had barely time to shelter themselves from the musketry of the soldiers.' In the aftermath of the battle, two rioters were sentenced to transportation for life, while a number of others received minor punishment; most of those arrested during the clashes were liberated. The magistrates and council made an attempt to bring Captain Bushel to trial for murder, but – screened by the powers that be – he not only got out of the trouble, but was promoted in the service.

Glasgow became a battleground in 1725. This illustration originally appeared in the historical works of John Cassell in 1860.

This was also an era in which the custom of duelling was at its height. Every gaming table, brothel, tavern, coffee house, masquerade, theatre and festival in the British capital produced its duellists, and the universal fashion for wearing swords allowed no time for passion to subside. A walk into the street or even into another room could produce circumstances that ended with drawn swords and mortal wounds. The most eminent of men succumbed to their violent passions. We learn that two doctors, Mead and Woodward, 'fought like a pair of butchers' at the very gates of Gresham College (where they were resident) in June 1719, having quarrelled over a medical question as they walked together along Bishopsgate. The two men had struck each other with their canes at first, and the affray had escalated into a clash with drawn swords in the 'Square of the College'. Woodward was seriously wounded by his opponent, and when Mead gloated triumphantly, 'Take your life!' the other replied, 'Anything but your physic!' Mead did not slay his adversary, contenting himself with breaking Woodward's sword; nonetheless, Woodward reportedly suffered several stab wounds during the encounter, and it was merely blind luck he did not die.

St Botolph's, Bishopsgate, today, where the two scholars began quarrelling. (Photo courtesy of John Winfield.)

But every drunken rake who staggered through the streets of the capital had it within his power to plunge his sword into the breast of a stranger for a fancied slight. Dead bodies were frequently found down alleyways, or else floating in the Thames or laid out on heathland: and those who had the capacity to leave the city for the countryside did so without looking back. Fellows who moved in the sphere of gentlemen often set the worst of examples. In 1717 an assembly of such rakes gathered one evening in a drawing room at 'the Royal Chocolate-house in St James Street'. A quarrel among the gamesters became general throughout the room, and soon a pitched battle was being fought with swords that resulted in the slaying of three among their number. A footman of

Colonel Cunningham, greatly attached to his master, darted through the swinging swords and flying fists to seize and literally carry the colonel out of the confusion. The melee was only interrupted by the arrival of 'Royal-guards' who broke up the brawl by indiscriminately hitting the participants on their heads with the butt ends of their muskets.

It was not just London that suffered from these depredations. Every town or city of any importance, from Bath to Cambridge, and Lancaster to Edinburgh, could cite its own examples of quarrels that had ended with swords drawn or pistols fired: for duelling was a unique way of upholding one's honour that dignified the winner with the label of a gentleman - rather than that of a fortunate murderer. As far away as England's remote northeast – where London must have seemed a strange, foreign place - men of distinction fought like animals to avenge their reputation. For instance, an attorney named Edward Riddell was tried at Newcastle Assizes on 12 August 1722 for killing one Captain Lilburn. Their duel had been fought 'in the Nun's garden' in that town, but Riddell was acquitted of murder, there being no *proof* he dealt the fatal wound.

John 'Jack' Sheppard became a hero to the mob because of his defiance of the law (personified by Jonathan Wild) and even Newgate. (This illustration originally appeared in The Criminal Recorder, or Biographical Sketches of Notorious Public Characters *Volume 1, 1815.)*

George's reign also saw the advent of a strange phenomenon: the criminal as a folk hero, or, as we might understand it today, a celebrity. The career of the famous 'Gentleman' Jack Sheppard, for instance, was rendered remarkable because of his most daring and ingenious escapes from the fortifications of Clerkenwell and Newgate. Sheppard grew up fatherless, and despite his mother's honest endeavours to secure him an apprenticeship, Jack fell into crime at an early age after making the acquaintance of the landlord of the Black Lion in

Drury Lane, at that time the haunt of the most notorious criminals in London. He began to spend his evenings there, falling into a life of drinking and whoring that his apprenticeship to a carpenter could not sustain financially. Resorting to the appropriation of other men's goods, he gradually became bolder and advanced from petty larceny to house breaking - so that at the young age of 22 he was condemned to death for burglary. A final escape proving beyond his ingenuity, Sheppard was executed at Tyburn on 16 November 1724.

This is Jonathan Wild, a man whose underworld criminal empire exceeded anything yet seen in the English capital. The illustration originally appeared in The Criminal Recorder Volume 2, *by a Student of the Inner Temple in 1804.*

Sheppard's ultimate downfall was engineered by an equally nefarious character called Jonathan Wild, who in many ways personifies the times. He professed to be the most zealous of thief-takers, employed by the London authorities to catch criminals; for, as a former valet and veteran of debtors' prisons, Wild's knowledge of the underworld network in the metropolis was extensive. His power became immense and his name was public property: even Daniel Defoe sang Wild's praises upon the latter's apprehension of a number of felons who had returned prematurely from transportation, remarking: 'And 'tis hoped Mr Wild will double his diligence for the future.' Wild's public life was dedicated to the pursuit and apprehension of felons, and he received a bounty of £40 for each conviction he secured, allowing him to live in style at No.68 Ship Court, Old Bailey: in fact, it is believed that Wild was instrumental in the executions of 35 robbers, 10 returned felons and 22 housebreakers, including, of course, the great Jack Sheppard. This was all much to the admiration of the authorities; yet Wild was a ruthless man, mocking the law even as he pretended to uphold it. From about 1712 his secret trade was the restoration of stolen property, via a clandestine confederacy of huge numbers of thieves, pickpockets, highwaymen and burglars in the capital. These thefts he directed, the method of his success being the sale of the stolen wares back to the original owner – they, of course, under the impression that Wild had recovered it through his crime fighting endeavours... when in fact he was the actual architect of the theft in the first place. The proceeds were split with the thief, and the opportunities for blackmail this presented – Wild was still officially the 'thief-taker general' and above impeachment - made him a master of the criminal underworld.

His success received some check by an Act of Parliament in 1717, which dictated that persons convicted of receiving or buying stolen goods, knowing them to have been stolen, were liable to 14 years transportation. Another clause specifically targeted traffickers of stolen goods who split the proceeds with the felon. For a while Wild's audacity and ingenuity enabled him to sidestep the law; but his grip on the criminal empire he had built began to slip and at length he was arrested for 'fencing' some £40 worth of lace and condemned to death.

Having failed in an attempt to poison himself in gaol (he vomited some laudanum back up again), Wild's execution on 24 May 1725 was a remarkable affair. Thousands upon thousands turned out to watch his exit, there (according to Defoe) being not a single pitying eye or compassionate word among the multitude, who actually cheered as the master criminal was taken to Tyburn. In Holborn the mob pelted the gallows cart with stones, one of which struck Wild in the head and covered his face with blood. Defoe recorded of his final moments: 'When he was *turned off*, there was a universal shout among the spectators. As the cart drew away, his arms being loose, he happened to catch hold of the coiner, but was immediately parted from him.' Three others were hanged at the same time, a forger and two highway robbers. (Wild's skeleton can still be seen at the Royal College of Surgeons' Hunterian Museum.)

Jonathan Wild's downfall was catastrophic and complete: here the mob pelt him with stones as he sits in the gallows cart. (Originally from William Jackson's New & Complete Newgate Calendar Volume 2, *1795.)*

Although Jack Sheppard, Wild's most famous catch, was not a killer, no one could survive in these times in the London criminal underworld without at some point being put in a situation where the circumstances threatened murder. We are told that Sheppard nearly committed murder when he fired a pistol at Wild's lieutenant, Quilt Arnold, on an occasion when the man came to arrest him in rooms above a brandy shop in Rosemary Lane on 22 July 1724; but the weapon misfired, and Arnold was able to march his captive off to a magistrate, who had Sheppard imprisoned in Clerkenwell.

'Blueskin' attempts to assassinate Jonathan Wild. (*This illustration first appeared in William Jackson's* New & Complete Newgate Calendar Volume 1, *1795.) The prisoner still managed to cut Wild's throat despite his irons.*

Jonathan Wild himself barely escaped with his life from a murder attempt. While in his guise as a thief-taker who upheld the law, he bribed for information concerning a group of highway robbers who were terrorizing Hampstead. He put all his energy into arranging these arrests, having learned that these men intended to assault him and shoot him through the head. Although Wild secured their arrest and execution, one among their number, Joseph Blake - a former confederate of Sheppard's nicknamed 'Blueskin' - managed to get near Wild in 'the bail-dock' on 15 October 1724. Outraged by Wild's observation that, 'I believe you must die; I'll send you a good book or two, and provide you a coffin, and you shall not be anatomised', Blueskin produced a clasped penknife and leapt on Wild, cutting into his throat. However, the blade was too blunt to do the work effectually and Wild managed to survive. It was while he recovered from this assassination attempt that his grip on the underworld began to slip through his fingers. Incidentally, the uproar caused in the courtroom by this event spread to Newgate, and the ensuing disturbance allowed Jack Sheppard – at that time incarcerated – to perform the last of his legendary escapes from gaol, even despite his being encumbered by leg irons.

In Scotland, this was the time of the great Rob Roy MacGregor, a 'Jacobite bandit' and outlaw. This celebrated Highland chief's real name was Robert MacGregor, although he assumed the name Campbell on account of the outlawry of the clan MacGregor in 1662. Born *c.*1671 (although there are conflicting dates), his mother was a Campbell of Glenlyon and his wife Helen a Campbell of Glenfalloch. Like other Highland gentlemen, MacGregor was a drover prior to the rebellion of 1715, which he joined on the side of the Pretender. Upon the suppression of the rebellion, the Duke of Montrose – with whom MacGregor had previously quarrelled and feuded – took the opportunity to deprive him of his estates, and the latter retaliated by carrying out a war of reprisals on the property of the duke. An English garrison was stationed at Inversnaid, northwest of Aberfoyle, the *clachan* (residence) of MacGregor; but his activity and courage saved him from the hands of his enemies, against whom he continued for some time to levy blackmail. The hunt for Rob was followed avidly in the capital, with Defoe recording on 24 August 1717: 'We hear three troops of Dragoons quartered at Edinburgh and at Glasgow, are ordered to search the whole country for that arch robber Rob *Roi*.' Defoe also wrote that Rob commanded an army of some 100 freebooters, who he kept loyal with wages and plunder. Eventually Montrose actually managed to secure MacGregor, but he escaped only to turn up two years later at the battle of Glenshiel. By the time he was arrested and taken south to Newgate in 1726, MacGregor was the most wanted man in Scotland; yet, strange to relate, in view of all the conflict Jacobitism had caused during his reign, virtually one of the last acts undertaken by King George I before his death on 11 June 1727 was to grant MacGregor a pardon.

A portrait of Rob Roy, the 'Jacobite Bandit', originally from Kenneth Macleay's 1818 Historical Memoirs of Rob Roy & the Clan Macgregor.

MacGregor became a folk hero, sometimes referred to as Scotland's Robin Hood, and died at his home in Balquhidder, Central, on 28 December 1734. Always true to his principles, and a legend even in his own lifetime, Robert Roy MacGregor is a rarity for the age: in that, although outside the law for much of his life, he never killed wantonly, and any killings he did carry out *appear* to have been on the field of conflict. Despite Rob's reputation, it was in fact his boys who were the most dangerous. The *Scots Magazine* noted in 1753: 'Rob Roy, alias MacGregor, son of the famous Rob Roy, and brother to James, was apprehended at the fair in Gartmore, by a party of soldiers from Inversnaid, committed to Stirling Castle May 19th, and brought to Edinburgh Tolbooth on the 26th. He was *fugitated*, first in 1736 for murder, and again in 1751 for the forcible abduction and marriage of Mrs Jean Kelly, heiress of Edinbelly.' Both Rob and James were tried for these crimes, and although James escaped from Edinburgh Castle in 1753, Rob was hanged on 6 February 1754.

Nothing in MacGregor's career was quite so degenerate as the lives endured by tens of thousands of ordinary people in big cities across the land, day in and day out. By 1720, shadowy societies such as the Mohocks and the Hawkubites had been reinvented in the form of other 'clubs' dedicated to casual violence and irreligion in the capital. These wretches associated under two groups to commit their outrages, the Bold Bucks and the Hell Fires.

The Bold Bucks' crimes appear to have been more specifically sexual in nature. A paper dated 20 February 1720 declares them to be deliberate abandoned villains, whose aim was to be as promiscuous as possible – using force if consent were denied. Grandmothers, daughters, granddaughters and even their own sisters feared their violence, and the paper observes: 'Blind and bold love is their motto, and their soul's faculties (are) strictly terminated in the participation of entertainment and judgement with brutes.'

The Hell Fires mocked all forms of religion, calling for 'Holy Ghost-pye' in the taverns in a deliberate attempt to offend the sensibilities of the religious majority. Despite their high degree of education, their level of blasphemy and vulgarity was shocking: furthermore, their gaming, drinking and dicing on the Sabbath was an open challenge to the norm in an era that – strange to relate – was actually more *literally* God-fearing than the centuries that followed. Their depravity was so notorious that it actually forced the king into issuing a proclamation in April 1721 that railed against these clubs: 'His Majesty (has) received information which gives great reason to suspect that there have been lately, and still are, in and about the Cities of London and Westminster, certain scandalous Clubs or Societies of young persons, who meet together, and in the most impious and blasphemous manner insult the sacred principles of our Holy Religion, affront Almighty God Himself, and corrupt the minds and morals of one another…'

Bustling Westminster today, once the haunt of 'certain scandalous clubs'.

The Gentleman's Magazine in 1852 tells us: 'The (Hell Fires) were content to kill watchmen and simple citizens. Such killing was with them but an act of "justifiable homicide", and the inclination for it one of those amiable weaknesses which the young gentlemen of the day looked upon as the most natural thing possible.'

Despite the dashing examples of Rob Roy and Jack Sheppard, this could truly be a dangerous time to be an ordinary British citizen.

CORONATION REJOICINGS

In 1714, when the Hanoverian line ascended the British throne and secured the Protestant succession, the arrival at Greenwich, London, of the king and prince-royal was met with jubilant celebrations: cannons discharged in the city, bells chimed noisily and bonfires illuminated the capital. However, the somewhat shambolic state of the celebrations can be evidenced by an event on the day of coronation, when George was crowned king with all due solemnity in Westminster. For we learn that as the procession was going by, several people were killed and injured by the fall of scaffolding in Palace-yard.

On 20 October, far away in Bristol, the national celebrations took a sour downturn as the evening wore on when a crowd engaged in 'coronation rejoicings' began to attack the houses of religious dissenters, breaking their windows. A bloody melee occurred in Tucker Street, where the property of a baker named Stephens was besieged; a Quaker positioned himself in the bakery doorway and implored the crowd to desist - but was knocked down by someone in the crowd, and then kicked and trampled with such ferocity that he died the following day. Stephens' son made a valiant attempt to defend his father's property, shooting one of the mob in the head; the injured fellow died some days later. Another he ran through with a rapier, but the injured man did not die. A number of others were wounded as the crowd fought their way into the bakery and systematically plundered the drawers and boxes for plate, bread and other items; interior partitions were also broken down in a frenzy of looting.

At some point the authorities managed to regain control. Thirteen people were arrested and committed to Bristol's Newgate; however, 'the greatest criminals absconded'. Upon an application by the magistrates, who were perhaps concerned that Bristol might be labelled a Jacobite enclave, the newly-crowned King George I sent a special commission to try the rioters in custody. Three judges and four counsellors arrived on 25 November, and the proceedings lasted nearly a week. About ten of those indicted were fined '20 nobles' and put in gaol for three months ('to give security for nine months more'). One, indicted for felony, was ordered to be whipped, and the others were freed. It appears those involved in the murder of the Quaker went unidentified.

These were dangerous times for the British Isles in general, for the Hanoverian succession roused passions between mobs affiliated with the Tories and the Whigs; two years later, these focussed on a Whig drinking hole, the Mug House in Salisbury Court. An attack was launched on this building by mobs of Tories shouting, 'No Hanoverian, no King George, no Mug House!' The Mug House was eventually plundered, gutted by arsonists and pulled down during the clashes in July 1716 – although not before the proprietor, Mr Robert Read, had shot dead one among the mob with a blunderbuss, in attempting to defend his property. Numerous others were wounded before the disturbances were quelled by a party of grenadier guards; had not many inside the Mug House managed to escape the fire, it is possible an atrocity might have occurred. Mr Read was acquitted of murdering the rioter, Daniel Vaughan, at the Old Bailey later that year.

An attack on a Whig 'mug house', as depicted in Walter Thornbury's Old & New London Vol. 1 *(1878).*

KILLINGS LINKED TO JACOBITISM

The threat of uprisings by supporters of Queen Anne's exiled Catholic half-brother James Francis Edward Stuart (named Jacobites) hung menacingly over parts of the kingdom. To be branded a Jacobite could have lethal consequences: for instance, on 21 September 1714 when a court was held at St James's an argument erupted between Colonel Chudleigh and Mr Charles Aldsworth, MP for New Windsor. Aldsworth was branded by the colonel with the title 'Jacobite', and in the end both carried themselves to 'Mary-la-bonne fields' to fight a duel. Aldsworth was slain on the spot.

Far away from the capital, in Stamford, Lincolnshire, the threat also had unfortunate repercussions. On the demise of Anne, Stamford favoured a Catholic succession, and when George took the crown a mob of townsfolk gutted and destroyed the Presbyterian chapel on market day.

Stamford, Lincolnshire, in 2012. The George Inn still stands, on the left of the road.

A company of Honeywood's dragoons was subsequently quartered in the town to intimidate the Jacobite supporters. The tapster at the George Inn – a man named Bolton – had the misfortune to be found by a dragoon while he was in the act of drinking on his bare knees to the memory of Queen Anne. This soldier ran Bolton through with a sabre, killing him instantly, and when word of this spread through the old coaching town a large number of people gathered about the inn. They smashed the windows, and threatened to pull down the George unless the murderous soldier was given into their hands; however, the dragoon managed to abscond via a rear exit, and the crowd was soon dispersed.

It is possible that the soldier read Bolton's actions as an ironic salute to the death of the queen, and the 1701 Act of Settlement that denied a Catholic succession. In toasting Anne's death, Bolton was displaying Jacobite sympathies; and for this act of bravado he had met his violent and passionate end.

Around this time many towns saw pro-Jacobite tumults: Taunton, Bridgwater and Frome in Somerset, Bedford, Worcester, Gloucester and Chippenham, Wiltshire. The worst disturbances were in Bristol – where the mob killed one Mr Thomas, for persuading them to withdraw – and Manchester, where the anti-

Hanoverian riots took such a serious turn that it was necessary for the military under Lord Cobham to quell them.

SCREAMS FROM THE FIELD

In January 1716, in response to rumours of a horrific murder occurring in the (then) county of Huntingdonshire, a fellow of that region took it upon himself to write to the *Stamford Mercury* – one of England's oldest provincial news-sheets – to ensure the matter was reported correctly.

At about five in the evening of 9 January 1716 cries were heard coming from a field called Thurning Field, which was about mid-way between the villages of Thurning and Luddington-in-the-Brook, northwest of Huntingdon. In fact, several people in Luddington heard the cries, but no-one ventured to help; these included a farmer, who could have been on the scene within two minutes – but who chose merely to go into his farm and complain about the noise he could hear.

The following morning the body of a widow called Elizabeth Pare was found in the field. She had been attacked as though by a raging maniac, and to all appearances looked like she had been struck with a hatchet: for her left hand was almost cut off, only being connected to the wrist by a piece of skin. Two of her fingers and one of her thumbs were actually lopped off, these being found in the field. The woman had been struck six or seven times in the face and throat, and had also been hacked violently on her legs.

The fellow who chose to write to the *Mercury* explained that he had known Widow Pare for several years and that she had suffered at least thirteen wounds: in fact, he would not have recognised her were it not for her apparel.

Great concern naturally swept the neighbourhood, and the men of the surrounding villages and hamlets were forced to present themselves and explain their whereabouts. In nearby Great Gidding one Henry Johnson did not present a very good impression of himself, and he was brought before Sir Matthew Dudley in Thurning. A strict search of his clothes revealed his shirt and the right hand pocket of his breeches were smeared with blood; whereupon Johnson feigned surprise and denial but failed to provide an adequate explanation for the bloodstains. Many strong circumstances suggesting his guilt, Sir Matthew ordered Johnson to be taken to Huntingdon and incarcerated in the town gaol.

The remains of Huntingdon Castle, which functioned as the gaol throughout the 1700s.

The hatchet used to commit the deed was shortly thereafter found, and it was subsequently established that Widow Pare had been robbed of £3 and her rings (which perhaps explained the lopped-off fingers). There was little doubt of Johnson's guilt.

The case contains a number of elements with which we will become familiar. The first is that the motive for the crime was robbery, as was so often the case, and the second is the level of brutality employed. A third common factor concerns the *ease* with which the felon was caught: in many similar cases there appears to have been virtually no effort to escape or even *avoid* being detected, which begs the question of why so many people behaved like this throughout the century.

However, the use of the *Stamford Mercury* in allowing the witness to get his story across first-hand indicates a developing understanding of how the media might be used in reporting violent crime, which is one significant aspect of this case: such a means of conveying details with this level of immediacy would have been difficult to perceive just a few years prior.

'LORD PAMP'S' MISSING MISTRESS

From murders reaching the public's ears we look at murders kept secret. In the early 1700s there stood a building called Papillon Hall about one mile west of Lubenham in Leicestershire. The building was inhabited by a man called David Papillon, known locally as 'Old Pamp' or 'Lord Pamp'. He apparently bore something of a sinister reputation, for it is said that many people in the district believed him to be some kind of rural wizard capable of putting the 'evil eye' on them or their livestock.

When a young man Papillon is said to have acquired a mistress, who many believed was Spanish; but if he did, then very little is known of her. This would seem to be on account of the stories that 'Lord Pamp' kept her hidden out of sight and incarcerated inside the hall as a virtual prisoner. When she was glimpsed, this lady was spotted as though taking exercise on the flat leads of the roof before disappearing once more within the hall.

Around 1715, sometime before David Papillon's marriage, the 'Spanish' lady disappeared for good and was never seen again by anyone in the neighbourhood, not even from a distance. This was when 'Lord Pamp' was aged about 24, and shortly before his marriage to Mary Keyser, daughter of a London merchant.

Papillon subsequently became quite a powerful man. He was a Member of Parliament for several years, and between 1742 and 1754 he was a Commissioner of Excise. After he himself died in 1762 it was said that the only proof of the existence of his Spanish mistress were her shoes – a pair of silver and brocaded slippers and a pair of pattens that the hall still retained. It became something of a custom to hand these relics to each new owner along with the title deeds to the hall.

It only remains to be said that when the hall was assumed by Captain Frank Belville in 1903 a woman's skeleton was (supposedly) found walled up during alterations he was carrying out. This, of course, was guessed to be the poor mistress, and it was suggested she had met with foul play – for the remains were found in (or near) the hall's attic. The hall was pulled down in 1950, and the remaining shoes were presented to Mrs Barbara Papillon (one of the pattens having been lost down the years).

Where the hall once stood there is now a farm called 'Papillon Hall Farm'. As history the murder that supposedly occurred here is very questionable, although – like Longleat House and a host of other places – it illustrates well the 'skeleton in the closet' type stories that are associated with the era. This author could name a number of similar locations across the country with these types of stories, but it is better we leave them here and move on to what we might call the 'real world'…although with perhaps one final observation. However dubious stories from the world of folklore might seem, they are undeniably intriguing - and one wonders if there is just the tiniest bit of truth in the story of David Papillon's missing mistress. For - amazingly - her shoes still exist, and have been dated to the correct era; they are also believed to be of Spanish origin. Quite why Papillon killed his mistress (if, indeed, he did) can now never be known, so again we must defer to local lore: writer Guy Paget recorded in 1934: 'There's a story that one of the Papillons married a foreign lady. She was carrying on with some other. He found it out by her dropping her shoe. Well, some says he killed her…'

DEATH BY THE MAIDEN

Murderer John Hamilton's chief distinction in the annals of crime is the manner of his death. Hamilton was born in Clydesdale, South Lanarkshire, and was related to the afore-mentioned ducal family of Hamilton.

His upbringing was comparatively well-to-do, for his parents – to whom he was an only son – were able to afford to send him to Glasgow for an education; but within time it became apparent he was drawn towards an army career, and so well-meaning friends attempted to procure him a commission.

It may have been that some could see young Hamilton was falling into an irresolute lifestyle, and so hoped to save him. For Hamilton was at this point losing heavily at the card table, having fallen in with a group of abandoned young gentlemen in Edinburgh. His parents were forced to provide him with money to bail him out, but after this they refused to fund his lifestyle from that moment onwards.

Using this money, Hamilton immediately repaired to a village near Glasgow where he met his companions at a public house and embarked on a marathon gaming session that lasted for several days and nights. In the end, his 'friends' deserted him while he lay asleep, and Hamilton awoke in the blur of hangover to find he had been left to pick up the group's tab. There next followed an argument with the innkeeper, Thomas Arkle, over Hamilton's ability to pay. During this 'discussion' Arkle removed Hamilton's sword from its scabbard, and threw him out. After a while Hamilton returned, however, and upon Arkle calling him several scandalous names, Hamilton managed to grab a weapon and stab the innkeeper to death.

Arkle's daughter was present when the murder was committed, and – despite being almost blind – she bravely tore off 'the skirt of his coat' when Hamilton attempted to run off. From his sword, which he left behind, and the torn item of clothing claimed by the innkeeper's daughter, it proved easy to identify the murderer. Hamilton, though, had immediately fled to Leith and thence to the Netherlands, making his capture impossible.

However, two years later John Hamilton heard his parents had passed away, and this drew him back to the British Isles. As a consequence of this he ended up being quickly arrested when it became known he was back in town. Hamilton was tried in Edinburgh and convicted of Arkle's murder, despite a spirited attempt at defence by the accused that rested mainly on the fact that he was intoxicated and Arkle had insulted him. He was sentenced to be beheaded by 'the Maiden', an execution machine constructed in the following manner.

The Maiden consisted of two strong wooden beams affixed on a scaffold, and between them ran another beam to which was fixed a sharp instrument in the form of a chopping-knife, weighted by a large quantity of lead on the uppermost side. The criminal put his head between the two side-beams, and the cross-beam, being drawn by a pulley, was suffered to drop quickly from four feet (guided by grooves in the side-beams) and sever the convict's head in an instant. In effect, this was an early precursor of the guillotine employed by the French at the end of the century to most notorious effect. It was also the method of punishment Robert, Lord Balfour, had escaped some years earlier.

In Scotland, many persons of rank had died by the Maiden since its implementation in 1574 (or 1564); but Mr Hamilton was the last to yield his life in this manner. This he did on 30 June 1716, despite great efforts by his (still) well-meaning friends, who attempted to secure the disgraceful young rake a pardon. To the end, and even at the place of execution, young Hamilton believed he had been justified in committing murder, as it was (he claimed) in self-defence.

Following its retirement, this unique instrument of execution was removed to a room adjacent to the council-chamber of Edinburgh, and today, in the 21st century, can be found in the National Museum of Scotland in Edinburgh.

A FORGOTTEN ATROCITY

In 1717 a horrific and mysterious discovery was made along the banks of the River Thames 'against Arundel-street in the Strand'. According to the contemporary *Historical Register* a bag was dredged out of the water on 15 April 1717 which, when opened, was found to contain something so awful as to be barely credible.

Within the sack were the decapitated heads of two children, together with the body, entire, of a third murdered child. The *Register* makes next to no comment on this atrocious find; unfortunately, though, the report somehow sums up the conditions of early 18th century London despite its briefness. That such a thing might happen is all too evident from better-documented cases of child cruelty later on in the century.

THE INCIDENTAL VICTIM

News from Dorchester, Dorset, dated 17 September 1717 reported how 'some days ago' a Dragoon had stepped upon the gallows ladder to receive his punishment, after being convicted of murder. While on the ladder he confessed not only this crime, but also that he had killed two men above and beyond that for which he was about to suffer. At the same time a woman was executed for murdering her 'bastard child', which had been found floating in a river (likely the River Frome) with two stone slabs tied about its head and body.

While on the ladder, she admitted her guilt – but made a startling admission. The Dragoon next to her (currently hanging lifeless by his neck) was the father of the murdered infant, and he had contrived with her to get rid of their inconvenient offspring. In doing so, he had brought her to the gallows: claiming a fifth victim incidentally, on top of the others he had murdered.

Watercolour of a double execution by the caricaturist Thomas Rowlandson (d.1827).

THE HANGMAN HANGED

In the year 1718 the man who filled the office of public executioner in London – vulgarly called 'Jack Ketch' – was John Price. He was born in the parish of St Martin in the Fields, and though of reputable parents his father had been killed in action at Tangiers, reducing his mother to poverty. Though unable to provide for her children's education, Mrs Price somehow managed to secure an apprenticeship for young John – who, after two years, fled his place of employment upon the death of his patron. He subsequently took a position as a waggoner and then went to sea, where he served 18 years on a number of ships in the royal navy.

Paid off and discharged from further service, the seaman returned to London; where (the position being vacant) he earned the job of public executioner. But for his extravagance, Price might have lived long on the wages earned by his dreadful occupation; but while returning in the gallows cart from an execution he was arrested in Holborn for debt. He paid off his creditors with his day's wages and also produced three suits of clothes that he had taken from the executed criminals. However, before long he was thrown into Marshalsea Prison for other debts, and since he could not afford bail his position as public executioner was taken by one William Marvel.

Price is arrested in the gallows cart, as first depicted in William Jackson's New & Complete Newgate Calendar Volume 1, *1795.*

With the help of another inmate, John Price managed to escape from the prison by breaking a hole in the wall. While at large, on 13 March 1718 Price encountered a woman called Elizabeth White in Moorfields, near ten at night.

Mrs White was the wife of a watchman, who made a living selling gingerbread in the streets. When he made an attempt to rape the woman, Price found that Mrs White was a more formidable victim than he had thought. His reaction was to 'beat her so cruelly that streams of blood issued from her eyes and mouth, one of her arms was broken, some of her teeth knocked out, her head bruised in a most dreadful manner, one of her eyes forced from the socket; and he otherwise so ill treated her that the language of decency cannot describe it.'

A number of people, hearing Mrs White's screams, laid their hands upon Price and imprisoned him in the watchtower. The woman was conveyed to a house, where, being unable to speak, she indicated what had happened using signs to a nurse brought to assist her. Mrs White died four days after the attack.

Price was brought to trial at the Old Bailey on 24 April, his defence being that he had found the victim in her condition and had been apprehended while trying to get her back on her feet. Witnesses, however, absolutely contradicted this and Price was convicted of murder.

He thereafter proceeded to drink himself into oblivion frequently, obstinately refusing to admit any guilt - even as the date of his execution drew nearer. Finally, on the day of his execution he admitted his guilt and blamed it on his being intoxicated. As he stood on the gallows at Bunhill Fields on 31 May 1718, Price begged in his last moments that the multitude might pray for him and learn by his mistake. He was then 'turned off' and his body later suspended in chains near Holloway: an ironic instance of London's public executioner himself meeting the same fate as those he had so often dispatched. After a number of years swinging in its ignoble position the cage was taken down and Price's remains were committed to the earth at Ring Cross, Holloway.

THE SIEGE OF SOUTHWARK

The following case is a good example of the volatile state of life Londoners enjoyed, and also how quickly mob situations could get out of control.

A Quaker potter by the name of Oades resided in Gravel Lane, Southwark. This gentleman had four sons, who he admitted into partnership with him; however, because he suffered them to carry on business on their own account this naturally created enmity – not only between the four young men, but also between them and their father. The running of the 'partnership' appears to have become somewhat acrimonious, with argument and competition taking over. In the end the quarrelling became so odious that the sons actually saw to it that Oades was arrested for a violation of the peace in May 1718.

This act attracted the notice of the populace, who – as London historian JP Malcolm put it in 1810 – 'seldom fail to adopt the right side of a question of justice'. Somehow thinking that it was some of their business, a crowd mobbed the Quaker's house, where the sons, an attorney and another person were secured within; consequently, the Riot Act was read by the besieged party.

Immediately upon this proclamation gunfire from within the house hit a woman in the crowd in the head, fatally injuring her. Upon this death, the mob became furious, and their assault on the house threatened to become a massacre. Persons were dispatched to Mr Lade, a Justice, who very quickly bailed Mr Oades Senior in order to supplicate the mob; he next demanded that the occupants of the house give up their arms and surrender. Those inside refused, and so a guard of soldiers were sent for who took up positions in the streets and on rooftops surrounding the property. The stand-off ended at two o'clock in the morning when someone courageously scaled a palisade on the back part of the property, next admitting the soldiers - who rushed in and secured the building.

One of Mr Oades' sons was tried for the murder of the woman who died after being shot. He was found guilty, but pardoned upon the intercession of his father – provided he banished himself.

Such were the unpredictable elements of daily life in early 18th century London.

THE DEATH OF DERBY'S MERCHANT-VENTURER

In the 18th century, the situation of Derby, on the banks of the Derwent, rendered it extremely favourable to the institution and progression of manufactures which required the assistance of water. The manufacturing industry in Derby grew by the judicious application of machinery, and cotton mills began appearing in the town and its vicinity, following which came the silk barons.

The Italians had long been the front runners in the art of silk-throwing, and so around the year 1715 a young British mechanic and draughtsman named John Lombe made a somewhat perilous journey to Italy to see what he could learn of the trade. His idea was to bring the industry back to England – specifically Derby; and so while in Piedmont he procured admission to the silk-works by 'corrupting' (i.e. bribing) two of the Italian workmen there.

With their assistance Lombe managed to inspect the machinery in private, and whatever he observed he wrote and drew in detailed schematics before he went to bed each evening. In the end Lombe's planning was discovered, although luckily by this time he had obtained all the information he needed; however, he considered his life to be in immediate danger and was compelled to board a ship leaving for England – accompanied by his two Italian accomplices, who also feared for their lives.

Upon his arrival in Derby John Lombe decided the ideal location for his silk mill would be on an island, or swamp, in the river, 500ft long and 52ft wide, at £8 a year lease from the city's corporation. The silk mill was built, and Lombe's industrial revolution began to develop so quickly and successfully that it became necessary to erect temporary machines in Derby's town hall and other places. By 1718 his operation was employing many people, making tens of thousands of pounds, and reducing the price of silk for the consumer as a by-product of its success.

18th century Derby, as depicted in William Hutton's The History of Derby *(1812).*

1718 was the year that John Lombe obtained a patent to secure the profits generated from his energy, enthusiasm and innovation for 14 years. But in the midst of all this celebration and success, he died: and there were rumours that treachery had brought him to the grave.

The Italian silk manufacturers – whose trade rapidly diminished in the wake of Lombe's success – cried for vengeance. Through the complicated machinations of a cabal, a woman was dispatched from Italy under orders to assassinate the Derby industrialist. When he died, it was suspected that Lombe had been poisoned to death, and this mysterious woman – whose name we know not – was apprehended and examined in an almost certain belief that she had been the engineer of Lombe's demise; however, the evidence was not conclusive and she was dismissed. In the meantime, John Lombe was given a splendid funeral in All Saints' Church (now Derby Cathedral).

If John Lombe had been poisoned in an attempt to halt his success, then the plot failed, for he was succeeded by his brother William. When William Lombe committed suicide, the organisation was inherited by a cousin, Sir Thomas Lombe: he was so successful in his inherited trade that folklore actually regards him as the man who introduced the silk mill into England.

The factory built by the Lombe clan stood for almost 200 years until it finally suffered a fire that put it out of business.

ROBBERY ON THE HIGHWAY

The suppression of the Jacobite rising and also of political rioting was followed by a great prevalence of highway robberies in and around the metropolis. Although romanticized in some quarters as 'gentlemen of the road', these bandits were more often than not seen as a curse; for the streets of London were not safe, even in the daytime. Ladies and gentlemen became forced to travel with their chairs and coaches guarded by servants armed with blunderbusses. It is perhaps only natural that, to the lower classes, the brazen audacity with which some of these criminals robbed their wealthy victims should turn them into folk heroes: for politicians, the noble elite and even members of the royal family could fall victim to their attacks.

A lone highwayman robs a coachload of travellers. This illustration can be found on the exterior of the Highwayman pub, near Sourton in Devon.

Crimes of violence during the course of such robberies were frequently reported in the London news-papers, and these are typical examples from a two week period in early 1720:

Thursday, 21 January 1720: About five o' clock in the evening, the stagecoach from London to Hampstead was attacked and robbed by highwaymen, at the foot of the hill, and one of the passengers severely beaten for attempting to hide his money.

Sunday 24: At eight o' clock in the evening, two highwaymen attacked a gentleman in a coach on the south side of St Paul's churchyard, and robbed him.

Sunday 31: A gentleman robbed and murdered in Bishopsgate Street.

Monday, February 1: The Duke of Chandos, coming from Canons, had another encounter with highwaymen, whom he captured.

Tuesday 2: The postboy was attacked by three highwaymen in Tyburn road, but the Duke of Chandos, happening to pass that way, came to his rescue.

These snippets were collected by historian Thomas Wright in 1848 and constitute but a fraction of the contemporary reports. On a certain day, *all* the stagecoaches between Surrey and London were robbed by highwaymen, and in desperation a reward of £100 was offered for the apprehension of any highwaymen within five miles of London. Among those captured in this dragnet operation were several persons of repute in their respective calling, including a London tradesman, a duke's valet and the keeper of a boxing school.

Sometimes, victims fought back: on 19 December 1719 an old army officer told a robber at the foot of Hampstead Hill he would have to fight for his money. The two men exchanged pistol shots, and the robber fled, bleeding from a wound to his arm. One exceptionally brave would-be victim was Miss Worsley, who was ambushed while driving in her chair over Banstead Downs, Surrey, on 20 July 1731. According to the *Gentleman's Magazine*, Miss Worsley lashed at the highwayman with her whip when he pointed a pistol at her, causing his horse to 'sheer off'. Her footman had actually failed to assist her during the encounter due to fright.

Nor was highway robbery an exclusively male profession, though female robbers were rare. *The Gentleman's Magazine* records that a butcher was held up 'in a very gallant manner' by a woman well mounted on a side saddle near Romford on 24 November 1735. She pointed a pistol at him and demanded his money, to which the nonplussed victim stammered that he did not understand what she meant. A gentleman then appeared on the scene (whom one suspects might have been an accomplice, or at the very least had an ulterior motive), who told the butcher he was 'a brute' to deny the lady her spoils, and threatened to shoot him through the head if he did not hand over his valuables! The butcher gave the lady his watch and six guineas.

This highwayman finds he is pursued, as depicted on a pub sign in Hurst Green, Lancashire.

THE SHOOTING OF MADAME NAPP

The wantonness of the violence dealt out by 'foot padders' (the less glamorous brethren of the mounted highwaymen) drew no distinction, as the following account illustrates. On Saturday 31 March 1716 a widowed gentlewoman named Madame Mary Napp was travelling with her son from Sadler's Wells, Islington, to their home in Warwick Court, Holborn. It was between 10 and 11 in the evening, and the pair had been to see a 'diversion of dancing' when they were attacked in Jockey's Fields 'on this side of Gray's Inn Garden Wall'. The son, in protection of his mother, flung one of the bandits to the ground by his collar, and entered into a fight with a second. Madame Napp, fearing for her son's safety, screamed, 'Murder!' – and was instantly killed when a third rogue fired a pistol into her. Her last words were, 'Lord help me! Help me!' The sound of the shot alerted a group of people in Bromley Street, who rushed to see what was happening; this put the robbers to flight, their only spoils being the son's hat and wig. A little after this murder, the same gang attacked a man called Thomas Middlethwaite Esq in his coach near 'the Pindar of Wakefield'. However, he fired at them with a blunderbuss, wounding one of them, upon which they fled.

The celebrated thief-taker Jonathan Wild made it his business to apprehend the murderers of Widow Napp. Such was his extensive knowledge of the London underworld that he recognised the whole gang from the descriptions presented by both Mr Napp and Mr Middlethwaite. They were: Will White, Tom Thurland, Tim Dun, Isaac Rag and Jack Chapman, the man wounded in the arm by Mr Middlethwaite's shot. One by one they were tracked down and taken uneventfully, with the exception of Dun, who kept one step ahead.

By the time White, Thurland and Chapman were indicted at the Sessions-House in the Old Bailey on 18 May, Isaac Rag had turned informant and betrayed an astonishing 22 people involved in various robberies, burglaries and the handling of stolen goods. Among the various felonies the three stood accused of, the most serious was the murder of Madame Napp; Will White was charged with being the gunman, the other two with being accomplices in the murder.

The three men, all in their early thirties, were sentenced to death, admitting the crimes they were charged with but nothing more. White was a Londoner, by trade a seaman who had served on numerous war-ships; Chapman was a gardener who hailed from Essex, while Thurland was a shopkeeper from Colchester. All three were hanged at Tyburn on 8 June 1716.

The hunt for Tim Dun continued; he was finally tracked to lodgings in 'Maid-lane, near the Bank Side in Southwark'. His location was revealed because Dun sent his wife out to Jonathan Wild's lodging house to see what information she could learn; when she made her way back to Southwark Mrs Dun was stealthily followed by one of Wild's lieutenants, who marked the pavement with chalk in front of the house she entered. Early the following morning, Wild dispatched one of his men, Abraham Riddlesden, to the address, and he shot Dun in the shoulder as the fugitive scrambled over the tiles in the back yard. After Dun had fallen into the yard, Riddlesden further incapacitated him by shooting him in the face with small shot.

On 24 July 1716 five malefactors were taken in two carts from Newgate to be executed at Tyburn; among them was Timothy Dun, wounded, blinded and convicted of Madame Napp's murder. Jonathan Wild gained great recognition for bringing the five bandits to justice, as well as winning a 10 guinea bet with one of his men that he would have them all before the next assizes; this was, of course, before he was himself exposed as the master of a criminal network that extended across the capital on a scale hitherto unthinkable.

'SUCH A GREAT RIOT'

An article in the *Original Weekly Journal* (21 May 1720) speaks of 'a great riot' being fought 'on Wednesday night last' in Windmill Street near the Haymarket in London. Nearly 100 gentlemen battled with swords, sticks and canes, occasioning many serious injuries. The watchmen who attempted to quell the disturbance were themselves violently attacked, and the affair was only quelled when a patrol of 'Horse-guards' rode into the midst of the battle laying left and right with their swords. It seems many were fatally injured, for the *Journal* reported: 'We hear of none that were killed upon the spot, though many, it is thought, cannot recover from their wounds.' Quite what was behind this is unclear, although possibly it stemmed from a collision between two of the gentleman's 'clubs' that prevailed during these times.

Barely a week later there was another vicious crime occasioned by the depravity of the loutish young rakes who wandered the streets looking for trouble. On 29 May 1720 Captain Maurice Fitzgerald and three companions stopped a sedan-chair in the Strand that was carrying a lady from St James's. This gentlewoman was returning to her lodgings in Cecil Street between three and four in the morning. The gang immediately tried to force her out but met stout resistance from the chair-carriers. Because of this the four hooligans drew their swords and started demolishing the vehicle.

The noise brought a watchman, Peter Parry, to the scene, who during the confrontation received a fatal stab wound to his back. Defoe wrote of the killing: 'The chairmen were about to pull out the poles, in order to secure her from violence, which the Captain seeing, drew his sword, and sheathed it in the body of a poor unhappy watchman, just come to their assistance, who instantly dropp'd down dead; the Captain was secured for that night in St Martin's Round-house, and the next day committed to the Gate-house; the coroner has since sat upon the body, and the jury brought in their verdict Wilful Murder.' Captain Fitzgerald was convicted of murder and hanged at Tyburn on 15 August 1720.

The George, in the Strand (believed to have been founded three years after the murder of the watchman).

Perhaps such vicious behaviour was understandable, however, if not condonable; after all, the aristocracy set a shocking example. During George's reign an Italian nobleman resident in the capital, Ferdinando, Marquis de Palleotti, (brother to the duchess of Shrewsbury), had, in a transport of passion, killed his own servant. Palleotti had chased John Niccolo into Lisle Street (where he resided) and stabbed the man a number of times with his sword on 11 February 1718. He appeared 'disordered in his brain', and his sister the duchess earnestly solicited the king and many other persons of distinction for a pardon. But the common multitude became so clamorous that it was thought dangerous to rescue him from the penalties of the law: these the marquis very ignominiously suffered at Tyburn on 17 March 1718.

The nobleman slays his servant in cold blood, as originally depicted in Knapp and Baldwin's Newgate Calendar Volume 1 *(1824).*

We learn that around this time the plague of duelling had gotten so bad that an attempt was made to outlaw it by Sir Joseph Jekyll, who presented to the House a bill against the 'impious practice'. The bill was read on 8 March 1720, and had been drafted following the slaying of an MP. Mr William Buckingham, Member of Parliament for Reading, and William Aldworth, Member for Windsor, had quarrelled after drinking too heavily and fought a chaotic duel in near-darkness in which the former suffered a wound to his arm so serious that it led to his death. It says much about the times that the bill was rejected by the House of Lords – and although Aldworth was brought before the courts, he eventually received a pardon. The combat between these two politicians is said to have occurred in Stanlake Park, east of Reading on 5 March, immediately following their altercation at a birthday celebration in Windsor. With his dying breath Mr Buckingham chivalrously admitted he had provoked his opponent; but it is clear that in the 18th century politicians – rather than engaging in a mere war of words – might literally try and kill each other over some perceived slight or political disagreement.

Returning to London, Defoe's observations provide a very good illustration of the murder here, murder there way of life in the British capital during the first quarter of the 18th century, much in the same way Walpole's writing would during the second half of the 1700s. On 4 June 1720 he recorded in his journal, 'Some days since, a soldier of the Marquis of Winchester's Regiment of Horse, after robbing two coaches on Hounslow Heath, was (in attempting the like on a third) shot by a young gentleman travelling therein; upon which unexpected reception, the fellow rode off, but by the loss of blood, which ran very plentifully from his wound, he soon fell off his horse; however, he was taken up by the country people, who carried him to a surgeon, by whose care, we hear, he is in a fair way *to live to be hanged.*' Around the same time: 'Not far from Acton, an old woman was robbed of a shilling, which she complained of to all she met on the road; upon which, some rode after the robber as fast as they could, and he perceiving they would soon be up with him, that he might lose no time in facing about, would have fired a pistol at his pursuers over his shoulder; but in the hurry he shot himself in the head, and dropt dead from his horse, to the disappointment of Squire Ketch (i.e. the hangman), who would otherwise have had a customer of him.' Defoe's correspondence under this date goes on to note numerous other acts of mindless violence and crime, as well as the carriages that ran down pedestrians in the road and the machinations of scheming fire-raisers. Defoe also implies that sheriff's bailiffs – 'the Catchpole Society' – were universally despised, in their meagre capacity of enforcing jurisdiction; he observes on 28 October 1721 that one poor fellow was grabbed by the populace and 'toss'd in a blanket as usual' merely for having been spotted leaving a public house 'near Westminster School' in the company of a bailiff.

Bailiffs assisted judges at assizes, served writs, collected fines and assembled juries, their subordination to the law making them despised at many levels of society; yet they were themselves wont to thoroughly exceed their authority, for Defoe notes: 'Two others of them, in the Execution of their Office, arrested a worthy gentleman (Captain Edward Luttrell) near Norfolk Buildings, treated him so roughly in the height of their modesty, that, it seems the poor gentleman was shot thro' the body, stabb'd in several places in the back; and, being since buried at St Clements Danes, the two bailiffs, it seems, lye in good strong irons for wilful murder, as charged by the Coroner's Inquest.' Another instance like this was reported in the *British Observator* in 1734: 'Yesterday (13 May) a Bayliff and his follower were committed to Newgate for the murder of a woman, by throwing her down and stamping on her head and breast in such a manner that she died immediately.'

Men of position and title were still occasionally killed in the most common manner. The *Historical Register* records that Mr Alexander Agnew, son of Sir James Agnew, Bart, died in a violent scuffle at the Lubeck Tavern in Maiden Lane on 3 August 1724. Agnew had gotten into a quarrel with one Major

Charles Harrison, in which the major had got the upper hand; although the circumstances were somewhat unclear due to the fact that the two men had been the only ones present at the time. Harrison had fatally stabbed his antagonist in the breast with his sword, but when he was tried at the Old Bailey the court accepted that the killer had acted in self defence. The pair had formerly been brother officers in the Garrison of Dunkirk, and although Harrison bore an inoffensive reputation, the baronet's son was said to be an argumentative type of fellow.

Perhaps the most informative snippet of London life Defoe recorded concerns the killing of a man in June 1718 – for this one entry above all others seems to sum up the madness, anarchy and self-destruction that gripped people so frequently that even the most outrageous tragedies became mere footnotes to coffee-house gossip, and then only for a while until the next event occurred. Defoe wrote on 28 June 1718: 'Some days ago one Kelly, an attorney, came to the Sun Ale House in Long Acre, and asking if Mr Ryan (a comedian at the New Play-house) was in the house? Was answer'd, no. Whereupon he swore Mr Ryan was above stairs, and that he would go up and kill him; he accordingly ran upstairs, and finding Mr Ryan at supper, made several passes at him, which Mr Ryan parried *with a plate* till he got to his own sword, which lay in the window, and then gave Kelly a wound on the left side, of which he instantly died. The Coroner's Inquest having sat on the body, have given in their verdict *se defendendo*. Mr Ryan absconds till the Sessions, when he will surrender himself and take his Tryal.'

It does not appear Mr Ryan was obliged to take his trial for this homicide. Ryan, at that period, was among the finest actors in the capital: yet his career was itself nearly terminated through violence. Going home one night alone from the play-house, he was attacked by two street robbers near Lincoln's Inn Fields and shot in the throat with a pistol as he drew his sword to protect himself. Luckily, surgeons managed to remove the ball and – despite his voice being greatly affected – he returned to the stage.

THE CRUELLEST OF CONSPIRACIES

Nichol Mushet appears to have been a young man of some fortune, being described as 'of Boghall', and we learn he had studied for the profession of a surgeon. However, for some time he had led an irregular and dissipated life in Edinburgh, where he had as one of his best friends a noted roisterer named James Campbell, of Burnbank, who was ordnance store-keeper at the city's castle.

Mushet was drawn into an ill-advised marriage with a lady named Margaret Hall, for whom he soon discovered he had neither affection nor respect; and he at length became so desperate to free himself of the connection that he planned with Campbell a means to obtain a divorce under false pretences. An arrangement was agreed between the two men to the effect that Mushet would pay Campbell an outstanding debt of £50 as soon as the latter could procure – or create - some incriminating evidence against the luckless wife that might facilitate the divorce proceedings.

According to one (1852) account by Scottish criminal historian JH Burton: 'They drugged the poor victim with opium, and caused a scene to be enacted and witnessed that *cannot be described*. Mushet raised an action of divorce against his wife; but his solicitor, hinting that the grounds on which it rested were suspicious, and might lead to an awkward exposure, he (Mushet) endeavoured to strengthen his case by the testimony of false witnesses.' Ultimately this unbelievably cruel conspiracy came to naught.

Following this failure Campbell suggested they remove the woman by poisoning her to death. Mr and Mrs James Mushet (Nichol's brother and his wife, who were in desperate circumstances) readily undertook the responsibility of secretly administering the poison to Margaret: but on each occasion the victim's stomach rejected the deadly substance.

There were by now four people engaged in the plot to murder Margaret. The plan was revived to rape or seduce Margaret Mushet, and the brother, James, agreed to undertake this act; however, for some reason it appears to have been aborted in favour of simply getting rid of her once and for all.

The victim appears to have been particularly resolute, if blind to what was going on - for dosing her with poison was resumed once more, but again without effect. James Mushet next agreed to beat his sister-in-law's brains out for 20 guineas, of which he was given one or two in advance; we are told this wretched man 'employed (himself) in burying a child of his own'. Thus, there is an implication an unwanted offspring was quietly dispatched by Nichol Mushet's desperate relatives.

These diabolically wicked schemes employed the attention of Nichol Mushet, his brother and sister-in-law, and Campbell for many months; not one of them, it appears, ever felt the slightest compunction towards the poor woman, despite it being evident she loved her husband and no real fault on her side was ever insinuated.

At length Nichol himself borrowed a sharp knife, and on 17 October 1720 took his wife for a walk out of the city to Duddingston. At a solitary place in the King's Park (Holyrood Park) Nichol Mushet put an end to his wife's life once and for all, and then hastened to tell his brother James what he had done. It is implied that Nichol may not have actually intended to slay his wife in such a way, for he is said to have been extremely agitated after the event; it may be that he just found himself presented with an opportunity in King's Park and took it, against all good sense and reason.

The following morning Margaret Mushet was found lying dead on the ground, her throat cut to the bone. Her body also bore numerous other wounds, which she appeared to have sustained in fighting off her husband's assault. Nichol Mushet was quickly seized and examined, whence he readily related the full circumstances of the murder and the developments leading up to it. He was adjudged to be hanged in the Grassmarket on 6 January 1721, and Campbell – his associate – was 'declared infamous' and sentenced to banishment. Prosecution of the other conspirators for the attempts to poison Margaret Mushet appears not to have been pursued, since the method that had been employed at the time was of such a circuitous route that it was not thought possible to secure a conviction.

Another interesting detail of this is that Jean Mushet, Lady Boghall, (Nichol's mother) wrote to her son in gaol while he awaited execution, and her letter ended up being published as a broadside. The first sentence sums up everything that follows: 'Nichol. I cannot now in writing give you such expressions of affection, as I formerly used, for you have by your wicked and abominable crimes, made me ashamed and sorry to own the relation of a mother to you...'

The Scottish historian Robert Chambers tells us of this tragedy: 'The common people, thrilled with horror by the details of the murder, marked their feelings in the old national code by raising a cairn on the spot where it took place; and Mushet's Cairn has ever since been a recognised locality.' Nichol Mushet's executed cadaver was hung in chains at the Gallowlee, Leith Walk.

Of James Campbell, we find a little more information: while confined in the castle under sentence of banishment, he and one George Faichney got hold of a man called James M'Naughton, who they made drunk. While he was in this state of insensibility they apparently set him on fire deliberately. For this outrage Campbell was again indicted, along with his friend Faichney. This occurred in 1722, and in all likelihood Campbell never left the country but died in confinement.

THE MYSTERIOUS MURDER OF OXON'S MP

On 25 April 1721 the Right Honourable James Herbert, Esq, of Tythrop House at Kingsey, Member of Parliament for the county of Oxon, took a walk into fields about his home in the parish of Dinton in Buckinghamshire. Mr Herbert had only lately returned from a trip abroad; and when his body was shortly thereafter found in a little spring, or rivulet, where the water was not above mid-leg depth, it was at first conjectured that the stress of his trip had induced an apoplectic fit while he walked in the direction of Thame and crossed a bridge. During this episode he had somehow fallen and drowned.

Herbert, however, was not an old man; he was aged about 33, in fact. When his body was taken out of the water and laid out, it appeared from injuries he displayed that he might actually have been garrotted. His disconsolate widow, Sarah, the daughter of Sir James Hallet of Bloomsbury Square, firmly determined to find out what had happened to her husband on behalf of herself and their six children.

Sarah Herbert was convinced that James had been assassinated, either by footpads or opponents, and to this end she petitioned King George I to agree a pardon for anyone (bar the actual killer, or killers) who provided evidence in the case of her husband. Her remarkable letter appeared in many of the news-sheets of the day, and read:

'I, Sarah Herbert, widow of the said James Herbert, Esq, do hereby promise to pay unto such person who shall first discover those that were concerned in the murder of the said James Herbert, the sum of £1'000 to be paid within one month after any person shall be by due course of law convicted of the said crime: witness my hand the 23rd day of August 1721.'

Sadly for Sarah's attempt it seems her husband's death went unsolved, even despite the immense reward she offered for information. Rewards were often offered in murder cases, but £1'000 was a record sum in those days: if the worth of a man's life might thus be measured then it would appear that James Herbert was a very highly-regarded man indeed.

'CRUEL FATHER, THOU ART THE CAUSE OF MY DEATH!'

William Shaw was an upholsterer in Edinburgh in the year 1721. His daughter Catherine had become passionately attached to a young man of dissipated habits (John Lawson, a jeweller); meanwhile Shaw was desirous she should marry a steady husband of his choosing. This was a young man named Robertson, who was the son of a neighbour and a friend of Shaw's.

On one occasion a quarrel between father and daughter over this matter became very violent, and Catherine was overheard screaming the words 'barbarity', 'cruelty' and 'death' by a watchmaker named James Morrison living in the same building, whose apartment was divided from that of the Shaw family by a single partition only. Sometime later William Shaw stormed out of his rooms, and not long afterwards the watchmaker perceived a low groaning from his neighbour's apartments. Becoming alarmed, he summoned people from the street - who listened attentively at the Shaw's door and heard Catherine gasp two or three times from within, 'Cruel father, thou art the cause of my death!'

When the room was entered, the girl was found bloodied and slumped, having clearly been stabbed by a bloodstained knife laid not too far from her.

Those present asked her if she attributed her wounds to her father, upon which she managed to weakly nod her head – after which she immediately died. Scarcely had she expired when William Shaw re-appeared and entered the room. When he saw the group of people stood round his daughter's body he became extremely agitated; when blood spots were pointed out on his shirt, it began to seem clear that he might have stabbed his daughter in a fit of rage before he had stormed out.

William Shaw was apprehended and tried at Edinburgh for his daughter's murder. He denied any act of violence against his daughter and explained that the blood spots on his shirt came from his own arm, which had been improperly bandaged following an operation involving bleeding some days before. Despite his denial it seemed clear he was the guilty party, and in November 1721 he was executed and his body suspended in a gibbet cage at Leith Walk.

In August 1722 there occurred a development that makes this tragic affair one of the most complicated of the 18th century. A young man, who had succeeded to the tenancy of the Shaw's apartments, found a folded piece of paper in a cavity on one side of the chimney in the chamber where Catherine had expired. The letter contained an avowal, in her own handwriting, that she intended to commit suicide in consequence of her father's cruelty towards her. 'My death,' the letter concluded, 'I lay at your charge. When you read this, consider yourself as the inhuman wretch that plunged the knife into the bosom of the unhappy Catherine Shaw.'

The magistracy of Edinburgh were thus convinced an innocent man had been executed, and they lowered William Shaw's body from the gibbet post at Leith Walk. It was delivered to his relatives, who buried him and 'directed a pair of colours to be waved over his grave'.

This case (if, indeed, it is true) is possibly unique. Catherine Shaw had, in effect, caused her hated father William to be murdered by the law after her own demise. It is unclear if this was the deliberate end; for the suicide note admitted he had not killed her. And yet she had apparently hidden this away rather than allow it to be found with her body. In implying – falsely - in her dying moments that her father had killed her, even allowing for her tumultuous state she *must* have known he would hang – leading one to suppose that this is perhaps an almost unparalleled method of patricide in British criminal history.

PETIT TREASON

Some of the news-sheets briefly recorded a grotesque public spectacle as occurring in Lincoln in the middle of July 1722: the execution by strangulation and burning of a woman called Eleanor Elson.

Eleanor had been convicted of *petit treason*: the murder of her husband. When the execution occurred, she was secured to a stake near the gallows, and the following can be gleaned from Andrew Williams' *Bygone Punishments* (1899), which paints a grim picture of the woman's awful demise: 'She was clothed in a cloth "made like a shift", saturated with tar, and her limbs were also smeared with the same inflammable substance, while a tarred bonnet had been placed on her head. She was brought out of the prison barefoot, and, being put on a hurdle, was drawn on a sledge to the place of execution near the gallows. Upon arrival, some time was passed in prayer, after which the executioner placed her on a tar barrel, a height of three feet against the stake. A rope ran through a pulley in the stake, and was placed around her neck, she herself fixing it with her hands. Three irons also held her body to the stake, and the rope being pulled tight, the tar barrel was taken aside and the fire lighted. The details in the *Lincoln Date Book* state that she was probably quite dead before the fire reached her, as the executioner pulled upon the rope (round her neck) several times whilst the irons were being fixed.'

While the punishment for male murderers was execution by hanging and then gibbeting, this ghastly public carnival illustrates that for women convicted of this offence the punishment still bordered on medieval. Examples litter the annals of murder throughout the 18th century; for instance, and staying in Lincoln, Mary Johnson was burned alive for poisoning her husband in April 1747 - while a man named Lynn, or Lyon, was hanged at the same time for poisoning his wife.

The most famous case of *petit treason* – that of Mrs Catherine Hayes – we have yet to come to; suffice to say that the method of execution suffered by Eleanor and her contemporaries does little more than reinforce (to the modern reader) what a shocking, hardened and pitiless facade the 18th century could present.

ROUGH JUSTICE

A sentence other than capital punishment imposed by the courts was no guarantee that lethal justice would not be dispensed anyway, although by the murderous hands of the mob rather than the authorities. Just such an indictment on London society is said to have occurred in 1723.

A brief report in the *Historical Register* for that year notes the curious death of John Middleton, who had been sentenced to stand in the pillory at Charing Cross by the Court of King's Bench. Middleton had been convicted of 'wilful perjury, in swearing treasonable practices against innocent persons'. He never saw out his sentence though, for his lifeless body was shortly thereafter taken down from the pillory: a subsequent coroner's inquest recorded the extraordinary verdict of '*accidentally* strangled'.

In all probability, Middleton – his crimes rousing the anger of the populace, while not warranting the death penalty – was garrotted by the mob while he was trapped immobile in the pillory. A later source (1766) makes the assumption that he was 'so severely treated by the populace that he was taken down dead'.

DESCRIPTION OF A ONE-EYED ASSASSIN

On 22 April 1723 Sir James Campbell of Lawers was foully murdered at Greenock, Renfrewshire, by Duncan Campbell of Edramucky. The facts are thus related in a contemporary letter:

'Lawers had been in a treaty of marriage with (Campbell of) Finab's daughter, which Edramurkle (Edramucky) was very active to get accomplished, out of a seeming friendship for Lawers. After the marriage articles were agreed upon, they went together to make a visit to the young lady, and, in return, came to Greenock on Friday 19th last (April), where they remained Saturday and Sunday - Edramurkle all the while *shewing* the greatest friendship for Lawers, and Lawers confiding in him as his own brother. Upon the Saturday, pretending to Lawers that he had use for a pistol, he got money from him to buy one, which accordingly he did, with ball and powder. The use he made of this artillery was to discharge two balls into Lawers's head, while he was fast asleep, betwixt three and four on Monday morning; and which balls were levelled under his left eye, and went through his head, sloping to the back-bone of his neck…he was found in a sleeping posture, and had not moved eye or hand.

The fellow (Edramurkle) went immediately off in a boat for Glasgow, and from thence came here (Edinburgh), the people in the house having no suspicion but that Lawers was asleep, till about 11 o'clock, when they found him as above, swimming in his blood. Upon recollection on several passages which happened with respect to Duncan Campbell, they presently found him to have been the murderer, and caused the magistrates of Greenock to write to the magistrates of Glasgow to apprehend him; but he being gone for Edinburgh, the provost wrote in to our provost here, whereupon there was a search here…but the villain is not as yet found.

The occasion of this execrable murder is said by the murderer's friends to be to prevent Lawers going back in the marriage, whereof he was then apprehensive; and being a relation of the bride's, and very active in bringing on that courtship, the Devil tempted him to that unparalleled cruelty. But we rather believe it was to rifle his pockets, for his breeches were from under his head, and nothing but a *Carolus* and four shillings in them; whereas it is most certain that Lawers always carried a purse of gold with him, and more especially could not but have it when he intended to celebrate his marriage.'

This correspondence was written by Andrew McDowall, later Lord Bankton, and what is implied is that the Scottish peer was assassinated by a relative of his wife-to-be who accompanied him.

However, the *true* motive does not ever appear to have been ascertained. Duncan Campbell was extensively advertised for as 'a tall, thin man, loot-shouldered, pock-pitted, with a pearl or blindness in the right eye'. He was dressed 'in a suit of gray Duroy clothes, plain-mounted, a big red coat, and a thin light wig, rolled up with a ribbon' and was 'betwixt 30 and 40 years of age'.

Despite the suspect's facial composite being circulated, and the offer of 100 guineas reward for his arrest, there appears to be no record of Campbell ever being brought to justice, according to Scottish historian Robert Chambers.

ASSASSIN OR INSANE?

The case of Edward Arnold is an interesting one, since it illustrates an early instance of manifest proofs of insanity being taken into account as an explanation for a serious crime – an assassination attempt, in fact.

The target was Thomas Onslow, 2nd Baron Onslow. While returning from a foxhunt on 28 August 1723 Lord Onslow found himself confronted in a lane running past a turnip field near St Catherine's Hill, Guildford, by a man aged about 39 who was armed with a loaded fowling piece. That this was no robber was abundantly clear, for it was the middle of the day and the man demanded no money; he simply fired at his lordship, wounding him in the shoulder and knocking him off his horse's saddle. As Lord Onslow lay on the ground, writhing in pain, the man walked up to him and said, 'Damn you! Do you kick? I'll soon put an end to your kicking!' He then proceeded, very coolly, to load his gun and was in the act of preparing to shoot his victim once more in cold blood when he was grappled to the ground by his lordship's retainers.

The assassin proved to be one Edward Arnold, and he went on trial on 20 March 1724 before Mr Justice Tracey at Kingston's Lent assizes. The motive for the shooting at first seemed to be political. Lord Onslow had been very vigilant as a magistrate in suppressing societies that were suspected of existing to disturb the government belonging to the new Hanoverian monarch. Arnold had frequently been heard to declare that Onslow would ruin the nation.

However, it was also evidenced that in and around Guildford Arnold was considered a man of wild and turbulent manners, who – just before shooting Lord Onslow – had attempted to destroy his own beloved child. Witnesses at his trial described him as at best exceedingly strange and different from other people, and at worst, unequivocally mad. Even his old school friends recalled him as a sullen, difficult and withdrawn child. His own family considered him mad, and let him live a life of solitude and near poverty, knowing full well Arnold slept in barns and under hayricks, yet not knowing what they could do to help him. He would enter into arguments with himself, only to laugh maniacally and smash objects. In his sleep, he perceived he was plagued by demons, imps and ghosts.

Lord Onslow lived in Arnold's neighbourhood, and he began to form the opinion that his lordship was responsible for all the violence and tumults the nation had witnessed; furthermore, he declared his belief that Onslow was sending the imps that tormented him so. These evil little creatures, he persisted, climbed into his belly and prevented him from eating: Arnold called them Bollies, or Bolleroys. Deciding that he cared not for his own life, he decided to slay his lordship.

The proofs of Edward Arnold's insanity were great. However, the court decided that his act had been, ultimately, born out of vengeance, and very deliberately directed at a powerful man who he had taken to be his enemy. To this end, Arnold was sentenced to hang on the gallows; but remarkably, at this point his victim interceded and demanded that Arnold be sentenced to life imprisonment.

The request was granted. Edward Arnold spent 31 years languishing in the New Gaol, Southwark, until he died aged about 70 in 1754. Although he outlived his victim (who died in 1740), one is left with the impression that Arnold was prepared for, and even desired, the gallows – rather than the living Hell of three decades in one of England's disgusting prisons.

THE WALTHAM DEER-STEALERS

In the early 1720s a desperate gang of poachers came to be considered so dangerous that it became necessary to create a new Act of Parliament in order to help catch them.

The gang's practice was to arm themselves with pistols, and – their faces darkened with gunpowder – enter the country parks of the nobility and gentry in *daylight* in order to steal deer. By the time they raided Windsor Forest they were notorious for the manner in which they brazenly and carelessly committed their poaching. The gang numbered about seven, and could be exceptionally dangerous to cross: on one occasion they took two countrymen who refused to join their criminal society, dug holes and buried them both up to their chins, leaving just their heads exposed. These two unfortunates would undoubtedly have perished, were it not for their accidental discovery by a third party.

This act of callousness had the effect of frightening away one of the gang, Edward Elliot. Elliot was a tailor's apprentice in Guildford, and in many ways his story is a pathetic one and his fate far worse that what he might have deserved. Elliot served for some time as a lady's footman, but in 1723 had the complete misfortune to run into some of his old comrades – who coerced him into going with them to poach deer on Waltham Chase. Upon being assured no harm would come to him, Elliot agreed.

While the rest of the gang hunted deer, Elliot himself chose to pursue a fawn, but while he was thus engaged he was ambushed by the Bishop of Winchester's gamekeeper and a number of assistants, who took him into custody. However, Elliot's protestations brought the rest of the gang running through the thicket to help him, and during a pitched battle the keeper was shot and instantly killed by a gang member called Henry Marshall (a sometime boxer who had earned a degree of fame earlier in his life when he broke the arm of a highwayman who was intent on robbing a coach).

The murder of the gamekeeper in this manner prompted the government to usher in a new law against going about armed and disguised with intent to poach, steal fish, tear down trees or commit any manner of this type of crime; those caught with their faces blackened in any forest, open heath, farm field, common land, outhouse, hovel, highway lane etc would suffer execution under the new move. It seems that blackening one's face in the daylight was enough to suppose that one might be on their way to commit a felony, and this measure came on the back of the hunt for the Waltham Chase gang – who now went by the moniker 'the Waltham Blacks' in the towns of Hampshire and the capital.

Their notoriety ensured they did not remain long at large. Richard Parvin, one of the group who mainly employed his time as a Portsmouth innkeeper, had the random misfortune to encounter one of his own maids in a countryside tavern, which drew her suspicions as to why he was there; this led to his arrest and imprisonment in Winchester Gaol. The unfortunate Elliot, who had only been with the gang on the night of the murder by sheer chance, was arrested shortly after and lodged in Guildford Gaol. The rest of the gang comprised of Marshall, the murderer; Robert Kingshell, from Farnham in Surrey; two brothers from Portsmouth called John and Edward Pink; and James Ansel, also of Portsmouth, who had been a highway robber before joining the gang round about 1721. (This last person may have been the 'James Russel' that the news-sheets reported in October 1723 had been lodged in Winchester Gaol suspected of being the 'king' of the gang.)

We learn that all were taken by 'vigilant exertion of the civil power', and afterwards brought as a group to London under strong guard, where they were imprisoned in Newgate. On 13 November 1723 they were all brought to trial in the court of King's Bench, Westminster, and being convicted on the 'clearest evidence' they were all (including the singularly unfortunate Edward Elliot) sentenced to die. It is said that Henry Marshall, upon being sentenced, was instantly deprived of the use of his tongue, and was unable to speak a single word until the day preceding his execution – when he apparently regained the power of speech.

Curiously, each and every one of the seven convicted men is reported to have behaved very devoutly in the days leading up to their execution, receiving the sacrament before they left Newgate on 4 December 1723 for the final journey to Tyburn. They were utterly resigned, and admitted the justice of their death sentence, and it is said that their final moments were engaged in trying to outdo each other in their cries to God for mercy; however, they do not appear to have been capable of the impressive public addresses the people of London expected at their executions. It was also reported that they were guilty of 'many crimes' besides that which they were tried for.

Their sentence is perhaps the most interesting element of the case, for prior to the murder their crime of poaching while 'armed and disguised' might not have warranted the death penalty. Marshall, in gunning down the keeper, had, in a strange way, doomed them all - for it brought in the law that condemned *all* of them, even those not directly connected with the murder, like Elliot.

BELLINGHAM'S 'LANG PACK'

In England's rugged and wild north, they knew how to deal with bandits; perhaps it was ingrained in them after centuries spent fighting Scottish raiders along the borders.

A famous story tells how one Colonel Ridley returned to Lee Hall, a mansion beside the North Tyne south of Bellingham, Northumberland, having made his fortune in India. He and his family repaired to London in the winter of 1723, leaving the hall in the care of the maid, an elderly retainer and a young ploughboy named Edward, who was aged about 16.

One afternoon there appeared at the hall a travelling pedlar, carrying a long, thick and enormously heavy-looking pack on his back, who requested a night's lodging. The maid refused, but was persuaded to allow the pedlar to leave his heavy pack in the parlour while he sought alternative lodgings.

After the pedlar had gone, the maid – to her utter fright – perceived the pack to move, as though something living were within; Edward ran to her assistance, and, perceiving the same, fired a huge old gun into the middle of the pack. When the three servants opened the pack they found the bloodied body of a fatally wounded robber, and it was clear that this man had been deliberately smuggled into Lee Hall by his accomplice, the pedlar. Worse, he had been armed with a cutlass, pistols, and a silver horn – this last presumably for use to signal his accomplices after he had unlocked the door to the hall during the night.

Edward immediately ran for help, bringing back a number of men armed with swords, pistols, pitchforks and cudgels to help defend the house. He next prompted the robbers out of hiding by blowing the silver horn, and when a group of horsemen rode into the yard those inside opened fire, killing four more of their attackers and putting the rest to flight. Before dawn, some gang members returned - but only to recover the bodies of their dead comrades. As a consequence, no one ever knew who any of them were.

This peculiar grave in Bellingham, Northumberland, marks the spot where the slain robber was interred.

Some say this event in fact occurred further south at Swinburne Castle, Great Swinburne, although this appears to be a mistake. In St Cuthbert's Church, Bellingham, can be found a peculiar gravestone designated 'The Lang Pack' that is said to mark the spot where the man in the pack was interred.

HALF-HANGED MAGGIE

The case of Margaret Dickinson (or Dickson) was one that created great interest in Edinburgh. On 2 September 1724 Margaret had been hanged in the Grass-market for infanticide (or 'concealing pregnancy in the case of a dead child'), and afterwards her body was cut down, placed in a coffin at the gallows foot and conveyed on a bier by her friends to the parish churchyard in Musselburgh. However, the jolting of the cart and the admission of air into the coffin (through some damage the receptacle had received) combined to resuscitate the woman. When the cortege stopped 'at Pepper-mill to refresh themselves', all present were alarmed by one among the group claiming that Margaret's breast was gently moving. They made frantic efforts to fully resuscitate her, opening a vein and pouring spirits down her throat.

Margaret very quickly became the sensation of Edinburgh, a contemporary report in the *Caledonian Mercury* declaring: 'She was that night carried to Musselburgh, and so far recovered next day, that she both sat up and spoke to the company. She is at present in her brother's house in Musselburgh, in perfect health and judgement, and has been visited by almost everybody here, high and low. She has had a great deal of money given to her, and several others have sent her money from this place. 'Tis thought the stir and motion of the cart whereon she lay, provok'd the circulation of the blood, and contributed greatly to her recovery.' Even Margaret's husband, relenting under a renewed affection for her, took her back in again; for the pair had separated prior to her execution.

Margaret is revived during her final journey. (Originally from Annals of Crime & New Newgate Calendar No.8, *12 August 1833.)*

Margaret lived creditably for many years after her curious preservation, raising a large family and making a living selling salt on the streets of Edinburgh. Here, on account of her adventure, she earned the nicknames 'Half-hanged Maggie' and 'Ill hangit Maggy Dickson'.

ANDREW HORNE'S LIFE OF DEBAUCHERY

William Andrew Horne was born in 1685, the favourite eldest son of a gentleman who possessed a small estate at Butterley in Derbyshire. William was given a classical education; but his privileged upbringing engendered in him a propensity towards sloth and self-gratification as he grew older, leading him to the debauchment of his mother's maids; and even – he later admitted – his own sisters.

In February 1724, when he was about 39, one of William's sisters was delivered of a fine baby boy thanks to his cohabitation with her, and so he enlisted his brother Charles' assistance in covering up this scandal. The brothers secretly bundled the infant into a long linen bag and rode on horses to Annesley, Nottinghamshire, in the middle of the night. The infant was well-dressed, and Charles explained later that he had intended to leave it on the doorstep of one Mr Chaworth of Annesley, whom he knew; however, Chaworth's barking dogs forced the brothers to simply abandon the baby in a haystack (still tied in the bag, although with an air hole cut in it), hoping it would be discovered the next day. Of course, it being February the infant died during the night.

Andrew Horne leaves his offspring to die, as depicted first in the Annals of Crime & New Newgate Calendar No.22, *1833.*

When the Horne brothers fell out some time later, Charles vindictively informed their father of William's crime; the old man ordered it kept a family secret, and this shameful knowledge was still clandestine when William's father died in 1747. Despite this, William was left his father's estate and revenged himself upon his treacherous brother by turning him off the property without a penny to his name. Charles was reduced to keeping a little alehouse at the gate of his brother's estate, and occasionally he would open the gate for him, doffing his hat to his brother in silent mockery of the grim secret they both shared.

Thanks to Charles' inability to keep the matter quiet (he informed numerous people of the incest and murder while in drink) the crime gradually became an open secret in the parish. However, no-one Charles talked to could advise how to resolve such a delicate matter - it had by now been nearly 25 years since the incident, after all.

As the years dragged on William got into an argument with a poacher who called him an 'incestuous old dog', and the slander ended up being heard in an ecclesiastical court held at Lichfield. The court finding against this man, named Roe, he went to the magistrates during Christmas 1758 and charged that William Horne ought to be arrested for murder on account of the stories his own brother was telling people.

In March 1759 a warrant was issued for William Andrew Horne's arrest, and he was discovered hiding in a large old chest within his house at Butterley. By now he was a bald-headed old man of 73, and said upon his discovery, 'It is a sad thing to hang me; for my brother Charles is as bad as myself, and he can't hang me without hanging himself.'

Andrew Horne's undignified arrest, as depicted in the Newgate Calendar Volume 2 *(Andrew Knapp and William Baldwin, 1825).*

William Horne went on trial on 10 August 1759 at Nottingham Assizes, before Lord Chief Baron Parker. Despite being married, his licentiousness and lofty arrogance had made him hated and feared throughout the parish, and there was no one who had a good word to say about him. He was convicted of murder and executed on 11 December 1759 - the day of his 74th birthday.

In a confession written by his own hand before his death, Horne confessed to two other murders: that of a servant girl who he had made pregnant, and also that of one Amos Killer, who he had dealt such a violent blow on one occasion that it had occasioned the fellow's death. This person had aroused Horne's wrath by coming begging at his door.

THE MYSTERIOUS AFFAIR AT MARTHAM

A very strange conspiracy was reported from Martham, Norfolk, in 1724. A man called Hugh Robinson and his son William had lately been hanged for setting fire to the house of a Mr Townsend in that village; however, the threat against Townsend's property appears to have been a continual one, with the result that guards were employed amid extra vigilance.

It appears that Robinson and Townsend had been embroiled in some kind of vendetta or rivalry for the previous two years, but it is unclear what the nature of this was; more so because Hugh and William Robinson had been convicted of setting fire to *several* houses in the area, and not just Mr Townsend's property. Both were sentenced to death at Norwich Assizes in August 1723, the son's body to be hung in chains near where one of the fires had been started.

This is Gibbet Hill, a slope that rises near Martham: the name of the place suggests a link to the mysterious affair in 1724.

Towards the end of August 1724 (following the Robinson's execution) one of Townsend's barns was set on fire and burned to the ground, proving that the threat against his property was an on-going matter for concern. Shortly thereafter a stable and outhouse were set ablaze around midnight one night in early September: it was after this that guards were posted to try and catch the arsonist.

This vigilance was rewarded when a man named Grice was taken up as he made his way to Townsend's house two nights later, apparently with the intention of setting fire to the premises: for he carried all the materials on him for just such an act. Upon being seized Grice called out that he was a dead man, and immediately declared he had been hired to commit the act of arson with the intention of burning Townsend's house with him in it.

Grice claimed that the person who had hired him was the executed man's wife, Mrs Robinson, and also implicated several other people in the plot: Mrs Robinson's new husband (a man called Bennett), one of Mr Townsend's own servants, and thirdly a man called Hales – who, bizarrely, had been one of the witnesses *against* the hanged Mr Robinson.

One by one, all the named parties were taken and lodged in Norwich Castle, while warrants were issued for a number of others alleged to be involved in this conspiracy. Grice, the hired arsonist, was made an evidence; and subsequently these events were reported (although in a confusing manner) in many of the news-sheets across England, the speculation being that the matter might be fully explained at the forthcoming trial – provided the evidence, Grice, was not tampered with, of course.

By the time the four accused were tried at Norwich Assizes in July 1725, Grice had totally changed his story. He denied knowing anything against them, and after a waste-of-time trial they were acquitted; in exasperation, the authorities waived Grice's rights as an evidence and brought in a special verdict against him of being an 'agent therein', for which he was sentenced accordingly.

Correspondence received on 3 August 1725 revealed the mysterious *denouement* to this affair. It appears that Mrs Robinson and the others so acquitted did not trust Grice to keep his mouth shut: for he died in Norwich Gaol the very day after the trial ended, there being great suspicion that he had been poisoned by the very people he had saved from the gallows. Grice, it appears, was assassinated to draw a line under the affair – which to this day appears to warrant a good deal more explanation.

PIRATES OF THE NORTHERN ISLES

Although piracy was by now becoming more readily associated with the Carolinas and the West Indies, it is interesting to consider the examples of domestic criminal buccaneers, freebooters, and common pirates who still menaced the remoter British shores.

Ten miles north of Caithness, on the top of the Scottish mainland, the archipelago known as the Orkneys was ravaged by the warlike and feared 'Stromness Pirate' John Gow during the later reign of King George I. It is said that Gow had earned his captainship through the murder of his vessel's former captain, whose throat was slit during a mutiny when the ship was seized off Santa Cruz. Gow had personally shot the captain full of bullets for good measure, and fellow conspirators had next cut the throats of three more who they did not trust to side with them. The seized ship was an English warship, re-named by Gow as the *Revenge*, and it bore twenty large guns and six smaller ones.

John Gow seizes his ship by bloodthirsty massacre. (Originally from Annals of Crime & New Newgate Calendar No.13, *1833.)*

Gow also went by the aliases Goffe or Smith. Trusting to the defenceless state of the Orkneys at that time, and needing a safe hideaway from the authorities, the crew of the *Revenge* entered the harbour at Eday via Calf Sound in January 1725, with a view to using it as a base to extend their depredations. It seems Gow's identity went unknown for some time, for he hosted dancing parties in Stromness and even received the troth-plight of a young lady possessed of some property. His identity did not stay a secret long though, thanks to an inherent lawlessness among his crew. The *Newgate Calendar* tells us that at one point they abducted two island women for three days, using them so violently that 'one of them expired soon after they had put them on shore'.

By this time the *Revenge* had begun attacking local shipping, and her crew had also raided the Hall of Clestrain. Gow's true identity as a freebooter became suspected following a damaging raid on Kirkwall during which ten of his men deserted.

His apprehension came about in the following manner. The *Revenge* had, for a while, appeared respectable; she had 35 hands, and was richly laden with figs, beef-wax and copper, managing to pass herself off as a merchant trader. However, shortly after the killing of the island woman, Gow sailed into Calf Sound with the intention of robbing the house of one James Fea, an old school fellow of Gow's who some accounts suggest came from Clestrain.

Most accounts suggest the following incident occurred in the bay of Calf Sound itself. Unfortunately, Gow all but ran the *Revenge* aground on a little island called the Calf, where Fea grazed his sheep. Since she had weighed anchor too near land, and was positioned in unfamiliar waters where the wind could not take her back out to sea, the *Revenge* was in immediate danger of being destroyed on the shore. So Gow, under the guise of friendship, sent a letter by small boat to Fea's cottage, which was quite near the shore, requesting immediate assistance.

Fea was aware of the rumours spreading throughout the Orkneys concerning Gow, and so ignored the request; but soon he found himself in immediate danger when five armed *Revenge* crewmembers came ashore in another small boat demanding assistance for their captain. Fea, in a masterly display of cunning, offered to entertain these criminals at the local alehouse, all the while plotting with his friends to destroy the pirates' small vessel, thus trapping them on the island; he next contrived to walk and talk outdoors with the boatswain personally, ensuring the man was grabbed as soon as possible and a gag thrust in his mouth. The other four pirates were arrested at gunpoint as they sat at table waiting for the boatswain to return. In his scheme, Fea was much aided by Mr Jas. Laing, grandfather of one Malcolm Laing Esq, an eminent Scottish historian. The following day the *Revenge* was driven by the waves upon Calf-Island, and Gow was forced to hang out a white flag. By degrees, the whole crew were brought ashore either by desperation or trickery and made prisoner: and in the end the *Revenge* was taken by Fea and the officers of the customs (who had been alerted) without bloodshed. When Gow was finally on land and disarmed, he begged that he might be shot rather than hand over his cutlass.

The captives were clapped in irons and imprisoned in the Hall of Clestrain. They were suspected of piracy and several murders, and it was generally hoped they would be tried at Kirkwall, the biggest town and capital of the Orkneys. However, James Fea sent a letter to Edinburgh, whose dignitaries in turn alerted the authorities in London, since the ship Gow had seized had been an English vessel formerly called the *George Galley*. The prisoners were subsequently loaded on board the *Greyhound* frigate in Edinburgh and brought south to the English capital.

Gow was eventually hanged at Execution Dock, Wapping, along with eight of his comrades. The executions occurred at noon on 11 June 1725, and Gow asked the executioner to put him out of his misery as quickly as possible. This the executioner attempted to do by pulling Gow's legs, but he did this so violently that the noose broke and Gow collapsed to the ground. He was immediately hoisted back up and more efficiently dispatched. His trial had been something of a farce; Gow, a Highlander, refused to acknowledge the authority of the court at the Sessions of Admiralty within the Old Bailey, and an executioner was brought to the bar of the court; he tied Gow's thumbs and wrenched them in an effort to get him to make a statement. This torture Gow bore with incredible obstinacy, and it was only the threat of being pressed to death the next morning that forced him to speak up in court. Even then he had very little to say, much like his co-accused; even the announcement in court of his death sentence failed to elicit much response. In all, twelve members of the gang were convicted on various charges of piracy and murder; three were acquitted.

Site of Execution Dock, on the Thames shoreline at Wapping. (Photograph copyright of Fin Fahay.)

John Gow was probably aged about thirty when he met his end at 'the dock'; this consisted of a scaffold for hanging near the Thames shoreline at low tide, which left the victims' corpses suspended from the noose until such time as the tide began to wash over their heads. Because of its position, the mob often got a better view from the water, and upon Gow's execution people turned out to see the notorious pirate in such numbers that it affected the local shipping lanes. Such was their excitement that an abundance of mischief was done, and several lives lost, both on the water and on the shore.

Sir Walter Scott would later use these events as the template for his work *The Pirate* (1822), after hearing of them from his mother.

If tradition is to be believed, the worst of the 18th century raiders of the northern seas, however, was Captain John Fullarton. Fullarton, who may have come from either Stromness or Orphir, had a lot of blood on his hands; his ship was seized from a cousin he had murdered, and it was said he forced prisoners to draw lots to decide which of them would hang. Following a running battle with the Scottish merchant ship *Isabella*, Fullarton boarded her and fatally shot the captain. However, Mary Jones, the captain's wife, managed to seize a pistol, and, clapping it to Fullarton's temple, blew his brains out as he was hauling down the *Isabella*'s colours. The *Isabella* returned safely to Leith, and Mary earned the nickname 'the Pirate Slayer'. Fullarton's demise calls to mind an international folktale, although his legend was considered credible enough when recorded by Ernest Marwick (d.1977), the premier historian and reporter of the Orkney Islands, and a founder member of the Orkney Heritage Society.

But if these salty tales remind us of the deeds of Edward 'Blackbeard' Teach far away in the Carolinas, and appear to have no place off the British coast at a time when the kingdom's navy was emerging as the very best in the world, then the evidence would suggest this was not the case: further south, the violence of coastal rogues out at sea was just as evident, and later during the century too, as we shall see.

A MASS FAMILY KILLING IN YORKSHIRE

A chap-book issued in 1725 explained that there had of late occurred a mass murder in 'Simer' (Seamer), Yorkshire. The perpetrator was one John Chambers, who had been married to a 'very good woman' for thirteen years. The marriage was to all outward appearances successful, for the union saw the births of seven children at various points; yet at some juncture Chambers grew 'jealous of her', and his response was unparalleled.

Chambers contrived to wipe out his entire family, and began with the children. He had committed murder upon the six youngest, and was about to kill the seventh (and eldest), a daughter, when the latter managed to escape. This, it appears, brought the matter to light; Chambers was apprehended and thrown into the county gaol where he lay until the next assizes.

Chambers, we learn, was executed on 6 May 1725. There is not much more information available than that, although the chapbook title indicates the case contained somewhat melodramatic moral elements: such as how 'the Devil appeared to him', for instance, and how Chambers was prevented from murdering his eldest 'by her prayers to God, who sent an angel to deliver her out of his hands'.

LUNATIC KILLING IN LINCOLNSHIRE

In Stickford, Lincolnshire, a maltster called John Bishop went berserk in his own home on the night of 10 June 1725 and cut his widowed mother's throat, before also viciously stabbing a second person; for which rampage he was committed to Lincoln Gaol. The motive for the attack was brought about by a dual combination of avarice and impotent rage, Bishop being continually frustrated in his desire to receive a £100 inheritance upon his mother's death.

However, the means by which he delivered her death are somewhat curious. Bishop simply left his bed – and sleeping wife – at one o'clock in the morning and went to the parlour where his mother Francis slept. Here he cut her neck through to the bone and stabbed her three times under the left breast and once under the right. The crime was enacted in the darkness, and all the more remarkable for the fact that a young child aged about four was in bed alongside the elderly gentlewoman, as well as a maid called Jane Hutchinson, who lay asleep on some bedding in the same room. Mrs Bishop's dying words were, 'Dear Jacky, you prick me, you have done enough, you have done enough!'

Stickford is still a small rural community near Spilsby in Lincolnshire.

The second person who Bishop knifed was a lodger in the house, who had come to Mrs Bishop's assistance when the clamour raised the household. He had been extremely fortunate not to be killed in the incident, and was forced to smash a window and scramble to safety in his nightshirt, along with Bishop's terrified wife. The lodger's belly had been ripped open to such an extent that part of his intestines spilled from the wound, although he subsequently recovered thanks to the miraculous attentions of a surgeon. Amazingly, when help was summoned, Bishop was found laid out on his bed as though ignorant of the whole tragedy; he had even put on a clean shirt to make it appear he had been asleep all the time. However, a second bloodied shirt was found stuffed under his bed, and it became clear that these pathetic deceptions were an attempt to mask the truth of the matter.

In July 1725 it was reported that Bishop had twice attempted to poison himself while in Lincoln's castle. After recuperating for five weeks the second victim – a man called Gibbons - was able to appear as a witness at Bishop's subsequent trial. Here, evidence was heard that Bishop had actually lured his mother to the property under the pretence of some business with her.

What is interesting about this case are the discussions concerning the prisoner's sanity. For the *Evening Post* (20 July 1725) reported, 'The coroner's inquest, after several consultations, had found the fact wilful murder; and that great endeavours were using to prove him (Bishop) *lunatick* at the assizes.'

This is another early example of such a consideration; unfortunately for Bishop, it meant nothing – he was executed anyway following his conviction at Lincoln Assizes.

THE HADDINGTON MURDERS

In the winter of 1725 a horrific double murder was committed upon the postmaster and his wife at Haddington, East Lothian.

A group of people managed to obtain entry to the house of Mr Johnston, ransacking the premises from top to bottom, breaking open the drawers and stealing all the gold, silver and plate they could lay their hands on. Worse, Johnston and his wife had their throats cut from ear to ear, before the group sat down by the fire and decided how they were to divide up the loot. Then, with callous disregard for the dead couple, they then went into the cellar and began drinking their victim's wine.

The case was solved very quickly. One of the gang, a young woman named Helen Hutton, immediately absconded to Edinburgh, dressed in men's clothes, where she had the misfortune to be 'seized by one that knew her'. When this fellow questioned her as to her attire, which implied a disguise, Helen resolved all his doubts by pulling out the murder weapon – a bloodied razor – which she then used to make an ineffectual attempt on the throat of this man.

Helen was apprehended after this melee, and while incarcerated she named her accomplices without hesitation: Alexander Napie (the man who tended the Johnston's horses) and Ralph Burnet, a dragoon from Carpenter's regiment who was quartered at Haddington. Both of these were taken by surprise on 7 December 1725 and committed to Edinburgh's toll-booth.

When Napie's commanding officer found out that one of his men had committed this murder he was outraged, and assisted the Haddington magistrates in the questioning of the suspects, which went on through the night. He was even more incensed by the suggestion that two more dragoons had played a lesser part in the conspiracy – and so he immediately saw to it these other soldiers were stripped of their regimental clothes and dismissed into poverty. The investigators managed to recover £160 in stolen money, putting the guilt of those taken beyond doubt.

Helen Hutton, Napie and Burnet went on trial at Edinburgh on 23 January 1726 and admitted their guilt. However, it could not be established with certainty who had committed the murders, since all three blamed each other for being solely responsible.

On 25 February Ralph Burnet was executed 'at the Gallow-lee' in Edinburgh. Remarkably, he presented his victims' son-in-law with a parcel containing guineas as an act of contrition. He was afterwards hung in chains. On the same day, Helen Hutton and Napie were hanged at Haddington, Napie's corpse also being hung in chains afterwards. A few days before her execution, Helen wrote a letter to her mother, which was afterwards published in chap-book form.

CRUEL AND UNUSUAL...THE CRIME OF CATHERINE HAYES

During the reign of King George I the law continued to prescribe strangling and burning in the cases of women convicted of petty treason – in other words, the slaying of their husbands. They were first garrotted, but it sometimes happened that, through the bungling of the executioner during the ceremony, the condemned woman might be burnt alive.

The story of Catherine Hayes is perhaps one of the most notorious of the 18th century. Catherine was born *c*.1690 to poor parents by the name of Hall, some four miles from Birmingham in the county of Warwickshire. Some accounts describe her mother as 'adult'rous and wicked', for she apparently abandoned Catherine as an infant. Uneducated and wild, Catherine later took up with a group of military personnel quartered in the neighbourhood when she was but a teenager, accompanying them to Ombersley, Worcestershire - where they unceremoniously dumped her.

Aged around 15, she found herself taken in by a good-natured man named Hayes and his wife, who had several children of their own. The eldest of these,

20-year-old John, was following a trade as a carpenter and he took an instant shine to Catherine: in private, the two made secret pledges to marry – and this they did, in Worcester around 1705. The pledges were made in secret because Hayes' father strongly disapproved of the union, and only backed down when young John threatened to cut his own throat: a strangely ironic portent, considering what was to happen 20 years later. On the wedding day Catherine somehow fell into a river or lake, and would have drowned had not Hayes waded in and rescued her.

By sheer bad luck the soldiers who Catherine had dallied with happened to be billeted in Worcester at the time, and learning of the marriage they decided to play a trick: in the middle of the night they barged into the newlywed's lodgings and dragged the unhappy John from the marital bed, telling him they would press-gang him into service. Thus was the young carpenter forced to seek financial help from his father in order to obtain his liberty. It is a curious fact that Catherine subsequently persuaded her new husband to enlist so that she might follow him to Spain; it was later reported that this was 'more for the love of the officers than him'.

Though the marriage appears to have settled down after this rocky start, John and his wife were, it appears, very different characters: he being 'a sober, honest and peaceable man, and a good husband'; while Catherine, we learn, was a 'very turbulent vexatious woman' always involved in quarrels with her neighbours and fomenting disputes. By 1719 the couple had returned to Britain and subsequently opted to move to the metropolis. John Hayes, having been to a certain extent reliant on the indulgence of his aging father, began to become somewhat successful in his own right, although his wife was still as passionate and argumentative with her neighbours as ever; nothing had changed on that score. A dual side to her personality was also developing; to John's friends she would extol his virtues, but to her cronies she would privately make comments like, 'It (would be) no more sin to kill him (John) than a mad dog.'

Hayes, who was possessed of some little estate by this time, as well as being involved in money-lending, lodged with Catherine in several properties, before finally they settled down at the house of a Mr Whinyard along 'Tyburn-road' (Oxford Street), a dwelling ascended to by two flights of stairs. Shortly thereafter one Thomas Billings, a tailor by trade in Monmouth Street, came to see Mr Hayes and - being a fellow countryman of Catherine - this young man was invited to lodge with the married couple.

In time it came about that John had to travel away on business for several days, and Catherine took the opportunity to host a drunken roister that had only just finished when her husband returned home. There was no keeping the event from him however, and a heated argument occurred between man and wife, in which more than one blow was struck during the quarrel: although who was the aggressor is not clear. This occurred about six weeks before a crime took place that was subsequently to engross the attention of the whole of London.

This depiction of Catherine Hayes first featured in The Criminal Recorder Volume 1, *by A.F., a student of the Inner Temple (1804).*

The argument over the party may have been the trigger for Catherine taking the decision to murder her husband. John Hayes had been doing quite well for himself financially, and it is possible the thought had been entertained in her mind for some time - although for motives other than domestic violence. At any rate, she began to persuade Billings, the young tailor, 'by all the arguments she possibly could' that she was a wife who was abused and beaten daily, and that it would not be a sin to commit murder upon her 'violent' husband. While these furtive conversations were afoot, it so occurred that one Thomas Wood (a neighbour's son and a former acquaintance of the Hayes' who came from the same part of England) knocked on their door seeking refuge from the press-gangs; John Hayes invited him inside and lodged him in the same room as Billings, promising to try and find the young man work.

It is a testament to the state of the atmosphere within the house on Tyburn Road that Thomas Wood had not been there four days before Catherine communicated to him the designs she had in killing her husband. At first Wood was outraged at such a proposal, but little by little Catherine wore him down with her tales of woe, wailing that her husband was, 'devoid of any religion or goodness, that he was a murderer, and had killed a man in the country, and destroyed two of her children, of which she had had twelve, one of which was buried under a pear tree, and another under an apple tree in the country'. Catherine also observed that should her husband die she would become mistress of £1'500, which she would divide between herself, Wood and Billings. Apparently Wood took a lot of persuading, and it is possible that Catherine used sexual favours to encourage him; Billings, who seems to have taken a lot less persuading, might also have been offered sexual favours from the outset to get him onto Catherine's side very quickly.

When it happened, the murder seems to have been opportunistic, despite the venomous planning that had gone before. Upon returning from a trip out of town young Wood had found the other three – John Hayes, Catherine and Billings – drinking merrily in their lodgings. John was saying that he and another fellow had drank a guinea of wine that day without 'being fuddled' – upon which Billings offered to bet Mr Hayes that he could not drink another six bottles of 'mountain' without becoming intoxicated.

Bets were placed and the wager was agreed; but as the three conspirators walked to buy the wine from the Braund's Head in New Bond Street, Mrs Hayes reminded the two lodgers of their pledge to help her dispatch her husband, and suggested this would be an ideal moment. Wood took not a little persuading; but Catherine - with Billings joining in - managed to coerce the young man into helping them commit the crime. It was the evening of 1 March 1726 when these events occurred.

Catherine had ordered a gallon and a half of wine to be delivered to their lodgings, as well as some beer for herself and the two others. However, Hayes proved to be made of stout stuff, and she was forced to send away for another bottle. At last, fully intoxicated 'and deprived of his understanding', John Hayes slumped across the bed in the other room, his feet dangling over the side and touching the floor.

At this point Billings entered the bedroom and struck Hayes an almighty blow on the head with a coal hatchet. The blow woke Hayes, whose feet clattered noisily on the floor in his death throes; the whole sorry affair was brought to a conclusion when Wood entered the room and hit Hayes on the head twice more with the hatchet.

John Hayes was aged about 41 at the time of his killing. There was a moment of fright for the murderers when a Mrs Springate, who lodged in the garret over Hayes' own room, knocked on the door and complained about the noise, it being night time by now. Coolly, Catherine told her that they had entertained company and people had gotten very merry, but they would be leaving now so Mrs Springate should not worry anymore.

Next the plotters held counsel about the best way to conceal the crime, and determined to mutilate and dispose of the corpse. With Billings holding the slain man's hair, Wood hacked off the dead man's head using a pocket knife, while

Mrs Hayes held a pail to catch the blood at the side of the bed. Although they caught most of the blood, some spots still dotted the bedclothes (the aforementioned Mrs Springate, not realising what had transpired, threw them away at Catherine's request the following day). The blood in the pail was poured out of a window into a wooden sink, with water poured in afterwards to wash away the telltale traces. An attempt was made to wash away remaining stains in the bedroom, but despite Catherine's best efforts some spots went missed: some blood had sprayed or been flicked onto the ceiling, for example.

The conspirators decapitate Mr Hayes: a grim and famous illustration from William Jackson's New & Complete Newgate Calendar Volume 2, *1795.*

At this point Catherine suggested to the two men that they boil the head until all the flesh came from it, but this gruesome advice was rejected on account that the procedure would take too long. In the end Billings and Wood carried the head (in the pail, under Billings' coat) to the Horseferry at Westminster later that night, and cast it into the River Thames near 'Mr Macreth's Wharf'. In this act they were observed by a lighterman, but it being dark and there being no cause for suspicion, he thought no more of it. While they were thus engaged away from the house, Mrs Springate called again at Catherine's door, again complaining about the noise – for it was by now 11 o'clock at night. Catherine, in a breathtakingly cool act of audacity, acted the part of the abandoned wife and explained sorrowfully that the door-slamming Mrs Springate had heard was Mr Hayes leaving the house on a journey to the countryside (in fact it had been Billings and Wood leaving to dispose of the decapitated head), and as such she now feared her husband might come to some harm during his travels.

The two men subsequently returned to the house in Tyburn Road about midnight, and all three retired to bed (the same bed is implied).

The following morning, 2 March, Hayes' head was spotted in the dock by a watchman named Robinson, the tide not having carried it away as the murderers hoped. The pail was found in the mud nearby. Upon the authorities being informed, the magistrate was of the opinion that a serious crime had occurred, and ordered the head be cleaned and the hair combed. It was then stuck on a pole and exposed to public view in St Margaret's churchyard, Westminster.

View of Westminster, London (2010). St Margaret's Church is the small church just right of Big Ben, and this is where the victim's head was put on display.

Throughout the day, Catherine and her two confederates set to work again, hacking off the limbs of the dead man before wrapping the various body parts in two towels. These the plotters then carried to a pond in Marylebone fields at about nine o'clock, where they dropped them in.

Among the hordes that turned up at the church to gawp at the ghoulish trophy in St Margaret's churchyard was a young man called Bennett; he perceived that the head bore a likeness to Hayes, who he knew, and so took himself off to visit Catherine. She, however, convinced him that her husband was alive and well, and she seems to have reassured Bennett that he had made a mistake - and that to suggest otherwise might bring trouble upon Bennett's head. A journeyman tailor named Patrick also went to see the head and returned to his fellow workmen, explaining that he was convinced it was Mr Hayes. This group of workmen made their own way to St Margaret's Church and looked at the head, coming to the same conclusion. It happened that Billings worked at the same shop where these men were employed in Monmouth Street, and upon being told of the circumstance he attempted to lull their fears by claiming to have left Hayes at home in bed that very morning.

Catherine may have escaped initial suspicion largely because the community believed the crime to be the work of a maniac who might have killed others; a friend, Mrs Longmore, gossiped to her that there 'was a report in the neighbourhood of a woman just found in the fields, all mangled and cut to pieces'. Meanwhile, Wood continued to dispose of Mr Hayes' belongings. On 3 March he wrapped the murdered man's white coat and some leather breeches in a bundle and took them to Greenford near Harrow on the Hill for disposal.

The gruesome tale of Mr Hayes' murder has fascinated Londoners for generations; this famous illustration from the Newgate Calendar Volume 2 *(1795) depicts the chillingly simple method utilised to identify the victim.*

After the head had been on display for four days the authorities had it pickled in spirits and placed in a jar at the home of a surgeon called Mr Westbrook, and in this state it continued to present melancholy evidence of a crime that - as yet - remained unsolved.

On the 6 March Catherine took Wood, Billings and Mrs Springate to new lodgings at a distiller's in the neighbourhood. There, she employed herself in obtaining as much of her husband's property as she could: even going so far as to coerce someone – who is not clear – into forging a letter in her husband's name and sending it to Hayes' brother-in-law threatening him with legal action if he did not pay up a due debt. Hayes' own mother received the letter, and taking it for a communication from her son, arranged for the money to be paid. And when a woman from Kingsland mistakenly identified the head as that of *her* missing husband, Catherine perhaps began to feel that she might have gotten away with it. She even began to put it about that John had absconded following a violent altercation in which he had dealt another man a blow on the head and so killed him. This story Catherine furtively passed to selected people, although it was naturally a lie, the untruth designed to gradually filter through to Hayes' acquaintances in the hope it would – in their eyes - explain her husband's absence.

This was the story told to one friend named Joseph Ashby, who made a connection with the decapitated head and asked Catherine if this was the man that John was supposed to have slain. Catherine told this gentleman that no, the head was nothing to do with her husband, as John's victim was buried entire. It appears her story ran away with her in her desire that it be believed: for Catherine also told Ashby that John had fled to Portugal with 'two or three foreign gentlemen' upon his failure to pay his supposed victim's imaginary widow a yearly bond to keep her quiet.

Ashby was quite understandably suspicious of this nonsense story, and next went to see one Henry Longmore, a cousin of John Hayes, asking him to visit Catherine in order to make his own enquires about her missing husband, and see if he were told the same. The two men would then, it was decided, compare the stories given them by Catherine afterwards.

Accordingly Longmore paid Catherine a visit, making earnest and concerned enquiries as to her missing husband. Catherine confided that John had killed another, and fled into Hertfordshire armed with a brace of pistols. Longmore expressed his concern that John might thus be suspected of being a highwayman: at this point, Catherine's lies appear to have been made up as the situation dictated, for she responded to this concern by saying that John always travelled armed, and had, indeed, once been arrested on suspicion of being a highway robber – and would have suffered gaol but for a passing acquaintance who stopped and vouched for John's good character. As Catherine's mouth ran away with her she further made lamentable comments as to her husband's ill usage of her, which surprised Longmore, since this was the first time he had heard Catherine say anything negative about her husband.

In comparing observations, Longmore and Ashby found the whole scenario extremely suspicious, and went to find a Life-guard man, stopping on their way through Westminster to look at the embalmed head in Dr Westbrook's property. Both viewing it, they independently came to same conclusion: it *was*, without doubt, Hayes' head. Upon finding a Life-guard man named Eaton, the party took their suspicions to Justice Lambert and stated that they desired an immediate warrant for the arrest of Catherine Hayes…and Wood and Billings too, for they entertained little doubt of their complicity in the murder. The Justice issued warrants for the arrests and at 9 o' cock that night the group, accompanied by two officers of the guards, marched round to Catherine's lodgings. Silencing the owner, Mr Jones, with a brief explanation, the group barged their way up the stairs, where Justice Lambert loudly rapped his cane on the door. Catherine at first expressed a desire to get dressed; she must have known at this point what was happening. Upon opening her door, she was seized, and so was Billings as he sat on the edge of the bed *sans* stockings and shoes.

The Justice barked at Catherine whether she had been in bed with Billings. Catherine – aware an admission of adultery might damn her – claimed Billings had been mending his stockings, to which Lambert replied, 'He had good eyes that could see to mend his *cloathes* in the dark' - there being neither fire nor candle within to light the gloom. For good measure they also arrested Mrs Springate, although Thomas Wood was not present at the time.

Lambert proceeded to interrogate Catherine and Billings, but they kept up the pretence of utter ignorance as to any murder; finally the exasperated Justice had them imprisoned in separate gaols. While *en route* to Tothill Fields Bridewell, Catherine requested of Henry Longmore that she might be permitted to see the embalmed head before her confinement. The cortege duly stopped at Dr Westbrook's apartment, and Catherine, upon being admitted to see the ghoulish trophy, performed a truly heroic piece of dramatic acting: she fell on her knees and wailed before all present, 'Oh, it is my dear husband's head!' Mr Westbrook, the surgeon, procured the head from its receptacle and brought it over in his hands right before Catherine's face: whereupon she caught hold of it and kissed it, displaying great agony and emotion. She expressed a desire to keep one lock of hair: Dr Westbrook coldly told her that he feared she already had too much of her husband's blood, and at this Catherine fainted dead away.

During these dramatic scenes a Mr Hoddle and his servant walking through fields near 'Mary-bone' found the limbs of the slain man in a ditch. The following morning Hoddle ordered the pond drained, and so precipitated the discovery of the torso. News that the other body parts had been found was carried to the Justices even as they continued to examine Catherine Hayes in the bridewell following her recovery from her fainting fit. Catherine was next carted off to Newgate, her ears ringing to the jeers and catcalls of the mob, which by now had learned of her arrest; they followed her through the streets and shouted their joy at the apprehension of the murderess.

Thomas Wood – the only one of the three who appeared to express some sort of guilt over the affair – presently returned from Greenford. Unaware of what had happened in his absence, he was tricked into believing that Catherine could be found at the Green Dragon on King Street, this in actual fact being the place where Longmore lived. Wood arrived here on horseback, being met by Longmore's brother, who (with the help of four others) unhorsed the murderer and dragged him into the house. Here they held him while the officers were fetched, and Wood subsequently found himself thrown into Tothill Fields Bridewell on 27 March 1726. Left to mull his fate, Wood realised there was no way out and asked to see Justice Lambert, who arrived to hear Wood's confession in the presence of two other Justices of the Peace.

Billings, in his own confinement, heard of Wood's confession and realised that there was no point in persisting any further in denial; the following day the young man himself made a full and plain admission of the whole affair.

The whole case, from start to finish, was as dramatic as could be imagined. Yet in criminal terms, Catherine's murder was not particularly remarkable. It was the *human elements* surrounding the crime (rather than the crime itself) that marked it out of the ordinary: the population of London gawping at the slain man's head on a pole in a churchyard, Catherine's incredible scheming, manipulation and dramatics, and of course her unimaginable fate yet to come. Since the case was recorded in very vivid detail (for the era), future generations would be afforded a glimpse of not only the machinations of a calculating murderess but also the pitiless society in which this barbaric crime occurred.

News of Wood and Billings' confessions were relayed to Catherine in Newgate, where she was informed that she was not only facing a capital charge of murder but also a simultaneous one of *petit* treason, for which the punishment was to be burnt alive. For her part, Catherine resolved to plead not guilty, reversing a previously-declared intention to plead guilty in the belief that the whole world could not save her. However, she gradually changed this viewpoint: might not Billings and Woods' confessions somehow prove guilt enough on their part? And somehow cast doubt on her level of involvement, if she continually declared herself innocent?

Upon the three conspirator's arraignment at the Old Bailey, Catherine entered a 'Not guilty' plea, and then stood and watched both Wood and Billings confess to everything; their only wish was that, having confessed, their bodies not be hung in chains after their execution, and that they receive a Christian burial.

That Catherine had not dealt any fatal wound was testified in the confessions of Wood and Billings, and the accusation she was the prime instigator and ultimate guilty party rested on an alleged comment she had murmured while in

Newgate. This was to the effect that, 'The Devil put it into her head.' This comment had, apparently, been followed up with a semi-confession that John Hayes was not the best of husbands, and that her biggest regret was 'drawing those two poor men into this misfortune'. This was when she had been resigned to pleading 'Guilty': of course, all that had now changed. On a point of law, these comments were still unclear as evidence of Catherine's actual level of guilt. She claimed that the first mention of murdering John Hayes had been during a conversation between Wood and Billings, when both men had been disgusted to observe Hayes drunkenly assault her. Billings had allegedly stated, 'This fellow deserves to be killed', to which Wood had replied he'd 'be his butcher for a penny'. Catherine testified that she was in another room when she heard the crime committed, and her later involvement was born out of fear that these two men would also dispatch her in a likewise manner. But, after all the drama, Catherine's admission that she had prior knowledge of a discussion to kill her husband condemned her, and the fact that she had been in the next room at the time and had not actually physically killed him herself mattered little: either way, she *knew* the crime might occur, and had assisted in its disposal. It is also likely that the Justices sincerely *believed* from the pathetic, miserable confessions of the two men that they were in no way the instigators of this murderous plot.

Wood and Billings were still pleading for mercy when they were sentenced – 'mercy' being to be executed and buried, rather than executed and gibbeted. But they asked pity of a pitiless society, and both men were duly ordered to be hung in chains. Catherine, likewise, pleaded that she not be burnt for petty treason; it was also in vain.

After sentencing all three were remanded back to Newgate, where Wood and Billings were confined to the 'Condemned-Hold' along with others under sentence of death. Catherine was placed in an apartment specifically for condemned women. Here, Mrs Hayes displayed great concern and anxiety over the fate of the two men, particularly Billings, as she had done before; she endeavoured to see to it that most of her remaining money, and what little was contributed to her case from charitable donators, went the way of the two men.

Of the three Wood alone appeared *sincerely* repentant, and very quickly he succumbed to a fever brought on by the 'unwholesomeness of the place'. His illness took him to the gaol chapel, where he preyed fervently in his final days. In his dying moments, he confessed his crime again before a clergyman, and expressed an incredible desire that he might live to see his sentence carried out upon himself – to atone for his sins and to serve as a warning to anyone else who might break the law. However, Wood died of his gaol fever after being taken back to the 'Condemned-Hold' of Newgate on 4 May. It is recorded that he was aged about 28 years old, and of good parents from '*Ombersly* between Ludlow and Worcester'.

There is a lurid allegation that stories were by this time circulating that Thomas Billings was, in fact, Catherine's own *son*. We learn that Catherine herself did not emphatically deny this: she merely admitted that Billings was her own flesh and blood, although she knew not how closely related they were. In her final days Catherine's attitude began to change: she began to show more concern for Billings' fate than her own, and expressed a worry that these rumours might reach his ears before he was executed. She even made attempts to downplay his guilt, and made daily enquiries from her own confinement as to the state of his health while he lay in the 'Condemned Hold'.

A few days before her execution Catherine suddenly affirmed Thomas Billings to be her own son, lawfully begotten to Hayes following their marriage. Her husband, she declared, had forced her to deliver the unwanted infant into the care of relatives. But none of her relatives knew of any such child, and the authorities suspected that Catherine's claim was a fabrication, along the lines of her allegations that John had committed several murders; although to what end she made this late claim was unclear.

Thomas Billings' background was something of a mystery. Billings was at the time of his death in his very early twenties, and he professed no knowledge of a previous relationship with Catherine other than that 'he believed himself to be a near relation of Mrs Hayes, but by what means he could not tell'. He also stated he believed himself to be a bastard child who had no other knowledge of his parents. Although Catherine apparently told Billings that they were mother and son in the days leading up to their execution, perhaps the most likely story is the one that Billings was found in a basket on 'Holt-Heath' near where Catherine lived in Ombersley, prior to her marriage. As an infant, he was originally nursed by a family called Billings, whose name he took. Catherine, always aware of these long-ago developments, possibly came to regard herself as the nearest thing to a *genuine* mother Billings had ever had. However, since Billings was 22 or 23 at the time of his execution, and Catherine had only been married 20 years and eight months, it was just *possible* that she was the one who left him on the common herself all those years ago following some early sexual misadventure.

Billings also ultimately expressed great remorse for his part in the crime. The salacious rumours concerning Catherine and Billings' actual relationship were reported at the time: 'Upon taking the sacrament at Newgate, she (Catherine) affirmed that Billings…was her own son, got by Mr Hayes, 'tis supposed, before her marriage with him, so that the son killed his father, and assisted in quartering him, had criminal conversation with his mother, and lay with her when his father's mangled limbs were under the bed.' In the end word that Catherine might be his mother *did* reach Billings' ears, and he called her a 'vile woman' for not disclosing the fact before they had relations.

Nonetheless, as the date of execution approached Catherine appeared remarkably unconcerned, expressing only fear of the *manner* of her death and concern over the welfare of Billings. After so much brutality, their final days alive were curiously sentimental. When in the gaol chapel they would sit next each other, holding hands with their heads laid on each other's breasts at times: for which Catherine was reprimanded. Notwithstanding, she ignored these reprimands and continued to behave in a like manner. Three days before her execution Catherine somehow managed to obtain a phial of strong poison, but a woman confined with her in her final hours tested it first, whereupon it burnt her lips. The liquid was poured on a handkerchief, which also burnt; this woman smashed the bottle, thwarting Catherine's attempt at suicide.

On the day of her execution at Tyburn on 9 May 1726, Catherine took her final prayers and received the sacrament in the chapel. She still displayed great concern and tenderness as to the well being of Billings, a contradictory woman to the end: quarrelsome, scheming, ruthless, manipulative...and yet at the same time capable of great compassion and remorse. At around twelve the prisoners were severally collected and, along with a number of others so condemned for other crimes, they were carted off to Tyburn. Billings and another eight under sentence of death were transported in three carts, while Catherine was drawn to Tyburn 'upon a sledge'. When the sledge stopped at the house where the murder had been committed, she turned her head and smiled before gulping down 'half a *quartern* of brandy'.

The day saw much drama: two of the others so condemned, a pair of highwaymen, attempted an escape during the journey to Tyburn, with one managing to get out of the cart. Such was the clamour to see the executions that several scaffolds fell down in a sequence of catastrophic accidents, killing at least five people and breaking the bones of many more. After having taken some time for their private devotions, Thomas Billings and the other eight with him were 'turned off' in a grim mass execution.

Catherine was the last to die. In the end her fate was perhaps far worse than what she might have deserved. Virtually her last positive act was to enquire of her executioner on the way to the stake whether he was the one who had hanged her 'dear child'. She was then chained to the stake before a vast crowd of people, the chains running round her waist and under her arms. A rope around her neck was drawn through a hole in the post at her back and secured. Faggots, brushwood and straw were piled around her up to waistline level and set alight in several places. Almost immediately the blaze flamed out of control, and in the middle of the burning debris Catherine's arms were seen to move feebly as she attempted to push away the embers and flames now reaching her body. As was customary, the executioner moved behind her to garrotte her using the rope round her neck, but the fire was by now so severe that it scorched his hands and he let go, retiring to safety. Catherine's last words were, 'Oh Jesus! What shall I do?' as she literally burnt alive in front of the crowds, some of whom were curious, some aghast with horror, some cheering and some sympathetically throwing more faggots onto the blaze to fuel it in order to end her suffering quicker. It is a sickening fact that the executioner managed to throw a piece of timber into the blaze, hitting her skull so violently that her brains came out: one assumes – almost thankfully – that by this point she was in all likelihood already deceased. In about an hour her body was literally reduced to ashes. Catherine Hayes was aged about 36 at the time of her execution.

The executioner's hands burnt as he tried to strangle Catherine, forcing him to let go of the rope. Another notorious illustration from the New & Complete Newgate Calendar Volume 1 *(1795).*

Billings' body, in the meantime, was encased in irons as it hung on the gallows. After being cut down he was carried to the gibbet post about 100 yards distant, and hoisted up in his chains. An 'anonymous punster' penned of this tragedy at the time:

> *God prosper long our noble king;*
> *Our lives and safeties all;*

And grant that we may warning take;
By Cath'rine Hayes's fall...

MURDEROUS BANDITS

If a scarcity of multiple murderers and serial killers during this time seems noticeable throughout this work, then it is likely that this was due largely to a chaotic policing system. It is also likely that many criminals killed time and again until they were caught, and even then only confessed the deeds they were convicted of and not any others they might have committed; this is at least what is hinted by a number of instances where felons were judged to be guilty of numerous, unspecified heinous murders upon the advent of their executions.

In England, news from Portsmouth dated 15 March 1726 reported on the execution of two men, George Cutler and John Winter, on the same gibbet at Waltham Chase. Several thousand watched them dispatched, and the next day three more – Richard Cutler (a grocer), Joseph Maddison and Benjamin Rivers – met a likewise fate at Winchester. Another person, William Shelley, also condemned to die, received a last minute pardon. According to reports, the Cutlers used the aliases of Miller and belonged to a gang guilty of 'several murders'. They had lived by the highway many years, making a career out of robbery, and had been imprisoned two or three times before fatal justice caught up with them. Perhaps they were linked to the Waltham Blacks gang, seven of whom were executed for murder and poaching in December 1723 in this neck of the woods.

Far away to the north in Edinburgh, on 29 August 1726 four 'gypsies' were sentenced for robbery and murder by the Lords of the Judiciary. David Maxwell and John Marishall were sentenced to death, while their wives were sentenced to be whipped through the streets of Edinburgh (and then banished) for complicity in what appears to have been a ruthless crime spree. On 30 September the two men were executed; it seems they killed more than once during their endeavours, for the *Derby Mercury* (1 October 1726) reported that the pair had paid the penalty for 'several murders and robberies'. Several others from the gang had lately been seized and imprisoned also.

Another ruthless bandit, John Humphreys of Bonvilston, went on trial at Cardiff in September that same year. Newspaper reports indicate his notoriety was already exceptional; he had confessed to numerous murders, robberies and rapes. Furthermore, he had perjured himself by falsely accusing other innocent parties of involvement in the killings he now confessed to. News from Cardiff on 4 October stated he had been executed 'last Monday', behaving very remorsefully before his demise. Making an ample confession to his crimes, Humphreys appeared particularly penitent towards his habit of sleeping with 'lewd women' from the age of 12, and warned spectators at his exit to shun wicked courses, lest they find themselves in his position. It was reported, 'He being hang'd in chains, his body, and the gibbet, were carried clean off the next night.'

Humphreys appears to have been an early example of a sexual serial killer, although – like the vast percentage of crimes throughout the age - robbery was as much a factor. At his trial in Cardiff on 5 September 1726, he not only admitted robbing his uncle of 'several sums of money' but also attacking a string of women during violent burglaries. He raped and murdered one Mary Miles, afterwards robbing her house. He also confessed to raping and killing a widow called Elizabeth Thomas, before stealing silverware from her. After this he committed two more sexual attacks: raping and robbing a servant girl he overtook on the road, and also attacking 'the wife of one Smith'. He broke into the house of one Mary Evens of Llancarfan, robbing and sexually assaulting her; finally he raped a single woman called Mary John of Bonvilston, and cut her throat afterwards. It seems that when he was questioned, his attempts to perjure others drew further attention to him - and in the end he admitted everything.

THE DROWNING HOLE

It seems that although John Smith, of the parish of Rosneath, felt he had got away with one murder, when he committed his second in exactly the same manner it was *too* suspicious. The identical deaths drew the attention of the Honourable John Campbell of Mamore, one of his Majesty's Justices of the Peace, who ordered Smith's arrest.

When he was first questioned, Smith denied any wrongdoing; but three days later he reversed his denial and made a full confession, first to his father-in-law and then before Campbell and other dignitaries of the parish. What brought this about was the discovery of a letter belonging to Smith that evidenced 'an intrigue' between him and a young woman of the parish.

Smith explained that in December 1725 he walked with his sister Katherine Smith to a rivulet, where he had thrown her in and then held her head beneath the water until she expired. Since there were no marks of violence upon her person, no suspicions were voiced; but in September 1726 Smith committed the same cruel act upon the person of his own wife, Margaret Campbell. This time suspicions *were* raised, and following his confession Smith was committed to Dumbarton tollbooth on 8 November 1726, charged with two murders.

Smith signed his confession, and in bizarre scenes he was subsequently taken to the parish church where he confessed his guilt in front of the multitude gathered there. His remorse seemed to be genuine; deeply affected, he admitted neither woman had deserved to be killed and his wife had been both kind and obliging. The *Caledonian Mercury* (14 November 1726) reported: 'He is shortly to be brought upon his trial, where 'tis not doubted he'll meet the deserts of his crimes.'

At his trial, the motive for the murders became known. Smith's personal life was somewhat complicated. He worked a farm on land owned by his stepfather, John Campbell. In order to secure his future he contrived to marry Campbell's daughter Margaret, while simultaneously carrying on an affair with a woman called Janet Wilson. The pair corresponded in secret, with Smith penning to his lover that if his wife died then he would surely marry her; he also promised Janet Wilson a significant sum of money if she rejected the advances of another suitor. When Smith found he could not fulfil this financial obligation, he got rid of his sister Katherine so he would inherit the bulk of the Campbell estate. Margaret Campbell was next killed so Smith could wed Ms Wilson.

If Smith had entertained the sense to commit the second murder in an equally ingenious manner to which he committed the first, he may have got away with it. As it was, two deaths in the same way naturally pointed the finger at him. He was convicted and hanged in Dumbarton on 27 January 1727.

AVOID TALKING POLITICS

Colonel Charles Stewart of Stewartfield had behind him a distinguished career in the military and Whig politics in Scotland, and his murder shows once again how men of position might kill and die in the most violent of circumstances.

By 1726 Stewart was still heavily involved in Roxburghshire politics, and his name still carried some weight; so much so that Sir Gilbert Elliot, 3rd Baronet of Stobs, took it as a personal affront when Stewart declined to vote for him in a 1726 Scottish by-election. Sir Gilbert was a fellow Whig politician, and despite being returned that July he still bore a great deal of animosity about this slight. On the evening of 9 August 1726 the two men found themselves simultaneously at a dinner in Jedburgh following a meeting of the Head Court to validate the freeholder's roll. Sir Gilbert was by this time naturally a very responsible man, with a political position of some authority; yet this did not stop him entering into a heated discussion on politics with Charles Stewart.

Such a discussion could have only one outcome, for both were worse the wear for liquor. Elliot expressed himself offended that the colonel had not given him his vote, whereupon the colonel stated he had explained the matter and that should be an end of it. Sir Gilbert, however, refused to let it go and in the end the colonel stated brusquely: 'Pray Sir Gilbert, you have said a good deal to provoke me; don't provoke me further.'

Sir Gilbert now became very rude and loud, so the colonel lobbed a wine glass at him, which hit him in the face. The peer unsheathed his sword, ran at the colonel and stabbed him in the gut as he sat in his chair: the wound proved mortal.

Evidence that the colonel had been murdered in cold blood was presented to the magistrates by two witnesses, soldiers from the Scots Greys who had spent the day with Stewart. Sir Gilbert Elliot was outlawed, having immediately fled Scotland on a ship leaving for the Netherlands.

Elliot's relatives - including his kinsman, another Sir Gilbert Elliot, of Minto – took an active interest in his case, and managed to secure the fugitive a pardon, although it was better than 10 years before the killer politician could return to Roxburghshire. He died on 27 May 1764 aged about 84; hundreds throughout the century were executed for far, far less than what his actions ought to have warranted.

THE CHILDREN IN THE WELL

In November 1726 it was reported that a multiple murder had been revealed.

The affair occurred in Netherbury, south of Beaminster in Dorset. Several years earlier a man of that parish confessed to his apprentice boy that he had had five children by his wife's sister – and that he had murdered them all. Three were buried in a well, but he asked the lad to conceal his knowledge.

The boy did as he was bid but in time he left his master and entered into the army. His conscience nagged away at him however, and at length he requested leave so that he might return to Netherbury and investigate any truth in his former master's claims. However, the lad could get no-one to help him on account of his master's good credit and reputation – and so he returned to the army in hopeless frustration.

The matter continued to prey upon his mind, and so – requesting leave again – the boy presented himself before a magistrate and swore on oath that he knew there was a well where three children were buried, and also that he knew who was responsible. It was reported that a warrant was issued and the well searched; whereupon the remains of three children were found wrapped in thick paper which bore the father's written name.

The boy's employer was taken and imprisoned in Dorchester Gaol. Follow-up data is lacking.

THE BALLAD OF MARY FARDING

Describing the town moor at Hartlepool, the writer Sir Cuthbert Sharp observed: 'A small rock detached from the moor, a few yards to the north of what is called the East Battery, cannot fail, from its singular situation, to attract the notice of the stranger. The yawning space which separates this rock from the main land, is known by the name of Maiden Bower, and many a tale of "plighted faith and broken vows" is associated with it.'

According to an entry in the parish register, this windblown spot on England's north-eastern coast was the site of the murder of one Mary Farding, or Fawden. Mary was a stranger to Hartlepool, having been brought there by a 27-year-old Northallerton merchant called William Stephenson, by whom she was pregnant. He killed Mary by throwing her over the precipice on 4 June 1727; the register records that she was buried three days later.

A coroner's inquest blamed her death on Stephenson, and he was in due course hanged at Durham on 26 August 1727 for Mary's murder. While awaiting execution Stephenson allegedly penned a ballad concerning his crime, which Sir Cuthbert Sharp observed was still recalled by old parishioners. In part it went:

> *I promised her fair, that I would take care*
> *Of her and her infant, and all things prepare;*
> *At Hartlepool town, where she would lie down,*
> *Poor soul, she believ'd me, as ever she'd done.*
>
> *Let all men beware, when married they are,*
> *Bad women are surely a dangerous snare;*
> *Then love your own wives: them men only thrives*
> *That always live pious and chaste in their lives.*

This ballad was entitled 'The Hartlepool Tragedy', and purported to be the dying words and confession of William Stephenson, taken from his own mouth on 25 August, the night before his execution. He apparently spoke the ballad to someone who was allowed to see him in gaol, who wrote it down as he heard it; other lines in the ballad indicate that Stephenson beat Mary with a whip before she fell over the precipice, and that he subsequently fled back to Northallerton in hopes that the woman's body would be washed out to sea; this not occurring, he was traced south to his home town and apprehended. If genuinely Stephenson's work, then – although from the lips of a killer – the ballad (and its survival) is nothing short of remarkable.

THE DOWNFALL OF AN 18TH CENTURY ROCK-STAR

On 20 November 1727 there came to London one Mr Richard Savage, Esq, returning to the capital from Richmond where he had some time since retired to pursue his studies. Having lodgings both in London and Richmond, he had come hither to pay off money owing on the former. Accidentally meeting two acquaintances called James Gregory and William Marchant, Savage went with them to a coffee house where they continued drinking until very late.

Savage's first night back in London was to be an eventful one. When Savage decided he was ready for bed, he was told that there was not room enough to put up him *and* his comrades: so the trio left, determined to wander the streets in rakish fashion and divert themselves by whatever events might occur until sunlight. In Georgian London this was almost a recipe for disaster, and after a while they saw lights on in Robinson's coffee house in Charing Cross – which they entered, demanding a room. The group were told that a room would be ready soon, but that it was at present being vacated by a company who were organising their bill. For some reason this answer angered William Marchant, who barged into the room and told the occupants to get out. They were still finishing their drinks, and angry words were exchanged: so Marchant kicked their table while Gregory and Savage drew their swords, Gregory taunting, 'Damn ye, you rascal, deliver your sword!' at their antagonists.

A violent scuffle now ensued between the two groups, in which one James Sinclair was stabbed in the gut with such force that the wound proved mortal. Upon being struck, he screamed, 'I am a dead man!', and in the melee Richard Savage's blade (for it had been he who struck Mr Sinclair) also accidentally wounded a female servant who was attempting to hold him back from the injured man. The perpetrators of this violent deed extinguished the candles in the room and then bolted out the door, but numerous people had been within Robinson's at the time and a group of soldiers were quickly summoned; they had little difficulty tracking down Savage and his two friends, in liquor as they were. The three were lodged in the round-house and then carried before a magistrate, who committed them to the gate-house; when Sinclair died the following day they were incarcerated in Newgate.

The victim had gasped to a clergyman on his deathbed that he had been stabbed before having time to draw his own weapon, and this circumstance was agreed upon by several present: leading to Savage being indicted for murder at the Old Bailey in December 1727, while his two friends faced a charge of aiding and abetting the commission of the murder.

Richard Savage was at the time of his incarceration aged about thirty. What marks his case out of the ordinary is not necessarily the crime, brutal as it was, but Savage's position in London society. He was by this time becoming exceedingly well known as a poet, playwright and satirist, who had performed the title role in his self-penned *Sir Thomas Ovebury* publicly on the streets as he attempted to earn a reputation in the artistic community. His background was also shrouded in controversy, for *c.*1718 he claimed to be the son of Richard Savage, 4th Earl Rivers, and Anne, Countess of Macclesfield. The complexities of his allegations (as well as the counter-allegations, muck-racking and blackmail) eventually earned Savage an annuity of £200, but the affair rumbled on.

Despite the countess's objections the scandal became very well known; although, without getting side tracked by this too much, she completely denied and disowned Richard. Nonetheless, there *was* some evidence in favour of his claim being true. Still, by the 1720s - and with some sympathy behind him - Richard was making a name for himself independently; and his *Miscellaneous Poems* had just been published by subscription when this promising young man was overtaken by the violent incident in Robinson's coffee house.

After a trial of eight hours an Old Bailey jury convicted Savage and Gregory of murder, while Marchant was convicted only of manslaughter, and branded on his hand with a hot iron before being discharged. The other two were sentenced to death on 11 December 1727.

While Savage and his friend languished in Newgate, immobilised with iron chains, the Countess of Macclesfield took the opportunity to prejudice none other than Queen Caroline against her 'son', by telling her majesty the most malicious stories and even downright falsehoods; and, while she had the queen's ear, all petitions that were offered in favour of this unhappy young man were rejected. At length, Savage's pathetic predicament raised in him a supporter in the form of the Countess of Hertford, a lady whose influence the queen would *not* ignore; and so, on 5 March 1728 Richard Savage and his friend were set free after the queen, no less, used her influence to secure them a pardon.

It might be interesting to the modern reader to consider that Richard Savage was assuredly the 18th century equivalent of what might be termed nowadays a celebrity: for poets were, without doubt, the rock stars of their day, their talent often squandered young through intemperance, addiction and self-destruction. Although Richard Savage gained his liberty, his latter days appear to have been spent for the most part in abject poverty, and the *Newgate Calendar* records of him: 'His distresses do not, however, seem to have overcome him. In his lowest sphere, his pride sustained his spirits, and set him on a level with those of the highest rank. After enduring numberless privations, and disgusting almost all his friends by the heedlessness (and we are afraid we must add the ingratitude) of his disposition, Savage expired at Bristol, where he had been imprisoned for debt, August 1743, in his 46th year, and was buried in the church-yard of St Peter, at the expense of the gaoler.'

This brief obituary by the *Newgate Calendar* merely hints at the complexities of Richard Savage's life: his attempt to be nominated poet-laureate, his £50-a-year pension granted by Queen Caroline, his intimate connections with the many better-known scribblers, satirists and poets of the day, and his eventual ruination upon the death of the queen. Virtually the last person to abandon him was the great poet Alexander Pope, who cut his connections with Savage shortly before the latter died in Bristol. Upon his death Savage became the subject of Samuel Johnson's famed *Life of Savage* (1744), and one is left thinking that, had he lived in our own era, the tabloids would have had a wonderful time with this fellow.

CHAPTER 4

THE REIGN OF KING GEORGE II (d.25 October 1760)

INTRODUCTION

In many cases this was a reign in which it was pitiable to see the outcome of protest: it is almost as though the demonstrators knew what they were in for, yet desperation and bravado forced David to take on Goliath repeatedly, and more often than not, lose bloodily. Perhaps the most straightforward example of this was the slaughter at Culloden on 16 April 1746, which put an end to the resurgent Jacobite dream of taking power. The 40 minutes of fighting became the last land conflict between two opposing *armies* on the domestic field of combat in Britain, although it was by no means the last insurrection, sea conflict or external threat faced by these islands.

Throughout George II's reign towns and cities frequently suffered localised uprisings and protests that ended in horrendous casualties: for example, riotous scenes occurred when a mob of weavers marched on Lawford's Gate, Bristol, on 29 September 1729 in protest at poor wages. While the city swore in the new mayor, Samuel Stokes, the weavers came to the house on Castle-Ditch of Stephen Feachem, a considerable manufacturer, and threatened to burn it to the ground with him in it unless he raised their wages from 7 shillings to 8 shillings per piece. Feachem was defended by some 20 soldiers, who repulsed the mob, killing seven of their number and wounding many. The sergeant who commanded the troop died from a gunshot wound in uncertain circumstances, having apparently been accidentally shot by his own side. Despite the carnage, crowds of weavers still hung about menacingly, drawing out the whole regiment and the sheriffs; however, it appeared the massacre had made them more cowed and reasonable. By the time the proclamation against them was read, many had dispersed, and the few that remained were arrested and committed to Bristol's Newgate.

At the ensuing sessions all those arrested were set free, there being no evidence presented against them – the whole event being an example of the pointless cycle of poverty, protest and ruthless retaliation that often marked the lot of the working man in Georgian Britain. Although only a reactive force, in the sense that they were largely brought in to *control* insurrection, it is clear that the authorities were guilty of worse atrocities than criminal elements within the crowds ever were. That said, the mob – particularly in the capital – was a curious feature of life in the 18th century; the crowd was almost a political force in its own right, and despite the violent clashes that could occur with the soldiery, politicians frequently respected the mob's prejudices.

Politics aside, the mob also came down hard on all minorities: Methodists, homosexuals, informers, Quakers, the French, Franciscans and so on. For example, on the evening of Monday 26 July 1736 a great crowd swelled in Shoreditch and Spitalfields, crying, 'Down with the Irishmen!' The mob's rage was not so much directed against *the Irish* as it was against the fact that they were 'working at under rates' as labourers and weavers. Windows were broken and two inns kept by the Irish community were all but pulled down; when one of these taverns in Brick Lane was attacked, firearms were discharged from within, killing a young man and wounding six or seven others. This carried on for three nights, the Justices, constables and 'train'd bands' being unable to quell the violence; in the end, a party of Horse and Foot Soldiers were called in. After committing six or seven of the rioters to prison, the tumult died down.

Such lethal collisions – over any number of issues - were unfortunately not a rarity. The price or scarcity of food could be a frequent cause for tumult, with such a circumstance occasioning a great riot in Newcastle in June 1740. After one among the mob had been fatally wounded by a local militia who were trying to protect the town dignitaries and corn supply, the Guildhall was almost demolished; it is thought the mob would have burnt down the entire town but for the timely arrival of the regular soldiery. What is interesting about this is again what it says about the state of policing, for the local militia should not be equated with the regular soldiery; they were in fact an amalgamation of local people who had volunteered to protect the town in times of trouble. In fact, this militia was comprised mainly of young men, several of whom were merchant's apprentices, who - under normal circumstances - were nothing to do with peacekeeping. On account of their white stockings, Newcastle christened these civilian defenders the White Stocking Regiment. Sunderland and Durham also suffered similar uprisings around this time.

By the 1750s it was again the price of corn that turned parts of the kingdom into battlefields. On 25 August 1756, several lives were lost in a great riot against the dearness of corn in Sheffield. A good indication of how serious this matter became can be gleaned from the *London Magazine* in 1757, which reported that on 23 November four people were killed by soldiers during violence in Newcastle, Staffordshire; simultaneously, twelve people had been killed in Manchester, where two corn mills were pulled down by the mob. That June, rioting had occurred in Coventry, Frome (in Somerset, where three people died), Oxford, Cambridge, Chichester, Manchester and Carmarthen, where four people were killed in a battle. 1757 also saw widespread rebellion against the hated Militia Bill, and by October rioting had been reported from Lincolnshire, Hertfordshire, Nottinghamshire, Bedfordshire, Yorkshire, Herefordshire and Kent. Such widespread disorder almost appears to transcend riot and suggest open insurrection.

The introduction of turnpikes (toll houses) along roads could also be a focus for the animosity of the rabble. On 22 September 1735 an angry mob pulled down Ledbury Turnpike in Herefordshire, despite an attempt to defend it by Justice Skip and an armed party, who killed two among the rioters and took two others into custody. Only two of the defenders were lightly wounded, but in the aftermath of the clash the people threatened to burn the Justice's house, or murder him whenever they met him. 1748 saw violent clashes in Bristol, when a mob of 'Somersetshire country-people' protesting the new Turnpike Act cut down gates at various parts of the city. At Totterdown the sheriffs, backed up by officers, parish constables, several of the commissioners and a party of sailors armed with cutlasses, battled the mob and took 30 prisoners. Many were wounded in the fighting. In Beeston, Leeds, ten people were slaughtered and many others fatally injured in 1753 during a bloody clash between the townspeople and a troop of dragoons over the issue of turnpikes. The massacre came at the end of two days of tumult in the West Riding of Yorkshire towards the end of June, when the mob began to break up the paving stones and hurl the pieces at the soldiers; 20 of the latter fired into a mob numbering hundreds, inflicting horrendous casualties. The rioting quelled, three arrested ringleaders were carted off to York Castle on 2 July 1753.

It was, by the 1730s, becoming impossible to ignore the impact that alcohol was having on the British crime rates. A report submitted by one Thomas Wilson to the House of Commons in 1736, part-entitled *Distilled Spirituous Liquors, The Bane of the Nation*, made it abundantly clear the effect that brandy, wine and (most notoriously) gin were having on the nation's health and morals. In London, the ridiculous over-consumption of cheap alcohol (spawning the notorious advertisement 'Drunk for a penny, dead drunk for tuppence, clean straw provided') prompted this observation by Wilson: 'Already we find, that all manner of vice increases, such as murders, robberies, firing of houses, and these attended with uncommon and 'till now unknown barbarities. Drunkenness is a vice of a heinous nature, but to be drunk with the poisonous spirits commonly sold in and about this city, has something peculiarly heinous in it; as if possess'd by an evil spirit, it makes them mad and desperate, ready prepared for the most bold and daring mischiefs... and when their spirits are raised by drinking to excess, they are often carried to a degree of outrageous passion, and become bold and daring in committing robberies and other offences, for an immediate livelihood.' He cites a typical example of the evils of drink 'fresh in everybody's memory' concerning a woman who murdered her own child and tossed the body in a ditch after having stripped it of some clothes presented earlier that day by a charitable person - all so she could pawn the clothes for 'nine pennyworth of gin'. (This is possibly a reference to Judith Dufour, who had been sentenced to death at the Old Bailey on 1 March 1734 for strangling her own infant, aged between 2-3 years, with a handkerchief.) In November 1737, it was reported two persons had been murdered in the capital in one week alone for informing against retailers of spirituous liquors; one victim was an informer who died after being mobbed and severely beaten in the Strand.

Gin Lane, *Hogarth's reflection on the evils of drink in London society.*

By the time of George II's accession to the throne, it is also apparent that smuggling was an organized criminal industry. The *Gentleman's Magazine* (1735) makes it clear that smuggling was now a way of life in many British coastal communities, a livelihood in which violence was frequent and death an occupational hazard on both the sides of the law. For example, on 22 August 1735 five customs house officers, along with five soldiers and a sergeant from the Tower of London, took away a coach containing bags of seized tea they had confiscated. Near the village of Lewisham (as it was then) four smugglers armed with seven blunderbusses, pistols and cutlasses ambushed them, and swore that they would kill or be killed before they lost their prize. There followed a brief shootout, in which the smugglers (reportedly) fired first. Two among their number were fatally wounded and an officer had his horse shot beneath him. One of the attackers was arrested and committed to Newgate, but the fourth escaped. The periodical observed: 'The smugglers in Norfolk and Suffolk meet with better success, they go not only armed, but 20 or 30 in a gang, so that they frequently make the customs house officers fly before them.'

Bloody clashes like this were frequent, often following the landing of smuggled goods at any point along the shores of Britain. Another typical incident is noted in the *Gentleman's Magazine* as having occurred on 8 September 1735. Seven smugglers, coming up Limpsfield Hill, Kent, with seven horses loaded with 900 weight of tea, were ambushed by some riding officers and a party of dragoons who lay in wait for them, hidden in a chalk-pit. A 'smart battle' ensued in which one dragoon was wounded and a smuggler had his thigh shattered to pieces; but the rest of the gang fled the field of combat, and both the tea and their horses were taken by the officers.

Portrait of a smuggler. (A reproduction of this illustration can be found in the Jamaica Inn.)

Another type of criminal peculiar to this era were 'the Incendiaries', blackmailers who attempted to extort money from the wealthy via threats of murder and burning their property. The *Caledonian Mercury* reported in 1730: 'The practice of the Incendiaries continues to spread daily, as well here (London), as in the western parts of England, and are become so audacious and terrifying, that everybody is concerned to think what the end of these villainies will be; and the more, since the authors of them cannot be detected, notwithstanding the great care and rewards that have been, and still are offered.'

Many crimes reported in what we might now recognise as the 18th century's version of 'the media' were frustratingly short on detail, perhaps an indication of a lack of empathy: the murder was simply an 'event' to be reported, yet another commonplace crime whose details were not too important. Or perhaps it is merely that the publishers of fledgling newspapers and periodicals found it too difficult – through lack of content space, time and distance – to collate more than the barest facts on some occasions. Either way, it is interesting to observe how some murder cases were brought before the public in the greatest of detail (particularly in the capital), while others could be incredibly slight on information.

Take, for instance, the *Gentleman's Magazine*'s observation in 1735 that: 'At Gloucester Assizes received sentence of death, Edmund Goodrich for the murder of Robert Gregory, a bailiff, who went to arrest him in an action of debt for £34 10 shillings by shooting him; Sarah Toiley and Sarah Baylis for the murder of their bastard children...' Sometimes it is little more than a collection of names and statistics, rather than actual reporting. Typically we learn from the same periodical that among six condemned to death at the Old Bailey Sessions on 24 May 1735 were 'William Hughes, a soldier, for the murder of his mother...and Elton Lewis for murdering his aunt. Hughes and Lewis pleaded guilty, the former indeed could not deny the horrid crime, because he shot his mother as she lay in bed with a woman lodger who was witness to the fact; but Elton's being a secret murder, when he was taken up and examin'd before Justice Roby, he continued 5 or 6 hours obstinate in denying it; but at length was prevail'd on by the *pathetick* admonitions of the Justice, to make a full and free confession of the affair, and to sign the same.' Ages, identities, motives and locations often seem superfluous. Hughes's crime in particular is missing a motive; other reports suggest he was a private sentinel from Colonel Haughton's Company in the 1st Regiment of Foot-Guards, and that he entered his mother Katherine Jones's bedchamber (she 'kept a public-cellar over-against Hungerford-Market in the Strand') deliberately to kill her. Hughes shot his mother through the head as she lay in bed – but *why* he would do such a thing is not recorded, at least not in this edition of the *Gentleman's Magazine*. We also learn Hughes was 'very penitent' as he was led to Tyburn.

Perhaps the most telling sign of the times was the sentencing to death of a 10-year-old girl at the Old Bailey on 16 September 1735. Mary Wotton had been convicted of stealing £29 out of the house of a Mrs Eason; she was 'repriev'd for 14 years', but the threat was still evident. Apparently there was little distinction in the eyes of the law between the child and the adult, and despite the reprieve the little girl is likely to have suffered some sort of brutalizing punishment one way or another.

By the winter of 1744 street robberies in the capital had become so commonplace that the king was petitioned '(so) that a speedy, vigorous, and exemplary execution of the laws might be made upon the persons of such offenders, as should fall into the hands of justice'. The plea, dated 13 October 1744, paints a disturbing picture of life in Georgian London, and in part states:

'That *divers* confederacies of great numbers of evil-disposed persons, armed with bludgeons, pistols, cutlasses, and other dangerous weapons, infest not only the private lanes and passages, but likewise the public streets and places of usual concourse, and commit (the) most daring outrages upon the persons of your majesty's good subjects, whose affairs oblige them to pass through the streets, by terrifying, robbing, and wounding them; and these facts are frequently perpetrated at such times as were heretofore deemed hours of security. That the officers of justice have been repulsed in the performance of their duty, some of whom have been shot at, some wounded and others murdered, in endeavouring to discover and apprehend said persons, *buy* which means they are intimidated from duly executing their offices, and others put in manifest danger of their lives.'

The foremost politicians of the day did indeed travel in danger of their lives; the great Horace Walpole, 4th Earl of Orford and one of the prominent Whig politicians of the age, was robbed by highwaymen in Hyde Park. During the hold-up, it is clear Walpole came close to being murdered, for he afterwards wrote: 'One night in the beginning of November, 1749, as I was returning from Holland House by moonlight, about ten at night, I was attacked by two Highwaymen in Hyde Park, and the pistol of one of them going off *accidentally*, razed the skin under my eye, left some marks of shot on my face, and stunned me. The ball went through the top of the chariot, and if I had sat an inch nearer to the left side, must have gone through my head.'

Plunket and M'Lean commit one of their many robberies. (Originally from Annals of Crime & New Newgate Calendar No.19*, 1833.)*

These two robbers - criminals called William Plunket and James M'Lean - captivated Georgian society more so than any other bandits in the capital that century. The pair lived as gentlemen, and their faces were extremely well known about St James's. M'lean in particular is described as having been a tall, showy, good-looking man, and a frequent visitor to Button's coffee-house, on the west side of Russell Street, Covent Garden. Plunket was a journeyman apothecary, a handy man for M'Lean to have with him in case he was wounded during their criminal endeavours. When M'Lean was eventually taken in the autumn of 1750, Walpole wrote on 1 September: 'My friend Mr M'Lean is still the fashion; have I not a reason to call him my friend? He says, if the pistol had shot me, he had another for himself.' One doubts the truth of this, but such affected grace and gentlemanly conduct on M'Lean's part fuelled his mythology. On 18 October Walpole lamented that M'Lean had been hanged, and observed that, such was his celebrity, 3'000 people had been to see him in the condemned cell prior to his demise. M'Lean impeached his companion Plunket before his death, but the latter fled London, and what became of him is unclear.

London's coffee-house society was itself still plagued by bored young rakes, all armed and addicted to ridiculous wagers that bore no respect for human life. 'One of the youth at White's,' wrote Walpole to Mann on 10 July 1744, 'has committed murder and intends to repeat it. He betted £1500 that a man could live twelve hours under water; hired a desperate fellow, sunk him in a ship, by way of experiment, and both ship and man have not appeared since. Another man and ship are to be tried for their lives, instead of Mr Blake, the assassin.'

In 1751 the Murder Act was passed, for 'the more effectual prevention of murder'. It also elaborated on the practice of gibbeting. The act decreed, among other things, that anyone so convicted must be executed on the second day after their conviction, and that the murderer's copse ought either to be 'hung in chains' or delivered to a surgeon for anatomisation. The act had very little impact, at least initially.

Despite all this, George II's era saw a huge leap forward in policing: although it was perhaps a case of political necessity in reaction to the surging crime rate, rather than a naturally occurring innovation. The inefficiency of the watchmen and parish constables had been clear for some time, and in the metropolis the imaginative Bow Street magistrate and popular novelist Henry Fielding called into existence a force of *professional* 'thief-takers' who, although originally referred to as 'Justice Wright's People' on account of the magistrate to whose office they were attached, later took on the moniker of 'Bow Street Runners'. They were distinguished by their activity, intelligence and vigilance; while not entirely immune from corruption – after all, like Wild before them many had dubious and intimate underworld connections – they were nonetheless the first manifestation of a professional police force in the land. This was mid-century, and it was badly needed, for as Horace Walpole observed around the same time, in 1752: 'It is shocking to think what a shambles this country is grown! Seventeen were executed this morning, having murdered the turnkey on Friday night, and almost forced open Newgate. One is forced to travel, even at noon, as if one was going to battle.'

'THE SUDDEN AND SURPRIZING FIRE WHICH HAPPEN'D AT THE PUPPET-SHOW'

In 1727 the village of Burwell, Cambridgeshire (four-and-a-half miles northwest of Newmarket), suffered a disastrous fire – a tragedy on an almighty scale, which question marks still hang over.

In September that year a group of puppeteers passing via Burwell on their way to Stourbridge Fair, Cambridge, hired a large barn in which to put on a performance for the people of Burwell and the surrounding area. On the evening of the performance, however, huge crowds swelled outside the venue - including an 'undesirable section' who the organisers wished to keep out. With the barn packed to capacity the decision was taken by the puppet master, Mr Shepheard, to nail the one and only access door shut.

Around nine o'clock fire broke out within the barn and spread rapidly, lighting bales of straw and spreading to the thatched roof. As the crowd made down a passage to the access door (having to move a stout table previously used for magic tricks that blocked the way) they found it nailed shut. It took some time to force it open from outside; within the narrow passage that led to the door, and more importantly to the fresh air outside, there was pandemonium. People were crushed in the scramble to get through, and it quickly became blocked with the bodies of those trampled and suffocated in the melee. The passage also became choked with thick black smoke, and those unable to enter it burned to death as the fire within the main body of the barn took hold.

Seventy-six people were killed in the disaster and two more died afterwards. Among the dead were 'several young ladies of fortune, and many children'. Out of the 160 people crammed in the barn, only six escaped physically unscathed. Bodies crammed the passage four-feet deep and a woman in an adjoining house also died as the fire began spreading. Mr Shepheard, the puppet master, died alongside his wife and daughter in the conflagration.

An ostler named Richard Whitaker was subsequently arrested and brought before the magistrates in Cambridge charged with having started the fire. Whitaker, from Hadstock in Essex, had been employed to look after the puppeteer's horses in a space within the barn near the locked and bolted main double doors. It appeared that, in order to avoid paying to watch the show, he had hidden himself in a hayloft where his unwatched lantern might have lit the straw and started the terrible blaze. On 27 March 1728, however, he was acquitted of the charges against him. The court heard how he had been the first to yell, 'Fire!' and was among the first to make it out the barn, along with the theatrical troupe putting on the show.

Forty-seven years later *The Cambridge Chronicle* of 19 February 1774 reported an enigmatic postscript to this sad event. An un-named old man had died a few days previously at a village near Newmarket, and on his deathbed implied that he had *deliberately* set the conflagration due to 'an antipathy to the puppet showman'. One assumes that it was Whitaker, the ostler, who made this confession to arson and murder.

These days, it is difficult to imagine a tragedy of such enormous proportions occurring in such a pleasant place as Burwell. In the churchyard of St Mary's today (2012), all those who perished are remembered by a small tombstone which displays a winged heart motif: a human skull is depicted beneath, and flames above. It displays the simple epitaph: *To the memory of the 78 people who were burnt to death in a barn at Burwell on Sept. 8th 1727.* Quite why all those people died, whether by disastrous accident or murderous intent, is now one of Cambridgeshire's most infamous historical riddles.

This gravestone at Burwell (with its fire motif) stands as a memorial to what might have been one of the worst criminal atrocities in Britain during the 1700s.

THE MURDEROUS MAGISTRATE

A murder enacted in 1728 is remarkable not for its detail – of which there is little – but for the participants.

The matter that led to the killing is unclear, except for the fact that it stemmed from a legal complication and subsequent sequestration; on Monday 6 May 1728 a bailiff, or sheriff's officer, took himself to the rural hamlet of Burton Pedwardine in southern Lincolnshire to take the cattle belonging to one Captain Thomas Mitchell, alias *Micael*, of that place. During the execution of his office, the bailiff, one Pennystone Warden of nearby Ewerby, was murdered, although it is unclear how: the 19th century Sleaford historian James Creasey merely tells us Warden fell victim to 'an awful instance of ungoverned passion and its fatal effects'.

The *Stamford Mercury* (16 May) reported that Captain Mitchell had been taken not long afterwards and committed to Lincoln Castle by two of 'His Majesty's Justices of the Peace' to await his trial for murder at the next assizes. What made this situation unique was that Mitchell himself was also a Justice of the Peace, or magistrate, for the county of Lincoln: meaning that those who dispensed summary justice in Lincolnshire had been forced to order the arrest of one of their own on the most serious of charges.

Mitchell's elevated position appears not to have saved him, for according to the *Mercury* on 15 August 1728 he had lately received sentence of death at Lincoln Assizes.

THE DEATH OF THE EARL OF STRATHMORE

On 9 May 1728, Charles Lyon, 6th Earl of Strathmore and Kinghorn, and a relative, Mr Lyon of Brigton, happened to both be present in Forfar, Angus, for a funeral. As was usual on these occasions, liquor was partaken of very freely, both before the interment and afterwards, when the mourners had repaired to a tavern. The Scottish peer was aged about 29 at the time, and during the wake his companion, Brigton, had the poor sense to abuse and insult a fellow mourner, James Carnegie, Laird of Finavon, using the most impertinent language. This man he drunkenly scorned for his unwillingness to marry, his having bore no sons and his debts, and also abused their hostess – who was, in actual fact, his own sister-in-law.

The argument spilling into the street, Brigton pushed Carnegie into a deep and filthy 'kennel' (i.e. ditch). On recovering himself, Carnegie drew his sword with the intention of immediately taking vengeance; however, the Earl of Strathmore had by now stepped in between the two warring gentlemen - and upon Carnegie aiming a thrust, the earl received the laird's sword deep in his body. The wound was mortal, and the peer died in the course of 49 hours.

Carnegie went on trial on 2 August that year charged with Strathmore's murder, although it was apparent that the earl had clearly not been the intended victim of his drunken vengeance. The accused, while not exactly admitting culpability for the slaying, nonetheless expressed great regret for his victim's death, having nought but the greatest respect for him and stating he had borne Strathmore no grudge whatever. His testimony was quite sincere: 'If it shall appear,' he said at one point, 'that I was the unlucky person who wounded the earl, I protest before God I would much rather that a sword had been sheathed in my own bowels.' At another point he admitted, 'I had the misfortune that day to be mortally drunk, for which I beg God's pardon.'

As a point of law, previous to this trial the verdicts of jurymen had uniformly been *proven* or *not proven*; but now they found Carnegie *not guilty* by a majority of twelve to three. In spite of this landmark legal verdict, Carnegie was probably most fortunate to escape the noose; for his actions still evidenced someone whose rage, when aroused, prompted such violence that it had accounted for the life of one of the most respected Scottish peers of the generation.

This same James Carnegie, Laird of Finavon, appears afterwards to have been out with Prince Charles in 1745, and notwithstanding his part in this attempted overthrow of the Hanoverian monarchy, he kept possession of his estate till his death. As another point of interest, the slain earl's brother, from whom he succeeded the title, had also died in violent, unjust circumstances. John Lyon, 5th Earl of Strathmore, was among the casualties at the Battle of Sheriffmuir in 1715, when the insurgents had some 7-800 killed on the field of conflict. The 5th earl was aged about 21 at the time, and according to one account, 'He was taken and *murdered* by a dragoon; and it may be said of his fate, that a millstone crushed a *brilliant*.'

THE INTERFERENCE OF GHOSTS

As observed earlier, and without digressing too much into this particular theme, it is clear that superstition featured in many a murder case: from the killing of suspected witches, to the blaming of Devils for an act committed by a man. This phenomenon is also apparent in certain murder cases which featured a strong supernatural element; at least, this is how some violent crimes were occasionally reported to the public. This implies that even if the stories were themselves journalistic inventions, they nonetheless played on the *genuine* fears of certain sections of the populace.

That some of the tales might be journalistic inventions, or elaborations, is clear from a general lacking of detail. The following story *may* bear an element of truth, however.

Correspondence in the *London Magazine* (March 1762) observed that a man in the county of Warwickshire had called upon a friend's wife one morning, and made enquiries as to the whereabouts of her husband. She professed to be very worried, for her husband – a farmer – had not returned from Southam market, despite being expected back the previous evening.

The visitor declared that her worries could not match his own: for, he claimed, the previous night the missing farmer's ghostly apparition had appeared before him while he was quite awake! Worse, the ghost had showed him 'several ghastly stabs in his body'. The spectre imparted that his corpse had been thrown in a *marle-pit* and went on to name a specific person as his killer!

After this, the farmer's wife raised the alarm; and her husband's stabbed body was found in a pit near Southam. Furthermore, the man named by 'the ghost' as the killer was arrested and thrown into gaol.

The accused murderer came on trial at Warwick before 'the lord chief justice Raymond'. The jury were eager to convict the man on trial, but Raymond reined them in, saying, 'I think, gentlemen, you seem inclined to lay more stress on the evidence of an apparition, than it will bear...I know not of any law now in being which will admit of the testimony of an apparition; nor yet if it did, doth the ghost appear to give evidence.' 'Crier,' continued Raymond, 'call the ghost!' The victim's name was called three times, yet the apparition did not appear. The judge declared the accused of unblemished character, and ordered him to be acquitted. More to the point, he declared the person who claimed to have seen the apparition to be the *actual* murderer, 'In which case he might easily ascertain the pit, the stabs, etc, without any supernatural assistance.'

The man who made the claim of ghostly intervention was thus himself arrested, and upon his house being searched 'strong proofs of guilt' were found. He confessed the murder, and was executed at the next assize.

Although reported in 1762, it is possible that this incident is meant to have occurred many, many years earlier. However, possibly the strangest story with this theme took place during the first year of the reign of the second George.

Around midday on Saturday 22 June 1728 the master of the school in Beaminster, Dorset, dismissed his scholars, twelve of whom hastened to the yard of St Mary's Church to play ball. After a short time four of them returned to their schoolroom – which was kept in a gallery of the parish church, and from which there was a distant entry from the churchyard – to search for old pens. Within the church they heard a noise 'like the sounding of a brass pan' which put them to flight. When these four regrouped with the other children, it was decided among them that someone must have concealed themselves within the church deliberately to frighten the boys. In greater numbers, they all returned and looked about – but could find nothing to account for the disturbance.

However, as they were returning to their game, all heard on the steps of the church a noise emanating from the gallery that sounded like a man striding about in 'great boots': this put them to flight, sending them scurrying outside – from whence they heard, when at the belfry, or west door, noises from within that sounded like a minister preaching followed by multiple voices singing psalms.

The boys returned to their game once the sounds of the mysterious congregation had faded away, it having lasted but a short time. However, after some time one of the boys returned to the schoolroom in order to retrieve a book, and here the story becomes somewhat eerie and rather incredible.

This boy afterwards declared that he saw lying on one of the benches, about six feet from him, a *coffin*. He immediately ran outside and told the other children, who thronged the schoolroom door, peering in: five of the twelve saw, very clearly, a boy named John Daniel sitting quite near the coffin in the schoolroom (the reason why they all could not see this person is because the narrowness of the door precluded it for many of them). One of those who saw the boy was his half-brother, who said: 'There sits our John, with just such a coat on as I have, with a pen in his hand, a book before him, and a coffin by him. I'll throw a stone at him!' This he did, shouting at the figure of the boy, 'Take it' - upon which John Daniel simply disappeared from view and the whole church plunged into darkness for two or three minutes.

What made this story doubly strange was that some three weeks earlier, John Daniel's lifeless body had been discovered in a deep ditch a little way out of town, and despite bearing several marks about the neck, breast and stomach that indicated violence, John – aged fourteen – was interred without the benefit of a coroner's inquest. John's parents were both already dead, and his stepmother Elizabeth's declaration that John suffered from fits probably went some way to the boy's burial occurring without a proper investigation.

Upon the group of lads reporting what they had experienced, they were questioned very closely by Colonel Broadrep. All the witnesses were between nine and twelve years old, and they each corroborated their story in great detail, even down to the type of hinges that adorned the mysterious coffin. One of the witnesses had arrived at the school *after* John had died, and so had never met him; yet he was able to describe him exactly from the schoolroom incident – right down to an observation of a white cloth or rag that bound one of John Daniel's hands. The woman who had laid out the boy's corpse prior to burial was brought in, and she confirmed she had taken just such a cloth from the deceased's hand, the boy having worn this for about four days due to a lameness in his arm.

Following these weird depositions, John Daniel's body was exhumed. Close attention was paid to the boy's neck, and although a surgeon could not positively affirm there was any dislocation, three witnesses declared that, without doubt, the neck *had* displayed black marks immediately after death. These witnesses comprised of two women of good repute who saw the boy's body two days after death, and the joiner who placed the body into the wooden coffin. Although wrapped in a shroud by this time, enough of the boy could be seen to allow the marks to be very visible to the joiner.

The coroner's jury decided the boy had been strangled, and brought in a verdict of 'Wilful Murder'. It transpired that John was worth some £800, and although several were suspected of his killing none were charged; but the fact that he was found 'about a furlong beyond the mother's house' perhaps led many in Beaminster to suspect John's stepmother Elizabeth was somehow linked to the crime. These events set the town by the ears, and there were other reported sightings of John Daniel's ghost, including one by a man who claimed to have spotted him on 25 June in the field where he had been found dead.

The whole case is a very strange one indeed. The source most usually cited for this story is a letter published in the *Gentleman's Magazine* half a century later in 1774, although a contemporary handwritten account at the time remarked upon the strange circumstances of the boy's death. Reports also appeared in some of the contemporary news-sheets concerning the appearance of the boy's ghost in '*Beamister*', which, while they do not name John Daniel, clearly referred to this case – making it abundantly clear that the appearance of John's ghost was a talking point at the time, and not a story made up in 1774. All the protagonists in the drama were without doubt real people, and while the logical supposition is that Elizabeth Daniel had her stepson strangled in order to provide for her own son Isaac (Daniel's half-brother mentioned earlier), no-one was ever charged with his murder.

This author can offer three possible solutions to the mystery. First, that John Daniel's corpse was either not buried, or was disinterred, and used as a prop by persons unknown in the hope of bringing the matter of his murder to light; secondly, that all the boys who claimed to have seen John's ghost were involved in a schoolboy conspiracy to some unknown end; thirdly, that John Daniel did, in actual fact, return from the grave to shine a light on the tragic truth about his end. Now that near 300 years have passed it is impossible to tell, but the matter remains an intriguing one nonetheless.

That the ghosts of murdered people might return from the grave to obtain justice continued to be a popular fancy, even 34 years later in the nation's capital. In the year 1762 the so-called 'Cock Lane Ghost' disturbed the dreams and haunted the imagination of half of London, until it was, at length, discovered to be the contrivance of a man named Parsons, the clerk of St Sepulchre's Church, who had formed the design to ruin a certain gentleman by having the supposed 'ghost' accuse him of murder. Parsons, with the aid of a child (his daughter), carried out the deception so artfully as to deceive many respectable persons. His fraud was at length discovered; he was put in the pillory and imprisoned for two years. His wife and another woman, who were privy to the conspiracy, were also punished by imprisonment, the remarkable thing about the whole affair being how close they brought their victim to the gallows – a truly strange method of attempted murder in one of Europe's leading metropolitan capitals.

Another case like this was reported in May 1768. According to the *Gentleman's Magazine*, a man named Ripdeth discovered a dead child in a pond while on his way to Alnwick, Northumberland. A subsequent coroner's inquest brought in a verdict of 'wilful murder by persons unknown'. A few days later Ripdeth visited Alnwick and announced that the ghost of the deceased child haunted him, and he had also seen the murdered child's mother in a dream; so sure was he of her features that if 10'000 women were put in front of him he would infallibly pick her out. Amazingly, the women of Alnwick were made to walk past Ripdeth one by one until her pointed at one and declared, 'This is the murderer!' on which the woman was apprehended, examined and committed to prison.

However, no instance of ghostly interference in a murder case remains so eerily compelling as the case of poor John Daniel.

THE 'HOUSE OF CORRECTION' IN HALSTEAD

The *Ipswich Journal* (12 October 1728) reported on the appalling culture of abuse at a 'House of Correction' in Essex, and their column provides a good example of the curious writing style of the times:

'We had an account yesterday from *Chemsford*, that Thomas Diss, whipman to George *Dowing*, late Keeper of the House of Correction in *Halsted*, committed to that *goal*, for assisting his master in the murder of a travelling lace-woman, his prisoner, whose bowels they cut out, her head off, quartered her lower parts and burnt them, was also charged with a *mittimus* from the Rev. Mr. Wagener, of Systed (Stisted), with the murder of a boy of fourteen years old, in the said house of correction. 'Tis very remarkable that the daughter of Thomas Diss, above-mention'd, seeing the barbarous fact committed, could have no rest till she had discovered it, though against her own father, who afterwards made and signed an ample confession before the Justices of the Peace of the fact, and also of 16 guineas and a box of lace being taken from the deceas'd.'

Although the woman was butchered, the other victim in the correctional house had died a different death, expiring after being whipped.

Houses of Correction were different from gaols in that their purpose was to educate and train as well as punish, although their inmates could comprise a motley mix: petty criminals, children, the insane and prostitutes. Dowing, or Dewing, the keeper of Halstead's correctional facility (and Diss's boss), had already stood trial himself earlier that year in March at Chelmsford for the murder of 'a bastard child begot on the body of one of his prisoners'. The crime had been barbaric; in his position of authority and power over the wretches imprisoned in his establishment, Dewing had solicited a woman, Susan Baldwin, to sleep with him, but she refused. After he threatened to whip her to death, she consented. Eight months later this woman announced she was with child, and so Dewing had one of his servants (probably Diss) tie her to a post - where she was lashed and scourged with a whip until she miscarried. At one point, the servant being exhausted, Dewing took the whip and thrashed her himself. The infant was picked from the ground (moving), squeezed and mangled, squashed into a chamber pot and tipped 'down the vault'.

Susan Baldwin apparently was not idle in making this murder public, and an arrest warrant was issued for Dewing. The crime outraged the people of Halstead, and mobs of local people armed with pitchforks searched every house in the town in an attempt to flush him out. They eventually found Dewing in a public house, in the act of begging his wife not to believe the rumours about him.

Dewing had originally been sentenced to death for infanticide on 20 March 1728, but he was later pardoned - although the case against him was resurrected in October when he and his man Diss stood jointly accused of complicity in the other two killings.

In March 1729 it was briefly reported that Dewing had yet again been acquitted of murder at Chelmsford Assizes, although he *was* found guilty of a misdemeanour felony for brutally abusing one of the prisoners in his custody. For this he was fined £50. It is unclear what became of Diss.

'*I'LL MARRY THE MAID AND DISINHERIT YOU BOTH!*'

The following story, recorded by the Leicestershire antiquary John Throsby in 1790, affords an insight into how folklore often misremembered village murders, and illustrates the difficulty sometimes faced by historians in trying to get to the bottom of such incidents. Throsby wrote:

'In this neighbourhood (of Shepshed, near Loughborough), about 60 years ago, an horrid murder was committed on the body of a Mr. Warner, a game-keeper to Mr. Philips of *Gerendon* (or Garendon) hall, for which a young man named Flawn was hung in chains in or near the forest. The story is briefly related thus: Old Warner was rich; Flawn, an acquaintance of his son, courted his daughter. Flawn had a good character, but no money; in consequence, Old Warner would not give his consent to his daughter's marriage, (and even) threatened that he would marry his servant maid, and disinherit both his son *and* daughter. At a public house, it is said that young Warner and Flawn agreed to murder the old man as he was coming from Gerendon hall, from whence he often came in the night, they being fearful that the old man would put (his threat) into execution. They, in consequence, a night or two after, secreted themselves near the road the old man usually passed, knocked him down with a bludgeon or hedge stake, with which, by beating him over the head, Flawn dispatched him. Nothing appearing on the trial to criminate young Warner, a bill of indictment was preferred against him for deer stealing; for which he was found guilty, and suffered the penalties of the law.'

However, there is an important third party missing in Throsby's narrative – a Shepshed carpenter called John Harris. Harris courted one of old William Warner's daughters, and it appears that Throsby might have misidentified 'Flawn' with this person. For some of the news-sheets reported that on 23 March 1729 this Harris was tried at Leicester Castle upon the word of young William

Warner (the victim's son) and one John Flawn, who were both privy to the murder. Being unable to prevent a satisfactory account of himself on the night of the slaying, John Harris was convicted and ordered to be hung in chains: he alone suffered the penalty of law.

Warner was not convicted of involvement in his father's murder (having impeached Harris and received immunity from prosecution). But he nonetheless ended up on the gallows anyway in 1732, for returning from transportation and deer-stealing. He was apprehended at Castle Donington, and following his execution he was put in a gibbet cage in Charnwood Forest next to the remains of his former associate, Harris.

Confusingly, 'John Flawn' *was* executed; but this was for forging the will of a Mrs Grey of Kegworth. Flawn was executed at Leicester on 25 August 1741 and buried at Shepshed.

THE SIGN OF GUILT

In former times it was believed that a corpse might bleed in the presence of its murderer: and there was supposedly a survival of this belief observed at Wincanton, Somerset.

In 1730 a traveller named Robert Sutton made the mistake of announcing that he had a great deal of money and important documents on him during a spot of respite at a tavern in Castle Cary. By the time he left he had attracted the company of a local trouble-causer called Jack White, and the pair apparently began fighting at the junction just south of Bratton Seymour, a little way from Wincanton, after White made an inebriated pass at two women along the way. Sutton was left slain by the roadside by the fleeing ruffian, his head bashed in and one of his eyes gouged out by his assailant using a piece of wood.

When Sutton was found, his corpse was taken to the inn at Wincanton where it was laid out on a table. When Jack White came with the rest of the neighbourhood to look at it, his guilt was betrayed by a thin trickle of blood that began to seep from the cold wound on the corpse. Others saw this, and accusing eyes began to turn in White's direction; he promptly fled, but was quickly caught and dragged back to the inn where he was physically forced to *touch* the corpse. At this the wound began to bleed more plentifully and in the minds of those present this *proved* White's guilt.

White was subsequently hanged on 19 August 1730, his body afterwards being encased in a metal gibbet cage and hoisted up at the Bratton Seymour crossroads – which to this day bears the name of 'Jack White's Gibbet'.

ROAD RAGE

The *Grub Street Journal*, a popular weekly broadsheet, reported on 2 September 1731 that 'on Wednesday last' a crime had occurred that bears a strange familiarity: for it appears nothing less than an incident of 'road rage'.

As a sand-cart was passing a turnpike at 'Kent-street end', Southwark, it was met by a coach coming from the opposite direction. The two vehicles simultaneously grazed each other on the passage through the gate, upon which the door of the coach flew open and a gentleman wielding a sword jumped out into the lane. He drew back his weapon and stabbed the driver of the sand-cart in several parts of his body; he then got back in his coach 'and drove furiously away, without being known who he was'. The victim had just enough strength to drive his cart home, and coming into his yard he lay down and died of his injuries.

Reports of Hackney Coachmen being fatally attacked in various parts of London were not unknown in the early years of the century, and it is interesting that a mere 15 years before the 1731 incident Defoe observed that London's roads could be as dangerous as today's, for he wrote in his journal of the rudeness of the coachmen, and their extortionate fares; and 'also the carelessness of carmen, draymen, carters &c., who, by riding upon their carriages, were frequently found to bruise, run over and kill people in the streets'. Typically, the *London Chronicle* reported at the end of January 1762: 'On Thursday night a carman was committed to Newgate, being charged with the murder of a man, by carelessly driving his cart over him, which was the cause of his death.' The general impression given is that there were little or no road rules in the environs of London: carriages and coaches tipped over, and ran down women and children; or else drunken or sleeping passengers somehow tumbled into the road to have their skulls crushed by the next vehicle that came along. Some attempts seem to have been made to control the situation: for when an act of road sense occurred that was obviously criminally negligent, sometimes the coach driver, or 'carman', might be charged with murder. But in a world where the streets were a chaotic confusion of vehicles at the best of times convictions for murder under these circumstances seem to have been very difficult to procure.

MORE ROUGH JUSTICE IN LONDON

Around this time there were two noteworthy instances of people being murdered while trapped in the pillory and at the mercy of the mob, proving once more that convicted felons could still receive a death sentence even if the courts were lenient.

On 30 April 1731 a notorious 'procuress' named Mother Needham was pelted with missiles with such ferocity that she died two or three days later; this was in spite of an attempt to shield her by constables and beadles in the face of the crowd's assault on the corner of Park Place in St James's Street. Elizabeth

Needham was at the time a notorious and celebrated brothel madam who also used the alias 'Bird'; she had been punished before – for instance, she had been committed to Newgate in August 1724 for 'keeping a disorderly house'. It appears she became the target of the mob while incapacitated in the pillory because of her trade in selling young country girls to depraved men. She appears to have known that the mob would hate her, for one report suggests she hired a group of fellows to screen her and so help her cheat the law – which required that her face be on display. Nonetheless, one can only conjecture that this attempt would simply *draw attention* to her.

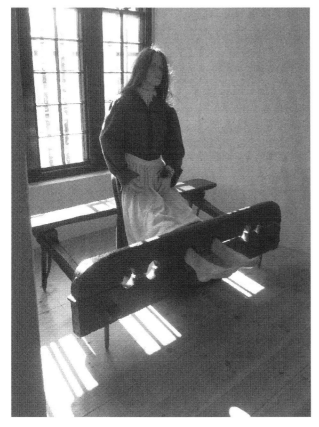

How Mother Needham might have looked; this lady is trapped in the stocks in Hexham's museum, Northumberland.

Another crime of this type occurred the following year, evidencing a depressingly miserable cycle of violence that perhaps surprised few in the capital. On 30 March 1732 one John Waller was committed to Newgate on a charge of perjury, having been accused of falsely testifying against several prisoners at Hertford and Cambridge Assizes, as well as against several more at other places.

On 29 May, upon the conclusion of the Old Bailey Sessions, Waller was convicted of giving false evidence (using the assumed name of Trever) against one John Edgelin, who he had accused of robbing him on the highway in October 1731. Edgelin and another so accused had been acquitted, and it had subsequently come to light that Waller was a habitual liar who followed the circuit judges and then swore false testimonies against people in order to claim rewards. Despite the fact that this practice could have had potentially lethal consequences for Waller's innocent victims, he was not sentenced to death: Waller was 'fined 20 marks, (and) two years imprisonment, to find security for his good behaviour during life'. He was also sentenced to stand twice a day in the pillory, bareheaded and with his crime written in great characters above his head, for an hour on both occasions. This ritual was to be performed at Seven Dials, where Waller – incapacitated in the wooden pillory – would face 'Hicks's-hall' on four different days.

Perhaps this part of the sentence worried him more than anything. His willingness to sacrifice complete strangers to the law – falsely, at that – for the sake of coin would have made him an instant target of hatred for the mob: in passing sentence, the authorities perhaps knew what was liable to happen. And so it did.

On 13 June, as he stood in the pillory at 'the Seven Dials', Waller was killed by a furious crowd of people in a savage and feral manner. He had only been in the pillory three minutes before he was pelted with cauliflower stalks and large stones. Bottles were smashed on his head and his hands were cut; then after this a chimney sweep jumped onto Waller and pulled him down from the pillory. The convict's clothes were torn from his body, although his shoes and stockings were left on his person, and - thus partially naked - he was kicked, beaten and jumped upon until he died.

Waller's body was carried back to Newgate where a coroner's inquest sat the following day, bringing in a verdict of murder by persons unknown that had used 'unlawful weapons'. Following this, Waller's corpse was buried at St Andrew's, Holborn.

Waller's miserable, squalid and public murder. This illustration first appeared in Knapp and Baldwin's Newgate Calendar Volume 1 *(1824).*

On 5 July, a grand jury at 'Hicks's-hall' found a bill of indictment against Benjamin Dalton, Lawrence Hughs and several others for the murder of Waller, who, after all, had been a state prisoner. Among nineteen people convicted at the Old Bailey in September 1732 were Edward Dalton (presumably the Dalton above) and Richard Griffith (a sergeant). They seem to have been the only fellows convicted of Waller's murder, the rest being found guilty of unrelated robberies. It also seems that there was some sympathy for the two convicted men. The *Stamford Mercury* (16 September 1732) was one newspaper that reported on attempts to win them a reprieve, declaring 'blind zeal' had led them to punish 'Waller's vile endeavours to take away the lives of several innocent persons'. But the ears of the king and nobility were deaf to these entreaties, and the pleas remained unanswered. Both of Waller's murderers met their end at Tyburn on 2 October 1732, along with 11 other convicted criminals.

Richard Griffith made a speech to the people as he was conveyed to 'the Tree' in the gallows cart. He declared he was innocent of Waller's murder, taking an oath upon the sacrament and denying his guilt to the very end.

MURDEROUS ENGLAND: REPORTS FROM THE 'GENTLEMAN'S MAGAZINE'

January 1731 saw the first publication of the famous *Gentleman's Magazine*. This periodical, founded by Edward Cave, began life as a monthly digest of news, poetry and commentary on the issues of the day, its wide-ranging subject matter gradually reaching the breakfast tables of the educated in society more thoroughly than any similar journal that had gone before it.

With hindsight, of particular interest is the section entitled *Monthly Intelligencer*, which reported the newsworthy events that came the way of the editors. These frequently consisted of fatalities, accidents, fires, suicides, scandals and murders; and despite the briefness of the reports, they shed an interesting light on crime in England during this time. In fact, in this author's opinion, it is the very vagueness of the reporting that captures the imagination – for these are glimpses of incidents *almost* lost to history, some of which paint a chilling, mysterious picture precisely *because* we know so little of what occurred. Disturbing inequalities in justice can also be observed, which the *Magazine* little remarks upon: death sentences were handed out left, right and centre, yet Sir Simon Clarke was acquitted of highway robbery at Winchester Assizes because of his youth, service record and 'the antiquity, worth and dignity' of his ancestors.

Some of the more interesting reports from the *Gentleman's Magazine*'s first year concern incidents in which whole families were destroyed: thus we learn of how one John Gerrard, a labourer, murdered his two young children in Norfolk before carrying their bodies on his back to Barney churchyard and laying them between two graves. This occurred in February 1731, and Gerrard – who 'appears to be lunatick' – was thrown into Norwich Castle. Elsewhere in Norfolk the wife of Thomas Denny ordered the family nurse to go for some milk: thus ensuring she was alone, Mrs Denny slit the throats of her 8-year-old daughter and 10-year-old son, killing both of them before cutting her own neck. Her suicide not being immediately effectual, she was taken in Caston for the murders. In Lincolnshire, an unnamed man killed his wife with a woodbill (a tool for lopping trees) before swinging his child against a wall and dashing out its brains; he was brought under control before he could murder his other three children, and confessed that he had committed his crime because he could not maintain his family. On 18 September 1731 he was incarcerated in Lincoln Gaol.

The shocking state of law and order in England can be gleaned from the myriad of reports; this is a selection of 'Accidents' from June 1731:

'A clergyman fishing in a river near Uxbridge (now part of Greater London), found a dead body with many tokens of it's being murder'd, which prov'd to be that of one Lock, who was seen the day before to go out with a young woman of that place, on which she was taken up, with two of her intimates, and imprison'd.'

'19. As Capt. Pigott and another gentleman were playing at billiards at a coffee-house near Leicester-fields, the Capt. gave the boy a blow on the head with his billiard mast, of which the boy dy'd in a few hours after.'

'23. Mr Stafford, a gentleman of quality, sent one Maywaring, a porter who ply'd about Grays-inn Gate, on an errand. The porter, on his return, insisting on more than the gentleman thought fit to give him, the gentleman drew his sword and wounded him in the left side, of which he instantly died. The coroner's inquest gave their verdict wilful murder.' (Stafford was tried later that year at the Old Bailey and appeared so deranged at his trial that he was brought in 'lunatick'.)

'24. One Kerry, a watchman was shot dead in a fray with 4 young sparks, 3 of whom were taken.' (This may have occurred in Dublin, but it isn't clear.)

'30. A gentleman kill'd by a *victuallar* (i.e. landlord) at Windsor, who on a quarrel about a reckoning, threw him over a table and broke his ribs.'

On 3 January 1731 we learn how a post-boy was fatally shot by 'an Irishman' on the road near Stone in Staffordshire, 'for which the gentleman was imprisoned'; we also learn of how a Gravesend blacksmith, recently parted from his wife, sent for the woman in October and simply fired his gun into her shoulder and breast, killing her; and of how a twelve-year-old boy fatally stabbed another child when they got into a playground tussle at Eaton School in March. Perhaps most gruesomely, we find that on 4 October the body of a man was found on the Bath to Bristol road, 'all his limbs cut off and mangled, and the skin *stript off his face*, supposed to be done to prevent his being known'. This summary does not even taken into account the shadowy extortionists known as the Incendiaries, nor the mysterious and disastrous fires that overtook towns like Blandford (Dorset), Cockthorpe (Norfolk), Tiverton (Devon) and other places.

Sometimes the victims are named, indicating that the case was perhaps more sensational than average; on 13 January, for example, 'one Mary Martin was found dead in a field near Hoxton; a piece of knife was sticking in her head, and a knife under her left ear; one Chapel belonging to the work-house in Bishopsgate-street was committed to Newgate for it, and has there confess'd it.' And intriguing mysteries are hinted at: in April, Mr Newcomen of Chester, 'who had received several threatening letters', was heard to cry out 'Help! Help!' one evening in the dark; he was afterwards found dead at the bottom of some steps in Fishmonger's Lane with his 'brains dashed out.'

Of these reports, perhaps the case of Mary Lynn is the most interesting; for her punishment mirrored that of Catherine Hayes – yet she was not convicted of killing her husband, rather her *mistress*, which made her fate somewhat unusual. The *Magazine* tells us: 'Mary Lynn, condemn'd last assizes for the county of Norfolk, was burnt to ashes at a stake, for being concern'd in the murder of her mistress; and Smith, the principal, was hang'd for the same fact. She deny'd her being guilty, and said Smith could clear her if he would. She behav'd with decency, and died penitent. Smith was drunk at the gallows; and seem'd to have but little sense either of his crime or his punishment; however (he) desir'd all masters to pay their servants wages on Saturday night, that they might have money to spend, and not run in debt; (he) said, "My mother always told me I should die in my shoes, but I will make her a liar"; so threw them off.' This was reported in April 1731.

This is an average cross-section of the reports carried by the *Gentleman's Magazine* in its first shaky year: but perhaps the most sensational murder it covered was the case of John Naden.

THE TALE OF JOHN NADEN

John Naden hailed originally from near Leek, Staffordshire; he was born of poor – but honest – parents, who provided him with an education in his youth. This education enabled Naden to take the position of manservant to a prosperous farmer named Robert Brough, who lived at White Lea, east of Leek.

Although John served his master faithfully, it became apparent before long that Brough's wife Mary entertained a healthy attraction towards the young man. By degrees she seduced Naden, even presenting him with a ring in 1728 and telling him that if Brough died she would be very happy with Naden. These were the first allusions that the woman made concerning the death of her husband; which over time became open efforts to persuade Naden to kill his master. In the end Naden agreed, and in June 1731 he made a half-hearted attempt to ambush

Brough as he returned from Congleton market; however, he found he could not go through with it, and his victim remained oblivious to the plotting going on behind his back.

Naden's mistress was furious that he could not find the courage to kill Brough, and her rage at him led him to again attempt the assassination a fortnight later on 23 June. On this occasion Naden followed Brough to Leek but waited until his victim was on his way home from a fair before committing the deed. Naden had been drinking heavily to steady his nerves, and in a moment of alcohol-fuelled passion he sprung on Brough, delivering him a blow on the head that knocked him down. He then attempted to cut the man's throat, but in his panic – or drunkenness – cut a great wound beneath his nose instead. His next attempt was more successful: he almost separated Brough's head from his neck. He also cut one of the man's wrists.

When he returned to White Lea, Naden told his mistress that the deed was done. After letting the household go to bed, Mrs Brough had the amazing coolness to slip out of the house in the middle of the night and locate her husband's dead body; she proceeded to rifle his pockets before throwing the knife over the hedge, in an attempt to make the attack look like a botched robbery. At three o'clock in the morning she returned and woke Naden up, telling him that if he was questioned he was to tell the authorities he had seen one William Wardle commit the murder.

When the murdered man was found, Wardle, of course, was vouched for by a number of respectable persons as having nothing to do with the killing. Such a patently absurd attempt to deflect guilt could not remain long believed, and both Naden and Mrs Brough were arrested on suspicion of murder. Naden was carried before Thomas Palmer, the coroner, and the evidence against him appearing plain from the start he was committed to Stafford gaol on 25 June 1731. On 19 August he was tried at Stafford Assizes, and – rather redundantly – pleaded 'Not guilty'. When he was convicted of murder he admitted his crime and begged pardon of Wardle, the man he had attempted to blame.

On 31 August 1731 John Naden was taken to his master's house to be executed. The day was exceedingly hot, and as he ascended the gallows ladder he lifted his manacled hands up, shook his head and once more desired Mr Wardle to forgive him. His last words were, 'Oh Lord, be merciful unto me John Naden, and show the greatness of thy mercy in pardoning a great and notorious offender. Amen.' Naden was executed at about midday; after hanging for about three quarters of an hour his body was cut down and taken to Gun Common, a height north of Leek, where it was encased in a metal cage and suspended from a 21-foot high wooden post to serve as a warning.

Gun Common, near Leek in Staffordshire; where Naden's body was suspended in view of travellers.

Curiously, the manipulative Mrs Brough was acquitted for want of evidence – despite it appearing clear she was a party to two deaths: her husband's, and by proxy that of her lover too.

A COMPLICATION OF MURDERS

30-year-old John Hewit must have been quite a charmer, for – despite being a married man of seven years standing – he was a confirmed adulterer whose romantic entanglements were so complicated that it manoeuvred one of his lovers into committing murder for him.

Hewit was a butcher in Stepping Lane, Derby, and for some time had been carrying on with Eleanor Beare, wife of Ebenezer Beare, a local publican. Not only this, but Hewit had also begun having an affair with the landlady's maidservant, young Rosamond Olerenshaw. Both women apparently knew of his dalliances with the other, and it is possible Mrs Hannah Hewit, his wife, was also aware of her husband's affairs; of her, we learn she was blatantly neglected, occasionally beaten by her husband and addicted to alcohol.

189

A fascinating contemporary description of Eleanor Beare – without doubt the most interesting person in this group of characters – is provided in William Hutton's *The History of Derby*: 'Eleanor Beare was a handsome woman, about the same age (i.e. thirty), with an education superior to her rank, and was mistress of that eloquence which insensibly wins over the hearer to her own side. She kept a paltry public-house, the White-Horse, nearly opposite the present gaol, in the neighbourhood of Hewit. But though she had the cypher of a husband, Ebenezer Beare, yet, as he bore no weight in the family, he was never mentioned; neither had he any more influence over her than a mouse over a cat, so that the residence always went by the name of Mrs Beare's.'

The wicked landlady was determined to be rid of Hewit's wife, Hannah, so that she might manoeuvre a marriage to the butcher herself. Therefore she obtained a large quantity of arsenic and mixed it into a pancake – which she then told young Rosamond to take to Mrs Hewit (who, it would appear, was a frequent visitor to the White Horse on account of her alcohol problem). The landlady encouraged her domestic to perform this chore with the promise of coin.

Hannah Hewit received the pancakes in grateful thanks and ate heartily: until she was seized with violent stomach pains that forced her to stagger into the yard, where she was violently sick. All the while, the hardened landlady stood in the parlour distractedly ironing some clothes.

A pig in the yard that was sniffing round the pool of vomit very quickly became ill and died, and Mrs Hewit herself died in excruciating agony about three hours after having eaten. The surgeons opened the body, which immediately revealed evidence of poisoning; the town of Derby became tumultuous, and the three participants – Hewit, Rosamond and the scheming Eleanor Beare – were committed to prison the following day.

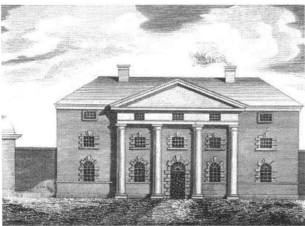

Derby Gaol, where the conspirators were incarcerated. A depiction from William Hutton's The History of Derby *(ed.1817).*

Eleanor Beare's plan was fiendishly simple; for she appears to have foreseen that the maidservant would be arrested for murder, thereby ridding her of another rival for Mr Hewit's affections…and so it turned out. The only flaw in the plan is that the landlady probably did not foresee that Mr Hewit would end up on the gallows also.

When the principals in this little drama were questioned, it appeared from the evidence that Mr Hewit knew of the plot that was taking place against his wife, and when it became obvious that he enjoyed 'criminal connections' with Rosamond Olerenshaw then a motive began to suggest itself. For her part, Rosamond confessed her part in the murder – but blamed her mistress, the landlady, Eleanor Beare, for instigating the whole thing.

Rosamond also admitted that an earlier attempt to poison Mrs Hewit had failed when an insufficient quantity of the deadly substance was stirred into her broth. Furthermore, this wretched young girl confessed a second murder: that of a 'bastard child' she had given birth to and which she had buried in a certain spot. When the site indicated was dug, the bones of an infant aged about seven months were accordingly found. Since it was suggested that Mr Hewit might be the father, this only added to the apparent guilt of both of them.

Now that the girl was a confessed murderer, all the wicked landlady had to do to escape justice was deny everything and call her maidservant a liar; for, if the girl were a murderer then lies would come all the more easily.

Following Rosamond's confession, John Hewit also admitted the murder. It is probable John entertained a genuine affection for the young maidservant, for at their trial, when he found he could not be saved himself, he attempted to save her. According to Derby historian William Hutton, the judge asked Rosamond directly whether Mrs Beare, the landlady, had played any part in the murder. John trod on Rosamond's toe, that she might repeat her accusation against Eleanor Beare; however, the wretched girl took the hint for its reverse, and answered, 'No!' loudly and clearly – thereby saving her wicked mistress's life and condemning herself infallibly. John Hewit and Rosamond were both convicted of murder at Derby Assizes, and soon afterwards both signed confessions.

The guilty pair were taken in a cart to the place of execution on 20 March 1732, amid a vast concourse of spectators. Ghoulishly, they were both already wrapped in their corpse-shrouds: these were usually reserved for the deceased post-mortem under normal circumstances, as convicted felons preferred to die in their finest clothes. Both seemed very penitent, and Rosamond appeared very doting towards Mr Hewit as the end approached. Hutton, who was there, wrote, 'I think she leaned upon his arm.' Hewit prayed very fervently in his final minutes, at one point saying that if he had a thousand lifetimes then he would give them all to live this one life again. This appeared to affect many in the crowd, who pitied and prayed for them as the cart was drawn away; both were left suspended and struggling by their necks, until finally their feet stopped kicking and they expired. Mr Hewit was praying for mercy even as the cart drew away.

There was great sympathy for the two felons, and Hutton wrote of the executions, 'He was pitied; but she, lamented.' A large part of the reason for this was that most people in the town blamed Eleanor Beare for the whole tragedy. The landlady was taken up on suspicion of felony and murder, but she did not meet the same fate as her companions and was acquitted. Which is remarkable, for she seems to have been responsible for multiple deaths: the murder of Mrs Hannah Hewit would appear to have been contrived by her, and the fact the murdered infant was buried in her garden suggests she knew of this also. Furthermore, it is likely that Rosamond was knowingly sacrificed to the noose, and by proxy Mr Hewit met his death also because of her scheming.

Such was the disgust in Derby at Mrs Beare's acquittal that earnest attempts were made to press other charges against her. It seems she bore a reputation locally, for Hutton records of her: 'She was remarkably expert at procuring gratifications for the men; an *exit* for those women who were troublesome wives; and abortion for those who were not.' To this end she was tried on Tuesday 15 August 1732 on charges of having attempted to coerce one Nicholas Wilson into poisoning *his* wife, and also procuring abortions for two women, one called Grace Belfort and the other unknown.

Eleanor Beare was sentenced to stand in the pillory in Derby's marketplace on 18 August 1732 and Hutton records: 'I saw her, with an easy air, ascend the hated machine, which over-looked an enraged multitude.' Eleanor's air of unconcern did not last long: once incapacitated she was so viciously pelted with missiles that it was thought she would be killed, although this she avoided by (somehow) disengaging herself from the pillory and running into the crowd. Rosamond Olerenshaw's brother was in the mob, and he dragged Eleanor back to the pillory by her hair 'looking like a moving heap of filth'. She was afterwards taken back to prison with great difficulty.

When she stood locked in the pillory again a week later, it was reported in the *Gentleman's Magazine*: 'As soon as she was fixed, such showers of eggs, turnips, potatoes, &c. were thrown, that it was expected she wou'd not have been taken down alive. She lost a great deal of blood, which running down the pillory, a little appeas'd their fury. Those who saw her afterwards in the gaol, said, she was such an object as was not fit to be look'd upon.' The gaol keeper at some point suspected from the bulk of her head-ware that something protected her head, and so removed her coverings to find that Eleanor had concealed a pewter plate over her hair to protect her skull. This he threw into the crowd, who then commenced their assault upon her prone person.

It is literally a miracle that Eleanor Beare was not killed by the mob: but being young and strong she did recover. Hutton records of her: 'She afterwards sustained the three years imprisonment, recovered her health, her spirits, and her beauty.'

THE JEERING OF HORNS IN LINCOLN

In the early 1730s two brothers called Isaac and Thomas Hallam carried out a sequence of daring robberies in the Lincolnshire area. These two in their depredations committed gruesome murders, and when their identities became suspected a government proclamation was issued offering a reward for their capture.

The brothers were suspected of the brutal murder of 18-year-old William Wright, who was found in a post-chaise at 'Faldingworth Gate', near Market Rasen, with his throat cut so violently that his head had almost been decapitated. A seat cloth had been laid over this youth's corpse, and his pockets had been rifled.

The brothers were also suspected of the murder of a post-boy called Thomas Gardiner, who had been found with his throat cut, laid out next to the body of his horse near Nettleham on the outskirts of Lincoln; the animal had also had its throat cut in what appeared to have been an unparalleled act of bloodthirsty violence. This 19-year-old youth had been employed in carrying the mail between Lincoln and Grimsby, the containers of which had been broken open and robbed. Both killings were carried out within two days, on 2 and 3 January 1733.

The brothers evaded capture for about a month, but at length they were taken (probably betrayed for the reward and by the fact that they haunted the same stretch of road) and committed to Lincoln Castle Gaol. When they were carted into the city it is said that the post-boys of Lincoln jeered their entry with the loudest blasts of their horns, their indignity aroused by the allegation that the killers of Thomas Gardiner had forced him to blow his own horn – and then told him he had just sounded his own death peal. One of the accused was observed to weep upon being subjected to this barrage of abuse.

The Hallam brothers were tried at Lincoln and convicted of both murders. There is some suggestion that the spree might have started due to one of the brother's antipathy towards a local post-master following some work-related disagreement. This explained their attack on poor Thomas Gardiner, and also perhaps helped identify them. Nonetheless, they accepted the justice of their sentence, albeit with an air of arrogance, and admitted carrying out 63 robberies and a *third* murder 'exclusive of that for which they were condemned to die'.

While they were incarcerated they made an attempt to escape, somehow procuring a case knife that they next notched like a saw. Thus fashioned, they used this implement to cut off the irons that bound them; then, with a spike-nail, they began digging through the wall of their prison, but in this they were detected.

On 20 February (or, alternatively, 10 March) 1733 Isaac was taken to the scene of Thomas Gardiner's murder near Nettleham at about 9 o'clock in the morning, where he fell into violent agonies of mind. There being no clergyman, he requested a spectator assist him in his devotions, and died very penitently. Thomas Hallam was forced to watch his brother struggling in his death throes, before - shrieking in torment - he was himself drawn to Faldingworth Gate about eight miles away. Here, the halter was placed around his neck and he too died in the 'utmost agonies of mind'. He appears to have been the weaker of the two brothers, confessing that he held the post-boy's hand while Isaac killed him. He also declared that Isaac was 'for murdering all they robb'd'. Both were encased in their 'chains' and suspended where they were executed.

Thomas Gardiner was buried in Nettleham churchyard, his headstone inscribed: '*Tho. Gardiner. Post boy of Lincoln. Barbarously murdered by Isaac and Tho. Hallam. Jan. 3rd 1732. Aged 19.*

Thomas Gardiner's sad grave is in Nettleham churchyard.

A LONDON EXPLOSION

On 17 January 1733 it was reported that a terrific explosion in St James's Street, central London, had occurred. When the dust cleared it was found to have claimed the life of one Mrs Warburton.

A coroner's inquest was held on this death, which revealed a surprisingly rare type of crime. Mrs Warburton had earned a living mending clothes 'under the Black-Swan, a grocer's in St. James's Street'. It was established an assassin had deliberately placed a quantity of gunpowder in a pot of charcoal that she had used to warm her feet, which ignited in a catastrophic explosion and set her alight. The coroner decided that 'some evil-designed persons' had set this trap in her stall, leaving her a 'most miserable spectacle'.

St James's Street today, where the explosion occurred.

A verdict of 'Wilful murder by persons unknown' was returned. Several residents in St James's Street put together a reward of ten guineas to find the murderer, but it appears it went unclaimed.

HOW TO BEAR A GRUDGE

In the case of murderer William Alcock, it is not so much the crime that he committed as the means which brought him to it which are fascinating.

Alcock came from Bourne in Lincolnshire. When he married, the union lasted just two years before he upped and left his wife, who was suffering with the palsy - he giving it out that he had caught her in bed with another man. He relocated to Colchester, Essex, where he remarried and set himself up as a miller – rather successfully, as it happened.

The problem arose when Alcock dismissed one of his employees, a man named Peck, following an argument between them. Peck was a vindictive fellow, and feeling himself slighted, he said to Alcock: 'I'll do as good a job for you; for I have heard you have a wife in Lincolnshire, and I'll travel the kingdom over till I find her, and send her to you.' This was no idle threat, for Peck spent an astonishing *two years* travelling from town to town in

Lincolnshire (working a few days at a time to sustain himself) before he found Mrs Alcock. He then went to the parish officers of Bourne, who were providing maintenance for the wife, and told them where Mr Alcock might be found. Two parishioners were dispatched to Colchester to force Alcock to pay his dues, and he came to an agreement with them to pay £20, then another £30: most problematically, he was also forced into agreeing to bring her from Bourne to Colchester to live with him.

On 22 August 1732 Alcock arrived in Bourne to collect his wife. He turned up on a horse bearing a new pillion for her to sit behind him; however, he made earnest attempts to persuade the parish officers to keep Mrs Alcock, saying that she was so disagreeable that he would rather be hanged than take her back again. Finding all offers rejected, he set off with her on 24 August.

The following day Mrs Alcock was found murdered in a ditch near the hamlet of Pilsgate, at that time part of Northamptonshire and about eight miles from Bourne. It was established she been strangled, for there was a short cord drawn about her neck; some accounts suggest she was actually hanged from a tree with some lace. Her new pillion was discovered some way along the road. Alcock was naturally the first and only suspect, and he was arrested in Colchester on 28 August by officers from Bourne and committed to gaol.

William Alcock's trial was almost a foregone conclusion, and he was convicted at Northampton Assizes on the clearest evidence. He appears to have understood his life was over on the day the parish of Bourne ordered him to take his wife back, and as a consequence he lived in a most shockingly cavalier manner in the days leading up to his death. He denied his guilt continually, refused the attempts of clergymen to get him to repent, and drank himself into a state of intoxication on the day of his execution. This was 9 March 1733, and it was in a state of drunkenness that he left the prison. He paid some money for a pint of wine, but this being denied him, he refused to get into the gallows cart until the money was returned to him. On the road to the gallows he sang an old song called 'Robin Hood', adding to each verse the chorus of 'Derry down!' Along the way he swore constantly, and kicked anybody who came near the cart.

When he reached the 'fatal tree' Alcock kicked off his shoes while he was being tied. A clergyman who was in the cart with him attempted to get him to repent and confess one last time – but Alcock dashed the prayer book out of the man's hands. He then damned the spectators (who numbered in the thousands) and called for more wine. Even as the final psalms were being sung, and prayers being read, Alcock ignored it all, idly conversing with acquaintances throughout. Finally, just before he was hanged, he urged his friends to remember him and drink to his 'good journey'…and with his last breath he once again bemoaned the injustice of his sentence.

ANIMALS AS MURDER WEAPONS

Correspondence dated 1 March 1733 posted to the *Ipswich Journal* related a ghastly murder that had lately taken place near Nottingham. A 17-year-old woman was on her way to service in the city, carrying a bundle of clothes and a small box, when she was accosted by 'a tinker and his trull (i.e. female companion)' in a field just outside Nottingham. These two robbed her, then stripped her naked before tying her to a tree. They then set their dog on her. The animal ferociously attacked her, 'and tore one of her breasts almost off' before the two robbers lost interest and simply left her, still bound to the tree with the dog continuing to tear furiously at her.

Presently the girl was found in this condition by a gentleman out riding, who at first thought the dog was savaging a sheep; when he saw it was a young woman, he whipped it away and unbound her, wrapping her in his greatcoat before leaving her propped against the tree. Leaping on his horse, he followed the dog, which led him to a pub about half a mile away: inside, the gentleman asked a woman on the property who the dog belonged to, and was told it was owned by a man and a woman in the next room.

The gentleman immediately sent to Nottingham for an officer, and bravely entered the room, keeping the tinker and his female companion in conversation until the officer arrived. Both were secured and their room searched, whereupon the stolen property was discovered.

After they were imprisoned in Nottingham Gaol, the female was brought before a magistrate, where she made a full confession to the crime. Upon this admission of guilt some persons were dispatched from the city to the scene of the deed – where they found that the unfortunate victim had since died of her injuries.

Although this brutal crime was reported in many news-sheets up and down England, it was later suggested to be an entire fabrication. But whether or not the Nottingham incident was factual, another case whereby an animal was used as the weapon most certainly *did* occur. On 22 March 1734 it was reported that 'last week' a farmer from Spaldwick had gone on trial at Huntingdon Assize accused of a bizarre killing. His servant boy, driving a loaded harvest time cart, had overturned it; fearing his master's rage he had run off into the fields to hide. The farmer found him and dragged him to a horse, roping him to the animal's tail. The intention (according to the farmer's defence) was to march the boy through the village by this method and so shame him. Unfortunately, at the next village the farmer got down from the horse's saddle: whereupon it (allegedly) took fright at something and trampled the boy to death. The farmer deposed that his servant was an 'idle, wicked lad', and there appeared to be some evidence for this; and so the jury gave him the benefit of the doubt and brought in a verdict of manslaughter.

THE FINAL WORD

When a man named Johnston stood about to be executed in Dumfries for horse stealing on 6 June 1733, it seems he thought he might as well clear his conscience; for since his sentencing he had 'confessed his being accessory to several murders and other *attrocious* crimes'.

There is little more by way of information, but it does indicate that many of the robbers who became household names during the 18th century may have had much more blood on their hands than came to light. This also might be a good point to reinforce just how epidemic in nature robbery was becoming. The *Gentleman's Magazine* reported that the month of September 1736 was particularly bad around the capital: 'The robberies talk'd of this month are very numerous, yet some have predicted more for next. Maidenhead Thicket, Hounslow Heath, Putney, *Barns* and Finchley Commons, and places adjacent, have been the daily scenes of action. In Whetson (Whetstone, Barnet), two highwaymen pursued a gentleman up to a house, but he getting in from 'em, they forc'd their way through the turnpike and rode off; three or four persons were murder'd by robbers.' The problem of robbery is worth emphasizing, in view of its being the supposed motive in the following crime, which became one of the most notorious of the age.

Hounslow Heath today is vastly reduced in size. To travel this way was literally to take one's life in one's own hands in the 1700s. (Photo courtesy of Ian Yarham.)

'MANY DIE SO SUDDENLY THAT THEY HAVE NOT TIME TO CALL FOR MERCY...'

The *Newgate Calendar* tells us: 'The Temple, and other Inns of Court (in central London), were built for the accommodation of lawyers alone', but these apartments were not ideally suited to lawyers bringing up families. Consequently many private tenants moved into these lawyer's chambers, one of them being a lady called Mrs Lydia Duncomb, who was about 80 years of age at the time of her residency in 1733. She kept two servants – Elizabeth Harrison, aged 60, and Ann Price, aged about 17. The apartments of the Inns of Court were desirable and fashionable, consisting of two, three or four rooms: each being attended by a hired laundress who made the bed and swept the floor, and thereby made a tidy income by the standards of the time.

One young woman thus employed as a laundress here was Sarah Malcolm. Sarah came from Durham, and was aged about 22 at the time of the following awful events, which engraved her name in the minds of Londoners for a generation. Her parents had moved to Dublin after Sarah's birth, this being the home town of her mother, and here her father's position in public office entitled Sarah to a good education. The parents apparently doted on their little girl, but in time they moved back to England and settled in London, where Sarah's mother fell sick and passed away. Her father remarried, and from this an acrimonious family split was occasioned - with Sarah going her own way out of dislike for her new stepmother.

Sarah Malcolm sought to make her own way in London society, and her education provided a good opening for her in the servitude industry. She worked, by all accounts, diligently for several reputable families, presently being employed as a domestic at the Black Horse, an inn near Temple Bar; from here she gained a position (based on a recommendation) as a laundress in the Temple. Among her employers here was a young Irish gentleman called Kerril; and also Mrs Duncomb, to who she officiated as charwoman.

On Saturday 3 February 1733 Sarah called at Mrs Duncomb's chambers, where she visited the elderly servant woman, Mrs Harrison (who was ill) and stayed until 8 o'clock. Mrs Duncomb was at the time entertaining a Mrs Love, the two elderly ladies making arrangements to dine together the next day.

The following morning Mrs Love arrived at the Duncomb apartment to collect her dinner companion, but – finding no answer to her raps on the door – enlisted the help of a Mrs Oliphant. The two formed the opinion that the ill servant, Mrs Harrison, must have died of her sickness during the night and thus the household was busily engaged; maybe Mrs Duncomb had forgotten about her luncheon appointment. Presently Mrs Duncomb's executrix, Mrs Rhymer, was engaged, and when further attempts to rouse the household brought no response the gaggle of women began to become alarmed. They climbed into the outside gutter through the window of Mrs Oliphant's employer, and from this vantage point they broke Mrs Duncomb's window pane and managed to gain access to her chambers.

Inside, a scene of horror greeted the three women. The first sight that befell their eyes was the body of the young girl, Ann Price, laid on her bed in the passage with her throat cut and the bedclothes soaked in blood. In the next room they found the frail Mrs Harrison; she had been strangled. And in an adjoining room they found the body of Mrs Duncomb herself. The elderly lady had also been strangled in her bed, it being observed that a box where she supposedly contained her valuables had been broken open and emptied, excepting a few papers. The neighbourhood quickly became alarmed, and a crowd began to gather, among them the young Irishman, Kerril, whose companion, Mr Gahagan, remarked, 'Mrs Duncomb was your Sarah's acquaintance!' In Covent Garden, the two gentlemen found the coffee houses abuzz with the news of the triple murder, the consensus of opinion being that 'some laundress' must have committed the crime. Kerril brooded on this, but did not return to the Inns of Court until near one in the morning. Upon opening his door he found Sarah Malcolm lighting a small fire in his chambers: he stormed at her, 'So Sarah, are you here at this time of the morning?'

Although Sarah Malcolm was Mr Kerril's domestic, and as a consequence had access to his rooms, her behaviour appeared contrary to her routine. The conversation edgily turned to the killings, and Mr Kerril asked Sarah what she knew. She declared her belief that a person who lived beneath Mrs Duncomb had been absent from his own apartment two or three days, and he was suspected. This was clearly erroneous, since Sarah herself knew that Mrs Duncomb had been alive the very day before, so how could someone who had been absent three days have been the guilty party? Kerril, clearly suspicious, stated, 'Nobody who was acquainted with Mrs Duncomb shall be in my chambers till the murderer is discovered; and therefore, look up your things, and be gone.'

After this, suspicion very quickly centred on Sarah. Two watchmen who had been called to the scene found two of Mr Kerril's waistcoats missing from his closet, and Sarah was trapped into admitting pawning them in Drury Lane for two guineas. She appeared sincerely repentant, but Mr Kerril stated that he was not so much concerned about his stolen clothing as he was with his suspicions that Sarah might be involved in the three murders. He then keenly observed a bundle lying on the floor near Sarah, which she said was her gown with some linen tied in it, and she hoped decency would prevent Kerril from inspecting it; he abided by this wish. However, a wider search revealed more items of Kerril's property that appeared to have been hidden, and so Kerril asked the watchmen to place Sarah under arrest. As she was led away, Kerril and his friend Mr Gahagan conducted a thorough search of her living quarters and found a piece of incriminating evidence: a silver pint tankard with a bloodied handle.

Sarah is arrested on suspicion of committing the triple murder. (This illustration first appeared in William Jackson's New & Complete Newgate Calendar *Volume 2, 1795.)*

There was now an element of farce, which shows how *laissez faire* the attitudes of the Georgians could be in the midst of serious crime. Kerril subsequently hailed the two watchmen - who said they had let their captive go because she had promised to surrender herself once again at ten o' clock the following morning! A number of watchmen immediately fanned out on the order of Kerril, and Sarah was found still in the Temple. She had not fled: perhaps the first indication that she might not have been the guilty party, and a constant niggling argument observed by those in favour of Sarah's innocence in the days that followed. Sarah explained that the tankard was her mother's, bloodied when she had recently cut her finger. As a consequence of these 'frivolous excuses' Sarah was again arrested. On searching her person a green silk purse containing '21 counters' was found in her bosom and she was committed to Newgate.

It appeared that Sarah Malcolm was, of late, at the very least a habitual thief; but things were soon to look worse. A turnkey at Newgate named Johnson discovered a small bag concealed under her hair containing a number of guineas, shillings and crowns. Taking Sarah into his confidence – after all, he now had incriminating evidence suggesting the prisoner was hiding stolen money – the pair talked. Johnson agreed to accept a substantial bribe from her to keep the matter of the hidden money secret: he also learned that Sarah had engaged three men to swear that the tankard belonged to her grandmother. Everything else against her was circumstantial, she confidently declared to the turnkey. Next she put a piece of mattress in her hair to give it the bulk it had before, since Johnson had taken the bag of money as per their arrangement. Sarah clearly felt that she could trust Johnson (perhaps she felt she had no choice), for the closest thing she made to an admission was in his presence: she stated that although she was *concerned* in the robbery, she had watched from the stair while two brothers named Thomas and James Alexander, together with a woman named Mary Tracy (all of whom she had met while working at the Black Horse), committed the *actual* crime. She herself knew nothing of how the murders occurred.

As her captivity progressed, Sarah's health appeared to deteriorate. Her mental condition worsened, and she fell victim to such fits in her cell that it was feared she had taken poison. She had not, and in London society the general opinion was that her guilt was now driving her into a frenzy of madness; however, it is possible that a maddening terror was dawning upon her that she was going to pay with her life for a brutal killing spree committed by others. When she was asked questions during her illness, little regard could be paid to what she said, raving and random as it was. But when it was decided to take the brothers Alexander and Mary Tracy into custody, Sarah Malcolm lucidly and gleefully stated: 'Ay, these are the persons that committed the murder' when they were presented before her. Accusingly, she turned to Mary Tracy and said, 'You know this to be true; see what you have brought me to; it is through you and the two Alexanders that I am brought to this shame, and death must follow; you all declared you would do no murder; but, to my great surprise, I found the contrary.'

Sarah Malcolm did not have to wait long for her trial, which occurred on 21 February 1733 at the Old Bailey. When her trial commenced, although the evidence against her was circumstantial, it was very strong, and after a parade of prosecution witnesses had been brought before the court not a single person present doubted Sarah Malcolm's guilt. This was in part due to her acknowledgement that she knew of a plot to rob Mrs Duncomb prior to the event.

Sarah persisted to the last that the robbery had been contrived by herself and Mary Tracy during a conversation at Mr Kerril's apartment while he was away. The plundering of Mrs Duncomb's chambers had been proposed, and at Sarah's insistence that she could not carry out such an audacious crime alone, her friend enlisted the assistance of the Alexander brothers to help ransack the old lady's rooms.

The crime, Sarah claimed, had come about thus. She had left Mrs Duncomb's rooms after visiting Mrs Harrison, the lady's ill servant, around 8 o' clock in the evening on 3 February. Meeting Mary Tracy and the two men, they proposed to rob the place immediately, as it was observed that the door was ajar. The young maid, Ann Price, had deliberately left it open when she had left the rooms earlier, knowing Mrs Harrison was too weak to open it for her upon her return. James Alexander took advantage of this and immediately sneaked into Mrs Duncomb's rooms where he hid himself beneath her bed.

Later that night, Sarah, Mary Tracy and Tom Alexander met on Mrs Duncomb's stair and heard the watchmen outside shout that it was midnight. The evening was a very stormy one, and the trio bided their time for another two hours, hiding on the stairs until James Alexander appeared from within the rooms and said, 'Now is the time.' For two hours Sarah (or so she claimed) sat on the stair acting as a guard, until finally the other three reappeared and (after ensuring the spring-loaded door was secured behind them) they retired to an archway by Fig-tree Court where they divided up the proceeds of the burglary. These were considerable, amounting to about 300 pounds. Sarah's cut included the tankard, and they warned her to hide her share under the earth and not to purchase anything with it immediately. They also stated that they had bound and gagged the occupants of the apartment, but did not elaborate.

The jury did not agree with this tale, believing it a fabrication. Sarah, as a laundress, would have had knowledge of the chambers she worked, and they believed that she committed the robbery alone in order to obtain finances to secure one of the Alexanders as a husband. The true meaning of her compassionate visit to the ill serving woman, it was thought, was to secrete the key of the door or spoil the lock so as to gain easy access later on that evening. The victims had been killed, it was suggested, because one of them interrupted her when she furtively slipped into the apartment. Naturally, Sarah would have been recognised, and this was why she had embarked on a horrid course to eliminate the witnesses.

Sarah Malcolm in her cell awaiting execution.

Sarah was convicted of the three murders and sentenced to death. Her jailer attempted to get her to confess as the time drew nearer, but although she was by now suffering more violent fits she refused to do so, remaining stubbornly immovable. However, she was still lucid: she attempted to console a man under sentence of death in the next cell by telling him: 'Your time is short as well as mine, and I wish I was to go with you: as to the ignominy of your fate, let not that trouble you; none but the vulgar will reflect either on your friends or relations: good parents may have unhappy children, and pious children may have unhappy parents; neither are answerable for the other. As to the suddenness of our death, consider we have had time to prepare for it; whereas many die so suddenly that they have not time to call for mercy.'

Although she behaved very devoutly in the days leading to her execution, many saw it as hypocrisy, her general attitude being one of denial, arrogance and insincerity. She was observed to contradict herself frequently when she talked, and her fits were seen as symptomatic of an inner guilt trying to express itself. This was at its most evident on the morning of her execution, 7 March 1733, when she wept bitterly and wrung her hands in the cart that trundled her to Mitre Court, Fleet Street. She fainted as the noose was placed round her neck, and after she recovered the executioner kissed her; whether this was a sympathetic act or a piece of pantomime for the crowd on the part of the executioner is unclear. It is possible it was the former, for another fellow present attempted the same but

Sarah denied him the chance. Just before the cart moved off and launched her into oblivion she turned towards the Temple and cried, 'Oh! My master! My master! I wish I could see him!' Her last action was to cast her eyes to Heaven and call upon Christ to receive her soul. Her final moments were witnessed by thousands, including many among the nobility who peered out of the upper windows of nearby buildings overlooking the spectacle.

After her execution, Sarah's body was taken to an undertaker's on Snow Hill and there exhibited for money. Among the crowd it was observed there was a man – some supposed him to be her late master, Mr Kerril - who stooped and kissed the corpse before presenting the attendant with half-a-crown. She was afterwards buried in St Sepulchre's Church, although her remains were later disinterred and her skeleton displayed in a glass case in the Botanic Garden, Cambridge.

The Alexander brothers and Mary Tracey were released from Newgate on 7 April 1733, a month after Sarah's execution. One wonders if there were any misgivings about the case when the brothers were arrested on 16 July in connection with a highway robbery. When they appeared in court, the judge – angry that no one could positively identify them – demanded to know how they made a living. In answer to this, one signified he was a shoemaker, the other that he was a hod carrier. The court saw fit to dismiss them 'with an admonition to behave themselves well for the future'.

The celebrated illustrator Hogarth painted Sarah Malcolm's portrait during a visit to her cell in Newgate on the day before her execution. She had worn red, claiming that it made her look better, although Hogarth's painting does not reflect this: it shows a stout-looking young woman in greenish bunched skirts, her sleeves rolled up and a white apron from her chest to her feet. She also wears a white mobcap-type affair that hides her hair as she looks distractedly away from the painter. A rosary is on the table at her elbows, there being some suggestion that she was brought up a Roman Catholic (or took the faith while in prison). All said, Hogarth's picture depicts a not-unattractive woman, but one who the artist undoubtedly considered evil: to Sir James Thornhill, who accompanied him, he observed, 'I see by this woman's features that she is capable of any wickedness...'

THE UNHAPPY LOT OF THE WATCHMAN

The following story, reported in the *Political State*, is a good indicator of the daily lot of a watch-man in the capital.

At about two o'clock in the morning on 17 May 1733, 'the watch' stopped two women with baskets on their heads near Chiswell Street, who said they were going to market. Upon examination the watch-men found the baskets to contain 117 pounds worth of tea. Suspecting the tea to have been smuggled into the country, the watch-men escorted the two women to the watch-house at the end of Bunhill Row, Chiswell Street, St Luke's.

After the tea was secured, the two women earnestly declared that if the duty constable would send a watch-man or two with them, then they would show them the house from whence they brought the tea, adding that they believed there was a great deal more in the house. The constable agreed to this proposal and ordered two of the watch-men to go with the women and investigate.

The group left the watch-house, and as they were 'passing along by the upper end of Bunhill Row' it became immediately obvious that the two women had led the two watch-men into an ambush. One of the women yelled out, 'Sam! Sam! We are robbed, and the goods taken from us!'

Immediately three men on horseback came up, and at this one of the watch-men scrambled off into the darkness in fright. The three horsemen rounded on his partner, and beat him ferociously about the head with the butt-end of their whips. In fact, they beat him so severely that they fractured his skull in a number of places and fatally injured him, for he died but a few hours after the assault. The *Political State* reported the victim's name was Samuel Alexander, 'a poor infirm old man'.

According to this report, '...the men and women went off together undiscovered'. A coroner's inquest, having sat upon the body, brought in a verdict of 'Wilful murder'.

Samuel Alexander's murderer turned out to be a famer-turned-smuggler called George Watson from the Hull area, who had earned the nickname 'Yorkshire George'. He was tried for murder at the Old Bailey in June 1736, although quite how his arrest came about after three years is unclear; suffice to say that one of his confederates, one Walker, was persuaded to appear in evidence against him. It appears that some months prior, George Watson had been arrested over some sort of financial problem, and while he languished in Newgate he entertained the idea of bringing the matter of Samuel Alexander's murder to light in order to blame someone else and perhaps manoeuvre his freedom. Unfortunately for Watson, Walker, one of his criminal associates also imprisoned, seems to have had the same idea and gone to the authorities first to blame Watson.

During the trial it transpired that George Watson had moved south from Yorkshire, first making a living as a servant, and then as a farmer on the Isle of Sheppey, Kent. This was where he had made the acquaintance of 'friends' who in fact turned out to be a smuggling gang, and it had all been downhill from there – at the expense of Watson's thriving farm and family. At the time of his trial, he was aged about 55, and virtually his whole adult life had been engaged in smuggling along the south-east coast, although he maintained he was not a desperate, dangerous man like many of his confederates – who, he said, frequently fought the king's customs officers and soldiers in clashes during which much blood had been shed.

Although he denied having been a participant in any battles in which murder had been committed, Watson *had* been arrested on suspicion of murder before. This appears to have concerned the fatal shooting of a customs officer named Hill about five years earlier on the Kentish coast, for which Watson was arrested and imprisoned in Southwark's New Gaol in heavy irons. However, when he came to trial at Maidstone Assizes Watson was able to persuade the court that he had been in London on the day of the shooting, having a damaged finger attended to by a surgeon.

On Saturday 12 June 1736 the Old Bailey sessions ended with George Watson being capitally convicted of Alexander's murder. Following his conviction, he admitted the killing and claimed it had been carried out with two fellows called John Hemming and Robert Hemming, not yet taken. However, he persisted in his denial that he had committed any other murders while part of the Kentish smuggling organization. On 5 August Watson, after taking an emotional leave of his family, was hanged at Tyburn, his execution causing something of a stir because of his position as a smuggler; executions of smugglers seem to have been quite rare in the capital itself at this time, it appears.

'HE SAW FIT TO MOVE HER OUT OF THE WAY'

In 1734 a terrible and baffling crime occurred in Steeple Morden, a village in rural Cambridgeshire, near the Hertfordshire border. Elizabeth Pateman was the 18-year-old maidservant of one James Hoy, of that parish. At about midnight on the day before Shrove Tuesday she had been 'making *Holliday*' at a party, and returned to her employer's residence in the company of a 14-year-old lad, also a servant at the house. The mistress of the house let them in, and Elizabeth retired to her room.

At about five in the morning a dismal moaning from Elizabeth's chamber awoke Mr Hoy, who knocked on her door and demanded to know whether she was alright. Receiving no answer, he lit a lamp and entered Elizabeth's room.

The scene within was shocking and horrific. Elizabeth lay on the floorboards, which were greatly splashed with blood. She appeared to have been struck in the face and body: her cheekbone was broken, and she was otherwise bruised elsewhere on her person. But her throat had also been cut, a large piece of flesh having been gouged out and exposing the jugular vein. From this injury she died three hours later, unable to utter a word about who might have attacked her.

At the south side of the house, a casement window was found to have been damaged. A small iron bar had been taken out of the middle of it, this being supposed to be the means by which Elizabeth's murderer entered the premises. The fact that a break-in had occurred appeared to eliminate anyone among the household as a suspect. The murder weapon - a bloody plough iron - was found under the window; but when its owner was traced two or three days later he proved unequivocally to have had nothing to do with the crime. Thus it appeared the murder weapon had been stolen by the killer.

The day following the girl's death a coroner's jury sat on the body; industrious efforts were also made to catch the culprit. Unfortunately, every clue led nowhere. Two Justices of the Peace examined the whole household as well as Hoy's nearest neighbours, with none falling under suspicion. It did not appear to be a robbery gone wrong, for nothing was stolen – despite there being seven silver spoons on a table near the window where the killer had entered the property. Bizarrely, three bottles of ale had been taken from the cellar by the murderer, but these he had left in the yard untapped: what did this mean? No one ever found out. Next, a rumour spread that Elizabeth might have been 'debauched' by a sweetheart, and then killed to cover up the rape; a skilful surgeon dismissed this theory by proving she was still a virgin. No sense was ever made of the brutal killing, and a contemporary report surmised: 'She had been privy to some mal-practices in a person thereabouts who has but an indifferent character, and for fear of discovery he thought fit to move her out of the way.'

Neither culprit nor motive was ever ascertained, however. It seemed someone had taken it upon themselves to stealthily enter the property, specifically with the intention of murdering the servant girl. Poor Elizabeth was interred on 21 February 1734; the fact that her killer was never identified was reflected on her tombstone in St Peter and St Paul's Church, which in part read: '*Therefore repent who ere you be; Or I foretell your destiny; In hell's hot furnace dark and deep; Your wretched soul shall wail and weep; While she I hope in Heaven high Shall reign above the lofty sky.*'

Over two centuries later, the Cambridgeshire folklorist and historian Enid Porter collected fragments of anecdotal evidence concerning this murder. She scribbled down popular theories of what was believed to have happened in Steeple Morden all those years ago, and these elements of the story were put together in her *Cambridgeshire Customs and Folklore* (1964). Elizabeth's place of employment had been an old farmhouse called Moco, by Cheney Water, which by Porter's time had been reduced to ruins. According to local gossip, an itinerant packman had sometimes stayed at Moco on his way to sell trinkets and wares; at some point it was noticed he had vanished without trace overnight while staying there. Nosey and gossipy neighbours also noted that a well in front of Moco was never used again and was subsequently filled in. Many believed Mr Hoy, the farmer (and Elizabeth's employer), had in fact murdered the traveller, and Elizabeth had had the misfortune to be overheard whispering to her sweetheart that she had a secret to tell him. Thinking that she knew the secret of the traveller's death, Hoy and his wife contrived to murder Elizabeth next.

Was this just rumour? Or had Enid Porter – over 200 years later - collected a version of the truth, passed down through successive generations in Steeple Morden, perhaps discreetly at first, before it became common knowledge as the events faded into distant history?

By now, of course, it is too late to ever know the truth behind poor Elizabeth's murder.

The Moco Farm stood here, along the Litlington Road in the vicinity of the war memorial at Steeple Morden.

THE ALBEMARLE STREET MYSTERY

Another mysterious crime occurred in the capital this year, as recorded by Westminster historian John Entick some 32 years after the fact. He wrote: 'On the 14th (of May 1734) we have an account of a *surprizing* murder. A fire being discovered by the neighbours in the house of Mr Cantillon, a French wine-merchant, in Albemarle Street (off Piccadilly), about three o'clock in the morning, they broke in, and found him smothered in his bed, with his head almost burnt, or cut off; and he having to the value of £200'000 in the house, and other circumstances, caused a suspicion of villainy in the affair. The servants were therefore secured and committed to prison. But the strongest suspicion was of the cook, who had been discharged about three weeks before, and now fled with a valuable cargo beyond sea, under a feigned name. The servants were tried and acquitted; and a reward of £200 was offered for a discovery; but this mysterious affair never could be found out.'

Richard Cantillon was aged about 54 at the time of his supposed murder, and Entick's account merely hints at the mystery surrounding this incident. Although his name is now almost forgotten, Cantillon retains a reputation as one of Europe's foremost economists and entrepreneurs. Formerly a London resident, he had around 1719 removed to Paris where he acquired a considerable fortune before returning to London and purchasing his current estate. After his murder the newspapers reported: 'His lady is still abroad but shortly expected here.'

While the building still burned Cantillon's corpse was removed from within, one periodical of the day noting 'his head (was) almost burnt off'. The servants also managed to save some of his belongings, such as jewels etc, but the blaze soon engulfed the property – also destroying the neighbouring property of the Honourable Mr Percival, brother to the Earl of Egmont. The fire was at first thought to have been an accident, occasioned by a candle lighting some paperwork that Mr Cantillon had been reading in bed; but soon two or three of the servants were taken up on suspicion of killing their master and torching the house.

A post-boy deposed that he collected a man at the King's Arms Inn in nearby Leadenhall Street who asked to be taken to Harwich in Essex; his destination beyond that appeared to be the Netherlands. The description provided by the post-boy matched that of the dismissed cook, a Frenchman named Joseph Denier, and the witness also observed that the fellow carried with him a large portmanteau (case) and seemed well provided with ready money. The dismissed servant had been seen drinking in a public house in St Giles's on the day of the murder and it was theorised he might have gained access to Mr Cantillon's property by way of a ladder that was left a few days earlier at the back part of his house.

A coroner's jury sat in a tavern on Albemarle Street and (Joseph Denier still being sought) brought in a verdict of murder against two of Cantillon's other servants and a maid, all three of whom were currently incarcerated in Newgate. They were ordered to be tried at the next Old Bailey sessions, but – as we know – this all collapsed and came to naught. Many witnesses appeared at the trial of the accused – Isaac Berridge, Roger Arnold and Elizabeth Pembroke – and testified to their good character; they were acquitted after five hours.

The whole affair remains somewhat curious to this day. Was it an accident? The circumstances *suggested* murder, but by whom? Some, such as writer Antoin E. Murphy in *The Demise of Richard Cantillon* (1989), have also suggested that the merchant faked his own death, having become embroiled in legal wrangles and the victim of conspiracies: for a certain 'Chevalier de

Louvigny' later turned up in Surinam with a collection of documents relating to Cantillon. This begs the question of who the part-decapitated man – his features conveniently obscured by the fire damage - lying in Cantillon's bed might have been…

TERROR IN A WELSH VILLAGE

Terror swept the little Welsh coastal community of Oystermouth, about three miles from Swansea, on 2 July 1734.

A ship's carpenter named John Maddock was that day working on a dredging oyster boat. Seeing his 'ancient' father walking on a stretch of beach locally called the Mumbles, Maddock stopped working, took an axe and ran up to the old man. With this weapon he delivered his father a mighty blow, which knocked the man to the ground. Maddock then ran to his father's house and there split his mother's head open with the same weapon. He continued striking her, dashing out her brains even while his sister (reportedly) attempted to cradle the injured woman in her arms. All the while the mother screamed at her daughter to prevent the assault, but in the end her cries were silenced by her maniac son.

The sister had by this time fled the house and the village. Maddock followed her, but saw that his father was not yet dead; in fact, the old man was on his feet on the beach being supported by a number of people, who were leading him in the direction of a nearby property. Maddock, enraged, stopped chasing his sister and charged at them instead, swinging his axe in such a deadly manner that these Good Samaritans were forced to let the old man go and flee for their lives. In full view of everyone Maddock proceeded to 'cut and mangle his father in the most unheard of manner'. By now all Oystermouth was in uproar, but the matter was brought to an end when someone deftly approached Maddock and bashed him violently over the crown with a club.

Maddock was carried, injured, before a Justice of the Peace and sent under the guard of parish constables to Cardiff Gaol. The story was reported in the English news-sheets when a coaster from Oystermouth landed in Bristol and told of the outrage. Little explanation was provided for the son's actions except, ''Tis said he had been delirious for some time before.'

THE SIEGE OF SKEWIS HOUSE

In 1734 an event occurred at 'Skewis' (Skewes), a manor in the parish of Crowan, Cornwall - England's most Celtic county and only lately a land where the rule of English law had fully penetrated. Many remote parishes still spoke only Cornish, and the land's distance from London – not only geographically but

211

in culture also - illustrates that for parts of the kingdom such as Cornwall, the capital at the time might as well have been a foreign land.

The estate of Skewis had for a long time been the freehold patrimony of a succession of proprietors by the name of Rogers. About this time there were two brothers, the elder of which was married but without children, who lived at the estate's farm, Skewis House. When he died, Skewis House was left to his widow – much to the annoyance of the younger brother, Henry, who was also married but *did* have children. Henry was by trade a pewterer in Helston; he was not a particularly violent man, but nonetheless one of great bodily strength who had difficulty in restraining his passions sometimes. Henry's opinion on the matter, which was generally prevalent in the area, was that freehold lands should descend through heirs, and this ought not to be subverted without the concurrence of the next heir. To this end, when Henry's sister-in-law Anne Rogers (whose maiden name was Millett) acquired Skewis, it inflamed his anger, and – despising legal assistance – he decided to take matters into his own hands.

Waiting until his sister-in-law was away from the property, Henry Rogers arrived at the farm and turned the servants out, taking forcible possession of the house. She in turn appealed to the law, and although the voice of the whole county was against her, including the local dignitary Sir John St Aubyn, Rogers felt the need to fortify his position and prepare for violence.

The law, in response to his greatest fears, sided with his sister-in-law. Henry Rogers refused to budge from Skewis, and consequently on 8 June 1734 the under-sheriff received a writ directing him to eject Rogers by force and deliver the property over to Anne Rogers.

By this time Henry had fully barricaded himself inside Skewis House, along with a number of friends and supporters who had agreed to stay with him and resist the authorities. When the date of eviction came on 18 June 1734, great numbers of curious spectators turned up (some two to three hundred people in fact), and in scenes of rowdy confusion the civil power was completely resisted. From within, Rogers was defiant and yelled that even if the King and Lord Chancellor came he would never deliver Skewis House over alive. Several guns were fired into the property, but without apparent effect.

On the following day the under-sheriff returned to the scene assisted by some soldiers led by Captain Sadler. From within, Rogers was heard to exclaim, 'Damn you, are you come again?' A gun was poked out through a hole cut in the house door, and a blast from inside felled a besieger called Carpenter, fatally wounding him in the back, while a second shot fired from elsewhere wounded Carpenter's servant, a man called Hatch. A surgeon who dressed Carpenter's wound before he died found that he had been shot from about the fourth rib to the buttock, lethally wounded by many slugs and jagged pieces of lead. From the later trial records, it appears that others were wounded among the besiegers, and the testimony of one Mr Black speaks of 'Carpenter *and* a soldier killed'.

This second fatality on the 19th June was an elderly soldier named Woolston; he died within an hour after a weapon was discharged from a window at him. At least three guns were being fired from the property, and Woolston's wound extended from his groin to his ankle. A volley of musket fire was poured back at the property by the soldiery – but again without apparent effect.

It is a sign of the times that, strange as it may seem, Rogers was allowed to remain unmolested until March 1735, when the siege of Skewis recommenced. (There is some suggestion that the whole affair was held up in legal complexities, and also that Rogers might have absconded; perhaps the siege commenced upon his return.) On 16 March a constable called Andrew 'Tubby' Willis was the luckless fellow ordered to take Rogers for the previous killings: Willis was felled by a gunshot fired from a window of Skewis House. Rogers was afterwards observed to leave the property and kneel over the slain constable, taking his weapon from him. There were at least two other armed people spotted within the premises, one of these being John Street, a servant of Rogers' who was also armed with a cutlass. Rogers, walking round the corpse backwards and forwards, shouted to those inside the house, 'Here lies the black bill!'

During the second assault on Skewis, some of Rogers' children were resident, and they became trapped inside the besieged house. Years later, Rogers' son Henry Jnr recalled the battle, telling local historian Davies Gilbert how he had seen his father cheat death when a shot that hit his thigh shattered a snuff box and powder horn in his pocket. He also recollected 'that while he himself was in bed, several (musket) balls came in through the window of the room, and after striking against the wall rolled about on the floor'. This child's brother and sister braved the threat by going outside to enquire what was wanted of their father and were swiftly gathered up and dragged away from the danger area.

At last it was ordered that cannon be brought from Pendennis Castle to the site of the battle, in order to threaten the defenders into submission. However, on the night following the commencement of the siege Rogers and the remaining others inside somehow managed to slip through the net and escape Skewis House. Rogers fled with his remaining son Henry –then aged about seven – and a maid. Amazingly they were stopped by two soldiers while crossing a field some distance from the house, but escaped suspicion by claiming they were an innocent party looking for a cow. After this Rogers left his son and the maid in a neighbouring farmhouse and set out to make his way *on foot* into Wiltshire, with the ultimate intention of making his grievance known to King George II.

Sir John St Aubyn now took the initiative, and became an active lead in attempting to secure the fugitive. He was, through marriage, connected to the Earls of Pembroke, who resided near Salisbury in Wiltshire, and in this capacity he secured their help in quickly distributing handbills dated 21 March 1734-5 around the county. These advertised the fugitive as wearing a drab fustian frock, with 'bastard peal buttons' and a blue riding coat, and offered £350 for his capture. Sir John expressed a great desire that 'Henry Rogers and his abettors' be brought to justice, lest they begin ravaging the countryside.

Henry Rogers' arrest came by the following circumstances. A post boy driving a chaise was stopped by a stout man with a gun in his hand who requested a ride; and so the post boy drove him to an inn, where the armed passenger secured a bed. The man's general description excited much suspicion that he might be Rogers, and so the inn was raided, with the fugitive being taken uneventfully in his sleep. He was at once returned to Cornwall to face the consequences of his actions.

At the assizes held at Launceston, Cornwall, Henry Rogers' trial opened on 1 August 1735. Also before the Justices was John Street, his chief assistant in the defence of Skewis: both men faced numerous charges, including the murders of William Carpenter, George Woolston (*alias* Wilson) and Andrew Willis (*alias* Tubby). Many present during the siege testified that the soldiers had not fired upon the house until they themselves had been shot at, and described the gruesome fatal injuries suffered by the wounded and dying.

(Some of this written testimony is somewhat clipped in the manner it was recorded and confusing in its chronology, but typically evidencing the chaos is the account of the under-sheriff, Stephen Tillie, whose testimony read thus: 'Mr Tillie gives the same account that he did before. Second day after Carpenter was shot, Henry Rogers came to the window with his gun on the east side, fired, and a shot went through his hat, and a soldier wounded. He ordered the soldiers to fire. Woolston was on the west side, and was shot there. No gun was fired by the soldiers, or any person in the assistance of the sheriff, nor a sword drawn, nor any force, till after Carpenter was shot and Hatch wounded, and Jeffries shot through the leg. Woolston declared that Rogers had shot him, on his asking him. Died in about half an hour after. Soldiers went to the assistance of him; ordered them to use no force till resistance.')

Both the defendants were found guilty of two murders, and - it being felt there was no need to proceed further with any of the other charges - Rogers and Street were sentenced to death. After their convictions both appeared to be very penitent, particularly Rogers himself, who refused any sustenance but bread and water. Rogers admitted he was guilty of one of the killings (that of Woolston), but denied any knowledge of the others; he also admitted, as well, that had it been within his power he would have killed as many of the besiegers as had been possible, and believed that fundamentally he was guilty of no crime. Street, Rogers' servant, had little to say; but what he did defended his master's actions. He also stated he was ready to die, because by the course of nature he was not long for this world anyhow, and he hoped God would receive his poor soul. An account of the end of the trial was reported in the *Gentleman's Magazine* at the time, for the benefit of readers largely based in the capital who no doubt completely failed to understand or empathise with the dynamics of the drama that had played out in the rural South West; perhaps for them it may as well have happened in Ireland, France, or Italy.

Henry Rogers after his capture. (This illustration first appeared in James Caulfield's Portraits, Memoirs & Characters of Remarkable Persons Volume 3-4*, 1820.)*

Rogers and Street were executed on 6 August 1735 at St Stephens by Launceston. In all, it seems certain that three people – Carpenter, Woolston and Willis - were killed throughout the besieging of Skewis House, with a further two or three possibly suffering fatal injuries. There were also numerous wounded; although there appears to be some little discrepancy between the events as reported in Davies Gilbert's *The Parochial History Of Cornwall* (1838) and the trial accounts he collected. Gilbert names elsewhere another victim, this one a civilian: 'A little later he (Rogers) shot one Hitchens, as he was passing the high road on his private business.' There is also mention of a man named Toby ('Tubby' Willis?) lying dead in front of Skewis for several days after being shot. The dismissal of certain charges after Rogers and Street's guilt had been proved early on means that some details are a little open to interpretation.

Gilbert wrote: 'On the 8th of January, 1816, I called at Skewis, and saw several holes in the partitions, made by shot of different sizes, when Mr Henry Rogers resisted the law in 1735.' Later that century, in 1867, local historian Joseph Polsue wrote of this remarkable event: 'Although no one attempted to justify the violence, and especially the murders committed by Rogers... long after the occurrence a strong feeling of compassion was entertained for him. The marks of the bullets are still to be seen in the house at Skewis; and there is a popular notion in the neighbourhood that none of the subsequent proprietors have prospered in its possession. The property is still in the family of Millett.'

'DRAGG'D HIS GUTS ABOUT THE HIGHWAY...'

On 10 September 1735 there stood before the new Recorder in Bristol one Captain James Newth, accused of murdering his wife. It was proved before Mr Michael Foster, Esq, that Newth and his wife had fallen into a violent argument at their house, she yelling at him, 'You dog, what, will you see murder committed in your own house?' Newth then knocked her down with a cribbage board, and when she screamed, 'Murder!' Newth replied, 'If you want a murder, I will give you a murder!' He then stamped on her two or three times, after which she never spoke. Newth was convicted of wilful murder and sentenced to death.

On 12 September, Newth, 'after taking leave of his children', took a large quantity of white arsenic and died in convulsive agony. It was discovered he had left a suicide note, in which he challenged the world to find him blameworthy; he also stated his wife gave the first provocation, insinuating she held a 'criminal conversation' with another man. However, despite his pretended innocence, it was not the first time Newth had faced serious charges. He had formerly stood trial for piracy and murdering his cabin boy in 1729, and was suspected of having killed three of his mariners.

The people of Bristol were so outraged at this criminal having cheated justice yet again that they assembled at the crossroads near the city where his corpse had been buried, and proceeded to dig it up. According to the *Gentleman's Magazine*, they then 'dragg'd his guts about the highway, poked his eyes out, and broke almost all his bones'.

In this instance, it is not necessarily the crime itself that stands out as remarkable, more the grim aftermath: for it is a stark example of the 'legitimacy' of the carnival atmosphere that so often accompanied the death of a felon in big cities.

'PRESS'D TO DEATH'

The *Gentleman's Magazine* in 1735 observes that during George II's reign one could not consider oneself safe in their own home: 'Street robbers and housebreakers abound, and are very barbarous. Mr Ryan, of Covent Garden Theatre, had two of his teeth shot out, and Mr Gisbon, a baker, of Islington, was almost killed and his house robbed.'

An atrocious instance of housebreaking is listed in the periodical. None of the participants are named, but the case concerned a mother who arrived home in May 1735 to find her house near Petworth, West Sussex, ransacked and her daughter slain at the property.

The mother was a widow, and was entertaining her daughter, who had 'just come from service sick'. That morning both had gone to visit a neighbour, but the daughter returned by herself some time later. It appeared from the evidence that she had opened her door and disturbed someone within, who had punched her to the floor and then cut her throat in a shocking manner. She had also suffered multiple stab wounds, including injuries to her hands that suggested she had tried to defend herself. A few hours later the mother also returned and found her daughter dead and the house rifled.

Upon this horrific discovery, 'she rais'd the country' and 'this man' (the suspect) was taken on suspicion of the crime. Several spots of blood were found about his person, and goods taken from the house were in his possession. The suspect was carried before a Justice of the Peace and committed to Horsham Gaol.

The suspect professed to be both dumb and lame, and when he was brought to the bar at the assizes in Lewes, Sussex, on 4 August he could not be persuaded to speak or plead. However, four or five persons swore that they had heard him speak, and so his defence was disbelieved; he was carried back to Horsham Gaol and 'gradually press'd to death', continuing 'obstinately dumb' until he expired.

There were suspicions he had committed the killing with a 'man and a woman not yet taken'. However, when these were apprehended and brought before the Justices of the Peace, they were found to be innocent of any involvement. As an additional point of interest, this is a rare incident of such a medieval form of punishment *allegedly* being used on a murder suspect in the Georgian era.

Horsham's Gaol stood in East Street. This was where a murder suspect was reportedly crushed to death by gaolers trying to get him to talk. (Originally from H Dudley's History and Antiquities of Horsham, *1836).*

Horsham Assizes had tried another case like this the previous year, also born out of criminal greed. This crime was - if anything - even worse. Richard Miles had kept a little alehouse near Ditchling Common, northwest of Lewes, and for the past two nights the family had entertained a guest at the house, whose name (as reported) was 'James, alias Jacob Hirsh, alias Harris, alias Davies'. At about nine o'clock on the evening of 2 June 1734 Davies had ambushed Miles in the stable while the publican groomed his guest's horse, cutting his throat from ear to ear with a hook-knife. He had then proceeded to slaughter Mrs Miles – who at that time lay in bed sick – and stab the family maidservant. Despite her injuries, the serving girl managed to flee the house, but fell over a nearby stile and was subsequently found dead in a ditch. Mr Miles did not die immediately, but lived long enough to describe his attacker: a known smuggler he knew as 'James' – who was a well-dressed chap with his own hair (rather than a periwig) and a powerful grey mare.

Davies is said to have been 'a Jew pedlar by trade'. It appears he was run to ground very soon afterwards at a place called Turner's Hill, his capturers being one John Oliver and his servant. He was afterwards committed to Horsham gaol.

Following his apprehension and conviction at Horsham Assizes, Davies was sentenced to be hung in chains on the common facing the house where he had perpetrated the massacre; the *British Observator* noted grimly: 'We hear that Jack Ketch (i.e. the hangman) has received orders to go into that county to perform the execution…'

Davies was executed on Saturday 24 August 1734, his body suspended from a gibbet post and left to rot on the common near the now-empty alehouse. It was recorded that as late as 1866 five or six feet of the gibbet post still remained on the Common, where it was referred to as 'Jacob's Post'.

SHROPSHIRE'S SERIAL MURDER

In the spring of 1735 an affair came to light which seems to suggest serial murder for profit along the English-Welsh border, although by any standards the reporting of the event in various news-sheets is somewhat confused.

A 'Scotch pedlar' had lately been robbed and murdered near Ludlow Castle in Shropshire. Not long after, a 'Welchwoman' was caught selling silk handkerchiefs in Worcester at six shillings a dozen, as well as 'hollands, cambricks, and other goods'. It appears that the cheap price she offered for these wares (the handkerchiefs should have gone for thirty shillings) drew attention to her, and on a Sunday night she was committed to the House of Correction in Worcester while further enquiries were made. This woman's name was Margaret Jones.

Ludlow Castle, from Thomas Wright's 1836 History and Antiquities of the Town of Ludlow.

A messenger was dispatched across the Welsh border into Montgomeryshire, presumably to arrange for the woman's husband to be taken in for questioning. When the messenger returned to Worcester he brought the news that Sir John Price of Newtown had committed the woman's husband, Evan Hugh Jones, to Welshpool Gaol on 28 March 1735. Jones' two sons were also incarcerated, and

Sir John had apparently elicited a very quick confession from Jones to the murder of the pedlar, a man named John Ree. Furthermore, Jones also confessed to murdering *another* Scottish pedlar - one John Burkley - several months earlier.

All four members of the Jones family came to be tried at 'the Assizes held at Pool for Montgomeryshire' on 5 July 1735, and all of them were capitally convicted. Jones was sentenced to be suspended in chains after being hanged. However, the circumstances as reported in the various periodicals of the time are not very clear in their detail; the *Gentleman's Magazine*, for instance, implies that the family killed *three* Scottish pedlars – Ree and Burkley in December 1734, and a third unnamed victim in March 1735. All the victims were robbed, and the implication is that the murderers were perhaps innkeepers or hostel owners who preyed on itinerant travellers in the assumption they would not be missed; but there is precious little information to be gleaned from the news reports other than this.

COMPOUNDING ONE'S GUILT

It seems a futile attempt to escape by a prisoner being conveyed to Warwick on a charge of horse-stealing resulted in a fatality; for we learn that on 5 August 1735 John Amus was sentenced to death at Warwick Assizes for killing Dodd, 'the turnkey of Oxford gaol', who was conducting him during his journey.

Amus was at the time of the murder being conveyed from Oxford to Warwick, where he was to be tried for horse theft. The turnkey was in the coach or chariot, guarding Amus with a brace of pistols. They were also accompanied by another horseman, who rode beside them and was also armed with pistols. During the journey they called at an alehouse, and Dodd – drinking too freely – fell asleep once the journey commenced. Somewhere near Lord Willoughby's seat at Compton Verney near Kineton, the prisoner managed to pick the weapons out of his sleeping guard's coat; he then woke the man and asked to be let out of the coach to answer the call of nature.

Amus immediately drew his pilfered pistols, and told the turnkey and the coachman they were dead men if they did not give him some money and remove his chains. Dodd refused to help him, and so Amus simply fired a pistol into his breast, killing him on the spot. Amus then pointed the pistol at the coachman – who immediately ran off, along with the second horseman who had been accompanying them.

These two raised the whole county and an extensive search was made for the fugitive, who was found the following morning in a wood, or thicket. Amus' failed escape indicates the measures people would go to: for horse-theft was a serious crime, and an additional murder made little difference once the wheels of justice were set in motion.

'ALL THOSE WHO DARE AVENGE INNOCENT BLOOD, LET THEM COME HERE...'

The story of Captain John Porteous charts a cycle of death so extraordinary that the infamy of the event was destined to last for centuries, particularly so in Edinburgh where the grim saga was played out.

Porteous was himself a native of the area, born near Edinburgh. He started off life as a tailor's apprentice, his marriage being facilitated by a dowry of five hundred pounds presented by a former lover of the woman who discreetly and painlessly wished to be rid of her. This gentleman had been Lord Provost of the city, and so when a vacancy appeared for the position of captain in a local regiment of peacekeepers he nominated Porteous. This was largely on account of Porteous' obvious disinterest in his work as a tradesman, and his wife's desperation to ensure that they did not succumb to poverty: she thereupon applied to her old paramour the Lord Provost to see if he could arrange John Porteous' move into the world of soldiery. Thus through nepotism rather than achievement did Porteous become captain of one of three companies of men employed to keep the peace in Edinburgh, with 25 soldiers under his command, a scarlet uniform and an annual income of eighty pounds.

If we are to believe the *Newgate Calendar*, Captain Porteous very quickly forgot his civility: for his new found power quickly brought out a different, rougher and more brutal side to his personality. Although his remit was to ensure the arrest of offenders and keep them in custody till a magistrate could examine them, this he often did with much violence and harshness.

An incident in Edinburgh - remarkable in itself - earned him the undying hatred of sections of the mob. It so happened that two young men were competing for a vacancy in the lectureship of a church near Edinburgh, and – both having an equal number of votes – the matter was referred to the Presbytery. Though the Presbytery preferred Mr Dawson, the other candidate, named Wotherspoon, had this judgement overturned by the synod, and on the day he was due to take his place at the pulpit and preach his first sermon a great tumult was occasioned inside and outside the church. His rival, Dawson, had gotten there first: and, the soldiery being called, Porteous simply marched up the steps and dragged him down from the pulpit. This started a violent melee in which Dawson – although the mob's choice - unfortunately suffered so many injuries that he died a few weeks later. Such was the confusion that Wotherspoon fared little better; coming in as Porteous mistreated Dawson, Wotherspoon was set upon by the mob and beaten so badly that he also died a few weeks later, around the same time as his competitor. Many in the crowd had also been seriously injured by Porteous' soldiers, who were in danger of running amok during the incident. Despite this, the captain was not disciplined. It seems that

221

Porteous actually enjoyed being in the middle of a furious, rioting mob, in which he was allowed to dispense violence freely under the guise of keeping the peace.

Scotland, like the rest of the British Isles, suffered greatly from organized smuggling, and the downfall of Porteous was set into motion by an event quite outside his sphere of influence. It so happened that an active revenue officer from Fife, named Stark, had raided the house of a smuggler called Andrew Wilson and confiscated goods that he suspected had been smuggled from France. Wilson, in response, had enlisted the help of a man named Robertson, as well as some others, who had marched on the customs house. Here, they had broken the door down and loaded Wilson's goods onto a cart in open defiance of the law. When Stark discovered this, he raised such a furore that the Sheriff of Fife ordered the culprits to be hunted down and punished. Accordingly, many were apprehended: most were acquitted, but Wilson and Robertson were convicted and sentenced to death.

On the Sunday 11 April 1736, before the pair were due to be hanged, Robertson managed to effect an escape as they were being taken to Tolbooth Kirk to hear their last sermon; Andrew Wilson, though handcuffed, managed to bite one of the soldiers escorting them, and also manhandle two others, while Robertson vanished into the crowd of Sunday worshippers in the confusion. The magistrates ordered Porteous and his company to search out the offender, but luckily Robertson – with the aide of friends – managed to break off his handcuffs and flee to Dunbar, where he boarded a ship to Holland. (He was still recorded as living 20 years later, as a publican in Rotterdam in 1756.)

In many respects, smugglers in Scotland were considered more worthy than their English counterparts; rather than criminal greed, their actions were brought about by an unwillingness to pay such duties as would support the government, and as Porteous ranged about Edinburgh looking for the escapee he knocked down many inhabitants merely for expressing this sentiment.

The mood was ugly when, the following Wednesday (14 April), Wilson was accompanied by Captain Porteous and fifty men under his command to a temporary gallows erected in the city's Grass-market. Porteous, anxious that an attempt would be made to liberate Wilson, persuaded the Lord Provost to enlist five companies of Welsh Fusiliers, commanded by a major, who took up position in the Lawn-market near the place of execution.

The stage was set for an almighty conflict. Initially, no tumult arose, and the crowds watched Wilson bravely ascend the ladder, where he breathed his last. After the corpse had been dangling for some time, the executioner took up position to cut Wilson's body down, at which point a stone hurled from the crowd hit him in the head and made his nose bleed. Almost immediately a hail of stones flew through the air as the mob showed their disapproval: Porteous, without a moment's thought, ordered his men to, 'Fire, and be damned!'

The captain himself drew first blood, discharging his piece at a confectioner's apprentice and killing him on the spot. Many of the soldiery chose to obey their orders by firing their muskets over the mob's head, but unfortunately this killed two or three persons who were looking out their upper windows at the drama being played out. Others among the soldiers, however, fired directly into the crowd, causing many serious injuries that later resulted in amputations. The crowd were by this time infuriated, and missiles of all types were being hurled at Porteous and his men, who began to withdraw – but not before another barrage of musket fire had killed a further three people in the mob. In all, Porteous' actions had accounted for nine dead and numerous critical injuries following Wilson's execution.

There next followed bizarre scenes, whereby the Welsh Fusiliers stationed in the Lawn-market were forced to accompany Porteous and his men to the guard-house for their own protection. Porteous was summoned by the Lord Provost, and after a long examination he was committed to gaol on charges of murder.

On 6 July 1736 Captain Porteous faced the Lords of the Judiciary, previously having made a confession to the massacre but pleading self-defence. His counsel then stated the following point of law, to be determined by the judges: 'Whether a military officer, with soldiers under his command, who, being assaulted by the populace, should fire, or order his men to fire, was not acting consistently with the nature of defence, according to the laws of civilised nations.' The counsel for the prosecution responded with the counter-argument: 'That if it was proved that Captain Porteous either fired a gun, or caused one or more to be fired, by which any person or persons was or were killed, and if the said firing happened without orders from a magistrate properly authorized, then it would be murder in the eye of the law.' The jury was empanelled, and forty-four witnesses – both for and against the captain – were presented before the court. For his part, John Porteous' counsel laid the ultimate blame higher up: the magistrates, in ordering Porteous to ensure Wilson was not rescued, had by implication ordered him to repel any display of force with equal force; and that powder and ball had been allocated to Porteous and his men validated this fact. Furthermore, Porteous averred that the situation under his command was chaotic, and he had only meant to intimidate the mob. He had even knocked a piece out of one of his own men's hands (he claimed), but found that he could not control them and bursts of fire boomed from their numbers despite his orders. Porteous had himself been outraged, and ordered that no weapon be cleaned so that an investigation would confirm who had fired. And he declared he had not fled Edinburgh in the aftermath of the slaughter – although he had ample opportunity to do so successfully, had he possessed a guilty conscience.

The arguments over the legitimacy of excessive force raged for quite some time. The prosecution stated correctly that Porteous's men had been deployed to prevent a rescue, and that after the successful execution of Andrew Wilson their mission was over, and the issuing of powder and ball an invalid moot point. Furthermore, only the reading of the Riot Act could legitimise lethal force, and it was argued the magistrates, whose duty it was to make this proclamation, had been conspicuously absent: in fact, they had hidden in a house during the clashes. The repeated argument in Porteous' defence was that he and his men were defending themselves with weapons lawfully placed in their hands.

The jury (after some considerable time) convicted the captain of murder. This is likely to have occurred for a number of basic reasons. Firstly, the attempt by the defence to pass the buck higher up meant that, in the eyes of the powers-that-be, Porteous would have to carry the guilt solely, to reinforce their blamelessness. Secondly, an outright acquittal would, in all probability, have caused more serious rioting and further casualties. Thirdly, although there is no way of proving it, it is possible that some in the judiciary believed that Porteous and his men were dangerously out of control, sections of the Edinburgh soldiery having fallen into degenerate methods based on Porteous' own example. Thus the captain had brought about his own downfall and forced himself to be made an example of... although in an era when lethal force was commonly used to suppress rioting this last is debateable.

At any rate, the case roused national controversy. Even the king (at that time in Hanover) took a great interest in the proceedings. Porteous had many supporters in the military and at higher levels of society, and Queen Caroline, on the advice of her counsel, granted Porteous a temporary reprieve until the king could return to Britain and consider his opinion on the matter. This respite roused the anger of the people of Edinburgh; their response was perhaps unique in the annals of crime, and in many ways awesome in its defiance of authority.

Their reaction might have been spontaneous, upon word spreading like wildfire of the queen's proclamation. On 7 September 1736, a huge body of men entered Edinburgh between nine and ten in the evening and seized the arms belonging to the guard. Groups of people then fanned out into the streets, crying out: 'All those who dare avenge innocent blood, let them come here!' In the meantime they shut the city gates and placed guards there. The main body of the mob marched to the prison, where, disguised and armed, they first took hammers to the door and then set it alight. When it was weakened enough, they broke it down and forced the jailer to take them inside, yelling at him, 'Where is the villain Porteous?' Porteous replied, 'Here I am; what do you want with me?' The masked men coldly answered that they meant to string him up in the Grass-market, scene of his crime against the town. Despite his protestations, Porteous was seized by the arms and legs and carried out of the prison to the site. On their arrival the mob broke into a nearby shop and procured a strong rope, which they fixed round Porteous' neck, throwing the other end over a dyer's pole. They then hoisted him into the air.

Captain Porteous is lynched by the mob in Edinburgh. (From Annals of Crime & New Newgate Calendar No.36*, 1833.)*

Porteous' last moments alive were engaged in trying to fix his hands between the halter and his neck to relieve the pressure. Observing this, someone in the crowd struck him violently with an axe, putting an end to his struggling. After the captain's death throes had subsided into stillness, the crowd gradually dispersed, injuring no more persons and themselves leaving unmolested by the local authorities. The captain's body hung from the pole throughout the night, finally being taken down about seven o'clock the following morning.

Afterwards a royal proclamation was issued, offering a large reward for the apprehension of the murderers. No one came forward; in fact, the closest thing to a reaction by the authorities was to arrest the magistrates of Edinburgh, who were summoned to answer for not quelling the disturbance. They were fined, and relieved of any position of responsibility in the judiciary. Although grenadier companies were quartered in the town and its suburbs, the trouble did not resurrect itself.

Thereafter an arrest *was* made, of one William Maclauchlane, a servant of the Countess of Wemyss, although he was not accused of murder: the charge sought against him was that he was one of a number of armed men standing guard near Beth's Wynd. The trial was something of a farcical exercise, Maclauchlane apparently being a tipsy drunkard in the wrong place at the wrong time, but the court nonetheless heard a number of first-hand accounts from alleged witnesses and non-participants in the lynching. These - whether fabrication or not - presented a disturbing picture of the events that occurred on the night of 7 September.

George Wilson, a workman in Edinburgh, stated that he had arrived at about 11 o' clock at night at the Tolbooth, and observed some in the mob set fire to the door by lighting a pile of faggots. He waited till he saw the captain brought up the Lawn-market, whence the crowd came to Stewart's signpost near the Bowhead, over which some of them proposed to hang Porteous. This was decided against, but it was clear the intention was to kill him – it was just a matter of where. Wilson contrived to get as near to Porteous as he could and heard it proposed that they should hang him over the Weigh-house stair. At this point Wilson was recognised as an intruder and punched to the ground, and then trampled on by the crowd as they made their way to the dyer's tree. Porteous was being dragged by this time, struggling to present his purse to a wealthy citizen who stood nearby in the hope that it might be passed to his brother. Wilson observed the noose placed about Porteous' neck, but the victim was not hoisted off the ground till a rumour swept through the crowd that the regular military were approaching the Grassmarket via the Canongate. Twice Porteous was hoisted up, and twice set back down again. The first time, the rope was not right about his neck, the second time he was observed to have his shirt pulled up over his face. Some in the crowd struck him in the head with their 'Lochaber-axes' and shouted that Porteous' ears should be cut off. When they were satisfied he was lifeless, having struck him more times as he scrabbled at the rope, they nailed the end of the rope to the pole, threw their stolen weapons away and rapidly dispersed.

Another depiction of the captain's murder. This first appeared in Knapp and Baldwin's Newgate Calendar Volume 1 *(1824).*

Porteous was buried in Greyfriars Kirkyard. These events lived long in the memories of Edinburgh folk, and during the following century family memories of the events, passed down through successive generations, purported to shed some light on who the ringleaders of Porteous' murder might have been. Apparently, 'men moving in the higher ranks of society' were heavily involved, with Lord Alva telling the writer Sir Daniel Wilson that his own great-grandfather had averred that 'Lord Haddington' had taken a direct role in Porteous' death, while disguised in his own cook-maid's dress. Wilson drew a line under such speculation, however, when he observed: 'There is little reason to anticipate the mystery in which this deed of popular justice is involved, will ever be further cleared up, now that considerably more than a century has elapsed since its occurrence.'

Porteous's gravestone in Greyfriars declares: *All passion spent.*

MURDER AT THE ROADSIDE INN

In the year 1736 Mr Hayes, a gentleman of some wealth, put up at an inn in the county of Oxfordshire, on the Oxford to London road. He was accompanied by a footman. That evening before bed Hayes supped with two gentlemen, also visitors to the hostelry, and unguardedly mentioned that he was carrying a large sum of money. In time the three retired to their respective chambers. The other gentlemen were sharing a two-bedded room, and as the night progressed one heard an awful groaning death rattle that seemed to be coming from the adjoining chamber, where Mr Hayes had retired. Waking his slumbering companion, the two gentlemen stealthily and quietly made their way into Hayes' chambers to see if he was alright.

To their horror, the gloom was lit by a dark lantern, held by a man who in his other hand clutched a bloodied knife. This sinister figure stood over the bed, upon which the two terror-struck witnesses perceived the prone and silent body of Hayes, drenched in blood. It was clear what had happened, and in the shock of the moment the knife-wielding criminal stared at the two men who had discovered his endeavour, before they - recovering their senses - rushed in and overpowered him.

The criminal proved to be the inn's proprietor, Jonathan Bradford, but by now he had recovered his composure. Bradford claimed that he had entered the victim's chambers with the same humane intention as the two gentlemen, to enquire why Hayes appeared to be sick. He had found Hayes already slain, he protested.

The following morning Bradford was taken before a neighbouring Justice of the Peace, who was so immediately convinced of the man's guilt that he commented, 'Mr Bradford, either you or myself committed this murder.'

The whole of Oxfordshire was abuzz with this crime, and when Bradford when on trial at the assizes at Oxford, it seemed ridiculous for him to deny his guilt. He tried anyhow: he had heard a noise, and enquired as to its cause; finding villainy had occurred, he immediately grabbed the nearest thing at hand to defend himself, which happened to be – much to his later chagrin – the actual murder weapon itself, left at the scene by the *real* killer.

A view of old Oxford, from T. Joy's Oxford Delineated *in 1831.*

The jury brought in a guilty verdict without ever having left the box, so clear was Bradford's guilt. Still protesting his innocence, he went to the gallows, disbelieved by all.

But – remarkably – Bradford's story had been in part true, and he was not guilty of the killing. Eighteen months later a remarkable deathbed confession by Mr Hayes' dying footman revealed that he, and not Hayes, had been the murderer. The footman confessed that he had fatally stabbed his master on the bed and then rifled his breeches for his money, gold watch and snuffbox, and then escaped to his own room seconds before Bradford himself entered. The footman died on his sickbed, having been responsible for two deaths: that of the man he murdered, and the man he let hang for it.

But as if this wasn't strange enough, Bradford himself was not entirely guiltless. Although innocent of murder, he had still had murder on his mind when he entered Hayes' chambers. Armed with a knife, and having heard Hayes talking earlier about the money he carried (as had the footman), Bradford had snuck into the man's room prepared to kill and rob him. What a surprise it must have been for him to discover that someone had already done the bloody deed: in his shock, Bradford had dropped his weapon on the bloodied corpse and in grabbing it again smeared blood all over his hand and the knife itself. This much he confessed to the clergyman who attended him after his service.

The case is a curious one indeed, and it is difficult to track down evidence of its reality prior to the very early 1800s. Suffice to say that it bears a moral (thieves never prosper) - and the sad detail that, any way one looks at it, Mr Hayes was a dead man from the minute he stopped off at the roadside inn.

ENGLAND'S WORST GRANDPARENTS

Some of the news-sheets reported a callous crime, the details of which almost beggar belief – for it concerned an aged grandfather's killing of his own grandson.

The 'old fellow' in question was Michael Morey, or Moorey, an ancient woodsman who lived on St George's Down, east of Newport on the Isle of Wight. Morey had raised his grandson, James Dew (or Dove), from an infant, but in June 1736 the boy – now aged about 14 years old – somehow or other offended Morey. At about six o'clock one morning Morey left the house with the boy on the pretence of their travelling to a market town about seven miles distant. However, he in fact took young James off the road and into woodland near Arreton – where he struck the boy on the skull with the back of a bill-hook.

Morey did not return home for a week, and when he did his grandson's absence was of course immediately noticed and commented upon. Morey did not have the intelligence to provide a satisfactory explanation for James's disappearance, and so was arrested upon suspicion; a search of Morey's property turned up a bloodied shirt (wrapped up in a clean one) inside a chest. Upon this suggestive discovery, Morey was committed for trial at the summer assizes.

The boy's body, however, remained missing, and this accounted for a delay in Morey's trial. No account of coercing could get him to admit any knowledge of what had become of his grandson, and it was only when the boy's remains were found in October 1736 that there came the necessary breakthrough.

The boy's remains were found in two 'wallets' (leather sacks) deep in the woodland. It appeared that Morey, after striking him with the bill-hook, had decapitated the poor lad, and 'mangled' the body; there appeared to have been an abortive attempt to set the body ablaze, and on the whole the remains were so decomposed that it was only possible to identify James Dew by his hat, shoes, breeches and stockings, which people had seen him wearing when he left his house with his grandfather. Incriminatingly, Michael Morey's gloves were also found at the scene together with the bloodied bill-hook.

The old man was tried for the boy's murder at Winchester Assizes the following year. He steadfastly refused to acknowledge any level of guilt in the boy's disappearance and murder, but the weight of circumstance was heavily against him. It was suggested that the motive might have been Morey's belief that his grandson was due to inherit some money: but if this was the case then the old man's belief that he could simply kill the lad and inherit the money in his place speaks to a stupidity almost as unbelievable as his monstrous crime. It is also unclear whether the victim's grandmother, Elizabeth, had any knowledge of the plot to get rid of him.

Morey was hanged on Saturday 19 March 1737 at Winchester, Hampshire, but afterwards his body was brought back to the Isle of Wight and gibbeted on a Bronze Age round barrow on Arreton Down. This spot now goes by the name of Gallows Hill, and the grassy Bronze Age relic upon which the gibbet post stood is now known as Michael Morey's Hump.

It is sometimes said that Morey tried to set James Dew's corpse on fire after bringing it back to his cottage, and in doing so torched the building down; this accounts for both a road and a farm in the vicinity known as 'Burnt House'. But if this is true, then Morey could not have consumed the body very thoroughly in the flames, since the clothing remained intact enough for the remains to be identified. As a further reminder of this grim case, the Hare and Hounds pub at the end of Downend Road contains (what is said) to be part of the gibbet post visible in its structure. It was also claimed until fairly recently that Michael Morey's skull resided within the pub, although this has lately been found to be a mistaken belief; the skull on show predates the 1736 murder considerably.

'THE DEVIL IS COME!'

On 16 May 1737 a truly horrific murder was committed at Ashcombe, near Chudleigh in Devon.

Of late a 30-year-old thatcher named John Collins had been showing increasing signs of a disordered mind; but the day in question found him going to his employer's house as normal. In Colway Lane, 'which parts the two Halldowns' (possibly Colley Lane is meant) Collins met his employer, Mr John Ball of Dawlish, in the road. Ball observed that Collins appeared highly agitated, both looking and sounding wild; when he asked the young man what ailed him, Collins replied he was troubled in his mind and could get no rest.

At this point three fisherwomen rode past. The first two greeted Collins with the words, 'How do you do, gaffer Collins?' However, the third – a young woman from Alphington called Jane Upcot - ignored him completely, and this seems to have been the trigger for what followed. Collins wielded a spar-hook, with which he struck Jane Upcot and knocked her from her horse. Mr Ball rushed to protect the woman and was dashed on the arm and forehead by

Collins; it was only by chance that the second wound did not kill him, Ball being hit with the *back* of the hook and not the fore part. Despite his injuries Ball managed to wrestle Collins to the ground long enough for Jane to remount her horse and ride after her companions.

Ball was somewhat hampered by his injuries, as well as a chronic gout complaint, and he couldn't hold Collins on the ground forever. Therefore he set him free upon the madman promising to leave the women alone, and go after his horse – which had been scared off during the scuffle.

Once liberated, Collins simply started off after Jane Upcot, speedily catching up with her and again knocking her from her horse. He then attacked her like a wild animal, hacking her head off and continually striking the decapitated head until it was dashed to pieces in the lane. He next opened her body up, from breast to navel, extracting her heart and sticking it on the end of his spar-hook. Collins then proceeded to march around Haldon with his trophy, being seen by numerous people who thought he carried a pig's heart.

Later that day two yeomen named Lakeman and Mole heard a dreadful wailing coming from the porch of St Nectan's Church in Ashcombe. This proved to be Collins, who was yelling, 'The Devil is come! The Devil is come!' When he saw the two men, he rushed at Mole to attack him, but Lakeman knocked him off his feet and the pair secured him. Collins screamed, 'I have done the thing, by God!' and when asked what he meant, he replied he had murdered a woman in Colway Lane and smashed her head to pieces. The two men properly secured their captive and hastened to the lane, where they found the ghastly evidence.

At 11 o'clock that night Collins was committed to gaol. Although he admitted the crime, there were, right from the offset, questions about his sanity; his wife stated that over the last year his mind appeared to have deteriorated, and he raved about the Devil frequently. In particular, Collins claimed he had lately stayed at his employer's house where he had been put to bed by a woman dressed in a man's clothing who he was positive had a cloven foot. The prisoner professed no previous grievance towards Ms Upcot, and ranted wildly to the Devil while in his cell; yet Collins' own father professed no knowledge of any instability in his son, and it seems this is the testimony that led Collins to the gallows rather than an asylum.

Collins was subsequently executed on 26 August. The *Newgate Calendar* (1824) implies that he and Ms Upcot had some sort of relationship, although the true motive for the crime is unclear; it also adds the detail that Collins 'left the horrid spectacle to the view of the passing traveller!!!'

231

The Devil's influence was still sometimes felt in murder cases. (This picture can be found in Clitheroe Castle Museum.)

MURDER IN THE TEMPLE

Within the chambers of the Temple in London, there resided 'up 3 pairs of stairs' a 70-year-old barrister called Mr Levinge. His chambermaid, Ursula Moore, lived with him.

In an adjacent chamber there lived a 33-year-old near-relative of the barrister, also called Levinge. A little before one at noon on 7 September 1737 Levinge Jnr went into the old gentleman's chamber and roughly seized Ms Moore, the maidservant. Levinge drew a razor across her throat with such force that he killed her immediately and almost separated the girl's head from her neck. He then turned his murderous rage upon his elderly relative, slicing him across the face, nose and throat with the razor and also severing the tendons of one of his victim's hands. However, the old man managed to escape into another chamber and thereby down some stairs, where he cried, 'Murder!' which brought a number of people running to his assistance.

Young Levinge's behaviour – already extraordinarily brutal – now grew even stranger. He slit open his own throat, but although severe the wound did not kill him. In this state, blood gushing down his neck and soaking his clothes, he got to

232

the window next to Hare Court, which he flung open. Levinge next threw out three notes, one for £400 and two for £25 each – all the time yelling to the people outside that he was being murdered for his money by the very people he had himself attacked.

Two porters dashed into the room and secured the madman; but Levinge managed to get one of his hands free, using it to literally tear out his own windpipe. He dropped down dead there and then in the room.

A Coroner's Inquest was held to try and solve the mystery of why Mr Levinge had committed such a horrific murder. According to the *Gentleman's Magazine*, he had for some time been disordered in his senses, and a laundress at the Temple explained that she had heard him wandering around in his chambers talking to himself and saying he was uneasy, and couldn't bear it; also that the bailiffs and Jesuits were coming for him. However, it appeared there might have been some kind of romantic connection between young Levinge and Ms Moore, for one of the documents he had thrown out the window was signed in her name and declared that she was not married to him.

A proper explanation not forthcoming to this mysterious and brutal affair, the coroner brought in a verdict of 'Wilful murder' upon Ursula Moore and one of *non compos mentis* (i.e. lunatic) upon Mr Levinge.

VICTIMS ON HOUNSLOW HEATH

What could George Price do when his wife threatened to expose him for poisoning the twins she had delivered at her lodgings in Hampstead? For him, the answer was simple: add her to the list of his victims. Price was at the time engaged as a servant, and his life was becoming increasingly complicated: Mrs Price suspected him of poisoning the two children under the guise of giving them a sleeping draught, and their relationship had become strained. Fearing for his finances, Price all but forced his wife to have an abortion when she fell pregnant yet again, and his marriage was also beginning to get in the way of a dalliance he entertained with a widow in Kent.

On 26 October 1737 it was reported that 'last Monday fortnight' Price (whose employer was Richard Coke, Esq, a merchant of New Broad Street, Broadgate, London) took his wife from the house on the pretence of visiting an uncle in Wandsworth; instead he took her to Hounslow Heath, at that time 4'000 acres of heath, scrub and woodland on the southern fringes of London. Here, Price made his wife strip and then stabbed her in the head and neck with a hanger, hacking with such violence that he almost decapitated her. He then threw the body into a ditch, where it was later discovered by a Life Guardsman airing his horse. Mrs Price's last words to her husband as he launched his attack were, 'My dear! My dear! If this is your love, I will never trust you more!' Price actually had the inhumanity to strip his wife's body of the rest of her clothes and mutilate her to such an extent that he hoped – mistakenly, as it turned out – she would not be identified. Worse, he left the corpse sprawled beneath a gibbet post upon which hung the chained bodies of executed malefactors.

In the shadow of a gibbet, Price callously murdered his wife. (From Annals of Crime & New Newgate Calendar No.12, *1833.)*

Price returned home, but his wife's absence - coupled with his unsatisfactory attempts at explanation - gave Coke's other servants cause for suspicion following his return to work. Upon their asking him if he had killed her, he immediately absconded. However, he was taken after the discovery of his wife's body and her subsequent burial in Twickenham, and his apprehension happened in the following manner.

Price had fled to Portsmouth, and as he supped ale in a public house he heard a bell-man loudly declaring that the hunt was on for him. This latter – a kind of cross between a town crier and news vendor – provided such an accurate description of Price that the murderer immediately betrayed himself by launching himself through an open window into the filthy water by the wharf and swimming for his life until he made the shore. He next fled to Oxfordshire, where he confessed his crime to his father and younger brother; however, his description was in all the newspapers, and when he next moved to Gloucester he found that a fellow-servant where he took employment had actually guessed who he was. At this, his conscience betrayed him, and - sick of running - he returned to London to surrender himself to justice.

On 18 January 1738 it was reported that he had been sentenced to death at the Old Bailey. However, Price fell severely ill while languishing in Newgate, and was found dead in his cell at the end of February before he could be executed.

These days it is difficult to appreciate just how big Hounslow Heath was. Once part of the Forest of Middlesex, it was for more than 200 years one of the most dangerous places in England. Between the 17th and early 19th centuries the Heath occupied perhaps 25 square miles. No-one was really sure where its boundaries lay, and no-one cared, for it was a tract of country to be crossed as quickly as possible. It supported (in Price's time) only a handful of tiny villages, such as Brentford, Isleworth and Teddington. Though Hounslow itself was not large, it was after London the most important of coaching centres: across the Heath ran the Bath Road and the Exeter Road, along which travelled wealthy visitors to the West Country and courtiers journeying to Windsor: all of whom provided rich pickings for highwaymen lurking in copses bordering the lonely ways. This was the melancholy region where Price chose to murder his poor wife, perhaps in hope that her slaying might be blamed on these very criminals. Typically, one periodical notes that the month after Mrs Price's body was discovered, 'A man was found murdered on Hounslow Heath, having his throat cut, and several marks of violence upon his person.'

EXTRACTS FROM THE 'EXPOSITION ON THE COMMON PRAYER'

Possibly the most depressing sign of the times was the cruelty meted out to children: some of the acts perpetrated upon the innocents were truly disturbing, all the more so for their frequency and casual detachment.

Laurence Clarke and Samuel Butler's contemporary journal entitled *Exposition on the Common Prayer* reported newsworthy events of the time, and the stories covered throughout the period between 3 August 1737 and 10 January 1739 give some indication of the level of appalling crimes that occurred against children. On 12 October 1737, for instance, Sarah Allen was capitally convicted at the Old Bailey of murdering her 'bastard child' by throwing it out of the window as soon as it was delivered. On 13 May 1738, Mary Lawrence (who lodged at Mr Keat's house in Milford Lane, near Temple Bar) slaughtered her six-week old baby girl by cutting its throat and tearing out its windpipe. She was committed to Newgate the next day by Justice Messer.

Later that year in November, news from Saffron Walden, Essex, explained that a young woman had recently been confined to gaol, having confessed to murdering her 'bastard child'. She had given birth in a barn, then cut the infant's throat and buried it in a pile of dung – where the body was uncovered by a hog snuffling around in the muck. On 21 January 1738 it was reported that Mrs Collins, a heavily-pregnant woman, had collected her 5-year-old daughter from her husband in Wells, Somerset, and taken the child to the moat surrounding the Bishop's Palace. Here, after waiting for members of the public to pass out of sight, she threw the little girl into the moat and left her to drown - even knocking the child's hand away when she scrabbled at her mother's handkerchief to save herself. After the little girl's body was dragged out of the water, a coroner gave a verdict of 'Wilful Murder'. There was no explanation suggested for the mother's behaviour.

Mrs Collins callously murdered her own 5-year-old in the shadow of Wells Cathedral.

The *Exposition*'s grim list contains many other incidents. On 21 September it was reported how a barmaid in nearby Bath had killed her newborn and shoved it under her bed, where it remained undiscovered for a week. On 25 September 1738 a newborn babe was found with its head, both legs and one hand chopped off, wrapped in a blanket in Hanover Yard on Oxford Road, London. Two nights later, a jury decided 'persons unknown' had killed the child. On 13 March 1738, 'John Manning was committed to Newgate by virtue of a warrant from Mr King, coroner of the County of Middlesex, for a rape and murder of an infant *two years old*.' (Manning was a shoemaker who lodged with a family by the name of Clay near East Smithfield. The parents, frequently going abroad, left little Eleanor in the care of Manning, who finally committed such a vile act of perversion on the infant that she died. The coroner's inquest, consisting of 24 persons, pronounced Manning guilty of murder without the least hesitation.)

The *Gentleman's Magazine* reported another case in September 1737: 'Two persons received sentence of death at Bristol, one of whom was a boy for the murder of a child about 20 months old, by throwing it into the tide.' However (and to return to the *Exposition*), even by these horrific standards, one crime stands out as particularly callous. On 27 July 1737 Margaret Wickers was tried at Rochester Assizes before Mr Baron Thompson, for the murder of Lydia Fagg, an infant about 18 months old who was daughter of Thomas Fagg, gentleman of Dover. It was established at the trial that Wickers had been employed by the family, and the day before the murder she had been upbraided by her mistress. In order to revenge herself, Wickers had absconded from her master's house at four a.m. on 28 May, carrying little Lydia with her to Dover Castle – where she had tossed the child into the sea. The child's body was later taken up in a fisherman's net off the Kentish coast.

Wickers was aged about 22 and single at the time of her trial, and she tried to convince the court that she had kissed the infant several times before taking her to the seaside - where a gigantic wave had washed the child out of her arms. Although she rushed into the water numerous times she was unable to help little Lydia, she asserted. The jury believed not a word of it, Margaret being unable to present any good reason why she would take the child to the coast at such an unsociable hour. Nor could she explain why she had been found hiding about three miles away in a cliff-side cave. Margaret Wickers – described as 'this hard-hearted creature' – was deservedly capitally convicted and afterwards hanged on 18 August 1737.

Margaret Wickers drowned her little victim near Dover Castle, Kent's coastal landmark.

In fact, the *Exposition* provides a very good illustration of the times: its news as reported consists of little more than a depressing list of robberies, fatalities and disasters, largely in the capital. The following is a selection of the more interesting reports, some of which paint a chilling picture:

On the morning of Saturday 19 November 1737, a woman was found with her throat cut from ear to ear near the Dog and Duck in St George's Fields, London. When the coroner's inquest sat later that month, it was established she was the wife of one Smith, formerly an apothecary in Dartford, Kent. According to the *Exposition*: 'A waterman swore that he carried them both (i.e. Smith and his wife) over the water; and brought only him (Smith) back again; his fingers being cut, and his clothes bloody, he pretended that he had been robb'd and beat in the Fields, and had left his wife behind at a relation's. The occasion of his committing this horrid fact, was his having renewed a policy on her life, and at her death was to receive £200. The said Smith is now closely locked up in the Fleet Prison.'

On 12 April 1738, another outrage occurred here: 'Last week a young woman well dress'd was found dead in the Fields between Stepney and Limehouse, with several marks of violence about her, from whence she was conjectur'd to have been first robb'd, and then murder'd.'

Fights broke out everywhere in the capital: on 24 August 1737, two butchers – one a pork butcher, the other selling beef – came to high words at the market in Honey Lane, with one flinging a knife at the other. The weapon stuck in the former's groin, and he died in St Bartholomew's Hospital. The beef butcher, named Runnington, was charged with murder.

Bodies turned up in ditches, down alleyways, and in the waterways: the *Exposition* reported, typically, on 26 July 1738: 'Last Friday a man was taken up *naked* from the Faulcon Stairs, very much bruised in the head, suppos'd to have been murder'd, having taken in no water, not being swelled.' And for some, a reprieve from the gallows meant nothing: on 29 March 1738, it was reported how Nathaniel Hillyard had been pardoned for the killing of 'a Sheriff's Officer in the Hay Market'; but despite having obtained his Majesty's Reprieve, he died anyway, succumbing to Newgate's notoriously filthy and disease-ridden conditions.

The *Exposition* also touched on dreadful events from across the kingdom. On 22 March 1738, the journal reported news from Lyme Regis, Dorset, where a 70-year-old farmer named Jenkins had his penis cut off by his wife while he slept. 'He died from the great effusion of blood from the wound' and his 50-year-old wife was committed to Dorchester Gaol. News from Bristol on 19 November 1737 spoke of a grim discovery being made by two women cutting furze on Durdham Down. Perceiving disturbed ground, they dug at the spot, thinking it might be a barrel of rum hidden by smugglers. However, they unearthed a sack containing the body of a young woman, whose head, arms and thighs had been hacked away by a hatchet, or some other such weapon. Two napkins were found within the bloodied mess, and together with the sack they were displayed at the White Hart in an attempt to identify where they came from.

Mob violence and crowds acting like packs of vicious animals were a persistent problem. The mob often came down hard on minorities, with politicians frequently respecting their prejudices. Correspondence from Preston dated 15 August 1738 explained that on 'St James's Day last' a Protestant named Robert Method had been brutally slain by a great number of Catholics at Plumpton, in Lancashire's Fylde district. Method was beaten by a crowd who dragged him out of an alehouse, the victim having given them not the least provocation; they then tied him to a pole and tormented him, before hauling him back into the alehouse. Here - fourteen in number - they throttled him so violently that he died six days afterwards. During his torment, the victim had cried out, 'Murder!' uselessly, as it did not help; but afterwards a number of suspects were thrown in Lancaster Gaol, and warrants issued for the rest. In Workington, Cumbria, a mason named John Burne was knocked down with the butt-end of a musket during ferocious clashes, and furiously beaten while thus incapacitated. He died, and the report states: 'The mob had sword and firearms, but we have not yet heard the verdict of the jury, nor the reason that occasioned (the riot).' In Deal, Kent, impressing the seamen aboard the *Louisa* caused a violent backlash from the townspeople, leaving one man dead and many injured.

Back in the metropolis, informers were still popular targets. On 9 February 1738 one Sikes reported a Broad Street, Carnaby Market, chemist to the authorities, accusing him of passing off 'spirituous liquors' as medicine. The allegation was thrown out, but Sikes (who belonged to the second Regiment of Guards) fell into the mob's hands. They pelted him and dragged him through a horse-pond, and ''tis thought he cannot recover'. On 19 November the crowd seized an informer in Dean Street, Soho, and 'after dragging him through the Channels' they threw him into a horse-pond, pelting him so viciously that he died.

This selection of extracts illustrates the squalid and dangerous day-to-day existences that many endured. What is noticeable are the precarious lives people led, for it is clear that through any combination of circumstances violence could flare at a moment's notice. Without doubt, and very sadly, these grim reports merely touched the tip of the iceberg.

PUBLIC ENEMY NUMBER 1

Many a notorious highwayman had been 'stretched' by Richard Turpin's time, those standing on the gallows platform often being the celebrities of their time thanks to their audacious – some might say anarchic - disregard for the laws that held the majority of the population in check. Some highwaymen entertained a reputation for flamboyant brazenness: but the reality is that these men were generally desperate and dangerous, and they often became more so as capture crept nearer.

One such gang, headed by Edward Burnworth (an apprentice to a Grub Street buckle-maker before he fell into a life of vice), rose to notoriety in the capital upon the demise of Jonathan Wild. Burnworth had graduated from pickpocketing and thievery to highway robbery and burglary, gathering about him a bunch of ne'er-do-wells as ruthless as himself as he went. At one point, they heard that Jonathan Wild's lieutenant, Quilt Arnold, was seeking them and so ambushed him in a public house in the Old Bailey. Burnworth forced Arnold to drink a glass of brandy mixed with gunpowder at pistol point, threatening to murder him in cold blood if he ever heard the man was on his scent again; he then struck the stricken Arnold a savage blow. It is possible that Arnold died of this mistreatment, which occurred in March 1726, as nothing is heard of him after this. The Burnworth Gang's open defiance of the law even led them to commit robbery at a magistrate's house in Clerkenwell, a crime born out of revenge rather than greed - for the fellow had been very active against thieves. In the end they naturally graduated to murder, upon hearing that a gin-shop keeper in the Mint, Southwark, intended to turn informer and betray them; Burnworth shot and killed this man, named Ball, in cold blood even as the fellow was on his knees begging for mercy.

Burnworth took to drinking in taverns with a loaded pistol on the table as he sat; but in the end he fell victim to a betrayal by a former gang member named Leonard, with whose wife he was having an affair. Leonard and his wife contrived to alert the magistrates and see to it that Burnworth was taken by six men who dashed into his lodgings via a door which his treacherous mistress had deliberately left unbolted. Mrs Leonard was actually targeted by an assassin while Burnworth languished in Newgate, being shot at near her own house – one of two murderous attacks aimed at intimidating anyone into not providing evidence against the criminals. These continued outrages made the gang the most wanted men in London.

Three of Burnworth's confederates – named Berry, Dickenson and Blewitt – fled to the Netherlands, but were caught following an application to the Dutch by the British Secretary of State. They were returned to London loaded with chains and kept on a boat near the Tower of London, which was itself guarded by three other boats.

Even after Burnworth was condemned, along with five members of his gang, they made a spirited effort to escape by way of a plot to drug their guards using wine mixed with opium, brought in by 'friends' who it was proposed would then set fire to parts of the prison. However, this came to naught due to the exceptional vigilance of the authorities, and in the end Burnworth accepted he was to die: he even told a gaoler 'if he did not see him buried in a decent manner, he would meet him after death in a dark entry, and pull off his nose'. All six were hanged on 12 April 1726, Burnworth and Blewitt being suspended from a gibbet post in St George's Fields. The other four were also gibbetted, two on Kennington Common and two on Putney Common. It is believed that they committed many more than 100 robberies in total.

HMS Belfast now lies on the waters of the Thames near the Tower, where once Blewitt, Berry and Dickenson were incarcerated on a vessel.

Another typical case closer to Turpin's time illustrates the average highwayman's brutality. Two mounted robbers named Udall and Raby held up the St Alban's stagecoach on its journey to London, with Raby actually cutting off the finger of a woman inside the coach to obtain her ring! On another occasion Udall had robbed a coach and horses on the road to Uxbridge, together with two accomplices called Wager and Baker; Baker had shot the coach guard to death when he fired at Udall and wounded the latter. Some six weeks later the robbers killed another coach guard during a hold-up on Turnham Green.

Less than glamorous: this highwayman is robbing someone returning from market of a goose. The mural is depicted at the Highwayman Inn, near Sourton, Devon.

William Udall was eventually sentenced to death at the Old Bailey for robbing a Mr Thorne on the highway near Islington. He was executed at Tyburn on 14 March 1738, aged just 22 and blaming his downfall on his association with lewd women. This young man had made a career out of robbery and violence, and his life story (as told in the *New & Complete Newgate Calendar*) evidences that Richard Turpin was far from unique in his chosen profession; yet most of these bandits, however much of a stir they caused at the time, now lie in unknown locations and remain largely forgotten.

There is, of course, one exception. Among all the notorious names the 18th century produced, Richard - or Dick - Turpin stands alone. Most modern writers take the care to point out that he was not the romantic highwayman of myth but a brutal, unattractive and deadly career criminal. The story of this romanticized, dangerous man is as follows: fact, as they say, is always more fascinating than fiction.

Richard Turpin was the son of a farmer from Thaxted, Essex, and having received a common education he distinguished himself from youth onwards by the impropriety of his behaviour and brutality of his manners. His first position was as an apprentice butcher in Whitechapel, but following his marriage to a young woman from East Ham he took to stealing his neighbour's cattle, which he would slaughter and cut up for sale. This occasioned his first known brush with the law: one victim of his rustling was directed to Waltham Abbey (where Turpin disposed of the cattle hides) and recognised a distinctive hide as coming from his own herd. A warrant being issued for Turpin's arrest, he slipped out of the back window of his house as the peace officers entered the property by the front door.

Turpin retreated to a place of security where he found the means to contact his wife, who furnished him with money. He retreated into the hundreds of Essex, where he became a career criminal, first joining a gang of smugglers and later a band of deer stealers who worked in Epping Forest. However, this business not meeting their expectations, the gang became bolder and determined to commence housebreaking instead. Their first attack of this kind was on the property of an elderly man named Stripe, whose chandler's shop at Watford they barged into after he opened the door in answer to their knocking. Stripe was robbed of all his money, but was not physically injured. The next victim fared worse; the group forced an entry into the house of an elderly woman in Loughton, blindfolding both her and a maid with handkerchiefs. When the woman refused to reveal the whereabouts of her reputed hoard of 700 or 800 pounds, Turpin threatened to set her on fire. When she still resisted, they placed her on the fire until the heat of the flames forced her to reveal the whereabouts of the money.

Turpin and his gang would threaten to put homeowners on the fire: a famous illustration from Knapp and Baldwin's Newgate Calendar Volume 1 *(1824).*

Throughout 1734, the gang grew bolder and greedier. They robbed a farmstead in Barking - literally breaking the door down - and bound the farmer, his wife, their son-in-law and a maid, and absconded with 700 pounds. When divided, this amounted to around 80 pounds each. Turpin is said to have gloated, 'Ay, this will do if it would always be so!' The next robbery occurred without Turpin, he having in the meantime gone to the metropolis: where he drank himself into a stupor and forgot about the appointment to rob the house of Mr Mason, the keeper of Epping Forest. Despite Turpin's absence the robbery went ahead anyway, the gang apparently having some sort of vendetta against Mason: for this home invasion was the most brutal yet. An oath was taken to break all his furniture, and this the gang did, ransacking the lower part of the house and breaking everything upstairs. Mason was beaten and kicked senseless, and his daughter only escaped by running out of the house and hiding in the pigsty. Finally the victim was 'killed under the dresser'. Remarkably, having gone that far, the intruders let alone a terrified old man who sat by Mason's fireside because he declared that he knew nothing of the killer's identities. Mason, it seems, was killed because a revenge beating got out of hand, and not because his attackers feared identification and/or capture. After this they travelled to London where they gave Turpin a cut, even though he had forgotten the appointment.

There was by now a hefty price on their heads. It was clear to the authorities that the same gang was committing these robberies, due to their proximity and the similarity of the methods employed. A proclamation was issued for the arrest of the gang, with £50 promised if convictions were secured. The idea was to get them to turn on each other, but the ploy had no effect, and - flushed with success - they continued their outrages in open defiance of the law.

During this spree the *London Gazette* (25 February 1734) issued descriptions of the gang members and their suspected lodgings: Samuel Gregory (a 23-year-old smith with a scar on his right cheek), Thomas Rowden (a 30-year-old pewterer) and Herbert Haines, a 24-year-old barber, were all listed. Turpin's description is recorded thusly: 'Richard Turpin, a butcher by trade, is a tall fresh-colour'd man, very much mark'd with the small pox, about 26 years of age, about five feet nine inches high, lived some time ago in White-chappel, and did lately lodge somewhere about Millbank, Westminster; wears a blew grey coat, and a light natural wig.' It appears this information might have been extracted from fringe members of the gang, a number of whom were in gaol - including, 'Mary Johnson, alias Brasier, alias Rose, committed to the Gatehouse Westminster, as being accessory in receiving the goods knowing them to be stolen'.

On 11 January 1735 Turpin and five of his companions raided the house of Mr Saunders, a rich farmer of Charlton in Kent. Knocking on the door, they politely enquired if Saunders was at home: when there came an affirmative from behind the door they forced an entrance and interrupted a card game that

Saunders was hosting with his wife in the parlour, telling those assembled that no-one would be hurt if they sat still. A silver snuffbox on the card table was grabbed immediately, then Saunders was dragged through the house and forced to reveal the hiding places of his coins, plate and valuables. A servant girl ran upstairs and barred her door, flinging open a window and yelling, 'Thieves!' before being grabbed and secured. Then, with utter disdain the group sat down with their victims and ate mince pies and drank wine. They encouraged their captives to do the same, and when Mrs Saunders fainted they helped her recover her senses with water. Some considerable time later the gang packed up their booty and left – but not without threatening to massacre the whole lot of them if so much as a word of alarm was given within two hours, or the marks on the stolen plate advertised. The robber's brazen and unpredictable behaviour probably convinced the occupants that they meant their threat entirely.

The gang's spree continued, with robberies at Croydon on 18 January (where they reimbursed their victim of two guineas, apologising for their conduct), and then Edgware near Stanmore, Middlesex, on 4 February. Here, in complete contrast to their courteous behaviour in Croydon, the pistol-waving group of marauders forced their way into the farmhouse of a Mr Lawrence, utterly ransacking the place and threatening him and his servants with a variety of gruesome deaths. One of them took a kettle from the fire and hurled its contents over Lawrence, but fortunately it was not hot enough to scald him. In the course of going from room to room for plunder, a maid-servant was found in the dairy, where she had been churning butter. This was despite her having blown out the candles to darken the room; and for the first time (as far as is known), the level of violence escalated to sexual assault, with one of the robbers – it is not clear who – marching the girl upstairs and raping her. The entire household was locked in the parlour and the key thrown away in the garden while Turpin and the others rode off in the direction of London.

However, the gang's next robbery - plotted at the White Bear Inn in Drury Lane, London, on 7 February - proved to be their last. The gang raided the house of a farmer named Francis near Marylebone, binding two servants in the stable; when Mr Francis arrived home they pointed their pistols at his breast and threatened to shoot him dead in an instant if he made the least noise. Inside the house they cruelly beat Mrs Francis, her daughter and the maidservant and rifled the house of a silver tankard, a medal of King Charles I, a gold watch, several gold rings, money, good quality linen and other effects.

These they once more appropriated to London, but time was running out: it was clearly only a matter of time before they were forced to murder someone, or an entire household. The authorities being roused like a sleeping bear, an increased reward of £100 was advertised and two of the group were taken into custody on the evidence of an accomplice. These two were tried, convicted and hung in chains, and afterwards the other members of the gang dispersed. One of them, Herbert Haines, was later executed on 8 August 1735 at Chelmsford after being convicted of several highway robberies. He walked to the gallows in his shroud and behaved 'very decently'. (Three others were hanged alongside Haines, and a woman called Margaret Onion, convicted at the same assizes, was burnt to death at the stake for poisoning her husband. A periodical noted at the time she was 'a poor, ignorant creature, and confess'd the fact'.)

Turpin, however, now went alone, taking to the road and indulging in highway robbery. It was during one of these depredations that a famous event occurred. On a journey towards Cambridge he met a man genteelly dressed and well mounted, and – supposing that the man would provide good spoils – he pointed a pistol at him and ordered him to deliver, bellowing, 'By God, I'll let daylight through you!' To Turpin's surprise the man roared with laughter, exclaiming, 'What? Dog eat dog? Come, come, brother Turpin; if you don't know me, I know you, and shall be glad of your company.' For this was no traveller, but another career criminal, named Tom (or possibly Matthew) King.

The pair became partners, committing many robberies and gaining such infamy that public houses began to turn them away. At length they fixed on a spot between the King's Oak and Loughton Road, by Epping Forest, where they 'made a cave' that was large enough to be used as a hideout and could also stable their horses. The cave was cleverly disguised with thickets, brambles and bushes, so that the pair could spy on travellers and yet remain unseen themselves. Throughout all this Turpin had – amazingly – not completely abandoned his wife: she frequently provided him and King with provisions and also often spent the night in the cave. At length robberies became so common on the Loughton Road that even lowly pedlars travelled armed with pistols.

In many ways, King epitomised the dashing, romantic image more than Turpin. When they espied two young women receive fourteen pounds for some corn in Bungay, Suffolk, King objected to holding them up, saying it would be a pity to rob two such pretty girls. Turpin ignored this and stole the money from them anyway. On the way home the following day they robbed a Mr Bradell of his watch, money and mourning ring. However, they allowed the fellow his ring back on account of its sentimental value, and when Bradell asked what it would cost for the watch to be returned as well, King said to Turpin: 'What say ye, Jack? He seems to be a good honest fellow; shall we let him have the watch?' On Turpin's reply – 'Do as you please' – King made the gentleman promise to leave six guineas for it at the Dial in Birchen Lane, and handed it back.

On 4 May 1737 Turpin – for the first time that we know of - became a murderer. A £100 reward had been placed on his head, and Thomas Morris, a servant of one of the keepers of Epping Forest, set forth to capture him accompanied by 'a higgler'. Turpin spotted them near his hideout while he was there alone; however, perceiving that Morris was armed with a gun he mistook them for poachers and tried to divert them elsewhere by saying there were no hares near the thicket. 'No,' said Morris, 'but I have found a Turpin!' and levelled his gun at the highwayman. Turpin remained unperturbed, and - speaking to Morris in a calm and friendly manner - he gradually manoeuvred his way backwards to his own gun, which in an instant he seized and fired at Morris. The keeper was killed instantly, and his accomplice immediately fled into the woodland. When word of the murder was carried to the Secretary of State, Turpin became England's Public Enemy No.1, with the following government proclamation being issued:

'It having been presented to the King that Richard Turpin did, on Wednesday, the 4th of May last, barbarously murder Thomas Morris, servant to Henry Thompson, one of the keepers of Epping Forest, and commit other notorious felonies and robberies near London, his Majesty is pleased to promise his most gracious pardon to any of his accomplices and a reward of £200 to any person or persons that shall discover him, so that he may be apprehended and convicted. Turpin was born at Thackstead, in Essex, is about thirty, by trade a butcher, about five feet nine inches high, very much marked with the small-pox, his cheek-bones broad, his face thinner towards the bottom, his visage short, pretty upright, and broad about the shoulders.'

Turpin shoots Morris dead in Epping Forest. (This famous illustration comes from William Jackson's New & Complete Newgate Calendar Volume 2, *1795.)*

Turpin decided to meet with his companion King as soon as possible, and in the meantime sent a letter to his wife arranging to meet her at a tavern in Hertford. When he met her, Turpin had the misfortune to be recognised by a butcher who knew him, and also knew of his notoriety; the man said, 'Come, Dick, I know you have money now, and if you will pay me, it will be of great service.' Turpin begged leave to get five pounds from his wife, and immediately fled the property after escaping through a window (it is not stated whether or not he took his wife). He rode off once more, taking up again with Tom King and a third member of the gang named Potter; however, on the road back towards London, the group committed a fatal mistake.

Near the Green Man tavern in Epping Forest on a Saturday evening they encountered one Mr Major, who was forced to hand over his steed, which Turpin (his own horse being jaded) then mounted and rode off in the company of his two comrades. Mr Major made his way to the Green Man, where he related his adventure; it was quickly suggested that the horse-thief had been Dick Turpin, and that Major might now be in possession of the robber's old horse, which had no doubt itself been stolen. Major was 'advised to print hand-bills immediately' and distribute them, and very soon word reached the Green Man that Major's distinctive missing horse was tethered at the Red Lion in Whitechapel. The landlord of the Green Man hastened to the Red Lion on Mr Major's behalf, where he roused a constable and others – the plan being to seize the person who arrived to take possession of the animal.

The person who turned up to collect the horse at four in the morning was in fact King's brother Robert, who was also found to be in possession of a whip that had a button on it engraved with Mr Major's name. Under the promise of release, King's brother admitted a 'stout man in a white duffel coat' was waiting for the animal to be delivered to Red Lion Street. When the company went thither, they found Tom King waiting.

King realised he was being ambushed and so pointed a pistol at his enemies and fired; however, the weapon flashed in the pan, and as King struggled to get a second pistol out his coat, Turpin appeared on the scene atop a horse. King yelled, 'Shoot him, or we are taken!' meaning the nearest constable: whereupon Turpin aimed his pistol in the darkness, fired, and fatally wounded King himself by accident. As he slumped over, King called out, 'Dick, you have killed me.' (The *Gentleman's Magazine* reported a slightly different version of this incident, differing mainly in the detail that 'Matthew King' (i.e. Tom King) was the man who collected the horse. He quickly gave up Turpin's whereabouts and was then fatally shot in the melee to apprehend Turpin. There are, in fact, varying accounts of the events in May 1737 that confuse the exact circumstances of King's shooting somewhat.)

King lived a week after being shot, but before he died *c.*19 May he gave evidence that Turpin's latest hideout was a house near Hackney Marsh.

However, when this was raided Turpin was found to have flown; although it was ascertained he *had* made one final visit there on the night following Tom King's shooting when he had been heard to lament upon the accident.

By the end of the month, according to the *Gentleman's Magazine*, Turpin had committed a robbery almost every day on the roads near the metropolis. He had also indicated he possessed a 'hit-list' of two men he wished to murder, and also that he did not fear being taken.

Turpin's previous hideout in Epping Forest had been raided following the shooting of Morris, and it was not safe for him to return. Therefore he skulked about the woodland for a while, somehow managing to evade armed posses that came after him - at one point even watching from the branches of an oak tree while a huntsman led a pack of baying hounds through the forest. Following this near miss, he determined to flee to Yorkshire, where he was less well known. By this time, we learn, one of his old gang members, Rowden, had been sentenced to transportation on 23 July 1737.

As he made his way northwards, Turpin was arrested at Long Sutton in Lincolnshire for horse theft, but managed to escape while he was being conducted to the magistrate. After his escape he continued to make his way towards Welton in Yorkshire. Here, he adopted the persona of a gentleman by the name of Palmer, who made a living as a horse trader (in fact he had taken to stealing horses in Lincolnshire which he would then take on the ponderous, lengthy journey back to Yorkshire to sell).

Turpin, in his role as 'Palmer', often accompanied his contemporaries on hunting and shooting trips, and during one of these he lit the fuse that led to his downfall. During one expedition he recklessly shot a cock belonging to his landlord. When a neighbour named Hall remonstrated with him, Turpin threatened to shoot the man dead and made as if to load his gun. Hall was slighted by this insult and informed the landlord, who took the matter to the magistrates. An arrest warrant was issued for 'Palmer', who was taken into custody for this offence; and when he could not provide 'security for his good behaviour' to the Justices then assembled at the Quarter Sessions in Beverley, Turpin was ignobly carted off southwards to Bridewell Gaol in London.

While he languished in this prison near the River Fleet, inquiries were made into 'Palmer's' background. His frequent returns from Lincolnshire, loaded with cash and fresh horses, raised the possibility of his being a horse thief and highwayman. Turpin had still not been positively identified yet, but the magistrates were suspicious of his 'background story' that he was a butcher from Long Sutton who had been forced to flee to Yorkshire to escape debts over consignments of rancid mutton. Investigations forced by the magistrates in London and Lincolnshire revealed that 'Palmer' had no discernible means of income and was suspected of having escaped from peace-officers when accused of sheep stealing. It was also suspected he was a horse thief. Upon these

249

suspicions being aired, Turpin was sent back to Yorkshire and incarcerated in York Castle, to face northern justice. Within a month two horses and a foal linked to 'Palmer' and his 'business' had been reclaimed by their proper owners; yet – amazingly – no one had so far identified 'Palmer' for who he really was: Dick Turpin.

After four months in York Gaol, Turpin wrote a letter, dated 6 February 1739, to his brother in Essex:

> *'DEAR BROTHER,*
>
> *I am sorry to acquaint you that I am now in York Castle for horse stealing. If I could procure an evidence from London to give me a character, that would go a great way towards my being acquitted. I had not been long in this county before my being apprehended, so that it would pass off the readier. For Heaven's sake, dear brother, do not neglect me; you will know what I mean when I say,*
>
> *I am yours*
>
> *JOHN PALMER.'*

Turpin now met with a phenomenally bad piece of luck. This letter being returned unopened to the local post office (because the brother would not pay the postage), it was by chance seen by a schoolmaster named Mr Smith - who had taught Turpin to write, and recognised his handwriting infallibly. Smith took the letter to a magistrate, whereupon it seemed from the schoolmaster's insistence that 'Palmer' might actually be England's most wanted man, Richard Turpin. Smith was dispatched by the Essex magistrates to York Castle, where he identified 'Palmer' as Turpin without hesitation.

The game was up.

Richard Turpin's chief distinction in the eyes of history, and the major contributor to his enduring mythology in folklore, is the manner of his behaviour in the final weeks of his life. Once word spread that Turpin was languishing in York Castle, thousands flocked from all over England to see him incarcerated like a caged animal where he lay weighted down with 28 pounds worth of irons. They debated furiously whether this was Turpin, or whether a mistake had been made: could the man who had terrorised eastern England really have been caught for shooting fowl? Turpin, for his part, seemed resigned: when a young know-it-all visited and declared the prisoner was *not* Turpin, and he would bet money on that fact, Turpin whispered in his jailer's ear: 'Lay him the wager, and I'll go you halves!'

Turpin's trial in York was something of a foregone conclusion, and he was convicted on two indictments and sentenced to death on 22 March 1739. After his conviction he wrote to his father and implored him to use whatever influence he could 'with a lady and gentleman of rank' to get his sentence commuted to transportation. Turpin's name was so notorious, however, that his father could get no one to take an interest in his son's case, despite his best endeavours. His hopeless attempt thwarted, Turpin proceeded to live in a most cavalier and thoughtless manner, often jesting about the unnatural fate that awaited him. Many still flocked to see him, and he drank wine freely on a daily basis while he awaited his fate. A few days before his execution he purchased 'a new fustian frock and a pair of pumps' so that he might look his best at his execution, and hired five poor men, at 10 shillings each, to follow his cart to the gallows in mourning. He presented hatbands and gloves to several acquaintances, and also made a gift of a ring to a married woman whom he had known in Lincolnshire. All the while, he refused to admit anything other than that he was indeed Turpin.

On the morning of 7 April 1739 Turpin was put in the cart and drawn to York's 'fatal tree', bowing with an air of utter indifference as to his fate in the direction of the spectators who thronged the route. He ascended the ladder with courage, but upon his right leg being seen to tremble, he stamped his foot to stop it - lest anyone think he might be frightened of his fate. He conversed with the executioner for about half an hour, finally confessing his robberies and admitting the two killings; then he bravely threw himself off the ladder, stretching his neck and expiring within a few minutes. At his execution he had a fellow sufferer in the person of a horse thief named John Stead.

The spectators, it is recorded, were somewhat affected by the bravery Turpin displayed, and afterwards the criminal's corpse was brought to the Blue Boar in Castlegate, York, where it was laid out overnight before being buried in the churchyard of St Michael's parish. His coffin, inscribed with his initials and age: *J.P. 1739. R.T. aged 28* (although he was in fact about 33 when he was executed), was buried remarkably deep. Unfortunately, almost immediately – at about three o' clock the following morning – it was secretly disinterred and conveyed to the house of a surgeon, no doubt for dissection and anatomical experiments; however, the populace soon recovered Turpin's body from the surgeon's garden and carried it aloft, almost naked and laid out on a board, through York's streets in a triumphant manner. They then filled the coffin with 'unslacked lime' and reburied the corpse. What is said to be his final resting place can be found today in an enclosed burial plot opposite St George's Church in York.

Thus ended the remarkable career of Richard Turpin, whose name has come to epitomise the mythology of the highwayman - despite it being clear he was primarily a housebreaker and horse-thief. It is folklore that has enshrined Turpin's place in British history as a dashing, daring rogue, despite the truth being markedly different. Most counties in the eastern portion of England have pubs, taverns or hostels where he is supposed to have stayed; if even half of the legends are true then Turpin must have been in a permanent state of inebriation throughout his whole career. But Richard Turpin was no dashing rogue, merely a habitual criminal: one who, although *historically* linked to only two deaths, is highly likely to have killed others during his career, or at least been *involved* in several other murders. For instance, it is sometimes suggested that one of the victims - an old woman, in fact - subjected to the ordeal by fire on her own hearth by Turpin's gang expired of her mistreatment. This author, having grown up in Lincolnshire, is also aware of a legend that Turpin is supposed to have committed murder upon a man called Christopher Wilkinson between Dunston and Nocton, and from the number of robberies hereabouts the idea for the 'land lighthouse' of Dunston Pillar was conceived. There are other eastern counties that harbour stories of one killing or another linked to him also. Nonetheless, it is likely that his reputation as someone who only fired when cornered, and not wantonly, enhanced his myth, and perhaps his fame also came about because of the geographically huge area in which he perpetrated his crimes.

Upon Richard Turpin's death poems were already being written about him. Two – one by a Yorkshireman, the other by an Essex man – were published in the *Gentleman's Magazine* and proffered differing viewpoints on Turpin's downfall, both in his support and against him. The myth had been born already, even before Turpin's own body was cold.

What is said to be Turpin's grave in York.

THE CAMBRIDGESHIRE DECAPITATION

In the year 1740 the following crime is supposed to have occurred in rural Cambridgeshire.

A woman living at St Neots was returning home from Elsworth, where she had collected a legacy of £12 that was due her. For fear of being robbed, she tied the money up in her hair. As she was travelling home she was overtaken by her next-door neighbour, a butcher by trade who also kept an inn; this fellow bore a kindly reputation, and the woman was pleased to see him, as it made her feel safer. Presently they fell to talking about the woman's journey, and she made the foolish mistake of not only telling her neighbour of her errand, but also of how she had hidden the money in her hair. The butcher very quickly found an opportunity to pull her from atop her horse, next cutting her throat and decapitating her in the lane before thrusting the woman's head into his pack and riding off.

According to the report, two fellow travellers - a gentleman and his servant - came upon the scene not long after and found the woman's headless body 'moving on the ground'. This we may take to mean that she still twitched. The gentleman ordered his servant to ride full speed ahead and overtake the first person he caught up with in the road, since this was presumably the murderer.

The servant caught up with the butcher about a mile up the road, and requested if the man might be able to suggest a good inn in St Neots. The murderer naturally suggested his own, and presently the gentleman caught them up: the trio rode into St Neots and stabled their horses at the butcher's tavern. Here, the gentleman said that he was going to take an early evening constitutional, and would be gone some time; in fact, he went and found the parish constable and led him to the woman's decapitated body on the road outside St Neots.

The constable was at first loathe to believe the butcher was responsible for such an atrocity, as he had lived in St Neots many years and bore a great reputation. However, when he accompanied the gentleman to the suspect's inn they located the man's pack and found the ghastly trophy still within its bloodied receptacle.

It only remains to be said that the constable was sick and horrified to see that the decapitated head belonged his own wife. The butcher was sent to Huntingdon Gaol, and shortly thereafter executed for murder.

It is difficult to know what to make of this narrative. It first appeared in the *Universal Weekly Journal* (8 March 1740) and ever after has been cited in collections on crimes strangely discovered. Rather than having the quality of a real news report, the story feels more like it was something someone was *told*, perhaps as they passed through Cambridgeshire – the narrative proving so exceptional that they felt compelled to tell the *Journal* about it. The lack of names is suspicious, so until a better account of this crime is forthcoming its authenticity must be classed as 'unproven'.

DOMESTIC TYRANNY IN SOMERSET

Men beating their servants and domestic help might not have been considered particularly remarkable around this time; but for women to commit such violence was somewhat rarer, especially when it was taken to the level of sadistic, runaway cruelty.

Mrs Elizabeth Branch was born in Norton St Philip, in the Mendip district of Somerset. She was of a reasonably well-to-do family, but from an early age displayed a bitter, vindictive and cruel disposition, often directed at her father's servants, and which seemed to increase as she grew older. So awful was her conduct that her parents actually told her that unless she controlled her temper she would never get a husband, and after this Elizabeth seems to have reined in her cruelty with a great effort.

Elizabeth afterwards managed to obtain a husband in the form of a gentleman farmer called Branch, and no sooner had she settled with him at Hemington than her old vindictiveness began to display itself; only this time it was directed at her *own* domestic help. The Branch household must have been a strange one, for while Mr Branch is described as a humane and gentle employer, Mrs Branch was the complete opposite: a domestic tyrant, who enforced all manner of petty humiliations and cruelties on the household staff – even forcing them outside in the midst of a winter's night. The prompt and continual payment of wages seems to have been the only factor that ensured the Branch household managed to retain its domestics. In time Elizabeth bore a daughter, Mary, who unfortunately grew up as bitter and petty as her mother.

When Mr Branch died he provided in his will an annuity of £300 for his widow and daughter. However, not surprisingly, ALL the servants quitted the household shortly after their master was buried...and so Elizabeth and Mary were forced to look to travelling vagrants and the parish poor for domestic assistance.

Without Mr Branch to rein her in, it appears that Elizabeth's tyranny progressed from mental cruelty and violence to outright sadism. She and her daughter became notorious in the village for their treatment of servants, whom they would throw plates, knives and forks at for any disobedience, real or imagined: until into their service there eventually came one Jane Buttersworth, a poor girl aged about thirteen placed with the Branch women by the parish officers.

Matters in the Branch household reached a head in the following violent manner. On 4 November 1739 Jane Buttersworth was ordered to fetch some yeast, but took a long time about it. When old Elizabeth Branch asked the girl to explain herself, Jane told an outright lie – for which Mary Branch punched her forcefully in the face before pinching her by the ears and twisting her head. Both mother and daughter then threw the girl to the floor, and while Mary knelt on her neck the mother thrashed their victim with sticks until blood began to run from her injuries. Poor Jane was then beaten by Mary Branch, who had taken off one of her shoes to strike her with. The injured girl managed to scramble away from her two mistresses, crying for mercy, but only made it as far as the parlour before they caught up with her and beat her with broom handles until she fell senseless to the floor. The daughter then threw a pail of cold water on the unconscious form, which did not revive her. Following this they abused her 'with other circumstances of cruelty too gross to mention'. This last, among other things, appears to have involved rubbing salt into the open wounds Jane bore from the thrashing she had received.

The Branch women beat their poor servant. From Knapp and Baldwin's Newgate Calendar Volume 1 *(1824).*

This much was seen and heard by another servant, a dairy maid called Ann Somers, who at this point opted to retire from the scene to milk her cows, perhaps fearing similar treatment. Half an hour later she returned to the house and found a ghoulish scene that must have terrified her: her mistress sat silently beside the fireplace, while Jane Buttersworth lay on the floor. A clean mobcap had been put on the girl's head, but it had turned red with the blood that had soaked through it. Ann Somers ventured to timidly suggest that Jane was dead, upon which her mistress turned in her direction and threw the most abusive language at the young girl.

Jane was, indeed, dead by this point, yet old Mrs Branch saw to it that the lifeless body was put in the servant's bed as normal. This was naturally also used by little Ann Somers, who thus spent the entire night laid in bed next to a murdered body, too terrified to utter a single word lest she be killed also.

The following day Ann Somers was not permitted to leave the house, and her two mistresses buried the poor girl they had murdered in secret.

It was this private burial that brought the affair to light. Jane Buttersworth being missed, and burial of such a young person without recourse to a coroner being viewed as suspicious (for the two women's temperament was very well known locally), the body was disinterred. A surgeon called Mr Salmon, who carried out an inspection, stated without hesitation that Jane had suffered a number of violent injuries, any one of which might have proved mortal. Mr Salmon observed that the deceased's body was quite literally a mass of bruises, and the skull was fractured also in more than one place. Some of the wounds, he declared, would have fatally injured the stoutest man.

On 31 March 1740 old Mother Branch and Mary, her daughter, were indicted for murder in Taunton, Somerset's assize town. At their trial an attempt was made to suggest that the deceased suffered from fits, and as such had suffered her injuries during a fall and subsequent spasms; but nothing was found to substantiate this (quite the opposite, in fact) and the two women were sentenced to death. Among the witnesses at their trial was a boy, Henry Butler, who deposed he had seen the deceased struck violently on the head numerous times by the accused. Henry was himself another of their servants, who was often beaten in a like manner and – on one occasion – forced to eat his own excrement after soiling himself. After their sentence Elizabeth and Mary immediately petitioned the judge for a pardon, but the best they got was five weeks respite to allow Mrs Branch to settle some of her affairs.

Mary Branch appeared to sincerely lament her fate, and begged the prayers of everyone she came into contact with. Elizabeth, however, appeared supremely unconcerned – until a sermon was preached before them on the night of 2 May 1740, upon which the enormity of what was happening appeared to strike her. Both women made due preparation for their exits, and between three and four on the morning of 3 May 1740 they were collected from gaol and taken to Ilchester for execution. As they were conducted on their final journey to the gallows (which was erected in a field called Gallows Five Acres about half-a-mile outside of Ilchester on the road to Yeovil), they were accompanied only by the gaoler and about half a dozen other people - the usual festivities of such an event being abandoned because it was feared the populace would tear them to pieces if they could lay their hands on them. This was also the reason for the unsociable hour that the two women were executed.

When the grim cortege arrived at the spot it was found the gibbet post from which the women were to be hanged had been cut down. A carpenter was immediately sent for to put up another, and this had the effect of delaying the execution of the two evil women by a couple of hours. Finally they were launched into oblivion just before six o'clock: still early enough to thwart the thousands of people who had come from all over Somerset in hopes of watching the grim spectacle.

At the time of their deaths Elizabeth Branch was reckoned to be around 67, while her daughter was aged just 24. Before they were turned off, Mother Branch addressed the few spectators and declared she had not meant to kill the object of her sadism. Her daughter, Mary, also made an impassioned final speech: 'Good people, pity my unhappy case, who young, was trained up in the paths of cruelty and barbarity; and take warning by my unhappy end, to avoid the like crimes. You see here I am cut off in the prime of life, in the midst of my days. Good people, pray for me.'

This brutal story of countryside servitude proved an early forerunner to a strangely similar case that occurred in the capital nearly three decades later: that of the notorious Mrs Brownrigg, whose atrocious behaviour we have yet to look at.

'I WISH SOMEBODY WOULD SHOOT THE OLD DOG...'

Suffolk's *cause celebre* of the era concerned the case of Charles Drew.

Charles' father was a prominent attorney called Charles John Drew. He was eminently successful, having married a lady of good fortune and settled in Long Melford, where he kept a respected practice. However, for all his personal success Charles Snr seems to have neglected his son – to such a degree that the boy, by the most reliable accounts, grew up largely uneducated. Although the lad was of a friendly disposition, and not entirely inferior to, say, the tens of thousands who grew up in poverty in the capital, it was simply the case that there was no way he would ever amount to anything respectable.

In large part this was due to his father. Sadly, Charles John Drew appears to have been incapable of displaying love to any in his immediate family. By the time of the boy's adulthood he lived separately from his wife and behaved in an unfriendly and reserved manner towards his five daughters also.

The son having arrived at maturity, he began to court a young woman called Elizabeth Boyer. She was a good catch, but Charles Jnr stalled marrying her for fear his father would disinherit him; Elizabeth, when told of this, was overheard to say in January 1740: 'I wish somebody would shoot the old dog.'

At some point in his past Charles Jnr had appeared at Chelmsford Assizes, where he had made the acquaintance of one John (or possibly Edward) Humphreys, a notorious coastal smuggler with a reputation as a hardened villain. Charles Jnr arranged to meet Humphreys at Ms Boyer's lodgings – where he offered the smuggler an annuity of £200 if he would shoot his father dead.

Humphreys took some persuading but at length agreed. At about 11 o'clock on the night of 31 January 1740 he approached Drew's house in Long Melford. It appears his intention was to knock on the door and then shoot down the old man with a gun loaded with slugs while Charles Jnr watched the whole affair from a hidden vantage point in the darkness.

However, at the last moment Humphreys threw down the gun and declared his nerve had failed him. Charles Jnr appeared from his hiding place, took up the gun himself and threatened Humphreys to keep silent; he then knocked upon his father's door and when the old man opened it he simply fired and killed him on the spot. The two conspirators fled the scene together, Charles remarking, 'It is done!'

Humphreys immediately left Suffolk altogether and joined a band of smugglers at Great Dunmow in Essex before leaving with them for the capital. Charles Snr was found dead in his house on 1 February. The slugs had made five wounds to his body, three of them having passed entirely out his back.

Following the discovery of the murder Charles Jnr actually had the audacity to travel to London himself and apply for the king's pardon towards anyone who might provide information – excepting the actual person who had pulled the trigger. In consequence of this an advertisement was placed in the *London Gazette* making this offer. Such was Charles's desire to appear innocent that he followed this up with a public offer of £100 for anyone who would provide the evidence that convicted the murderer. He does not appear to have been trying to point the finger of suspicion at Humphreys so much as to point it *away* from himself.

In the meantime an inquest was held upon the body of the deceased in which Humphrey's name was mentioned as a potential suspect. This appears to have been based on the gossip of neighbours, who knew that the smuggler was acquainted with the victim's son. Word of this reaching Humphreys in London, he felt it better to return to Suffolk and try and convince the authorities he was innocent – for the longer he avoided Suffolk, the more guilty he would look. Humphreys was, of course, immediately arrested upon his return and imprisoned in Bury Gaol.

Since the victim's house had not been robbed, the authorities were – quite naturally – beginning to wonder whether Charles Jnr might have something to do with the shooting. Investigations suggested that he might have used a gun given to him by Elizabeth Boyer, and by now there was every reason to believe that she also may have known more about the incident than she was letting on.

However, although Charles had returned to his home county from London, it was proving difficult to shape a case against him.

As time went on John Humphreys' explanations of any association he may have had with Charles Drew Jnr proved not a little indifferent; but more to the point he had somehow obtained £20 while incarcerated in gaol. This money the authorities suspected had come from Charles, who was attempting to bribe Humphreys to keep his mouth shut.

Humphreys' evasive attitude heaped more suspicion upon him. In reaction to this Charles Drew went so far as to publicly declare that the smuggler was *not* the man who had shot his father; but of course this only drew further suspicion against the son, for how could he know such a thing with *certainty*?

Charles was by this time beginning to feel the breath of justice on his neck and so swiftly departed Suffolk to live in London. Here he changed his name to 'Thomas Roberts' and began corresponding with the still-imprisoned Humphreys back in Suffolk, who replied using the name of 'John Smith'. Unfortunately Humphreys, in one of his letters requesting money (dated 9 March 1739-40), mistakenly addressed the correspondence to 'Charles Drew'. Whether this was the result of drunken forgetfulness on the part of Humphreys or a deliberate attempt to bring the matter to a close is unclear: but the latter is likely, since Humphreys was, after all, innocent of any murder.

When the Bury coach brought the letter to London, of course no-one knew who 'Charles Drew' was, since he now went by the name of Roberts; and it is at this point that Charles Drew fell victim to a singularly unlucky circumstance not unlike the one that had identified the late Richard Turpin.

The letter being given to a Mr Mace when it neared the destination address, he endeavoured to find out who 'Drew' was; and in the end he was directed to a Mr Timothy Drew Esq in Holborn. This was a namesake, but a man of formidable intelligence and natural cunning who was aware from news-sheets like the *London Gazette* that Charles Drew was linked to the murder of his father in Suffolk. (It appears that by this point there was an open warrant out for Charles Drew's arrest on suspicion, following his departure from Suffolk in the wake of the growing case against him.) Timothy Drew Esq was also an attorney, who took a very keen interest in the murder of his brother-attorney even though it had occurred far away in Suffolk. Thus Timothy Drew took it upon himself to scour London to see if he could track down Charles Drew. From his discourse with Mr Mace, Timothy Drew suspected that 'Charles Drew' and 'Mr Roberts' were one and the same, and – armed with the correspondence address – he started at 'Roberts' lodgings in Sheer Lane and began to hunt his quarry down from there.

Timothy Drew's efforts to hunt 'Roberts' – or Charles Drew – were at first unsuccessful, for it appeared that his prey had paid people to deny ever having seen or heard of him. But by sheer determination and refusal to give up Timothy eventually found himself directed to Eastmead's bordello in Leicester-fields. Here, the conspiratorial nature of the landlord and a waiter when questioned roused the suspicions of Timothy Drew and he bravely shouted out in hearing of the entire place: 'Mr Roberts is in this house. But his real name is Charles Drew and he had murdered his father. I will see to it that all the people in this house are apprehended for concealing a murderer.' This authoritative attitude produced a reaction and the waiter showed Timothy Drew to his quarry - who was indeed hiding on the premises.

Charles Drew was taken before a magistrate, Justice de Veill, and then imprisoned in Newgate on suspicion of murdering his father. While imprisoned, Drew managed to bribe a turnkey, Jonathan Keate, to help him escape, but was betrayed to Akerman, the keeper of the gaol. After that Drew was watched continually; he had, of course, further implied his guilt now by trying to escape.

In the end Charles Drew Jnr was carted off on a dismal final journey to Bury St Edmunds, where he was told he would face trial on 27 March 1740. Humphreys was admitted in evidence, and his testimony helped convict Drew of the murder; an alibi Drew attempted to procure for himself on the night of the shooting also proved false, and only strengthened the case against him. Following his conviction he admitted his offence but seemed unable to grasp the severity of what he had done, saying that his father had denied him necessary money for his expenses; and had also refused to make over his estate to him. In gaol Drew was visited by his sisters, who tried to console him; perhaps they sympathised with his predicament, having suffered their father's harshness also.

Charles Drew Jnr was hanged just outside Bury St Edmunds on 9 April 1740 before a vast crowd of spectators. He was 25 years of age, and is reported to have attempted to delay his execution for as long as possible by begging the clergyman attending him (who happened to be his brother-in-law) to continue his devotions until the last possible moment. Afterwards his body was taken back to Long Melford in a hearse for a decent burial; which is somewhat curious, since he had been sentenced at his trial to be gibbetted. Perhaps this was due to the intervention of an unnamed 'great man' who tried to procure Charles Drew a pardon.

John Humphreys was discharged from gaol later that month, although just as swiftly re-arrested after a gentleman brought a charge of breaching the peace against him; this appears to be the last we hear of him. No charge was brought against Ms Boyer, although the suggestion is that she knew more of the affair than ever came out.

THE YOUTH WHO LIVED TWICE

17-year-old William Duell was one of five languishing in Newgate under sentence of death, having been convicted at the late assize in November 1740.

His crime was not particularly remarkable for the time; on 7 September he had, under the pretence of kindness, showed a woman called Sarah Griffin to a barn in Horn Lane, Acton (at that time a district west of London famous for its springs). The woman was travelling to Worcestershire, and required somewhere to lay her head; while she bedded down in the hay Duell – at the time 16 – had left her to seek out four ruffians, who could loosely be termed 'friends'. Perhaps wishing to show off, he had led them to the woman in the barn. However, this group were degenerates of the worst sort, who proceeded to rape the woman, subduing her by repeated blows from their fists and threats to murder her. In the end, they stole her possessions and her money, and left her in the barn, bloodied, battered and violated. Remarkably, she was still alive when found, and although Sarah Griffin couldn't describe the group of men (it had been dark), she *could* describe William Duell, who had been responsible for bringing the others and had also participated in the gang rape.

Sarah Griffin died the day after she was found, and Duell was the only one tried at the subsequent assizes: one other, George Curtis, who had beaten the woman badly and raped her twice, died in Newgate, while a third suspect – John James – had only recently been taken. The other participants in the crime remained at large. The coroner, being unable to say for certain that the outrage was the *direct* cause of the woman dying, brought in the extraordinary verdict of 'Death by Natural Causes'. Despite this, William Duell was convicted of raping and robbing her.

At his execution on 24 November 1740 at Tyburn, four others so condemned – various criminals convicted of burglaries and other felonies – died in the usual manner. William Duell was launched into oblivion at the same mass execution, and hung by the neck for a full 22 minutes before being taken down. His body was conveyed by hackney-coach to the Surgeon's Hall so that it might be anatomised; and it is here that nothing less than a miracle occurred.

When he was laid out on a table within the hall, the surgeons and assistants - while preparing to cut him up - heard the 'corpse' groan. They examined Duell and found other symptoms of life, and so bled him. After they took several ounces of his blood, Duell stirred; and within two hours he had managed to sit himself up on the slab, mumbling inarticulately and apparently unable to speak coherently.

The grim decision was made to carry Duell back to Tyburn and re-hang him, but in this the authorities were thwarted by the threat of a huge crowd that hung menacingly outside the hall. At midnight Duell was recommitted back to Newgate, where he was wrapped in a blanket and given some hot broth. Although he had by now regained the power of speech, he could remember nothing of what had occurred after the noose was placed around his neck.

William Duell became a celebrity in the eyes of the mob, and a curiosity among the apothecaries and surgeons of the era. It only remains to be said that his sentence was afterwards changed to one of transportation. The Lord, as they say, moves in mysterious ways; the young man had earned his punishment, yet providence saw fit to not only allow him to survive the hanging (quite how this happened is unclear) but also see to it that he stirred minutes before a surgeon's blade would have silenced him for good. Even then the surgeons could have ended his life on the slab; yet they seem to have fought to resuscitate him *merely to see if they could* – since they appear to have supposed he would only be re-hanged anyhow. In this providence helped the fortunate young man a third time, for it ensured his delivery back to gaol…rather than back to Tyburn.

Failed executions had occurred before, rousing the emotion of the mob. Two men called Bayley and Reynolds had been sentenced to death under the new Act against 'going arm'd and disguised', following an attack they had made on a turnpike. Reynolds was hanged at Tyburn on Monday 26 July 1736 and afterwards cut down as usual. However, when he was placed in the coffin he suddenly became animated and thrust back the lid as it was being fastened. Reynolds was still alive, and when the executioner made to tie him back up again the mob prevented it. The unfortunate prisoner was hustled away to an alehouse, where he vomited three pints of blood and then expired when he was given a glass of wine. Bayley, in an incredible piece of good fortune, owed his own salvation to this mishap: for the affair caused such tumult that he was reprieved.

KING OF THE ROAD: HENRY COOKE'S 100 ROBBERIES

Although the case of Richard Turpin had been a talking point across the nation, it served not as a warning and the proliferation of banditry continued unabated.

One of the more interesting cases concerns a young man named Henry Cooke, or John Stevens as he sometimes went by. Cooke was originally a shoemaker from Stratford, at that time a distinct village near London; but he is recorded as having fallen afoul of the law in October 1740, when he was apprehended on suspicion of having robbed James Thomason. The prosecution not proving very effective, and he providing an eloquent defence, Cooke was acquitted on this occasion.

Not learning from this, Cooke immediately returned to highway robbery accompanied by his journeyman, William Taylor (a former smuggler), and together they frequently robbed the Essex and other stage-coaches. This was until their *modus operandi* became so predictable that one Captain Mawdley chose to conceal himself in a basket attached to the back of the Colchester stage-coach: and when Cooke and Taylor ambushed the vehicle, they were themselves surprised by Captain Mawdley, who sprung up and opened fire on them. Cooke was hit in the shoulder, but the pistol balls did not seriously hurt him; Taylor was shot in the head and collapsed, dying at the scene. It was all Cooke could do to leap a gate and escape across fields in the direction of Upton before the approach of a mob that had come to investigate the fracas.

Cooke would later claim to have robbed the captain before fleeing, although this was judged improbable, and Mawdley himself denied the fact. Cooke also vowed to avenge Taylor and come looking for Mawdley: this was no idle threat, but happily the path of the two men did not cross again after this.

Cooke subsequently took up with four other highwaymen. Just before Christmas 1740 they held up a coach between Mile End and Bow, which happened to be carrying children. This did not stop two of the gang committing murder upon one of the occupants, Mr Cruikshanks, when he resisted; and although Cooke claimed to have had nothing to do with this killing, his denial is questionable – for he would later admit that Cruikshanks was a Stratford barber who actually recognised him and pleaded for his life. This probably doomed him, for in all likelihood it forced the gang to beat him to death to avoid being identified. At the very least, Cooke was guilty by association, although he claimed afterwards he tried to prevent his comrades from killing the man.

Nonetheless, Cooke would later claim that Cruikshanks' murder forced him to part company with his gang. He would give little away about them, except that one was since dead, one (he believed) had gone to sea, and the other two he would not name as they were still, to the best of his knowledge, committing robberies and had not been taken.

Cooke next took himself to Birmingham, where – using the alias Stevens – he set up business as a shoemaker. For a while he was quite well-to-do, but this was largely due to the fact that he continued to go out committing robberies at night while running his legitimate establishment during the daytime. After some months he felt confident enough to return to London, where he held up and robbed a Mr Zachary.

Unfortunately for Cooke his return to the capital was somewhat premature, as he was suspected now of involvement in many robberies. Like Turpin, Cooke's apprehension came about by an unlikely circumstance: on 28 July 1741 he was spotted passing St Mary-le-Bow Church in Cheapside by a woman called Martha Underwood, whom he had been acquainted with in Stratford. This woman knew Cooke to be suspected in numerous villainies, and so doggedly pursued him through the streets until her quarry entered a public house in Shoreditch. She presented this information to a constable called Haines, who with assistance managed to secure Cooke without incident. The prisoner was carried before a Justice, and when Mr Zachary's watch was found upon his person Cooke's guilt appeared clear and he was thrown into Newgate to await trial.

On 28 August 1741 Cooke was capitally convicted at the Old Bailey of robbing Mr Zachary. He at first refused to plead, but when 'the press' (a torture device) was prepared he entered a fruitless plea of 'Not guilty'. On the same day, one James Hall was also convicted of murder at the Old Bailey, and his case is worth briefly digressing into; Hall was convicted of robbing and murdering his master Mr Penny, late principal of Clements Inn, of the prestigious Inns of Chancery in the City of Westminster. Hall pleaded guilty, confessing that he had for some time plotted the murder – which he perpetrated on 17 June between 11 and 12 at night. He first struck Mr Penny down in his bedchamber and then stripped himself entirely naked before cutting the unconscious man's throat. This odd circumstance was to avoid getting any bloodstains on his clothes. He then carried the body out of the room and 'threw it in one of the holes of the Bog-house' where it was discovered ten days later. Hall was arrested on suspicion, and circumstances appearing against him, he was committed for trial.

Cooke and Hall were confined in the same room in Newgate while they awaited execution. It is reported that they conspired to escape, and actually managed to get some pistols smuggled into their cell thanks to the assistance of a comrade on the outside, a Hadley butcher. But they were betrayed by a fellow prisoner, and were surprised at midnight by Akerman, the gaol-keeper, who rushed into the cell and, with the help of one of the turnkeys, wrestled the weapons from the condemned men. The butcher, coming into Newgate the next day with more useful tools to assist the breakout, was arrested.

James Hall was conveyed via a hurdle on 14 September 1741 to the end of Catherine Street in the Strand, and at about ten in the morning hanged. His body was afterwards hung in chains at Shepherd's Bush in the Acton Road. Henry Cooke was taken from Newgate two days later and hanged at Tyburn alongside a horse-rustler named Hudson, a burglar named Bourne and one Mary Harris, convicted of 'stripping a child about ten years of age'. Cooke denied participating in the murder of Mr Cruikshank to the end, although he admitted he was guilty of over 100 robberies.

A land of criminals: this is highwaymen Johnson and Stockdale shooting dead a postman at Winchmore Hill, Enfield – a crime for which they hanged at Tyburn on 2 July 1753. This illustration originally appeared in William Jackson's New & Complete Newgate Calendar Volume 4 *(1795).*

STRANGULATION ABOARD THE RUBY

The city of Bristol's most infamous *cause celebre* concerned the murder of a baronet, Sir John Dineley Goodere, who – owing to squabbles with his younger brother over the latter's disinheritance – was forcibly abducted by a group of ruffians on College Green, Bristol. This was as he made his way home on 23 January 1741 following a lunch during which the two brothers had apparently reconciled. Their meeting had occurred at the house of a city attorney named Smith.

The baronet was dragged forcibly through Bristol's streets by this motley gang and violently hustled onto a boat floating on the water of the Avon 'near the Hot Well'. Along the way the company had been joined by the baronet's brother, Captain Samuel Goodere - who had (of course) organised the abduction and paid his crewmen to stage it. Bristolians who witnessed the abduction, or saw the struggling baronet, were told that the captive was insane, or was a murderer who had been apprehended. Sir John was thence conveyed by water along the Avon to the *Ruby*, a man-of-war lying in Kingsroad in the Mouth of the Severn that was commanded by his brother.

Captain Goodere, murderer of his brother. The illustration first appeared in James Caulfield's Portraits, Memoirs & Characters of Remarkable Persons Volumes 3-4, *1820.*

The baronet was kept captive in the purser's cabin aboard the *Ruby* until about five the following morning. The scheme was to kill him immediately, but this did not occur quite as planned. The reason for the delay appears to have been because the captain had hired two assassins to dispatch his brother, one of whom – Elisha Cole – drank himself into such a stupor that he was utterly incapable when the time came. Therefore the captain and his second assassin, an Irish crewman called Matthew Mahony, were forced to enlist another Irishman, Charles White, at the 11ᵗʰ hour. At first, White resisted; but he appears to have been induced by being told the *Ruby* held a 'Spanish prisoner' who had to be gotten rid of.

White must have realised very quickly that this was not the case, but he went along with the plot anyhow, no doubt persuaded by the thought of the money he would receive. The captain, Mahony and White were with their prisoner all the time from now on, and the latter was forced to listen to them discuss how the two Irish crewmen would be paid £200 and £150 respectively for killing him; and also how the criminals would divide up whatever money Sir John had in his pockets, together with his gold watch.

Sir John was then ruthlessly strangled by the two Irishmen. His treacherous brother Captain Samuel Goodere stood sentinel before the cabin door, sword in one hand and pistol in the other, should the sounds of struggle be overheard by the rest of the *Ruby*'s crew. White held the prisoner's hands while Mahoney tied a handkerchief round Sir John's neck and began to strangle him in cold blood. However, the handkerchief was too flimsy to be efficient, and Sir John struggled and yelled, 'Murder! Murder! For Christ's sake, don't kill me! Take all I have, but save my life, my dear brother! What? Must I die? Help! Help!' At this the captain ordered his two hit-men to use a cord, and to shut the victim up: Mahony garrotted the victim more efficiently on the second attempt, kneeling on his stomach while White held his hands tightly. Sir John was aged about 61 when he was murdered.

The murder was as brazen as could be imagined, and the captain was quickly arrested under the following circumstances. After the crime, he allowed the two Irishmen to go ashore again, and shut himself in the cabin. However, other crewmembers had seen the drama played out through crevices in the cabin wall, and the ship's cooper went to Goodere's lieutenant and informed the man that murder had been committed by their captain. The lieutenant was appalled; he ordered the cooper to knock on the purser's cabin door and tell Captain Goodere a chest had been forced open and rifled; thus deluded into promising to investigate this fictitious robbery, Captain Goodere opened the door a fraction to the cooper - at which a number of men barged their way in. They found the captain to be sharing the cabin with the corpse of his garrotted sibling, and seized him. Mahony and White were taken shortly afterwards, with all three being committed to Bristol's Newgate. Here, Mahony confessed the whole plot, and asked only that a priest provide him with absolution.

Mahony and White, Captain Goodere's hired assassins. (From James Caulfield's Portraits, Memoirs & Characters of Remarkable Persons Volumes 3-4, *1820.)*

Possibly Captain Goodere was over-reliant on the supposition that his crew would keep their mouths shut; he made a pathetic attempt at defence, claiming his brother was a suicidal lunatic, but despite this his trial was a foregone conclusion. On 26 March all three accused were tried at Bristol and (after nine hours) convicted of Sir John Dineley Goodere's murder.

Captain Samuel Goodere's service record in the navy was impressive: he had been at the taking of St Sebastian, Ferrol and St Antenio, at which last he burnt three men-of-war and also the magazine and stores. The assassination of his brother brought a sad and squalid end to his naval career, the twin passions of avarice and rage overwhelming all common sense and judgement in the mind of the captain – who, from the moment he ordered his victim taken on College Green, had effectively thrown his own life away as well.

Mahony alone was sentenced to hang in chains after his death, at the mouth of the River Avon. Three other men involved in Sir John's abduction were sentenced to twelve months in prison and were also fined 40 shillings; one Jane Williams was sentenced at the same assizes to be executed for the murder of her 'bastard child'.

Immediately following his conviction, the captain chose to walk from the Guildhall to Newgate. It was reported he wore a scarlet coat and doffed his hat to numerous passers-by. Less than a month later, on 15 April 1741, 'The wretched fratricide was executed within sight of his own ship…an attempt at rescue having been frustrated.'

On the day of execution, Mahony, White and the infant-killing Jane Williams were all drawn by cart from Newgate to St Michael's Hill gallows. It was about one in the afternoon, and the captain followed them in a mourning coach accompanied by the Rev. Mr Penrose. All three old salts behaved very penitently, and at the place of execution the captain kissed and shook the hands of his hired killers: then the captain dropped his handkerchief in a prearranged signal. The horse drew away the cart and all of them were launched into oblivion together. The captain was aged about 54 at the time of his death.

'CORONER'S VERDICT, LUNACY'

On 17 April 1741 a farmer's wife named Mrs Charlton, who lived at Fishburn, near Sedgefield in County Durham, picked up a meat cleaver and used it to kill her 14-year-old son. With the same weapon she then killed her two younger children before stabbing herself under the ear and expiring almost immediately.

This seemingly senseless multiple murder had been accomplished while her husband had been outside, trying to get a cow out of a ditch. The coroner recorded a verdict of 'Lunacy'.

RYE'S INFAMOUS ASSASSIN

Before the sea receded and its harbour silted up, Rye in East Sussex was an important town, its prosperity through membership of the confederation known as the Cinque Ports illustrated by the development of Mermaid Street during the 1700s. The place also hosted the Mermaid Inn, a focal point for smuggling gangs who drank with their pistols laid on the table, unchallenged by the law. However, Rye's most famous murder appears not to be linked to this pastime.

In 1743 there resided in the house on the southwest corner of Pump Street a butcher named John Breeds. Breeds entertained a violent animosity towards Mr Thomas Lamb, Rye's mayor and one of the leading dignitaries in the town. The cause of this hatred is unclear (it may have been due to a property dispute); but 17 March found the butcher armed with a knife and skulking around the rocks, waiting for a vessel to depart (from what is now near the present fish-market). The reason for this is that Breeds believed Mr Lamb would be waving the ship off, carrying as it did a relative off to France.

When the vessel had sailed, Breeds hid himself in the shadows of St Mary's Church and waited for Lamb to walk through the churchyard: for the road from the rocks to Lamb's house ran in this direction.

Between two and three in the morning - the moon being up but partially clouded - Breeds espied a figure coming in his direction. He struck, leaping out on his enemy and stabbing him ferociously with his butcher's knife, before throwing the weapon away and running off. Unfortunately, however, Breeds had attacked the wrong man. Mr Lamb had been unable to watch the ship depart and so had requested his brother-in-law and neighbour, Allan Grebble, go in his stead: and it was he who Breeds had fatally wounded as the man returned home. Grebble managed to stagger to his house in Middle Street, where he sat down and expired. It was found that he had suffered two stab wounds to his left breast.

Breeds ambushed his victim by St Mary's Church in Rye.

Grebble's murder caused great shock, for he had formerly occupied the position of town mayor for ten years. At first Grebble's servant was suspected in the killing, but this suspicion was soon allayed by Breeds' unhinged behaviour: he was considered of an ungovernable temper generally, and was subsequently arrested running nearly naked through the streets of Rye shouting, 'Butchers should kill lambs!' Clearly implicating himself, Breeds was taken and committed for trial; while languishing in jail, he confessed the murder, and also confessed he had attacked another man earlier, wounding the fellow in the arm.

Breeds' trial subsequently took place in a warehouse on the Strand, the town hall then still in the process of being built. He made a spirited attempt at a defence, attempting to convince the jurors he was insane, and claiming to have encountered a party of devils in Dead Man's Lane just outside the town; but it made no difference. He was found guilty following a trial presided over by the current Mayor of Rye, and sentenced on 8 June 1743 to be executed and hung in chains. For this purpose a gibbet was erected in the marshland at the west end of Rye (which quickly earned the name Gibbet Marsh). Interestingly, a Victorian gazetteer records of this, '(The) gibbet is down, and all that remains of the miserable culprit is his skull, which is now laying in the upper chamber of the town hall.'

This – together with the assassin's final suit, the metal cage – is still within this building, and it presents what might be considered a truly unique antiquity from the 18th century.

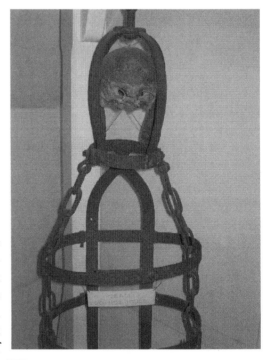

John Breeds' skull remains in his gibbet cage. (This can be found in Rye's Town Hall.) He hung for many years on the Gibbet Marsh near Rye, and the rest of his bones either fell victim to the elements or wildlife – or else were taken piecemeal by superstitious locals, who thought them a cure for rheumatism.

TRIAL OF AN 8-YEAR-OLD

In May 1742 there occurred the strangest case of the era: that of an 8-year-old girl who had been tried at the last Carmarthen Assizes for the murders of her 6-year-old brother and 4-year-old sister. A coroner's inquest had previously brought in a verdict of wilful murder against the little girl, but the thoroughly bizarre circumstances of the case did not come out until the trial.

The three children lived in a cottage near the Welsh coastline, and appeared to have been raised on fearful stories of atrocities committed by Spanish sailors, as well as the ever-present danger of them landing on the beaches. One day the children were left alone, and in the parent's absence a ferocious thunderstorm broke. The children became petrified with the belief that this heralded the landing of a Spanish vessel, and so the eldest made a decision to destroy herself with a hedging-bill. Seeing this, the two younger children cried out repeatedly, 'Pray sister, kill us first!' – upon which she actually dispatched them. She then fearfully wounded herself and ran out of the cottage into the rain to throw herself into a nearby river. In doing this she was spotted by some neighbours, who confirmed to the court that the terrified child had told them she was going to drown herself 'for fear of the Spaniards', and had slain her siblings because of this same reason.

Happily, this tormented little girl - the reality of whose actions was likely to haunt her a lot longer than tales of imaginary Spaniards - was acquitted of the killings.

THE EXAMPLE OF THE MILITARY

What could poor townsfolk do when the soldiery were quartered in their locale? The question was a worrying one, for some sections of the British military were a law unto themselves, and, if offended, the threat of mutiny and their running amok was always present.

At the end of September 1742 four soldiers were causing such a clamour in the Black Boy tavern in Kettering, Northamptonshire, that the innkeeper asked them to keep quiet. One of the 'scarlet gentlemen' slapped him across the face for his trouble, and then hit him again when he complained. The two struggled, with the innkeeper winning the fight; and so the soldier's comrades roused the rest of their troop, which numbered near 40, and returned to the inn. By this time, the townsfolk had also amassed in great numbers too, and the first person to confront the soldiery in an effort to mediate (who happened to be the landlord's brother) received such a violent blow from a sword that it almost severed his hand from the wrist. The poor fellow was then stabbed 20 times, and killed.

News of the trouble reached the ears of the commanding officer, who hastened thither. At a great risk to his own life he managed to talk the men into surrendering their swords, and saw to it that five principally involved in the murder were committed to gaol.

Sadly, this type of arbitrary lawlessness among the soldiery had been a continual problem: it was almost as if sections of the military saw themselves as above the law, and many of the crimes they committed were common murder of the worst kind. As an example, by this time there had long been a tomb in St Mary's Church, Hinckley, Leicestershire, lamenting the sad demise of 19-year-old Richard Smith, who '*a fatal halbert this body slew*'. Smith had been murdered in cold blood on 12 April 1727 by a recruiting sergeant in the town, whom he had affronted with a trifling joke.

Another incident had occurred on 2 July 1726. One Charles Fox was returning home in the company of some soldiers following their attendance at a boxing match at Holloway Mount, Shoreditch, when he was fatally stabbed by one among their number. A fracas had erupted over the result of the contest, which had occurred between a soldier and a baker, and Mr Fox had had the impudence to suggest the baker had lost through cheating. Fox was killed instantly, and two among the company of troops – Peter Percy and William Jones – were just as quickly incarcerated in Newgate on a charge of murder.

A final example goes to show this type of thing was not unduly uncommon. On 16 April 1756 it was reported that two officers belonging to Lord Charles Hay's Regiment, on a recruiting drive in Gravesend, Kent, had brutally killed the driver of a post-chase because the boy wasn't carrying them fast enough up Shooter's Hill to a playhouse in the capital. They knocked the lad off his feet and thrust a sword so forcefully through his body that it stuck in the ground; they then beat and stabbed him as he lay mortally wounded in the dirt road. The two killers were apprehended by another post-boy up ahead (armed with a whip) and a hedger carrying a billhook, both of whom had watched the tragedy unfold. When one of the officers attempted to flee, he was wrestled to the ground by a quick-thinking butcher who came upon the scene. Both were committed to Maidstone Gaol, it being reported that one of them was heir to a £600 annual fortune.

On 13 August that year, the officers – named Brown and Lauder – were tried at Rochester; the former was acquitted, the latter found guilty of the murder. Lauder went to the gallows three days later on Pennenden Heath for killing the post-boy, a lad by the name of William Forster. The point is that these two felons were *officers*; and if this was the example the officer class set, then what discipline, realistically, could be expected among those they commanded?

MASSACRE BY MISTREATMENT

In 1742, Horace Walpole recorded in his letters to Sir Horace Mann an appalling episode that amounts to a massacre. He wrote:

'There has lately been the most horrible scene of murder imaginable; a parcel of drunken constables took it into their heads to put the laws in execution against disorderly persons, and so took up every woman they met, until they had collected five or six and twenty, all of whom they thrust into St Martin's

Roundhouse (in St Martin's Lane), where they kept them all night, with doors and windows closed. The poor creatures, who could not stir or breathe, screamed as long as they had any breath left, begging at least for water; one poor wretch said she was worth eighteen-pence, and would gladly give it for a draught of water, but in vain! So well did they keep them there that in the morning four were found stifled to death, two died soon after, and a dozen more are in a shocking way... Several of them were beggars, who by virtue of having no lodging, were necessarily found in the street, and the others honest labouring women. One of the dead was a poor washerwoman, big with child, who was returning home late from washing. One of the constables is taken, and others absconded; but I question if any of them will suffer death.'

In the wake of this mass killing the mob attacked the Round House, demolishing it, and nightly pulled it down when attempts were made to rebuild it. The keeper of the gaol, William Bird, was subsequently arrested for the atrocity, and when he was brought before Colonel de Veil it was found necessary to sneak him to his examination via Hyde Park Corner – for an angry mob numbering in thousands had gathered. Bird was incarcerated in Newgate to the cries of ''Huzza!' by the crowds, and subsequently tried for multiple murder at the Old Bailey throughout September and October 1742. On 15 October, he was convicted of murdering one of the women, Phillis Wells, a sober, honest and industrious woman swept up in the dragnet when the ineffective and drunken constables had embarked on their purge.

When he was sentenced to death, Bird wept openly in the court. However, it was later reported that his sentence was commuted to transportation for life.

Sadly, this was not the first case like this; for a trial forced over events in Marshalsea Prison illustrates how truly appalling the conditions were in the capital's gaols. In 1729 it became necessary to try William Acton, deputy-keeper and turnkey at Marshalsea, on multiple counts of murder. He was accused of mistreating some of his prisoners so badly that, in effect, it became torture. Acton (and a subordinate named Rogers) were in particular accused of murdering an inmate called Thomas Bliss. Bliss, for the crime of attempting to escape, was thrust into a dismal prison-cellar called the Strong Room - a damp, lightless cell crawling with rats and toads, where inmates were secured to the wall with iron collars or other chains. Following a second escape attempt from this Hell-hole, Bliss was dragged back by his legs over the stonework, beaten violently with 'ox sinews' (leather straps) and had an iron cap forced on his head of an archaic manufacture used to steady prisoner's heads when they were being branded. He was then tortured mercilessly until he confessed who had provided him with the rope he had used in his latest escape attempt. Even when he was released from the Strong Room, Bliss was kept chained – his legs swelling so grotesquely that his leg irons buried themselves in his flesh; and a blanket thrown over him seems to have been the only concession towards humanity he was granted. After several months of this Bliss was released. He took himself to work as a carpenter in Southgate, but soon fell sick, blaming 'inward bruises' inflicted by his gaolers. He died soon after, and William Acton was brought to trial at Kingston Assizes on 1 August 1729.

Acton was acquitted of murder. Other charges against this man (including three further murder indictments) terminated in acquittal at the same assizes. The whole affair illustrates the utter want of any proper management in the prisons of this period, as well as the habitual cruelty and tyranny of turnkeys and deputies allowed to indulge their sadism by the all-too-absent governors. In each case Acton escaped not because he was innocent, but because it was difficult to decide how far the cruelty had been Acton's deliberate policy, and how far it had arisen from an exaggeration of his orders by the turnkeys under his command.

PSYCHOPATHIC HOUSEBREAKERS

If a man could be hanged for a lamb as much as a sheep, then why should he care if he killed the whole flock? Any criminal who broke into a house to commit burglary knew that there was a good chance they might end up committing murder also: for the greater crime might be necessary to conceal the lesser, seeing as how the penalty was the same anyway. Often, house robbers didn't simply kill in panic during their desire to escape: when the situation commanded it, they deliberately slaughtered the occupants to avoid being identified at a later date.

A typical example of the way that robbers preyed on vulnerable homeowners occurred in Coventry, at the time a growing manufacturing town in the county of Warwickshire. A man named Thomas Wildey earned a living as a wool-comber, but business was not good; he was forced to approach his aunt, a widow called Mrs Susannah Wall, who ran the White Lion public house in Smithford Street, and request a loan. Mrs Wall refused his request for money, and so on the night of 22 January 1734 Wildey next visited the house of Mrs Wall's daughter's in order to make a similar request. He found this premises empty; and so in desperation he returned to his aunt's house at midnight and knocked on the door.

Mrs Wall opened the door of the White Lion and Wildey immediately knocked the candle she carried out her hand. He then thrust her to the floor and viciously cut her throat from ear to ear. Running upstairs, he was in the process of rifling the bedroom when he perceived the daughter, Mrs Anne Shenton, laid in bed. Mrs Shenton had come to stay the night with her mother, and although nearly deaf she was now fully awake and staring right at Wildey. Mrs Shenton looked at his bloodied hands and said in fright, 'Lord have mercy upon me, what are you doing here in that condition?' Wildey told her that he had just killed her mother, and now had to dispatch her also; marching over to the bed, he grabbed the younger woman and cut her throat so forcefully that he almost decapitated her. Afterwards, he took a large quantity of gold and silver coins from a chest and fled the premises.

The next day Wildey went into Coventry and paid some money he owed – seemingly the cause of his desperation. When he returned home at eleven that night he was taken on suspicion of the killings, his guilt having apparently been intimated by comments his wife made earlier that day: these were to the effect that she hoped 'he was not concerned in the murder'. While in jail he confessed the atrocity and seemed very penitent, admitting that he had carried it all out in a quarter of an hour. He also claimed he had no desire to kill the younger woman, as he had not expected to see her there; but under the circumstances he had murdered her anyway. Thomas Wildey was hanged on 7 May 1734, his body afterwards encased in an iron gibbet on Whitley Common.

When the wrong type of person gained entry to one's house, the consequences could be truly horrific. On the afternoon of 16 June 1737 Catherine, the wife of Mr Robert Long, apparently admitted a man into her house on Limekiln-hill, Limehouse, a district of East London. Neighbours saw the man go in; quite how or why he gained admittance is unclear, although promiscuity does not appear to have been the reason; for Mrs Long had another visitor in the shape of a 4-year-old neighbour's boy called Robert Hooper, of whom she was very fond. Two hours later Mrs Long still entertained her guest, but at some point the man sent the boy out of the house for a penny's worth of cherries. In the child's absence the visitor dispatched Mrs Long by striking her on the skull with a hammer that happened to lie nearby before cutting her throat so forcefully that he almost severed the poor woman's head from her neck. Unfortunately, the boy returned with the cherries while the murderer was in the process of ransacking the Long's house; the man cut the child's throat also and threw the bairn's body on the floor beside that of the slain woman.

The two bodies were found when the boy's mother came to collect him at about six o'clock in the evening. The man had long gone, taking with him two silver watches, a silver chain and two seals, one plain gold ring and three silver teaspoons. He was last seen heading in the direction of Greenwich. Shortly afterwards, a man named McConnell was arrested in Goodman's Fields attempting to pawn the ring at a pawnbrokers. This man was put on trial at the Old Bailey in July, but – owing to the confusion of various witnesses as to whether he was the man glimpsed at the Long's home – he was acquitted.

Another appalling crime like this was reported in January 1741. On 9 January one Mrs Saunders returned to her home one morning near Fenny Stratford, Buckinghamshire, having visited Fenny Stratford the previous night. She found the house broken open and her husband, Edward Saunders, murdered; not only this, but George, the 7-year-old son of Mr Forster (who kept the chandler's shop near St James's House), had also been killed by the intruders - 'his head almost cut off'. We may surmise that perhaps the boy was on an errand, and was killed by the intruders merely for being in the wrong place at the wrong time. Both bodies were found in a booth or hut used by Saunders to sell ale 'to persons that travell'd the west Chester road, contiguous to the Highway just opposite to Rickley Wood, by a place call'd Gilbert close in this parish'. Both victims were interred on 11 January 1741; we learn that several persons were taken in on suspicion of this horrific crime.

A final example illustrates that this type of thing was not unduly uncommon. The same year, one Richard Pilgrim committed a horrific double murder in the parish of Knebworth, Hertfordshire, made all more remarkable for his ridiculous but determined attempts to deflect guilt from himself.

At around eight in the morning Pilgrim had called at an alehouse run by a 70-year-old woman called Mary Woodland and her son, aged about 20. Some time later the woman and her son were found dead, with both showing clear signs that they had met with foul play. The woman displayed a bruise which indicated she had been violently knocked down, then 'struck below the ear like a sheep'. Quite some time later she had been cut across the neck right to the bone. The son had been killed beside the fireside, stabbed at least seven times under the chin with a *blunt* penknife; this last was evidenced by the fact that determined attempts appeared to have been made to decapitate him, which had almost succeeded. The two bodies were afterwards dragged and thrown over each other in a bloody, untidy heap in a dark passage. Their attacker had then ransacked the house and literally broke the chests within to pieces in his hunt for plunder before making off. The two victims were interred in Knebworth's parish church on 14 October 1741.

Richard Pilgrim stood no hope of escape right from the start, and was captured within four hours. This occurred when he attempted to sell the clothes of the two victims, and following the observation that there were two bloodstains on his coat a search of his person ensued; the bloodied knife was then discovered in his pocket. While he was in custody, and before he appeared in front of the Justices, he accused two persons of being his accomplices in the crime. Both of these were dragged out of bed in the middle of the night, but it was quickly proven they were not guilty of anything, and Pilgrim confessed his deception. One of those accused was a shoemaker, and it seemed the murderer had pointed the finger of suspicion at this man because of an argument they had had over a pair of shoes a week earlier. It is likely that Pilgrim hoped his accusations would drag the poor shoemaker to the gallows along with him, thereby adding him to the list of his victims.

Pilgrim next attempted to blame the whole occurrence on a shocking accident. When he was examined by two Justices, he claimed that upon his arrival he had been drawn some beer by the son, which he found to be off. Pilgrim stated that during a quarrel about this with the old woman, she had casually fallen on a knife he was using to eat bread and cheese; this had pierced her neck and as a result she had died. Pilgrim had subsequently entered into a scuffle with the son, William Woodland, who had been fatally injured by accident. The whole event had been a tragic mistake, Pilgrim told Edward Searle and Thomas Shalcross, Esqs.

Of course, none of this was believed and on 5 March 1742 Pilgrim pleaded guilty to both murders at the assizes held in Hertford. After his execution he was hung in chains on Rableyheath, not too far from where the crime had occurred at (what is now designated) Old Knebworth. He was aged about 34 at the time of his death.

A DREAM OF DEATH

Around the beginning of April 1743 a soldier belonging to Fleming's Regiment, being quartered in Reading, Berkshire, deserted and fled into Lincolnshire. Here, he fell into company with a man who he subsequently robbed and murdered, stealing 5 guineas from him and also taking the victim's silver shoe buckles. The deserter tipped the corpse down a well, but was shortly thereafter arrested for desertion and returned to Reading.

The body of the murdered man was found by a singular circumstance: a lad in Lincolnshire who kept sheep twice dreamed that a missing lamb of his would be found in the afore-mentioned well, and (despite mockery) determined to look for himself. Of course, he found the victim within. A hunt began for the missing silver shoe buckles, which were very recognisable, and these were traced to the man who now possessed them – who stated he had bought them off the soldier in good faith.

Warrants were issued for the suspect's arrest in Lincolnshire, and these being received in Reading, he 'was taken up in the Forbury and committed to the Town Jail'. Here, the soldier relieved all question of his guilt by hanging himself.

THE VIOLENT TIMES OF SIR JOHN WITTEWRONG

It is difficult to imagine how a wayward great-grandson could bring a noble family into more disrepute than in the case of Sir John Wittewrong.

The Wittewrong line were of Flemish Protestant descent, and the first Sir John enjoyed a remarkable and distinguished career. He was knighted in 1640, but during the Civil Wars he fought on the side of Parliament; later, he was appointed High Sherriff of Hertfordshire in 1658 and made a baronet in 1662. He owned land at Wheathampstead and Stantonbury, and purchased Rothamsted Manor on the western fringes of Harpenden.

277

When Sir John died in June 1693 the title was inherited by his son John, who became the second baronet. When he passed away in 1697 it was another John who became the third baronet; and this fellow became MP for Wycombe. The Wittewrongs were certainly among the elite of the time.

Unfortunately the fourth baronet was of a different mould. This Sir John – his future already catered for – fell into the traditionally debauched way of life following an army career.

On 2 May 1721 the fourth Sir John Wittewrong committed murder when he 'barbarously' wounded a man called Joseph Griffith with his sword during a disagreement at the Saracen's Head Inn in Newport Pagnell, Buckinghamshire; this fellow is described as 'a mountebank', meaning a purveyor of patent medicines in public places, and some accounts suggest he was a surgeon from Chatham in Kent. Griffith died soon after being stabbed.

Sir John was aged about 26 at the time. He fled overseas following his crime, but we are told by Buckinghamshire historian George Lipscomb: '(Sir John) came over again, after some years, into England, got into the Fleet Prison, and there died of the wounds he had received, by being sadly beaten, in a drunken quarrel, about 28 March 1743.' He appears to have been aged about 49 at the time of his murder.

This opulent family having fallen thus into decay, Sir William Wittewrong succeeded the title upon the demise of his unhappy brother, and was the last baronet. What is interesting about this is the manner in which the fourth baronet conducted himself, for he seems to have behaved almost like a common gang member; it is also noteworthy that, when it came down to it, his noble heritage made little difference to the fellow prisoner who fatally attacked him inside London's notorious debtor's prison.

MURDER AT THE MANOR HOUSE: A FAMILY TRADITION

Here we return briefly to the realm of old family traditions. In Kineton, Warwickshire, the old Manor House stood in the fields near Little Kineton, and it was inhabited by a well-loved family called the Bentleys. Historically the place was the home of Sir Charles Bentley, Sheriff of Warwickshire, but by the 1740s it was occupied by his three daughters, Charlotte, Anne and Grace – the latter being engaged to Edward Nicholas, curate of St Peter's.

According to a tradition recorded by writer Charles James Ribton-Turner in 1893, the house was the scene of a brutal murder in 1744. The family's coachman had cast covetous eyes upon a valuable silver tea service in the possession of the sisters, and so formed a plan to rob the house when everyone was at church on a Sunday morning. However, when he put his scheme into operation he found the cook maid still on the premises, as well as Harriet Nicholas, the curate's 5-year-old sister (or possibly, niece). When the cook caught the thief bundling the silverware into a sack, he grabbed a meat cleaver and struck her on the head with it, killing the woman.

When the family returned home they found the cook lying in a pool of blood and little Harriet missing. At first they were frantic with worry, fearing the murderer had kidnapped the child; but at length she was found hiding inside the old brick fire copper in the corner of the kitchen. She had witnessed the attack on the cook maid and hidden before she could be spotted, which was incredibly quick-witted on her part; for very likely the murderer would have dispatched her also. It is said that she was unconcernedly playing cards with herself when she was found.

The coachman is said to have ended up on the gallows for his crime: but if he did then this author can find no record of it. Still, the little girl was made much of for her escape and her composure, and she had her portrait painted in which she held the self-same playing cards that she had been found with. (The whereabouts of this portrait are currently unclear.) The crime, however, appears to have affected this genteel household quite badly, for the curate died in 1745 and Miss Grace passed away around 1752 aged just 35 (it is said of a broken heart). Little Harriet died *c.*1746 aged about seven, and the house itself was pulled down after being purchased by Lord Willoughby around 1834. The stones were used to build the bridge at Compton Verney.

Stories of this nature, vaguely substantiated, are legion across Britain. One particularly intriguing tale also recorded in 1893 concerns the Glebe Farm, or Bumble Bee Hall as it was known, in Sharnford, Leicestershire. A boy who tended sheep in the fields near the farm overheard one day some thieves conspiring to rob the place. He told his master and the plot was thwarted; but the boy was waylaid early one morning by the gang, who flayed him alive and hung pieces of his skin on a nearby thorn bush. Afterwards they killed and skinned a sheep, wrapping the boy in its hide. When he was found, the boy was still alive and gasped that, 'It didn't hurt him much, except when they pulled it over his fingers and toes.'

This story was recounted by numerous old local people, including a 94-year-old local man who heard it when he was a boy and could even point out the actual thorn bush upon which the skin had been draped. Since the story was recorded in 1893 (in *Leicestershire and Rutland Notes & Queries*), this suggests it originated from an event that occurred in the 18th century. According to *Lincolnshire Notes & Queries* in 1891 this gruesome fate also befell a page-boy who worked at Girsby Hall in the Wolds.

The only question with stories like this is – how much of it is true? Whatever the case, they certainly do make intriguing reading.

WAR CRIMES AND RETRIBUTIONS

The site of the Battle of Culloden. The encounter was the last land battle fought between two opposing armies in Britain, though not the last conflict to engulf the British Isles – sea and air conflicts, revolts and riots would occur through the next 250 years.

Following the complete routing of the Jacobites at the Battle of Culloden (16 April 1746), a war crime occurred throughout the Highlands of Scotland. The victorious Duke of Cumberland marched from Inverness to Fort Augustus on 23 May with the main body of his army, where he arrived the next day. Here, he dispatched parties all around the Highlands, who committed the greatest excesses of atrocity in pacifying the land and rooting out rebels and Jacobite sympathisers. Vast numbers of the common people's houses were reduced to ashes, their cattle were driven off in thousands and many innocent people were either massacred or died from the effects of their mistreatment: many women and children were found dead in the hills, having simply starved to death after fleeing or being turned out. In Edinburgh, the colours of fourteen standards taken at Culloden were symbolically burnt by the hangman.

Typical of these events was the 'justice' meted out to a poor man named Alexander Kinnaird, from Culvie in the parish of Marnoch. On 10 November 1746 the duke's troops marched through Banff and tore down the Episcopal chapel; they also spotted Kinnaird notching a stick and surmised he was recording in this fashion the number of boats passing the river with troops in.

Taken for a spy, he was immediately dragged to a tree and hoisted up, where he was allowed to hang until he expired. It was recorded in 1845 that this arbitrary murder occurred 'near the site of the present chief hotel'.

Without digressing too much into atrocities committed in the wake of the war, it is clear that this is a complex subject. A letter to the *Westminster Journal* (26 July 1746) seems to sum up the for-and-against scenario of the unhappy state of Britain following the decisive Culloden battle: 'A letter to the journalist suggests the severities practised against the Highlanders, in destroying their habitations and killing their cattle, are become necessary and justifiable, since continuing still in arms, they rob and murder the English... But the letter writer wishes the work might be done without bloodshed.'

Prince William Augustus, the Duke of Cumberland, ever after went by the name of 'Butcher' in the Highlands for his role in ruthlessly stamping out the Jacobite threat forever. These were cruel times, for the army also dealt ruthlessly with *loyal* subjects in an effort to stamp out dissent; on 23 April – a week after the battle, and at the other end of the country – five deserters were shot in Hyde Park.

It was in this dangerous atmosphere that intrigue and murder occurred. At the beginning of June a certain John Catanach, servant to Mr Ogilvy of Kenny, Angus, who had been in the Highland army with his master, was arrested by a party of St George's Dragoons.

However, after a short time Catanach was set free by the authorities, and on one or two subsequent occasions he was observed to make his way between the place of his former residence and Lieutenant-Colonel Arabin's quarters. It being suspected that Catanach had become a government informer against the Jacobites, he was 'barbarously murdered' on 11 June 1746.

We learn that a number of people were arrested. Francis Anderson and Andrew Fithie were held in Kenny, and – tellingly – another servant of Mr Ogilvy's, one Barbara Couts, was also detained. All three were brought to Edinburgh and indicted, and when the trial opened in September the truth of the matter came out.

Local suspicions being certain that Catanach had become an informer to save his skin, a general concern swept the small communities hereabouts that Cumberland's purge would claim neighbours, friends and loved ones. Anderson and Fithie entered into a conspiracy to get rid of Catanach (that this might bring down more heat on them does not seem to have been a consideration in their plot), and others openly expressed a desire to join them. However, the two men went it alone, and soon found Catanach to be at Meikle Kenny, a tiny hamlet northeast of Alyth. Both men confronted him, saying, 'Now John, you are come to ruin the country and honest folk.' Catanach declared: 'I have not informed against you or any of yours', and upon this admission the two men knocked him down. Anderson held him while Fithie struck him an almighty blow on the head

281

with a large stone, using such violence that blood shot all over Anderson's breast. Then both men struck him again and again on the head until he died. A decision was made to hastily bury Catanach's body, but it did not stay long undiscovered.

Unfortunately for Anderson and Fithie, several local people appeared against them at their trial, although perhaps they expected this: the community wanted to be left in peace from the attentions of 'Butcher' Cumberland. Both men were sentenced to death, and on 10 September 1746 Francis Anderson was hanged between Edinburgh and Leith. Fithie was hanged the following day at Forfar. Barbara Couts was acquitted.

Anderson, in his last speech, declared that Ms Couts, as well as those who had testified against him, had all known of the plot; indeed, the whole community had rejoiced when news of Catanach's killing came to light.

Although the Jacobite's final and legendary last stand at Culloden is more suitable for another book, the whole campaign does provide some interesting examples of civilian violence outside the arena of the battlefield. For instance, on 15 February 1746 (while the rebellion was still in progress) Lieutenant George M'Farlane of the Argyllshire Militia decided to take a constitutional with a companion, Captain James Campbell, before dinner. The pair walked about a mile out of Fort William to the scene of the Civil War-era Battle of Inverlochy and the ancient castle. On their return home, as they were stepping the River Nevis, a 'rebel officer' called Evan Cameron of Inverlochy ambushed the pair: firing a gun from behind a rock, Cameron shot M'Farlane through the body, killing him immediately. This shooting was carried out in the presence of numerous witnesses. Although the British Isles were in a state of rebellion at this time, Cameron's action was nonetheless a premeditated assassination, and when he was finally run to ground on 16 December 1746 Cameron was charged with the lieutenant's murder. He was incarcerated at Fort William. M'Farlane's death was greatly lamented in military and government circles – but most of all by his wife and six children. Cameron was thought to have committed the murder in conjunction with two others; one of the suspect's houses was torched by the militia in the immediate aftermath of the shooting.

Another crime that stands out is the killing of Colonel James Gardner, who fell at the Battle of Prestonpans on 21 September 1745, aged 57, when he was struck down with a Lochaber axe by the Highlanders during the first significant clash of the rising. He received his death wound while lying injured on the ground, and afterwards the Highlanders stripped his body to the waist before the colonel was recovered by a servant and taken to Tranent, where he expired. In August 1746 some of the news-sheets reported that among 350 rebel prisoners held at Carlisle was the man who killed Colonel Gardner – an act that the Hanoverians seem to have viewed almost as an assassination, despite it occurring on the field of conflict. This was because intelligence indicated that the attacker – who seems to have been very young – came up behind the colonel while he battled two or three opponents, and struck him an almighty blow with a hedge-bill. This person – John McNaughton – was identified by a foot soldier, who claimed to have been within five yards of the man and seen the killing committed with his own eyes. On 15 September 1746 McNaughton was tried along with a number of other 'rebels' and sentenced to death for the murder of 'brave Col. Gardner'. Three days later, he was executed on 'Gallowhill near Carlisle' along with eight others convicted of crimes relating to the rebellion.

The English news-sheets were ever ready to report the Highlanders as murderous traitors; for instance, news from Scotland on 2 November 1745 read: 'Messrs John Soly and Thomas Ayres, Surveyors of the Excise in that kingdom, have been kill'd in cold blood by the rebels, near Hamilton-Castle, for not readily delivering up the produce of the revenue in their hands.' A particularly interesting report from Perth implies that differing loyalties among Scots played themselves out in violent incidents of factional warfare. News from that town reported that on the evening of 30 October 1745 a party of 'loyalists' (i.e. loyal to the Hanoverians) murdered seven Highlanders who were there to guard a number of government officers imprisoned following the battle at Prestonpans. The following day 100 more Highlanders arrived in Perth, demanding that the murderers be delivered over to them; this being refused, the principal persons among the Perth loyalists were obliged to flee the town and seek safety on board a government man-of-war – this led to Admiral Byng leading a force of marines into Perth to rescue the captured officers. Perth seems to have suffered divided loyalties, to say the least, and the atmosphere in the town must have been very threatening throughout the revolt.

There were some interesting incidents in England too. The memoirs of one Captain Daniel evidence that during the rebels' withdrawal from Wigan in late 1745 someone actually attempted to assassinate Prince Charles Edward Stuart, the second Jacobite pretender to the throne who was popularly known as 'Bonnie Prince Charlie'. However, the assassin – who remained unidentified – got the wrong target, and fired at Quartermaster-General Mr O'Sullivan. Despite their being in the middle of a strategic manoeuvre, a futile search was made for the responsible party. Sections of the Jacobite army were by this time becoming resentful of the prince's clemency towards Englishmen who treated them hostilely, and blamed this compassion for encouraging the shooting. Captain Daniel, in his notes, recalled a previous instance that had roused the Jacobite troops' anger: in Manchester, a woman and her son had been brought before the prince, accused of brutally killing a young English volunteer. They confessed, but Charles would not allow them to be put to death.

On 19 December 1745, as part of this strategic retreat, the Skirmish of Clifton Moor was fought between Penrith and Kendal, in which some 25 died in a desperate, violent action between the Hanoverian forces and the Jacobite rebels.

This has sometimes been called the 'last battle fought on *English* (not British) soil', although this is contentious and there are other candidates for this honour depending on one's opinion of what constitutes a 'battle'. Either way, the moniker does not address the fact that some of the riots seen in Britain later in the century were far more destructive than the Skirmish of Clifton Moor; nor does it acknowledge the *sea* and *air* conflicts seen during later periods of conflict in these isles.

Then there was the case of Father Germain Helmes. Helmes (generally called 'Holmes') was a native of Goosnargh in Lancashire, and a member of an old local family. Father Helmes was stationed at a chapel that had opened about 1715, in close proximity to White Hill near Grimsargh. He was a Franciscan and former lecturer in Catholicism at Douay, who during the conflict served at Lee House north of Longridge. During the hostile anti-Catholic persecution that followed the rebellion of '45-46 Helmes was apprehended by a mob at Lee House and incarcerated by magistrates in Lancaster Castle, loaded with iron chains, simply for practising his religion: the Stuart rising would, of course, have placed a Catholic on the throne - meaning that Helmes was a 'threat' during the campaign in England. After four months in these appalling, unsanitary conditions Father Helmes died in 1746, there being a great suspicion that his end was hastened by an unnamed 'wicked woman' who administered him poison. For his grossly unjust death, the father obtained the status of martyr.

Lancaster Castle in the 18th century: behind these walls, Father Helmes was allegedly assassinated. This picture is in the nearby Priory Church of St Mary.

Even as late as 1752 the threat of Jacobitism still lingered. The *Westminster Magazine* reported on 18 January that a genteelly-dressed man had lately been taken up in St James Park for dispersing papers to passers-by declaring that 'the two sons of the Pretender' were plotting to remove King George II by poison. Shouting that this was no secret to many at St James's, he was conducted to the Guard-room by soldiers.

'YOU HAVE KILLED YOUR PRINCE!'

One of the most remarkable murders connected to the Rising of '45 is credited with being an instrumental factor in allowing Charles Edward Stuart, the 'Young Pretender', to escape the British Isles.

In the middle of July 1746 one Roderick Mackenzie, an Edinburgh merchant who had been out with the prince, was skulking among the hills about Glen Moriston when he had the misfortune to bump into a platoon of soldiers at that time ranging parts of Scotland looking for the Pretender. Mackenzie was a genteel man, well dressed and about the prince's age and height; he was also not unlike him in appearance. The soldiers believed they might actually have chanced upon the prince, and so pursued the man. Mackenzie knew he stood no chance of escape and resolved to die with his sword in his hand, perhaps in his dying moments realising that fate had presented him with a manner of serving the prince more intimately than on any battlefield.

Mackenzie's bravery is said to have further strengthened the soldier's belief that they had run their quarry, the prince, to ground; one of them shot him in cold blood, and as he expired Mackenzie gasped, 'You have killed your prince! You have killed your prince!'

The soldiers were overjoyed with their supposed good fortune, and so decapitated their victim and took the head to Fort Augustus in the hope of claiming a £30'000 reward. The monumental (as it seemed at the time) news was carried immediately to the Duke of Cumberland, who - believing that his business was done in Scotland – started the long journey south from Fort Augustus to London on 18 July. He took the head with him.

This act of cold-blooded murder, committed on (as was supposed) a prince no less, does indicate what a terrible state the nation was in during the 45-46 rebellion; but it is also important because the soldiers and militia out looking for Charles Edward Stuart, the Young Pretender, became less strict, and not so vigilant as before: by which means he escaped from place to place, with less danger.

SCANDAL AND MYSTERY AT CAMBRIDGE UNIVERSITY

A rather bizarre and mysterious affair occurred at hallowed Cambridge University in 1746.

When the matter was reported at the beginning of April, it seemed straightforward enough, if a little usual for the respectable seat of learning that made Cambridge world-famous. The affair had reportedly begun when a scholar named Ashton, together with two fellow students, robbed another student at the same College, St John's, of a pair of silver buckles. By some means the victim discovered who had stolen from him, and when he began voicing his suspicions aloud the three villainous students entered into a conspiracy to kill him.

Ashton, however, had second thoughts about this, and so betrayed his two companions by telling the proposed victim that he was in danger. Because of this, the two others next formed a scheme to murder Ashton for his betrayal, and this they put into practice. The crime was performed by one of them, a young man called Brinkley, who found an excuse to stay in Ashton's chamber that night – where he stabbed the unfortunate young man in the neck and killed him.

Ashton had been enrolled at St John's College in November 1745, while Brinkley had only been there since January 1746. The matter shocked and scandalized the University, which prided itself on its discipline; yet the coroner employed to sit on Ashton's body could not find enough evidence to bring a charge of murder against Brinkley. Therefore the wayward student was confined to his rooms by the College authorities, with two persons guarding him at all times lest he try and flee, while the matter was investigated further.

St John's College Gate: the suspicious death occurred within this College.

An alternative version of this, purporting to come from someone at the College with first-hand knowledge, afterwards appeared in the news-sheets of the day, which put a somewhat different light on the death. This claimed that Ashton and Brinkley had spent the evening in question in Peterhouse College Gardens with two other scholars. At about 11 o'clock, they returned to their respective Colleges, Ashton and Brinkley sneaking through St John's Gate past the watchman lest he report them to the Master. According to

Brinkley's subsequent explanation, Ashton asked him to lie with him that night, to which Brinkley consented, this having apparently been a common practice of theirs. However, when they got to the top of the stairs Ashton changed his mind about this liaison and ordered Brinkley away; Brinkley, however, was not to be dissuaded and forced his way in – upon which the two young men undressed in the dark and lay on the bed together.

At some point, according to Brinkley, Ashton requested the chamber-pot, and so was passed it. The accused then declared that he heard Ashton simply fall off the bed and the pot smash; he dragged his friend back onto the bed, but – perceiving he did not stir – Brinkley left the room and engaged a neighbour and a porter to help. They found the young man dead on the bed, a great quantity of blood staining the bedclothes and the floor, with a stab-like wound above his collar bone.

A surgeon was next employed to look at Ashton's body, and he declared that the wound would have been immediately fatal, and must have been dealt by a shard of the chamber-pot, since no other object capable of inflicting such an injury could be found. Furthermore, he judged Brinkley's explanation of the 'accident' highly suspicious and unlikely, based on the nature and form of the wound – although, when pressed, he would not say it was *fully* impossible. On this basis, Brinkley was committed to the prison near the remains of Cambridge Castle charged with murder.

Cambridge Castle mound: the gatehouse was the town gaol in the 18th century.

Young Brinkley was tried at Cambridge Assizes in July 1746, but after five hours he was acquitted and set free. The matter remained unexplained, but what is curious about all this is the story that was first put out about Ashton being the victim of a criminal conspiracy. Perhaps this began with the Masters and Fellows, anxious that it be believed the killing stemmed from a villainous plot – rather than resulting from a homosexual misadventure…which is certainly what is implied.

The University of Oxford was not without its scandals either. Horace Walpole recorded on 10 April 1747: 'We have some chance of a peer's trial that has nothing to do with the (Jacobite) Rebellion. A servant of a college has been killed at Oxford, and a verdict of wilful murder by persons unknown, brought in by the coroner's inquest. These persons unknown are supposed to be Lord Abergavenny, Lord Charles Scot, and two more, who had played tricks with the poor fellow that night, while he was drunk, and the next morning he was found with his skull fractured at the foot of the first Lord's staircase. One pities the poor boys, who undoubtedly did not see the melancholy event of their sport.'

MURDER FOR NO REASON

On 21 May 1745, as a farmer named Mr Thomas Alder was walking through his fields at Hilton Park-house near Sunderland, he was attacked by a raging maniac.

The attacker knocked Mr Alder down and then cut his throat from ear to ear, before ripping open his belly. Alder's servant arrived on the scene carrying pails of milk, and at this the attacker threatened to murder the youth also. The young man ran terrified all the way to Sunderland to raise assistance, and when he returned with a group of people they found – amazingly – that the attacker still stood over the mangled body of his victim, screaming that he would kill the first person who came near him.

The standoff ended when the servant lobbed a large stone at the killer, stunning him long enough for the others to race across the field and secure him, disarming him in the process. The killer turned out to be a Sunderland keelman called Nicholas Haddock, who while in confinement confessed that he had borne his victim no malice; in fact, he said, he had never seen him before in his life to the best of his knowledge. He confessed the deed, and so suffered the penalty of death at Durham on 26 August 1745. At the time of execution, Haddock explained his crime merely by saying he was 'distracted at the time'.

'NOW OLD PARR'S YOUR NEIGHBOUR…'

On 7 March 1747 Banbury in Oxfordshire was the scene of an atrocious murder, committed on an elderly widow called Lydia Wilde.

Widow Wilde was found dead in the kitchen of her house in the Horse Fair, her skull having to all appearances been shattered with a hammer; her killer had also slit her throat almost from ear to ear. The house had been plundered of about £20, a gold watch and some silverware. The exact location of the murder is said to have been 'the second in the Horse Fair, reckoning from West Bar Street'.

Poor Lydia was interred on 11 March, and shortly afterwards her killer was arrested. He turned out to be an Irish shag weaver named Parr, and it proved no great task to find him; when his lodgings were searched his shoes were found bloodied up the heels, with further sprinkles of blood being detected on the upper leather. He had betrayed his guilt by leaving the town, and 100 people formed groups to track him down.

However, it is not necessarily the crime that is of interest, tragic though it was, but the aftermath. Parr was tried at Banbury, convicted and subsequently hanged in the Horse Fair opposite the scene of his crime. His body was gibbeted 'on the south side of the way leading from Easington farm-house towards Broad Street' and today one of the roads here is denominated Old Parr Road. Parr's execution appears to have created a great deal of carnival, and this shows that people were just as likely to engage in tasteless festivities in the small towns as they were in big cities upon the advent of what perhaps ought to have been a solemn occasion. A tradesman named John Baxter, who was noted as Banbury's chief wit, penned a humorous poem upon the gibbeting and dedicated it to the farmer who lived at Easington (who appears not to have been popular):

> *Rejoice and sing, Old Farmer Wells,*
> *Proclaim your joy with ring of bells;*
> *For now Old Parr's your neighbour*
> *And if the tree had been made like a 'T',*
> *It would have served both him and thee…*
> *And saved Jack Ketch some labour!*

Parr's body subsequently fell to the ground when the gibbet post collapsed, and some chimneysweeps took up the corpse and paraded it around Banbury to much applause and laughter. 100 years later the chains that immobilised Parr were still retained in the town for the attention of the curious.

Another example of the lack of any sort of compassion on 'hanging day' in Banbury is told by the town's historian, Alfred Beesley. Some years prior to Parr's execution some tinkers were hanged in the Goose Leys, adjoining the bridge, and their pet dog became so excitable that the spectators are said to have ceremonially hanged the animal next to its dead masters.

289

ROBERT FAWTHORP'S BUSY WEEK

The first week in October 1748 was quite a busy one for Yorkshireman Robert Fawthorp. In broad daylight on 3 October he broke into a grocer's at Church Fenton, North Yorkshire, and bloodily murdered two women on the premises, Elizabeth Ferrand (or *Terrand*) and Mary Parker, before rifling the house of everything of value. Having killed the women with a cooper's adze, or some other such blunt instrument, he decamped with his booty in preparation for his marriage – which took place the following day on 4 October.

The barking of a dog attracted the attention of neighbours, who broke into the grocery and 'discovered the two lifeless bodies, mangled in a most awful and shocking manner'. Fawthorp was arrested on the 6 October and confined in York Castle, and following his conviction he was executed at the Tyburn without Micklegate Bar on Saturday, 26 March 1749.

York, the assize town for the county, as it is today.

Fawthorp was hanged at the same time as two other men. He denied the murders to the very end, and when he was asked if he knew who (if not he) might have done it, Fawthorp replied that he 'knew nothing at all about the matter'. But the case is interesting nonetheless since Fawthorp had committed a double murder, got married and been arrested – all within the space of four days.

THE HAWKHURST GANG

In April 1748, the *Gentleman's Magazine* reported: 'Stephen Pettit, a smuggler, was executed at Ipswich, and afterwards hung in chains, for the murder of Mr. Hays, sergeant of that town, whom he stabb'd as he was carrying him to prison.'

This brief report typifies the war between smuggling gangs and the authorities. By the middle-18th century smuggling - principally in tea, wine and tobacco - had reached near-epidemic proportions, with one typical report presented before the Committee of the House of Commons in 1745 explaining: 'From Chichester it is represented in January, 1745, nine smuggling cutters sailed from Rye (East Sussex), in that month, for Guernsey, in order to take in large quantities of goods, to be run on the coast; and they had intelligence that one of the cutters had landed her cargo. Smugglers overawed most of the riding officers, and bribed many others, so that the peaceable inhabitants of coastal villages were completely at the mercy of these lawless bands.'

In fact, nowadays it is difficult to comprehend the immense scale of this organized crime; which at its heart existed to sidestep the government revenue imposed on such imported goods. Those participating in what – for some – was almost a career were not only daring seamen but armed and ruthless too: forming small armies, they frequently clashed bloodily with the officers of the customs. A typical offensive is recorded as having taken place against customs men and a troop of five dragoons on 13 June 1744, when these were ambushed on the seashore near Pevensey. A 100-strong army of smugglers attacked them *en masse*, firing about forty shots and lashing out with their swords 'in a dangerous manner' before disarming their opponents. These bandits then loaded the beached booty – which the forces of law had utterly failed to recover and protect – onto 100 horses before making off in the direction of London. Battles like this were common along the blustery, rocky and dangerous shorelines of many parts of the British Isles, often being fought in the moonlight against a backdrop of booming waves and sea spray. One incident, however, is particularly remarkable.

The most formidable gang that infested and terrorized the counties of Sussex and Kent was the 'Hawkhurst Gang', who by 1747 had become not only brazen in their attacks on people, property and perceived enemies, but also incredibly numerous. This gang ravaged the area like a band of Viking marauders, until famously - at the mercy of their extravagances and under threat of having to leave their homes - the people of Goudhurst in the Kentish Weald formed their own band of militia to defend themselves. Numerous persons subscribed to this force, which took the appellation 'The Goudhurst Band of Militia'; at its head was a young man named William Sturt, a 29-year-old native of Goudhurst who had recently received his discharge from a regiment of foot under the command of General Harrison, and whom the local people had persuaded to be captain of their resistance.

Intelligence of this confederacy reached the Hawkhurst Gang, who contrived to abduct one of the militia, and by means of torture and confinement they extracted a full detail of the intentions of his colleagues. The leader of the gang, Thomas Kingsmill, was outraged at the prospect of a tiny militia defying him, but he allowed his captive to return to Goudhurst – after forcing him to swear not to bear arms against the gang, and demanding he inform the militia that on 21 April the town would be attacked. Every house would be burnt, and every person who had not fled would be massacred, Kingsmill promised.

Upon word of the threat reaching Sturt, he organised his little band: some gathered firearms, while others were engaged in casting balls and making cartridges. At the time appointed, Kingsmill led the smugglers into Goudhurst, meeting the entrenchments of the militia at St Mary's Church. After some horrid threats a burst of fire was directed at the defenders, who returned a volley of fire at the smugglers, killing one among their number. Two more of the smugglers died in a further firefight, and numerous among their number sustained injuries: whereupon they quitted the battlefield. They were pursued by the militia, with some of them being taken and subsequently executed.

The *Gentleman's Magazine* noted this gun battle, the briefness of its report implying that such an event was not wholly surprising: 'Two smugglers, George *Kingsman*, and Barnet Wollit, both outlaws, the first of which formerly kill'd a man on Hurst Green, were kill'd in a skirmish with the townsmen of *Goodhurst* in Kent, who found it necessary to arm against these desperadoes, who rob and plunder, and live upon the spoil, wherever they come.' 'George *Kingsman*' was actually George *Kingsmill*, Thomas Kingsmill's brother.

(Some accounts of this incident, such as a letter from Goudhurst dated 27 April which was published in a number of news-sheets, suggest the skirmishing was not confined to the church, and the two men who died together may have been killed after firing into a house occupied by 14 militia men, who fired back.

Intriguingly, a pistol seized from a smuggler during the fighting is now retained in the Maidstone Museum; the weapon – ominously – has four distinct notches carved into the handle. The gang certainly appear to have had a lot of blood on their hands, at any rate; according to the Tunbridge Wells antiquarian Jasper Sprange, writing in 1797: 'Their leader, *Kingsmell* by name, proclaimed aloud, - "That he had been at the killing of *forty* of his Majesty's officers and soldiers, and swore that he would be damned if he did not broil four of their hearts, (meaning the town's people) and eat them for his supper."')

The road to St Mary's Church, Goudhurst, today: two or three smugglers died in a gun battle with a local militia hereabouts in 1747. (Photo courtesy of Ron Strutt.)

In fact, the *Gentleman's Magazine* noted numerous stories about the gangs in this part of England throughout the next few weeks: on 14 August 1747, for instance, a group of 24 smugglers rode through Rye in Sussex: stopping at the Red Lion to refresh, they fired their weapons to intimidate the customers, and then abducted one James Marshall, a young man too curious about their behaviour: 'He has not been heard of since.' The *Gentleman's Magazine* also noted this month: 'Four soldiers have been shot by these people (smugglers generally, not in connection with the Rye incident), and they threaten the printers for publishing advertisements against them.' In another edition, the periodical lamented the unprecedented levels of robbery within ten miles of London that October, a phenomenon that was blamed on smugglers: 'What is worst, they being desperate, have killed some persons and ill-treated others.' That November, 12 persons, armed and masked, broke into Maidstone Gaol to rescue four notorious smugglers, wounding the jailer and his assistants in the process. 20 more gang members waited with horses to convey the escapees away to freedom. And when an atrocious storm blew the *Nympha* onto the shore at Beachy Head in December, multitudes flocked to the beach for spoil; many perished on the sand in the freezing cold conditions, one woman being found dead with two children crying beside her. A great number of smugglers

293

attempted to take the vessel, but by this time Mr Belchier, Southwark's MP and part owner of the *Nympha*, had ordered soldiers to the coast. They fired into the mob of smugglers, killing two and dispersing the others.

Such reports provide but a glimpse of just how thoroughly this form of organised crime gripped many of Britain's coastal communities. But to return to our story, Thomas Kingsmill escaped for a time; he was aged about 27, and is described as being a native of Goudhurst himself, a bold, resolute man thoroughly opposed to the king's officers. He also used the alias Staymaker, and although his enterprising spirit could have made him a worthy member of society, he was a born criminal who (after recovering from his heavy defeat at the Battle of Goudhurst) next led a band of 60 smugglers in a daring midnight raid on the customs house at Poole, Dorset, on 7 October 1747. This assault, to recover tea, brandy and rum brought from France by the smuggling cutter *The Three Brothers* on 22 September, was carried out by the group armed with cutlasses and pistols - despite the threat of a sloop-of-war lying opposite the quay with her guns pointed towards the customs house.

In the wake of the Poole raid a reward was offered for the arrest of the culprits, and it was this circumstance that occasioned a barbaric and notorious crime.

On 14 February 1748, two men – William Galley the elder, a custom-house officer at Southampton, and Daniel Chater, a shoemaker from Fordingbridge – were travelling on the road to Major Battine's at Stansted. Galley was accompanying Chater to an appointment where he would provide a deposition in evidence against a suspect who had been arrested over the Poole raid. Along their route the two men stopped at the White Hart Inn at Rowland's Castle, where the landlady, surmising their mission, sent for two local gang members named William Carter and William Jackson to investigate the situation. As the two travellers were made drunk, more gang members were sent for; the alcohol was flowing, but Galley and Chater were unaware that the White Hart was steadily filling with men whose intention was to get rid of them.

During the night the two men were awoken and dragged roughly from their beds. They were forced outside and both tied behind a single horse, with their legs under its belly, and mercilessly lashed with whips. They were then taken to a well in Ladyholt Park, northeast of Horndean, where the gang threatened to throw Galley into its depths. This they did not do, but they instead tied him once more to the horse and literally whipped him to death before burying him on the South Downs. (The *Gentleman's Magazine* tells us that Galley's nose and privates were cut off, his eyes were gouged out by a 22-year-old conspirator named Stevens using a fork, and that he was dispatched after several hours of casual torture.) Having seen Galley murdered before his eyes, Chater stood no chance, and his torture is representative of the brutal 'justice' faced by informers under these circumstances.

Galley's body being buried by the smugglers. A famous illustration from Smugglers & Smuggling in Sussex, *by a gentleman at Chichester, 1749.*

Chater was taken to Old Richard Mills' house near Trotton and chained in the turf-house, where his nose and eyes were mutilated with a knife. As time went on, he was continually kicked and beaten by men who came into the turf-house. Some fourteen people were involved by this point, the captive only being kept alive so that the group could detect what information he possessed and what the authorities might already know. In the end a scheme was considered whereby a pistol would be set against Chater's head, with a string attached to the trigger that all might pull, so that everyone present would be simultaneously guilty of the shoemaker's murder: however, this plan was abandoned. Instead, in the dead of night Chater was conveyed back to Harris's Well out in the countryside of Ladyholt Park, where Benjamin Tapner, a former bricklayer from Aldrington, fastened a noose around his neck. The other end of the rope they tied to the pales of the well, before pushing Chater into it in the hope he would hang. One contemporary account states that he hung in this miserable position for some time, with the group going away and leaving him, only to return some time later. They found the rope had not worked, however, and Chater had refused to expire: so they hauled him out and untied him before throwing him headfirst down the well. They then pelted him with the well's rails and gateposts, as well as large stones. In this wretched situation Chater finally died.

Chater is lynched at Lady Holt Well. (Also from Smugglers & Smuggling in Sussex, *by a gentleman at Chichester, 1749.)*

The gang next proposed to get rid of their victim's horses, which had been stabled throughout the event. Galley's horse, which was grey, was killed, skinned and the hide cut into tiny pieces. Chater's bay horse, however, slipped from them and thundered off: the sole mute witness to one of the most barbaric crimes ever perpetrated in those parts. Galley's bloodied great coat was found in the road not long after, leading to the supposition that the pair had met with foul play; hefty financial rewards were offered for information, but it was some months before anything came to light.

Throughout the investigation into the missing men the murderers boasted openly about their crimes while on boozing sprees, and so it was not too difficult for the authorities to begin to track down the responsible parties. They were also betrayed by an informant in October, who confirmed the whereabouts of the corpses: 'The person who gave this information, however known to the magistrates, was in disguise, lest he should meet the like fate.' Galley's body was found by a Mr Stone while hunting on the Downs, hidden in a fox earth some seven feet deep. Curiously, his hands were found over his face, leading to an awful supposition that he might, in the end, have been buried while still alive. According to the *Gentleman's Magazine*, the corpse was 'so putrify'd as not to be known but by his cloathes'. This was 'near a place call'd Rake in Sussex'. Next, Chater's *headless* corpse was found six miles away in the well north of Horndean, with three feet of earth and stones covering him. When his body was drawn out the well, one of his legs came off, stuck in its boot when the rest of the remains came free.

The murder of Galley and Chater is one of the few cases from this era that *genuinely* shocked the establishment: that a customs officer and a federal witness could simply vanish into a nest of vipers and be killed so barbarically was tantamount to a declaration of war by the smugglers, and the crimes even shocked smuggling communities which were to some extent almost immune to violent deeds.

When their trial opened at Chichester on 16 January 1749, the seven accused were Jackson, Carter and Tapner; John Hammond, a labouring man from South Bersted; John Cobby, the illiterate son of a Sussex labourer; a horse-dealer from Trotton called Old Richard Mills (described as one of the most hardened of the group) and his son, also Richard. The trial was held at a special assize for smugglers before three judges: Sir Michael Forster, Sir Thomas Birch and Mr Baron Edward Clive. Two people privy to the murders had turned king's evidence against the accused, one of them being the young man named Stevens. The trial was short, and all seven were convicted of various levels of involvement in Chater's murder, while Jackson and Carter alone were convicted of Galley's murder. Jackson died in gaol on the night he was condemned, four hours after his conviction - probably given a good beating and killed in the confines of his cell in an act of brutal vengeance by Galley's comrades. It was put out, however, that he had died from pure fear of his forthcoming public execution.

The rest were executed at Chichester on 19 January 1749. Carter was hung in chains 'near Rackley' (Rake), while Tapner was suspended on Rook's Hill near Chichester; Cobby and Hammond were left on the heathland of Selsey Isle, where they sometimes landed their smuggled goods, and where their gibbeted corpses could be seen from a great distance both east and west.

During the trial, John Mills, another son of Richard Mills, actually saw the judges travelling over Hind Heath on 13 January 1749 on their way to Chichester Assizes, and proposed to hold them up and rob them; he was talked out of this by his cautious associates. However, not long afterwards John committed a murder of his own. He met with one Richard Hawkins, put the man on horseback, and carried him to the Dog and Partridge on Slindon Common, south of Slindon. Here, Hawkins was accused by Mills and his associates of having stolen two bags of tea: and upon his denying it the group flogged and kicked him to death. They carried his body twelve miles, tied stones to it and sank it in a pond in Parham Park.

John Mills was entrapped at the house of an outlawed smuggler named William Pring at Beckenham, and there betrayed. He was tried and convicted during the assizes at East Grinstead, and hanged on 12 August 1749 (according to William Jackson's *Newgate Calendar*) - being conducted to the place of execution by a guard of soldiers, lest a rescue attempt be carried out by other smugglers. After his execution, Mills was hung in chains on Slindon Common.

There is some suggestion that John Mills also participated in the murders of Galley and Chater, alongside his now-deceased father and brother. It is clear the authorities were on a war footing in Sussex, determined to try and stamp out the plague of smugglers: for throughout 1749 a number of others were condemned to death by the courts in the county, including two more men convicted of direct involvement in the murder of William Galley. These were Henry Shearman and Edmund Richards, who were executed on 21 March and 19 August respectively.

Richard Hawkins is brutally murdered. (Another well-known illustration from Smugglers & Smuggling in Sussex, *by a gentleman at Chichester, 1749.)*

In the meantime, two of the witnesses who had given evidence against their smuggling brethren at Chichester next gave information as to the meeting place of Thomas Kingsmill and three others who had participated in the raid on the

Poole customs house. (These three were named Fairall, Perrin and Glover. Perrin had been the skipper of the intercepted cutter *The Three Brothers*, and had managed to escape in another boat at the time). Glover was recommended for mercy and pardoned, but the other three were sentenced at their trial to be executed at Tyburn on 26 April 1749. Fairall, who had behaved most insolently during the trial (even publicly threatening a witness) was hung in chains on Horsendown Green, while Thomas Kingsmill's corpse was displayed on Goudhurst Gore, Kent.

As if to evidence that this way of life was not exclusively a southern phenomenon, the *Newgate Calendar*, in telling the story of Hawkins' murder, relates similar outrages in East Anglia. About this time, a battle to the death atop horses occurred in the Suffolk fens near 'Milden Hall', between three excise officers and two wanted smugglers named Rich and Cock. Rich tried to kill one officer by aiming an axe at his head from atop his horse, and then managed to fire a pistol into the man's mouth, shooting out two of his teeth. The officer recovered the gun and fired two shots into Rich's body and then furiously beat him over the head with the butt-end, until the man slid from his mount, fatally injured. Cock managed to escape during the melee. (The *Westminster Magazine* indicates this happened in March 1752.)

The ruthlessness of the East Anglian gangs is further exampled by a bloody incident reported in June 1735. A shooting battle had erupted between a group of smugglers and a contingent of dragoons near Ipswich, in which one gang member was fatally wounded. This so enraged the smugglers that they overcame the soldiery and murdered two of their number in cold blood. It was subsequently reported in September that two men linked to this incident, which occurred near Hadleigh, were tracked down in London and returned to Suffolk; John Wilson (alias 'Old York') and John Biggs (alias 'Young York') were hanged after their convictions at Ipswich Assizes.

In neighbouring Norfolk it was no better: on 11 December 1750 a smuggler named John Watling, from Horsey, was hanged for leading a brutal attack on a customs house watchman, among other 'numerous enormities he committed'. Abraham Bailey had been pulled from his bed, whipped by a group of 11 men and then hung by the neck from a tree. Bailey was, however, let down before he choked to death, it appearing the gang needed him alive to answer questions. He was left half-dead, and made to swear to his own damnation if he ever revealed his mistreatment.

MURDER BY A CHILD

In 1748 it was reported that on 16 May a 10-year-old boy, William York, had been committed to Ipswich Gaol, Suffolk, for murdering Susan Mayhew, a five-year-old girl who was his bedfellow in the poorhouse belonging to the parish of Eyke.

The boy confessed that a trifling quarrel had occurred between them three days earlier, at about ten a.m.: William had slapped the little girl across the face, making her cry. When she left the house to go to the 'muck hill' opposite the door he followed her with a knife and grabbed her left hand, cutting the girl to the bone all the way around her wrist. He then threw her down and did the same just above the elbow. He then put his foot on the little girl's stomach and did the same round her right wrist and elbow. He then retrieved a hook, and hacked 'her left ham to the bone' before striking her three times on the head, killing her.

Children killing children: William York's brutal act. (Originally from The Newgate Calendar Volume 2, *Andrew Knapp and William Baldwin, 1825.)*

William took great care to conceal his crime; in fact, his case is remarkable in that he went to more lengths than the average adult to cover up what he had done. He filled a pail with water from a ditch, stripped and washed the child's body of blood, then buried her in the muck heap and levelled it as best he could to cover the blood that had splashed on the ground. He then took the weapons indoors and washed them, also cleaning the blood off his own person. The child's clothes he stashed in an old chamber; finally he came down to eat some breakfast. When the man and wife of the poorhouse – under whose care the children had been – came back, William disinterestedly told them that he knew not where little Susan had gone.

A thorough search soon turned up the child's body. There was no one on the premises who could have committed the crime except the boy.

When he was examined, William displayed very little concern, even appearing 'easy and cheerful'. As an explanation, he said the girl had fouled the bed in which they lay together, that she was sulky, and he didn't like her much.

In reporting this odd case, the *Gentleman's Magazine* observed: 'Judge Hale order'd a boy of the same age to be hang'd, who burnt a child in a cradle.' However, although William York was convicted of murder, a panel of judges sitting on his case could not agree to sentence him to death, and a legal merry-go-round ensued, with the boy earning a number of reprieves from the gallows while remaining in custody. In the end, after nine years, William York – by now old enough to be executed - earned the benefit of his majesty's pardon at the Summer Assizes in 1757: upon the condition that he immediately enter into the sea service.

'THE MAN IS HANGED... AND NOBODY CAN HURT US'

Given the times, it is possible – even likely – that many more people went to the rope unjustly than was ever known. One of the most famous miscarriages of Georgian justice in England concerned the murder of Sarah Green in London.

On 23 July 1748 Sarah had attended a bean feast in Kennington Lane, and as she returned home to her lodgings at a late hour she was joined by three men who bore the appearance of brewer's servants. Two of them raped her in the Parsonage-walk, near Newington's church, and 'otherwise used her, in so inhuman a manner as will bear no description'. After the horrific ordeal, Sarah managed to make it home at around two o'clock in the morning, but she had been seriously injured; and the following day she told numerous people about her mistreatment. It became necessary to remove her to St Thomas's Hospital as her condition deteriorated, and when she was questioned Sarah stated that she thought a clerk in Berry's brew-house was one of those responsible.

It was supposed that Sarah was referring to one Richard Coleman, a clerk to a brewer who was married with two children. Two days after the attack he was drinking in the Queen's Head alehouse in Bandyleg-walk, Southwark, with a man named Daniel Trotman: Coleman was heavily intoxicated, but Trotman was perfectly sober. While they sat, and Coleman stirred his rum and water, a third party asked him if he was familiar with Kennington Lane, and whether he was aware of the woman who had lately been attacked there. Coleman replied in the affirmative, asking, 'What of that?' The fellow asked him: 'Were you one of the parties concerned in that affair?' To this, Coleman replied angrily, 'If I had, you dog, what then?' and threw the spoon at his antagonist.

On 29 August 1748 Trotman, having heard this transaction and wrestled with his conscience, presented himself before a magistrate called Clark and explained that he thought Coleman might be one among the guilty party. Coleman was arrested and taken before the injured girl, who still lay in St Thomas's Hospital: she thought that he *might* have been one of the guilty ones, but could not swear positively.

Coleman next found himself ordered to be taken before the girl again. This time he brought with him the landlord of an alehouse to speak in his defence; for this witness believed he had seen the three attackers leave his establishment in pursuit of Sarah Green, who he also recognised as having been there on the night in question. The publican was adamant in his denial that Richard Coleman was one of these three men, but during the second interview Sarah Green, when pressed, swore an oath that Coleman *was* one of the men who had assaulted her.

Sarah was by this time dangerously ill, and died shortly afterwards in the hospital. A coroner's jury brought in a verdict of wilful murder against Coleman and two others as yet unidentified. A warrant was issued to take him into custody, but Coleman did not help his situation by fleeing: in fact, he absconded as far as Pinner, near Harrow on the Hill. A £70 reward was offered for his capture, but Coleman – reading of this in the *Gazette* – took the extraordinary step of having a letter published in the newspapers insisting upon his innocence. It read: 'I, Richard Coleman, seeing myself advertised in the *Gazette*, as absconding on account of the murder of Sarah Green, knowing myself no way culpable, do assert that I have not absconded from justice; but will willingly and readily appear at the next assizes, knowing that my innocence will acquit me.'

By this, Coleman appears to have betrayed his location, for he was apprehended at Pinner on 22 November and incarcerated in Newgate on a charge of murder. Then he was next imprisoned in the New Gaol, Southwark, pending his trial to be held at Kingston Assizes, Surrey, in March 1749. The accused man was convicted of murder, principally on the evidence of Trotman and the dying girl, despite the testimony of witnesses who swore he was in another place at the time the crime was committed. This was ignored by the court, and Coleman was sentenced to death; he was hanged on Kennington Common on 12 April 1749. Before his death he delivered a letter to the Rev Mr Wilson, in which he declared his innocence, and in the cart he expressed only his sadness that his wife and two children would be un-provided for.

Unfortunately for all concerned, Coleman had been telling the truth. Two years later one James Welch was walking with a fellow named James Bush on the road to Newington Butts. Their conversation turning to those who were executed without good reason, Welch brought up the case of Richard Coleman, adding that he *knew* the man was innocent because he and two more – Thomas

Jones and John Nichols – had committed the murder for which he had hanged. Welch added that Jones and Nichols had raped the girl, but injured her so badly that he had refrained from carrying out a similar outrage himself.

James Bush did not pay this much heed. But sometime later, finding himself ill, he told his father of what he had heard. While Bush and his father drank in an alehouse a little while afterwards, it so happened that one of the named parties – Jones – passed by the window, and so they called him in, sat him down and with no small-talk asked him if he had attacked Sarah Green. Jones turned deathly pale, but then recovered himself, saying, 'The man is hanged, and the woman dead, and nobody can hurt us.' To this he added, 'We were *connected* with a woman, but who can tell (if) that was the woman Coleman died for?'

It only remains to be said that, because of these incriminating comments, Jones, Nichols and Welch were taken up for questioning. The case appeared to rest on the hearsay of James Bush – until Nichols cracked and was admitted in evidence for the crown (in a move to literally save his own neck). The prisoners being brought to the bar at the next assizes for the county of Surrey, Nichols testified that he and the other two had been drinking at an alehouse called Sot's Hole, and afterwards they had bumped into Sarah Green, whom they persuaded to go with them for a drink in another tavern called the King's Head. Following a pot of beer, these three had assaulted her in Parsonage-walk with such violence it had occasioned her death. At the time, all three had worn white smocks, and Jones and Welch had deliberately called Nichols by the appellation 'Coleman' in a move designed to steer blame in another direction – a circumstance that evidently led to the conviction of that unfortunate man, as it caused the dying girl to mistake their persons.

The court did not hesitate to find Welch and Jones guilty, and as the end approached they behaved with utmost contrition: for they were in fact guilty of two murders, firstly that of Sarah Green and secondly that of Richard Coleman by proxy, whom they had lied and framed to the courts before allowing him to hang by inaction.

Both were attended by the Rev Dr Howard, rector of St George's, Southwark, to whom they readily confessed their offence. They likewise signed a declaration, which they begged to be published, containing the fullest assertion of Coleman's innocence; Welch also wrote to Coleman's brother, begging his forgiveness and asking for his prayers. Jones wrote to his own sister in Richmond, asking her to use her position in the service of a genteel family to procure him a reprieve; she wrote back saying his crimes were of too great a magnitude to make such an endeavour worthwhile. She merely begged him to prepare for death – and this the two malefactors suffered on Kennington Common on 6 September 1751.

Richard Coleman's name has been cleared in the eyes of history...but one cannot help wondering how many others so convicted will forever be judged as guilty because a similar set of circumstances did not rescue their reputation from damnation.

CRUEL TIMES IN THE ISLE OF ELY

7 November 1749 was a cruel day in Ely, for the little Cambridgeshire market town, dominated by its magnificent cathedral, saw the execution of not one but two murderers.

John Vicars, one of those so condemned, was born at Doddington, in the Isle of Ely, and at thirteen he was apprenticed to a gardener at Holkham, Norfolk; however, a sexual intrigue some time later with a married woman of that place forced him to flee, and hereafter he seems to have been restless in his occupation. For although he worked as a gardener in various different locales throughout the years (at Kensington, Chelsea, Maidstone, Hackwood, Chichester, Brompton, Epping Forest and Thorney, near Peterborough) and his employers were often landowning men of standing, he was frequently forced to move on following some new sexual misadventure or criminal escapade. That he was criminally-minded is clear, for after working at Kensington Palace he first enlisted aboard a man-of-war and then, nine months later, took up with a smuggling gang for about a year. He was even taken prisoner by a custom-house smack near Rye, and committed to the New Gaol in Southwark for a time.

In time he naturally gravitated back towards Cambridgeshire, and following his departure from Thorney he took the road south over the River Nene to Whittlesey. Here he took lodgings at Adam England's, at the sign of the Dolphin, where he appears to have lived respectably for some three years, gaining employment with several gentlemen in the general area.

During his time here, Vicars married one Anne Easom, and they lived happily for seven years – until Anne fell ill, and it occasioned much discontent between the couple; so much so that Vicars, ever restless, enlisted in the Duke of Bedford's regiment for about a year. Still, he did return and take up with Anne again after this: although unfortunately she died after twelve months, and Vicars became a widower.

John Vicars would appear to have been an incorrigible ladies' man, and he next sought to woo Mary Hainsworth, who – despite having several beaus – was attracted to Vicars and very quickly fell for him. Throughout their liaison, the question of marriage was not brought up on his part, but after a while Mary began to press Vicars to marry her. When he backed off from this suggestion, Mary next told him that she was pregnant, and he had better make an honest woman of her or else she would obtain a warrant forcing him to marry her. Vicars was equally obstinate that he would not be cornered like this and so Mary, in her desperation, threatened to commit suicide.

Over time, Mary Hainsworth pleaded, threatened and begged Vicars to marry her, and in the end he agreed, somewhat reluctantly, it being apparent that his overactive libido kept bringing him back to her bed time and again, despite her having a number of other suitors in the area who he could have let take her hand were it not for his lust.

Predictably the newly-married couple enjoyed just two months of wedded bliss before they fell into a routine of constant arguing, which, in turn, led to violent blows being struck between them on occasion. At length Mary went to live with her mother, who (if Vicars' testimony is to be believed) was a venomous old woman who gradually poisoned Mary against him to such an extent that all hopes of reconciliation were dashed. Vicars even claimed that one day he had passed by his mother-in-law's house and, entering with a fruit basket as a gift, he had attempted to persuade Mary to come back to him; unfortunately, the old woman at that moment appeared, striking Vicars and yelling at her daughter – who held a knife – that she should stab Vicars to death! Vicars managed to scramble out the door, wounded in the hand from a half-hearted attempt made by Mary to knife him.

To add insult to injury, Vicars next learned that his mother-in-law was planning to have him arrested. This is the point that Vicars appears to have lost his reason. On 24 April 1749 he visited a gentleman about three miles from Whittlesey in order to ask his advice. This fellow suggested that Vicars make a bill of sale of his goods and go off (i.e. sell up and leave), and this Vicars resolved to do. He arrived back in Whittlesey about six o'clock in the evening; however, before he put any of his plans into action he observed his wife inside the shop which her mother had provided for her. Fuelled with rage at the thought that they desired his ruination and imprisonment, Vicars stormed onto the premises and walked up behind Mary, who was in a sitting position. He placed his left hand under her chin, and at this she (apparently) smiled, thinking her husband was going to kiss her hair; instead, Vicars cut her throat and stabbed her in the neck beneath the left ear. She cried 'Murder!' once, and as she died Vicars said into her ear, 'Molly, 'tis now too late, you should have been ruled in time!'

Vicars then simply ran into the street and shouted that someone should arrest him, or he would do more damage. At length, a man called Thomas Broome warily approached him, grabbing his arm and taking the weapon off him; Vicars did not resist at all, and allowed himself to be taken prisoner.

While in jail John Vicars admitted his guilt, claiming that his 'damned whore' of a wife had provoked him into his act of cruelty; he also declared that his initial intention was to dispatch himself afterwards, although he failed in his resolve. Interestingly, in the town it was rumoured that Vicars had killed a number of other people in his life, and he himself admitted one other murder, if it might be called that; when he had been gardener to Mr Mann, Esq, in Maidstone, Kent, he took it upon himself to catch a thief who often made into his master's garden and stole things. Armed with a gun and a cutlass, Vicars had waited upon this person and confronted him in the darkness. When the intruder fled, Vicars had managed to stab him in the leg with his cutlass and chase him into the path of a gigantic man-trap. The trap was so big that when the razor-sharp teeth snapped shut on the wounded man, they reached almost to his waist and wounded him so badly that he afterwards died of his injuries in Maidstone gaol. Vicars, it seems, was not prosecuted for the man's murder, however.

Following his conviction for murder at Ely Assizes on 10 October, Vicars was conveyed to the place of execution on 7 November 1749 to be hanged. At the fatal tree his attitude was a curious one of genuine penitence – for he owned his love for his slain wife – mixed with apparent unconcern as to his own fate; he even chatted gaily with many people from Whittlesey who had turned out to see their neighbour die.

Unusually for a county assizes like Ely, Vicars had a fellow sufferer in the shape of a young lady called Amy Hutchinson, also convicted of spousal murder in Whittlesey at the same time.

Amy was but 17 at the time of her execution. She too had fallen victim to a set of circumstances partly her own fault: for she had agreed to marry her husband John immediately upon her being deserted by her true love, a man identified only as 'T.R.' T.R. had been in the act of travelling to London, and so swift had Amy's decision been to marry a rival suitor – John Hutchinson – that the wedding arrangements were literally made for the next day. T.R. had not got very far from Whittlesey when a messenger caught up with him and told him the development; upon which he returned to Cambridgeshire and actually accosted Amy (surreptitiously) on her wedding day at the church door.

T.R. began to persuade Amy to kill her new husband by poison, and Amy could not resist her former gallant. John guessed very quickly that Amy still entertained feelings for T.R., and on occasion beat her with a stick. He also took to drinking heavily and keeping the company of his mates, rather than her, which only made it easier for T.R. to meet her secretly and persuade her that John Hutchinson had to die so that they might be together.

After a mere ten weeks, Amy mixed arsenic into her husband's ale, which he drank: John died in terrible torment later that very same day. Her mother-in-law was immediately suspicious, commenting to Amy: 'I am afraid you have done something to your husband!' A coroner's inquest had John's body exhumed not long after he had been interred, and determined he had died from arsenic poisoning.

Whether Amy was a cold-blooded murderess is dependent on one's point of view; she seems to have been an incredibly naïve young woman, for she was all but raped by a fellow prisoner (a male) while awaiting trial, who persuaded her that it would somehow help her case; this malefactor actually gagged her mouth with an apron during her ordeal. By this time, Amy had also been utterly deserted by T.R., who seems to have distanced himself from her as much as possible upon her arrest and incarceration.

Amy was sentenced to suffer death in Ely upon the same day as John Vicars. She was aged seventeen, and wrote an impassioned final letter in which she advised young people that the institute of marriage ought not to be mocked, as she had seen fit to do: 'They should never leave a person they are engaged to in a *pet* (in a momentary passion), nor wed another to whom they are indifferent, in spite.'

The double execution would have occurred within the shadow of Ely's majestic cathedral.

The worlds of these two murderers – John Vicars and Amy Hutchinson - came together on 7 November 1749 at Ely; and one wonders if they actually knew each other in and around Whittlesey prior to this. The pair sang psalms together as their end neared, and Vicars made it known that he wished his gaoler to be paid out of his effects, worth £30, which, unfortunately, had all been taken from him. He also reminisced on a number of named people in Whittlesey who he wished might remember him fondly. He then asked that his body not be hung in chains after death (which was denied him) and that he might watch Amy be executed first (which was conceded to).

Since she had been convicted of petty treason, Amy's fate was of the gruesome, medieval type with which we are now familiar. Secured to a stake, surrounded by woodchips and faggots, her face and hands were smeared with tar. The garments she wore were also smeared with pitch. After a short, final prayer, the executioner emotionlessly strangled her, and 20 minutes later set her afire, letting her body burn for half an hour. The executioner then moved on to Vicars, who with an undaunted air helped him affix the knot around his own neck – before throwing himself off the gallows cart. It is reported that he struggled and kicked for several minutes before his own body weight subjected him to strangulation by the noose.

KILLED BY SUPERSTITION

There must have been a sincere belief in Hertfordshire that Ruth Osborne was a witch and her husband John a wizard - for agitators had it so proclaimed throughout Winslow, Leighton Buzzard and Hemel Hempstead that the pair would be ducked on Monday 22 April 1751 at Tring. In fact, such was the conviction that the Osbornes *were* witches that Hemel Hempstead's town crier, William Dell, was paid fourpence to make this declaration: 'This is to give notice that on Monday next a man and a woman are to be publicly ducked at Tring in this county for their wicked crimes.'

In order to protect the couple, the overseer of the poor in Tring removed them to the workhouse; they were further moved on the night of 21 April to the vestry room adjoining the church. At about 11 o'clock the following day a great mob numbering about 5'000 assembled at the poorhouse, and, pushing the master of the place out of their way, they rushed in and systematically ransacked the building searching for possible hiding places where the Osbornes might be. They looked in the most absurd, tiniest of cubbyholes, in the belief that the pair (being witches) could hide in spaces so small as would fit a cat. One of the ringleaders appeared to be a certain Thomas Colley, who - upon spotting a hole in the ceiling - directed the others to get up there and have a look. Not finding the fugitives, Colley directed a wall to be pulled down, and next windows and window frames to be smashed, threatening to burn down not only the building but the entire town of Tring. The master, fearing the possibilities, gave the couple's hiding place up, and they were borne triumphantly out of the church vestry.

The couple were carried to a pond called Marlston Mere, where they were bound separately with cloth and sheets. A rope was tied under the armpits of

Ruth Osborne, and she was hauled into the muddy water. Two men, who stood on either side of the pond, grabbed each end of the rope and dragged her backwards and forwards through the water. After this she was thrust on the pond's side and her husband served similarly: both suffered this punishment alternately until, upon the conclusion of the third ducking, Ruth Osborne died on the water's edge.

Ruth Osborne's murder occurred in an almost carnival-like atmosphere. (As depicted in The Newgate Calendar Volume 2, *Andrew Knapp and William Baldwin, 1825.)*

Colley's behaviour throughout the event had been astonishing. Upon each ducking he had entered the pond, at a point where it was not quite two-and-a-half feet deep, and turned the woman over using a stick, pushing her under the water several times. Afterwards, he had emerged and moved among the crowd collecting money for the sporting nature he had showed in ducking the old witch, as he referred to her aloud. Someone clearly more compassionate than the rest implored Colley to let the woman alone lest he find himself facing a murder charge; but Colley, full of bravado and acting up before the crowd, refused, pulling off the cloth Mrs Osborne was wrapped in and leaving her quite naked. He also jabbed her on the breast with the stick he carried. While still alive, Ruth Osborne had feebly attempted to push the weapon away, but ultimately she expired through suffocation in the water and mud. She was in her 70th year. It is recorded that her husband John was afterwards tied to his wife's corpse; some accounts have it that while he did not die immediately – he was aged 56 and stout made – he expired some time later of his mistreatment, possibly succumbing to the long-term effects of exposure. However, he lived at least long enough to testify at Colley's trial, and it is reliably recorded that no-one would employ him afterwards; the parish of Tring was obliged to support him in the workhouse after his wife's murder.

Colley was charged with Ruth Osborne's murder, although 21 others were indicted at the same hearing. Two had absconded, and the others remained unidentified. Colley went on trial at the assizes at Hertford that autumn, and – there being no chance of denying a crime so publicly carried out – he was sentenced on 30 July to be hanged. Two others being tried with him, William Humbles and Charles 'Redbeard' Young, were cleared.

The jury had been selected from the gentlemen class, for it was recalled that there had previously been a similar case of murder in Frome, Somerset, where the jury had been selected from the lower middle-class, who would not convict the prisoner. This earlier case had been reported in the *Gentleman's Magazine* in 1731. In 'September last' some 200 cheering rioters subjected an old woman to a ducking, or ordeal by water, at Frome on suspicion of witchcraft. The woman had been blamed for the strange fits that the son of a man named Wheeler was suffering, and the mob dragged the old lady two miles out of town to a mill-pond, where they stripped her, tied her legs together, and – with a rope tied around her waist – threw her in. She 'swam like a cork' despite being repeatedly pushed under, and was eventually thrown on a heap of litter where she died an hour later. The coroner, although aware some forty people had actively participated in the murder, could get no one to announce who the ringleaders were, and in the end they were only able to charge three who appeared principally guilty with manslaughter.

The day before his execution on Saturday 24 August, Colley received the sacrament at Hertford, administered by the Rev Mr Edward Bouchier, before being moved to St Albans Gaol – in all likelihood to confuse the mob, who had thwarted his execution on the originally-set date by hanging around threateningly outside the prison. On that occasion some 10'000 people had refused to allow Colley out of the prison, and the execution had to be deferred until a military detachment could be dispatched. But in the end there was no escape from the law. On the day of justice Colley was escorted to his destiny in a one-horse chaise, in a slow and solemn procession guarded by 108 soldiers, officers and two trumpets. The grim cortege halted at *Gubblecut* (Gubblecote) Cross in the parish of Tring: for this was the place of execution. The mob was curiously absent at this point, although many felt that Colley was a hero for ridding their parish of the witch's threat. Multitudes refused to watch him die, although thousands stood at a distance muttering that it was a disgrace Colley should be executed for ridding the county of Ruth Osborne.

Colley's last act was spent in prayer for half an hour, before he was 'turned off' at 11 o'clock by the minister of Tring, the Rev Mr Randal. He was immediately hung up in chains on the same gibbet post he was hanged from.

Before his earthly departure Colley had a letter read out to those present; he appears to have been sincerely repentant, for the letter in part read: 'I beseech you all to take warning by an unhappy man's suffering; that you be not deluded into so absurd and wicked a conceit, as to believe that there are any such beings upon earth as witches. It was that foolish and vain imagination, heightened and inflamed by the strength of liquor, which prompted me to be instrumental (with others as mad brained as myself) in the horrid and barbarous murder of Ruth Osborne, the supposed witch, for which I am now so deservedly to suffer death…'

THE SURGICAL FATE OF EWAN MACDONALD

At about 10 o'clock at night on 23 May 1752 a quarrel erupted between a company of drinkers and a soldier in Mr Pinkney's tavern in the Bigg Market, Newcastle. Blows were thrown, and the soldier – one William 'Ewan' Macdonald, a recruit in a Highlander's regiment quartered in the town – pursued his antagonists when they made their way into the street. In the entrance of the public house, 19-year-old Macdonald laid his hand on one Robert Parker, a cooper; without any further ado he stabbed the fellow in the neck with a knife, killing the unfortunate man immediately.

Returning to the tavern, Macdonald continued to abuse those inside, breaking one man's arm in a second fracas, before eventually being marched out of the place by a file of musketeers who had been sent for. The young man was conducted to Newcastle's Newgate, and in the days after his incarceration he appeared sincerely penitent, regretting very much Parker's murder and saying Parker had been an inoffensive party when the brawl had kicked off.

On 28 September, pursuant to his sentencing, Macdonald was led to the Town Moor, Newcastle to be hanged. Unfortunately, he battled the executioner on the ladder of the gallows in an unseemly effort to escape his fate, attempting to throw the man from the steps. But it made no difference, and after his hanging Macdonald's corpse was taken to the Surgeon's Hall and anatomised, becoming the subject of a lecture by four surgeons.

It is said that when Macdonald was initially laid out for dissection, the surgeons involved were called away to attend an emergency at the Infirmary, and upon their return they were shocked to find the young recruit *alive* and groggily sitting up. Seeing the surgeons enter, Macdonald immediately begged for mercy; but a young surgeon snatched up a wooden mallet and violently dashed

Macdonald on the crown, killing him a 'second' time. Local author John Sykes, writing in 1833, observed of this: 'It was further reported as the just act of vengeance of God, that this young man was soon after killed in the stable by his own horse. They used to *shew* a mall at the Surgeons' Hall as the identical one used by the surgeon. I have thrown this note together from the report current some years ago, but which is now fast dying away.'

THE STRANGE CASE OF MARY BLANDY

Mary Blandy was the only daughter of Francis Blandy, an eminent attorney and town clerk in Henley-upon-Thames, Oxfordshire. It is recorded that Mary was possessed of a good education, common sense, intelligence and the manners of a privileged upbringing so sorely lacking in great sections of society at this time. It was also put about that she was expected to inherit a dowry in the region of £10'000.

Before her arrest, Mary Blandy's life was one of genteel luxury. (From James Caulfield's Portraits, Memoirs & Characters of Remarkable Persons Volumes 3-4, *1820.)*

Consequently, Mary – who was not unattractive – caught the eye of numerous suitors, and her father Francis obligingly entertained them at his table in the Blandy home on Hart Street. None, however, appeared more distinguished than Captain William Henry Cranstoun, the 46-year-old representative of an ancient Scottish family. His titled uncle had procured for him a commission in the army, and he had been sent on a recruiting drive to Henley - where he made the acquaintance of the Blandy family in 1746. Mary was at this time about 26 years old, and somehow Cranstoun managed to ingratiate himself into her affections; this was despite him being already married and having fathered a son. He was also badly marked with the smallpox and somewhat short on funds. But he possessed the gift of witty small talk, and Mr Blandy, being familiar with Cranstoun's uncle, permitted the soldier to court his daughter.

Cranstoun was honest enough to admit that he was involved in a lawsuit with his wife in Scotland, although he neglected to impart the whole truth, telling Mary the woman (one Anne Murray, of Edinburgh) merely *claimed* to be his wife. For her part, Mary stated that as long as her parents had no objection, she would wait until the disagreeable affair had terminated, and then permit the captain her hand in marriage.

This was the problem. Cranstoun's uncle, Lord Mark Ker, having learned of the liaison, wrote to Mr Blandy and informed him Cranstoun was a married man, and Blandy should preserve his daughter from ruin. When presented with this information, the captain made light of it, and although Mary and her mother were persuaded that reports of another wife in Scotland were erroneous, Mary's father was deeply concerned.

Cranstoun privately mulled the matter over, wondering how he could obtain a divorce. Seeing his meal ticket slipping away from him, he resolved to write to his wife in Scotland, telling her that if she would consent to a divorce then it might advance his career in the army if he was seen to be a single man. Writing that this would 'necessarily include your own benefit' and declaring himself 'your most affectionate husband', Cranstoun by this cowardly subterfuge eventually managed to get his wife to sign a letter disowning him in matrimony. However, Mrs Cranstoun's subsequent destitution led the matter before the courts, where the shameful ruse was seen through and their marriage declared legally bound. Cranstoun had to pay the court expenses and his wife's maintenance, added to which the matter was now in the full glare of publicity.

Cranstoun's wife had also written to Mary Blandy, informing her of the fact that her suitor was presently married; so Mary in turn wrote to the captain while he was in Scotland, demanding to know the truth of the affair. With breathtaking audacity, the captain wrote back and explained that the matter of his marriage, though legalised in Scotland, would be going to a higher court in London to be overturned.

This whole affair was also subtly confused by Mr Francis Blandy's own wife, Mary's mother, who could see no wrong in Captain Cranstoun; in fact she appeared as infatuated with the man as her daughter. Francis, however, could see that the captain's lies were having the desired effect on Mary: she believed everything he told her, and as a consequence the couple's relationship, far from ending, began to span the years.

Cranstoun appears to have been a suave charmer, but it was all manipulative to his own ends. For example, on one occasion, he disinterestedly threw £40 into the lap of Mrs Blandy, while she and her daughter were weeping in a London office in consequence of a debt they could not afford. Thirty pounds of this debt had been incurred in buying Cranstoun expensive treats while he stayed at Henley during one of Francis Blandy's absences. Shortly after this, Mary's mother died on 30 September 1749 and Cranstoun vocally expressed a fear he might be arrested over the £40 – to which Mary not only procured the money for him, but also (for some reason) felt compelled to give him her watch as well!

Mr Francis Blandy was by now beginning to take exception to the captain's continued visits. Using a vague explanation upon the infatuated girl, Cranstoun declared that on his next visit to Scotland he would send her some powders in an envelope marked 'Powders to clean Scotch pebbles'. These she was to administer to her father for the purposes of 'conciliating his esteem'. In fact, the powder Cranstoun posted turned out to be arsenic, although it is unclear if Mary knew this. At the very least, she seems to have taken leave of the good sense she was renowned for when the envelope subsequently arrived for her attention at the Blandy residence in Henley.

On the first available night, which happened to be a Sunday, the maidservant, Susan Gunnel, made Mr Blandy some 'water-gruel', and into this Mary furtively conveyed some of the deadly powder. She presented her father with the sustenance, and over two nights he partook. Shortly thereafter, he began feeling extremely unwell, being tormented by the most violent pains in his bowels and chronic vomiting. When the old gentleman's disorder worsened, a physician was called for on 6 August 1751, and Mary - in his presence - came into the room. Falling to her knees, she pleaded to her father, 'Banish me where you please, do with me what you please, so you do but forgive me.' As for Cranstoun, she uttered, 'I will never see him, speak to him, or write to him, as long as I live, if you will but forgive me.'

Upon her father forgiving her on his sickbed, Mary told him what had transpired: but said she had put the powder in his gruel without knowing what it was. The old man, turning in his bed, declared, 'Oh such a villain! To come to my house, eat of the best, drink of the best my house can afford; and in return take away my life, and ruin my daughter. Oh! My dear, thou must hate that man!' Mary implored her father not to curse her, to which he said such a thought would never occur to him. He then told her to leave his room and go and stay with her uncle, and to not say anything more lest it prejudice her situation. Mary *appears* to have understood at this point that she had been used as an instrument in murder, and if she were *truly* unaware of the consequences of her actions then the captain was guilty of engineering her death too, for he must have considered the outcome of this scenario.

Mary pleads for forgiveness at her dying father's bedside. (This illustration first appeared in The Newgate Calendar Volume 2 *by Andrew Knapp and William Baldwin, 1825.)*

Francis Blandy died shortly thereafter. Mary was quickly arrested upon suspicion of administering him the poison deliberately, and conveyed to Oxford Gaol where she had irons clamped on her person, it being thought she may attempt to escape; this was largely because she had been observed to flee the house upon her father's death. A coroner's inquest was held on 15 August 1751, and the autopsy clearly demonstrated Mr Blandy had been poisoned to death with arsenic.

Mary's trial opened on 3 March 1752 in the Divinity School before Mr Baron Legge. Many witnesses were called to give evidence of her guilt, testifying that she had cursed her father and 'wished him at Hell'. In an incredibly educated defence, she denied that any carelessly dropped phrases had been uttered with murder in mind, and presented herself as a victim: 'Your Lordship will judge from the hardships I laboured under. I lost my father. I was accused of being his murderer. I was not permitted to go near him; I was forsaken by my friends, affronted by the mob and insulted by my servants.' Upon being accused of fleeing the house when her father died, she explained that she was not in her senses, having nothing on but 'an half-sack and some petticoats', and had to be rescued from an angry mob gathering about her: 'Was this a condition, my lord, to make my escape in?' This appeared true, for Mary had in fact been arrested in the Angel Inn, terrified by the crowd of people that had begun to hound her when she fled along Hart Street towards Henley Bridge over the Thames. Beyond this, her defence was simple: she had not known the powder was poison, and she had seen to it that Francis took it involuntarily because 'it was intended to make her father kind to her'.

However, it was all in vain. The jury saw motive in the crime, and were outraged at the thought of such a prominent man being killed by his own daughter; to some extent, they were also probably influenced by printed and published depositions taken before the coroner, despite Mr Legge telling them to disregard such below-stairs tittle-tattle and servant gossip. The jury delivered a verdict of 'guilty' without even leaving the room, deciding Mary's whole excuse for the tragedy was a lie. Possibly the most compelling evidence the jury saw of her guilt, thus putting the matter beyond doubt, was that upon Mr Blandy first falling ill, the old man had given some of the gruel to the maid, Susan Gunnel, who herself became ill. An apothecary was sent for, who mixed them both a draught to take to remedy their illness. It was suggested that Mary had managed to contaminate the draught intended for her father - thus accounting for the fact that the maid recovered, while her father got worse and died. Thus, if Mary continued to poison her father, despite his growing sick, then it clearly demonstrated that her intention was to kill him.

Mary behaved very devoutly in the days before her execution. She received the sacrament the day before at the hands of the Rev Mr Swinton, declaring to the end she knew nothing of the possibilities of administering the deadly powder. At nine the following morning she was taken to the place of execution at Oxford Castle, dressed in a black bombazine and her arms bound in black ribbons. To the end, she acknowledged her father's death was her *fault*, but by accident and not design. Mary also made a curious comment perhaps aimed at Cranstoun: 'I die in perfect peace and charity with all mankind, and do from the bottom of my soul forgive all my enemies, and also those persons who have in any manner contributed to, or been instrumental in bringing me to the ignominious death I am soon to suffer.' Her bravery on the scaffold caught the attention of many; perhaps life now meant little to her following her betrayal and the deaths of her parents.

On the steps of the ladder she said, 'Gentlemen, don't hang me high, for the sake of decency.' Told she must go on, she expressed a fear that she might fall, and so the noose was placed around her there and then. A handkerchief was pulled over her face, and upon her signalling by holding out a book of devotions, she was hanged. The execution occurred on 6 April 1752 in front of a huge crowd; after she had been exposed to the elements the customary time she was cut down and taken in a hearse to Henley, where she was interred beside her parents at one o'clock in the morning.

Famous illustration of Mary Blandy's end, as depicted in William Jackson's New & Complete Newgate Calendar Volume 4 *(1795).*

When she died Mary was aged about 32, and in the days after her execution her case was discussed nationally by the British public. Very possibly she was an innocent dupe, although all descriptions of her suggest that she was in no way this naive. Cranstoun, the real villain of the piece, had committed an act of murder so fiendishly simple in its execution that there was no way it could ever be proved that it was his intention to kill the old man; the only flaw was that he probably did not intend Mary to go to the gallows, wishing her hand as he did…although he must have been aware of the possibilities. As such, by keeping his distance during the trial, he was as much a guilty party in Mary's death as he was in that of her benevolent and loving father.

Perhaps fittingly, Cranstoun did not last long. Upon Mary's arrest he fled Scotland for Boulogne, France, but was forced to keep on the move because some relatives of his Scottish wife, in the French services, had vowed to murder him if they ever got their hands on him. His last days were spent in Furnes, Flanders, where he died on 30 November 1752 following a severe fit of illness.

'WHAT GRIEVES ME…IS AFTER AGES SHOULD THINK ME CAPABLE OF SUCH A HORRID AND BARBAROUS MURDER'

The trial of James Stewart, which created a general sensation throughout Scotland, arose out of an ancient and deadly feud between the Stewart and Campbell clans. Like the case of Mary Blandy in England, the matter of Stewart's guilt or innocence continued to split opinion long after the events concerned.

Following the legendary and doomed Jacobite Rebellion in 1745-46, Charles Stewart of *Ardshiel* was imprisoned in Fort William as a traitor, and his estate forfeited to the crown. The gentleman employed as commissioner to confiscate such forfeited properties was Colin Campbell Esq, of Glenure, a man known as 'the Red Fox'. On 14 May 1752 during the execution of this dangerous duty Campbell was shot and fatally wounded by an unseen assassin. James Stewart, the brother of the attained Charles, was arrested for the killing, precipitating a trial before the Circuit Court of Justiciary in Inveraray between 21 and 25 September 1752.

Many at the time (and indeed to this day) saw James Stewart's trial as an exercise in revenge, based on the fact that the great head of the house of Campbell sat in the judgement seat, and the jury were mostly Campbells. Archibald, third Duke of Argyll and Lord Justice General, together with the lords Elchies and Kilkerran, sat as judges – Argyll's position meaning that it was the first time a Lord Justice General had sat as a judge at a circuit court. The charge before them was that two persons – James Stewart and Allan Breck Stewart – had assassinated Colin Campbell as he did his duty: although Breck, otherwise Vic Ean Vic Allister, had fled Scotland and been outlawed – leaving James Stewart to face trial by himself. Breck was accused of being the *actual* gunman; Stewart was accused of complicity in the crime.

The prosecution alleged that James Stewart, having previously been turned out of his possessions by Campbell, harboured a natural animosity towards the deceased, and in this capacity had repeatedly threatened vengeance. To this end he had recruited Breck, 'a man of desperate fortune', who waylaid Colin Campbell in the wood of Lettermore on the afternoon of Thursday 14 May 1752 and shot him through the body, killing him. Breck, it was held, then immediately fled, helped by the financial assistance of James Stewart, who had procured this blood money from some friends.

From the outset the case of the crown was riddled with circumstance and hearsay, based on the automatic supposition that Breck was the murderer - and the further supposition that Stewart *must* be involved because he had helped him escape. To this end, long speeches by the defence on the opening day of the trial, 21 September, declared that Allan Breck ought first to be caught and convicted before any case proceeded against James Stewart.

Lengthy observations on points of law were argued by the prosecution, in violent and inflammatory speeches. But the main evidence procured by the prosecution came from one Mungo Campbell, an Edinburgh writer and the murder victim's nephew.

Mungo asserted that he had set out from Edinburgh on 7 May, in the company of the deceased, to assist in the ejection of some of the tenants upon the fortified estates of Ardshiel and Lochiel. These tenants refused to budge, and so the two Campbells went to Fort William for legal back-up before embarking on their mission once more on 14 May.

The two men took the ferry to Ballachulish at around four or five in the afternoon and thence proceeded to their destination. When Colin and Mungo Campbell (and a servant, John Mackenzie) entered the wood of Lettermore, it was an ideal place for an ambush: the trees were thick upon both sides and the road so rough and narrow that they could not ride two abreast. Mungo went foremost, and suddenly from behind him heard the crack of a shot followed by Colin saying repeatedly, 'Oh! I am dead!' Mungo dismounted and ran back up the road, where he found Colin Campbell slumped on his horse. He recognised that Colin was clearly dying, and lifted him from the saddle before running up the hill from the road to see who had shot his kinsman. From some distance away he spotted a man wearing a short dark coat who was carrying a gun, and took off after him; this mysterious figure, knowing himself to be pursued, took flight and was lost to sight when he disappeared in the high ground that interjected between him and Mungo Campbell.

Upon his return to the wounded Colin, the latter leaned for some time upon Mungo's shoulder, trying to unfasten his clothes so that he might see where the shot had exited his body. He was unable to, but Mungo observed there were two holes in Colin's waistcoat, indicating the victim had been hit in the back with the gunfire exiting through his stomach. After half an hour of distressing agony, Colin Campbell expired. It was a dramatic location for such a shooting, happening as it did so near the banks of Loch Linnhe.

William Hole's depiction of Campbell's assassination, as featured in Robert Louis Stevenson's Kidnapped *(1893)*

As James Stewart's murder trial progressed, John Mackenzie, Colin Campbell's accompanying servant, deposed that he had been riding about a gunshot behind his master in the wood, when he heard a sound he took to be musket fire. Presently he encountered his master on the ground, covered in blood and unable to speak, while Mungo Campbell supported him and wrung his hands. Mackenzie was ordered to go and find a Campbell kinsman who lived at Ballieveolan, and in seeking help during this endeavour he encountered James Stewart, who observed Mackenzie's bitter weeping and enquired as to the cause. Stewart, on being told of the shooting, appeared shocked, and declared that he hoped innocent people would not be arrested in the rush to apprehend the assassin.

By this time, a number of people had gathered around the corpse of the slain man, including a servant of James Stewart's called 'Big' John Maccoll, whom (the trial heard) the Campbell party had observed in an agitated state when they used the ferry crossing at Ballachulish earlier on that fatal day. A local man, John Roy Livingstone, deposed that he had also seen Maccoll on the journey from the ferry to his master's house at the same time, and conversed with him: it became clear from this conversation that Big John Maccoll knew of Colin Campbell's destination later that day. Livingstone also claimed to have spotted Allan Breck in Ballachulish, wearing a dun-coloured great coat. Two further witnesses testified that they had heard Allan Breck vocally display his hatred for the Campbells earlier that year in April, making veiled insinuations that he would shoot them. He had a particular hatred of Colin Campbell of Glenure, who he blamed for trying to have him arrested upon his return to Scotland in the aftermath of the '45. Apparently, many of these threats were made during drinking sessions. One poor ploughman testified that Allan Breck had referred to fetching 'the red fox's skin', which he – with hindsight – took to mean that Breck desired the death of Colin Campbell, who was also called Colin Roy, Red Colin or the 'Red Fox'.

Next to testify was Catherine Maccoll, servant girl at the home of the accused James Stewart, who declared that Allan Breck had visited her master at Aucharn on 11 May and the two (in company) supped till quite late: and although Breck had arrived at the property in a long blue coat, red waistcoat and black breeches, when he left the following morning, having slept in the barn, he wore a dun-coloured great coat. However, it was also posited that Breck and James Stewart spent no time in private discussion, and others were always present. On the afternoon of 13 May - the day before the murder - Allan Breck turned up at the home of a kinsman in Ballachulish, leaving at midday the following day, and still wearing the dun-coloured great coat. He did not return that evening. On the evening of the 15 May – the day after the murder – Catherine Maccoll testified that she was ordered to hide a long blue coat and red waistcoat, clothes that she took to be the ones Allan Breck had left following his visit. She was then later ordered to retrieve them and give them to her mistress, James Stewart's wife: whereupon these incriminating clothes vanished for good.

There next came critical, incriminating testimony, which if true linked Allan Breck back to James Stewart. A certain Donald Stewart met Breck on the 15 May in Ballachulish, whereupon the latter professed great regret upon being told of Colin Campbell's slaying. Breck then made a strange comment to the effect that he knew of one Sergeant More, who had apparently threatened Campbell's life in France; however, Donald Stewart *knew* without doubt that this personage had not been in Scotland for some 10 years at least. Allan Breck's automatic deflection of guilt arose his suspicions, and when Breck furtively asked for an audience with Donald later that day, Donald accused him of being the person who had shot Colin Campbell of Glenure. Allan Breck Stewart was at this time dressed in the great coat, and wore a short dark coat with white buttons underneath this. He vehemently denied any involvement in the shooting, but declared he was worried he would be suspected; and could Donald go to James Stewart and see to whether James could arrange for some money to be sent to him at Caolasnacon near Kinlochleven…

This was how the case was built against James Stewart. This witness went on to testify that James Stewart, the accused, in arranging for this financial transaction to take place, had professed surprise: if Breck had wanted money, he commented, why did he not visit and ask for it himself? Upon being told by Donald that Breck feared being taken for murder, James Stewart had expressed a worried hope that Breck was neither the criminal nor the subject of a huge manhunt. As for Allan Breck Stewart, it appears he was last seen on 17 May, in a wood at Caolasnacon by a woman called Mary Macdonald.

Turning now to the evidence specifically against the defendant, one Alexander Campbell of Teynaluib deposed that in April that year James Stewart had stopped off at his house to refresh his horse, where a sour conversation had ensued. During this back-and-forth veiled animosity, James Stewart was found displaying a certain vehemence against Colin Campbell of Glenure in view of his position as eviction commissioner. Worse evidence against him was to come, however. The court heard that another of James Stewart's servants, Dugald Maccoll, was ordered by his master to hide a large Spanish gun in the barn under the girnel, after news of the murder came to Aucharn on the evening of 14 May. Stewart had already admitted that he himself had earlier hidden another smaller gun in the same spot, and also that these two weapons were subsequently taken from the barn onto the moors and re-hidden in the cleft of a rock. The Spanish gun, which was loaded, was observed in court to be - without doubt - one that Allan Breck had previously used for shooting black cockerels. Four swords were also hidden at this time, Stewart's actions coinciding with a rumour that a group of soldiers were coming into the country. Stewart's other servant, 'Big' John Maccoll, confirmed this sequence of events, but stated that it occurred on account of the supposition that a party of soldiers would soon be arriving: *any* weaponry would be doubly incriminating in the wake of the '45, especially in the hands of a Stewart. Maccoll affirmed that for months both firing weapons had been in poor condition, and implied they would not have been the first choice in *any* planned assassination.

Captain David Chapeau of General Putney's regiment, however, had been the man charged with recovering these weapons, and in his opinion the smaller of the two, which was unloaded, gave the appearance of having been lately fired.

Further circumstantial evidence came out, sometimes corroborating either the defence or the prosecution: that the prisoner had sent five guineas to Allan Breck while the latter was hiding in the wood, which the latter received from a pedlar acting as a messenger; while other witnesses testified that they had indeed heard the aforementioned Sergeant More threaten to shoot Colin Campbell on account of his harsh treatment of the tenants of Ardshiel. But at the end of it all the jury found James Stewart guilty of the murder, although of 'art and part' - that is to say, being concerned in the crime to such a degree that he shared responsibility. The court sentenced the accused to be taken on 8 November to the south side of the ferry at Ballachulish and hanged on a gibbet till he be dead, his body then to be suspended in chains and his personal estate to be fortified.

To his discredit, the Duke of Argyll, Lord Justice General, in summing up, made it clear that his political sympathies had interfered with his impartiality. He finished his partisan speech with the words: 'Though you don't now stand accused as a rebel (i.e. a Jacobite), nor am I permitted to call you a traitor, because his Majesty's undeserved mercy to you did several years ago restore you to the state of an innocent man; yet I may say, which great force of truth, that this murder has been visibly the effect and consequence of the late rebellion.'

The duke, in fact, might equally have been talking about the sentence he was himself imposing upon James Stewart, but the prisoner was resigned, declaring simply: 'My lords, I tamely submit to my hard sentence. I forgive the jury, and the witnesses, who have sworn several things falsely against me; and I declare before the great God, and this auditory, that I had no previous knowledge of the murder of Colin Campbell, of Glenure, and am as innocent of it as a child unborn. I am not afraid to die; but what grieves me is my character, and (that) after ages should think me capable of such a horrid and barbarous murder.'

On the fatal day the prisoner was escorted under strong military guard to the place of execution. He carried with him three copies of his dying speech, the first of which he delivered to the civil magistrate and the second to the commander of the troops who guarded him. His final moments were spent in reading out the third and final copy to the multitude of spectators that had turned out to see him hang; it is recorded that when James Stewart was finally launched into oblivion on a specially-commissioned gibbet above the Narrows there raged an extraordinary tempest. These appalling weather conditions did little to appease the minds of the superstitious among the spectators, many of whom were inclined to think that an innocent man now hung lifeless before them, thirty feet in the air.

What became of Allan Breck Stewart is unclear, although there is some suggestion he may have enlisted in the French service and fought against the British in North America during the French and Indian War. Sir Walter Scott wrote that a friend of his believed he had met Breck in Paris in 1789: by that time he was a 'tall, thin, raw-boned, grim-looking old man…his visage was strongly marked by the irregular projections of the cheek-bones and chin. His eyes were grey.'

In many ways, James Stewart's concern about how 'after ages' might regard him is poignant, in view of the fact that his case is one of (it has to be said) a mere handful of 18th century criminal cases that still continue to excite historians well into this 21st century. His chained remains hung for over two years before disintegrating, yet after this his bones were wired together and re-hung, so that his fate might continue to set an example. It is almost universally agreed that James Stewart was not the gunman, and although Campbell's death cannot have weighed heavily on his mind, perhaps he was only guilty by association and/or accidental circumstance after the fact. Scottish folklore has it that descendants of the Stewart line are all familiar with the name of the *actual* murderer, there perhaps also being a sneaking implication from this that it *wasn't* Allan Breck, whose name remains so well known as the top suspect despite his mysterious – and unproven – role in the murder. As late as 2008, a Glasgow lawyer was reported in the British media to be attempting to get Stewart's case reopened and reassessed by the Scottish Criminal Cases Review Commission: we can only wonder what James Stewart might have thought had he known, on his way to his execution, that in 260 years time his case would still be being debated.

What is said to be the gun used in the shooting can be found in the West Highland Museum, Fort William.

'A TALL GENTLEMAN, DRESSED IN BLACK'

There is a singular suggestion that the Devil played awful tricks on the minds of some. The *Westminster Magazine* reported on 11 April 1752 that John Davy, otherwise Young, had been convicted lately at Exeter Assizes of murder; Davy, an adulterer, had been found guilty of murdering his wife upon 'Ingolsby-Common' near Hatherleigh after luring her there upon the pretence of a reconciliation. The couple's relationship had ended about a year earlier, when Davy had deserted her for another woman. However, Davy and his new partner had determined to return to his old house, and – fearful that his ex-wife might impede their lifestyle – he arranged to meet the poor woman on the common.

Davy confessed that he previously bore his wife no particular ill will, but, 'Happening to be at the place before his wife, he never was so uneasy…while he was thus waiting he saw a tall gentleman, dressed in black, pass by him, who spoke to him, and told him he must kill his wife, and then disappeared.' That it was a Sunday morning is telling; for in the 18th century the Devil was indeed still believed to tempt those who were Sabbath-breakers.

Davy described 'much pleasure in his mind' when he subsequently saw his wife approach, yet after they had 'reconciled' (in a carnal sense) he throttled her to death while knelt upon her chest. Davy was executed at 'Heavy Tree Gallows' in Exeter alongside four other convicted criminals on 3 April, his body afterwards being hung in chains at the site of his crime as a warning to others.

Perhaps the only demons were the ones in his mind, but the implication in Davy's confession is that he believed he was 'led' by an agent of evil into committing his wicked deed. Or, to put it another way, Davy's defence rested on a unique point of law: an attempt to blame the *actual* Devil for his own wickedness.

AN ARGUMENT OVER SHOES

A report in the *Westminster Magazine* (11 April 1752) reads: 'Monday morning a woman carried home a pair of shoes to a man in George's-court, King-street, Westminster, and asked two shillings for the mending them, but he refusing to give it, words arose, on which the woman struck him on the temples with one of the shoes, which killed him on the spot. She was immediately secured, and is now in the Gatehouse.'

This incident, unremarkable in itself, nonetheless underlines the ridiculously unnecessary levels of anger and passion that could be aroused in all peoples during this time, to such an extent that even a *shoe* might be used as an improvised murder weapon by a lady during the most commonplace of disagreements. This phenomenon can be observed also in a curiously similar murder related in the *Gentleman's Magazine*, which tells us that on 5 May 1772 one Judith Whalen contrived to hang herself in Newgate using the material that bound her hair. She had been incarcerated some days earlier following an argument with a man who refused to mend her shoes; she had simply snatched up a knife and stabbed the shoemaker in the heart.

'A VIEW OF SWAN'

In the case of John Swan and Elizabeth Jeffreys, who were convicted at Chelmsford's spring assizes in 1752 of the murder of Joseph Jeffreys, the uncle of the female prisoner, it first appeared that the deceased was murdered in the night by an intruder. The prisoners had given the alarm of murder from within the house at Walthamstow; however, the undisturbed state of dew on the grass outside rendered it certain that the parties implicated were resident on the property. The crime had been born out of Elizabeth's fear of disinheritance following a quarrel with her uncle, to the extent that she enlisted Swan (the gardener and her lover) and another domestic named Matthews to kill the old man in the hope that robbers might be blamed. When Matthews' nerve failed him on the fatal night of 3 July 1751, Swan shot the victim himself in an upstairs room, and when Mary perceived her uncle not quite deceased the injured man was stabbed twice in the neck. Some 17 witnesses appeared against the pair, including Matthews.

Both were sentenced to be executed on 28 March 1752 'at Buckets-Hill near the Bald-faced Stag, on Epping Forest, near the place where the fact was committed'. Contemporary newspaper accounts suggest Elizabeth was aged about 26, with a ruddy complexion; she apparently confessed her guilt while awaiting execution, and on the due date both felons were hanged near the sixth milestone in Epping Forest. Afterwards, Elizabeth's body was presented to friends for interment, but John Swan's body was hung in chains in a different part of the forest.

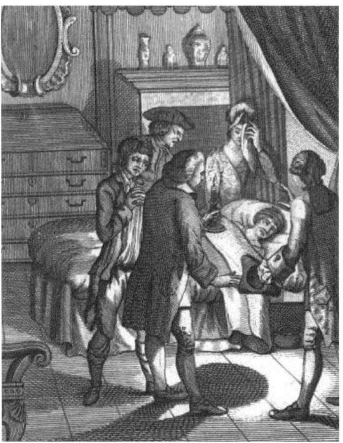

The wounded Mr Jeffreys dies in his bedchamber, as originally depicted in William Jackson's New & Complete Newgate Calendar Volume 4 *(1795).*

Although the crime caused a minor sensation at the time, correspondence printed in the media provides a fascinating glimpse of what it must have been like to happen across a body suspended in a gibbet cage. The *Derby Mercury* (24 April 1752) was just one newspaper that published this letter:

'To the printer & c. SIR, riding over Epping Forest, I had the curiosity to take a view of Swan, who was hanged in chains for the murder of Mr. *Jeffryes*; and as there is something unusual in his manner of hanging, I have sent you a description of him, if you think it worth inserting. He is hung by the side of a wood, on a very high gibbet, beyond the ten mile stone: he seems to be above six feet high, has on his head a white woollen cap, a light grey waistcoat, red everlasting breeches, grey stockings, and very black japann'd shoes; his irons are formed in a singular manner, having, besides those usual about his body, iron braces around his legs, and stirrups under his shoes to support his feet; which, when the wind blows, makes him appear as if he was vaulting in the air; and by which he must remain entire many years longer than usual, the legs of other criminals generally dropping off before the body is half consumed.'

A PERFECT STORM

Anne Whale, the woman at the centre of this next story, was born of respectable parents in Horsham, Sussex. Her father died when she was very young, and at an early age – under the sole guardianship of her mother – she displayed evidences of an ungovernable temper. For instance, when she was a young woman, Anne argued so badly with her poor mother that it led to her wilfully taking herself away from home: she subsequently began to consort with people of a poor reputation. It took all her mother's powers of persuasion to convince Anne to return home again and save herself from ruination.

Soon after this Anne was courted by a sober young labouring man named James Whale. Having reached maturity, she had lately been left a legacy of £80 by a relation, and following on from this Anne and James were married. For a while they lived at Steepwood Farm, south of Billinghurst, but at length returned to Horsham where they took up residence with one Sarah Pledge, who was distantly related to James Whale.

There next followed a remarkable sequence of events. Anne and Sarah initially did not take to each other at all, quarrelling so badly that Mr Whale forbade Sarah to enter his apartment, despite it being within her own house. This caused the two women to continually cross swords, until by some strange occurrence they were privately reconciled. What brought about the reconciliation is unclear; what is even less clear is how they entered into a criminal conspiracy to get rid of the obliging and sober Mr Whale. It is implied that the women were simply wicked (there is no suggestion of lesbianism, and both women were mothers), for while Mrs Whale was laying abed, having been ill, Sarah Pledge came into her room and said, 'Nan, let us get rid of this Devil!', meaning Mr Whale, who was at that time out of the house.

The wife said, 'How shall we do it?' to which Sarah replied, 'Let us give him a dose of poison.' Poor Mr Whale could have had no knowledge that these two women had joined forces to destroy him; as far as he knew, they hated each other. First the women attempted to kill him by putting roasted spiders into his beer, but finding this had no effect Sarah Pledge took herself off to buy some poison from an apothecary. She visited a number of premises in several market towns – but each time either fancied she saw someone she knew, or else was stricken with an attack of conscience. Finally – inexplicably – she visited an apothecary in Horsham itself and purchased a dose of poison.

The whole affair, from start to finish, is as curious as can be imagined. The two women stood virtually no chance of ever escaping interrogation, and this knowledge appears to have been behind Mrs Pledge's last minute nerves; yet still the two women pursued their plan, and although it had been Sarah who apparently first suggested killing Mr Whale, Anne, the treacherous wife, now took control of the situation. She actually mixed the poison into a pudding for her husband's supper while watching him cradle their child, upon whom he doted: shortly after partaking of the contaminated substance, Mr Whale was racked with gut-rot and terrible convulsions. He died in utter agony the following day, his symptoms having got unbearably worse as the corrosive substance ate his insides.

When the two women were taken into custody, Sarah Pledge immediately incriminated herself by implying she wished to turn king's evidence, and on being examined separately both women confessed and were committed to Horsham gaol. On their being tried in July 1752, their confessions (which they had signed) were read, and some corroborative evidence being presented to the court, they were convicted of murder and sentenced to death.

After her conviction Sarah Pledge took to behaving in the most hardened manner, swearing profusely and making it known she would fight the hangman on the day of her execution. Mrs Anne Whale seemed to understand the enormity of what she had done; she was but 21-years old and had been told she was to face the traditional punishment for *petit treason* – strangling and burning, as Catherine Hayes had suffered a quarter century earlier. On 14 August 1752 both women were taken to Broadbridge Heath on the western side of Horsham, where a huge crowd of people first watched Sarah Pledge suffer execution by hanging, then witnessed Anne Whale be garrotted and burnt to ashes while tied to a post.

Quite what was behind their crime is somewhat unclear, although there is a suggestion that Sarah Pledge had taken offence at Mr Whale through petty slight and jealousy; whereas Mrs Whale simply wanted rid of her husband. When both these women came together, it created a 'perfect storm', as it were.

A REMARKABLE ACQUITTAL

In April 1753 The *Gentleman's Monthly Intelligencer* reported on two rare acquittals for murder, evidencing that though the age was cruel the letter of the law, rightly or wrongly, could function.

The periodical reported that one William Hewish was executed on 31 March 1753 after being convicted at Exeter for the murder by poison of his father. Hewish had previously been tried in October 1751 for murdering his mother, but acquitted at the time; this was in spite of very strong evidence that Hewish had beaten, kicked and dragged his mother about by the hair of her head. He had frequently been heard to remark he would kill the poor woman, and shortly before her death she had told several people she was dying due to being hit in the stomach with an iron bar.

Despite this, Hewish had not been convicted following his eight-hour trial. However, the law caught up with him two years later when the Exeter Assize found him guilty of killing his father in December 1752. Bizarrely, as he stood on the gallows platform, Hewish denied murdering his father – but admitted he deserved death for his ill usage of his mother. He had, he admitted, cruelly beaten her several times. That he might deny the crime he was hanged for, while admitting the one he wasn't, seems somewhat curious. Nonetheless his body was delivered to the hospital for dissection after his own death. A newspaper at the time declared Hewish a ruthless criminal in the making, reporting: 'He was a genteel young fellow, and extremely well dressed on his trial. He robbed his master when (an) apprentice, fled, and afterwards had the benefit of the last pardon. If he had been acquitted of the above offence (i.e. murdering his father) he would have been indicted for forgery.'

Remains of Exeter Castle, where Hewish – the murderer of his own parents – was incarcerated.

Around the same time there stood trial at Warwick Assizes Miss Dorothy Smith, accused of poisoning her aunt, Mrs Dorothy Martin, 'relict of the Rev. Mr Martin, of Curdworth near *Colehill*'. Dorothy pleaded not guilty, although there was little doubt her aunt had died in an extremely suspicious fashion: the gentlemen who performed the autopsy were of the opinion, by the appearance of her stomach and bowels, that the old lady had been poisoned to death with arsenic. However, it could not be ascertained conclusively how this event occurred.

It did certainly not appear that Mrs Martin had committed suicide. The jury heard that the old lady had been in poor health for some time, but she became irrecoverably ill following a breakfast meal of milk porridge prepared for her by her niece. Feeling sick, she had desired a visiting neighbour to taste the porridge, and this lady confirmed that the spoonful she partook made her throat and mouth burn very much. Mrs Martin died that evening, although the other woman recovered, not having tasted as much of the contaminated breakfast. A greenish sludge was found lining the bottom of the bowl, and a subsequent coroner's inquest brought in a verdict of wilful murder.

The astonishing thing about all this is that Dorothy Smith had initially confessed the murder! She admitted in the presence of two clergymen that she had risen on the day of the crime and simply been tempted by the Devil – a temptation she could not withstand. However, it was suspected that the true motive might have been Dorothy's desire to get her hands on a £500 dowry her aunt had willed to her, to be given to her at age 25.

Dorothy had been raised from childhood by her aunt, and many simply refused to believe the girl could commit such a wicked act. This was to some extent evidenced by the fact that half the town threw out oatmeal they had purchased, believing that the market traders must have poisoned it for unclear reasons, and this was how the elderly woman had died. Dorothy's salvation, however, rested more on a point of law. The person who had purchased the arsenic for her was a girl under nine years of age, and it was argued for above two hours whether her evidence was admissible in court. In the end it was decided that it wasn't, and (together with the appearance of a number of witnesses who testified her good character towards her aunt since her infancy) Dorothy Smith was acquitted of murder.

A curious (to the modern reader) point of law is the allowance of suspects to be reported as guilty pre-trial: the *Derby Mercury*, for instance, had no qualms in declaring just days after the victim's death: 'On Wednesday last Mrs. Martin…was poison'd by her niece, a girl about 19 years of age.' But in both these cases we see – perversely – that what seemed to be two very clear cases of murder resulted in acquittals; all the more stranger for occurring in an age when to stand before a judge charged with *any* crime was tantamount to a death sentence.

And as if to reinforce that acquittals could and did occur, the 1756 autumn assizes at Chelmsford, Essex, was remarkable for the number of people it freed. Ten prisoners in all were set free, including two accused murderers and also 'Samuel Gouge and John Ovington, who were charged with the murder of three sailors near Harwich'. This last concerned an incident on 18 June 1756 when 60 pressed men took control of the *Delight* tender in Harwich Harbour, securing the officer and men before running the vessel ashore near Landguard Fort, Felixstowe. Some forty escaped onto land, or died attempting to, and the remaining twenty fought a sharp gun battle with a party of soldiers from a sloop. Several men were killed and wounded in this encounter.

THE GOOD FRIDAY MURDERS

When William Smith's mother married her second husband, a butcher called Thomas Harper of Ingleby Manor, Smith saw the inheritance of his late father's estate slipping away, and determined to remove not only Harper but also Harper's children by his first marriage. The relationships of the participants in this little drama were complicated; William Smith was aged about 22 and married to one of Harper's daughters – which made Harper both his step-father and father-in-law.

Smith, a fairly well-to-do farmer from Great Broughton in North Yorkshire, pondered several means to achieve his deadly aim. Finally he purchased two pennyworth of arsenic in an apothecary's store, ostensibly to kill rats in his barn. Instead, he mixed the deadly powder into the flour that was being prepared for a large cake, to be eaten on Good Friday 1753 at Ingleby Manor. Providentially, it happened that some neighbours invited to the dinner table that night could not come, so when the cake was served up only Harper and his two children, William and Anne, partook. The moment those sat at table became stricken, Smith prepared to set off for Liverpool and fled on Easter Sunday - which very quickly arose suspicion against him where before there had been none. The unfortunate victims languished in excruciating torment, all of them having died by six o'clock the following morning. All three were buried in one giant grave, and a maid-servant almost became the fourth victim, having also partaken of the contaminated cake. Luckily she recovered from her illness. Had the neighbours also been there and eaten the cake, five more people could have died.

However, in Liverpool it appears Smith's conscience betrayed him, and he very soon returned to Great Broughton, completely abandoning a plan to escape to Ireland. Here, he was in the end arrested some two miles from his late father's house by a member of a posse that had fanned out in different directions following his flight. Upon being taken he was carried to Great Ayton to be examined by Mr Justice Scottow and Mr Justice Beckwith, before whom he would confess nothing. However, upon being taken back to Ingleby under the guard of four men, Smith cracked and confessed to murdering his father-in-law and the two children: a confession he repeated soon after when he was next presented before the two Justices.

The apothecary who sold him the arsenic and a maid who spotted him mixing it into the flour appeared against him, and Smith was convicted of murder, his air throughout the trial being one of unconcern and insensibility. On 14 August 1753 he was executed at the Tyburn without Micklegate Bar, York, before his body was carted off to the county hospital to be anatomised and dissected.

'TO ARMS': THE BRISTOL COLLIER'S REVOLT

The ways by which tumult could so quickly spread is evidenced by a bizarre event reported in some of the British newspapers in March 1753. News from Newcastle declared that there had been great agitation occasioned in Warcop, Cumbria, owing to squibs and rockets going off, guns being fired and loud shouting being heard in the vicinity. At first, terror swept through the villagers, for it was feared that some kind of invasion was at their door; in the end, it turned out to be the work of a group of loutish young men who had assembled themselves, battered their way into a smith's shop and 'mortally wounded two landlords'. Little explanation is provided for this mysterious incident, although it does illustrate the agitation and tension that could alarm a population centre.

All the more so, then, when the threat came from a genuine force of numbers, armed and with angry grievances. On 26 May 1753 an army of several hundred colliers entered the City of Bristol at 'change-time' and made their way to the Council-House where they vocally registered their anger at the price of bread. They demanded twelve pounds weight for a shilling, but although the magistrates listened and tried to reason with the crowd no agreement could be reached. Presently the mob of colliers marched on the Quay where they boarded a vessel loaded with corn for export, broke open the hatches and began to plunder it. A party of constables came down to the Quay and in violent altercations they forced several of the colliers overboard and into the mudflats. The enraged colliers then marched *en masse* back to the Council-House, where they smashed the windows with stones and injured a number of people within and without. Eventually the constables, backed by a swelling group of Bristol inhabitants, forced the rebellious colliers out of the city gates, some through the waters of the River Avon.

On the Thursday after, the colliers, backed up by a force of country-folk, regrouped at Lawford's Gate, and so the two sheriffs – named Woodward and Whatley – bravely proceeded there from the Guildhall to engage them, backed up by the constables. A violent fracas ensued in which some of the rebels were injured, and some taken prisoner – although they refused to disperse and at this point the Mayor, John Clement, decided to take decisive action. Drums beat throughout the city, and the call 'To arms!' was heard from every quarter. This, it seems, rattled the colliers – who were found to have withdrawn upon the Mayor leading his force to the city gates. The gates were kept shut, and guards were posted to watch for the mob's return.

The following morning the gates were opened to admit a company of Scots Greys, newly arrived from Gloucester. But just as they were quartered, the drums once more began to beat throughout the city – intelligence suggested the mob of colliers was returning, and the Scots Greys were called to arms along with the city-guard.

The rumours were true. At about midday a huge mob reassembled at Bridewell-Gate with the intention of freeing one of their number taken prisoner the day before. The colliers succeeded in forcing the gate open: however, they were quickly surrounded and a number of shots were fired into their ranks. This panicked the colliers, who had little expectation they would be 'vired at wi' baal', and many among the crowd scattered in various directions, vanishing into the maze of Bristol's side streets and alleyways. Violent skirmishes took place in different parts of Bristol, in which four persons were killed and 29 taken prisoner (some of whom were critically wounded). The Scots Greys were drawn up with the intention of allowing them to open fire into the ranks of the rebels, but this proved not necessary - as by this time the mob had generally dispersed. A small party of gentleman pursued a band of the last colliers into the countryside outside Lawford's Gate, leading to a battle in which one of the rebels – a man named Fudge – died and three of the gentleman's party were seriously wounded. Two among the posse were also held captive for a time, including one who had taken refuge in a 'hay-talhot' until the rioters exposed his hiding place by thrusting pitchforks into the hay. By nightfall, however, the action had died down, and this captive was brought back to Bristol in safety.

In the aftermath of the uprising, the ringleader - a man called Job Phipps - and eight others were carted to Bristol's Newgate, where a specially commissioned court subsequently sentenced most of their number to two years in prison.

CORRINGDON'S DEATH HOUSE

On 6 August 1753 a labourer named William Prowse knocked on the door of Joseph Harvey, a farmer of Corringdon, near South Brent, Devonshire, in order to offer work. Calling twice more, his knocks received no answer, and so three days later Prowse and a neighbour called again; they looked through the kitchen window and perceived a motionless body on the floor.

The pair alerted Harvey's brother Anthony, and together they forced an entry at the window. They found Joseph Harvey's bloodied body laid out near a blood-stained razor, hone and billhook; his legs were under the kitchen table and his throat was cut. Going upstairs, the investigators found a scene of horrendous carnage. Mrs Jane Harvey, her throat cut and her 'head clove like a calf's head', lay on a bed beside her similarly mutilated 20-year-old daughter Elizabeth. Both women had a bed sheet pulled up over them. Harvey's son William, a stout man of about 23, was found in another bed, his throat cut and his skull cleft in by the billhook. One of his fingers was also lopped off, and a hatchet was found by this fourth body.

At a coroner's inquest, it appeared that old Mr Harvey had sent two servants and the maid on an errand to buy some hay, knowing this business would detain them for a week; he had been observed to be in a delirious state of mind for the past three months, and it seemed from the evidence that he had returned home from Totnes market at about nine at night on 4 August and systematically begun to slaughter his family.

There had been no robbery perpetrated at the farmhouse, which would usually have been the motive behind this type of crime had a stranger been guilty. Although the *exact* reason was unclear, the inquest on 14 August judged Harvey guilty of the three murders while in a lunatic state, it having been observed that he had been 'greatly out of his senses' for the past three months. Harvey had also killed himself, the inquest ruled.

'TO BE BURNT AT CURE-GREEN, WELLS'

By mid-century women who murdered their husbands still faced the medieval punishment of being burnt in public, and a typical example of this comes from Somerset.

On Monday 3 September 1753 a grim spectacle was occasioned near Wells when Susanna Bruford, a 19-year-old of '*Mounton*, near Taunton', was burnt at Cure-Green.

Susanna is believed to have hailed from 'Huntstile in Chilton', a farm set in the beautiful, rolling foothills of the Quantocks. She had been convicted of poisoning her husband John to death, he being a farmer of good repute at West Monkton. The pair had only been married in March 1753, and she had committed the deed in May.

At the trial it became clear Susanna had made an earlier unsuccessful attempt to poison her husband by putting arsenic in John's ale. He perceived it gritty, and soon after found himself seized with violent stomach spasms. By purging and vomiting, the effects of arsenic were prevented; it seems that John suspected his wife of trying to kill him following this, but took no action against her.

The next time Susanna tried, she succeeded. While John recovered, an apothecary ordered him to take flour of brimstone, and Susanna took the opportunity to mix in enough yellow arsenic to wipe out twenty men. Her husband did not eat the whole, but soon collapsed in pain, continuing to live in great torture – bowels and gut burning – before dying four days later in utter agony.

Susanna stood virtually no chance of getting away with the murder. The amount of arsenic used ensured the cause of her husband's death was obvious at the autopsy, and she was already suspected of the previous failed attempt on John. There were also allegations of an affair…the evidence was stacked against Susanna almost soon as her husband was cold.

Susanna was convicted of murder. A little before her execution, she declared that the beginning of her misfortune was a 'too near intimacy' with an attorney's clerk who had seduced her when she went to see some fireworks in Taunton. She behaved very penitently, and acknowledged the justice of her sentence; but the case is interesting from the point of view that it illustrates how courts across England still inflicted burning as a punishment upon certain female murderers, almost 30 years after the infamous case of Catherine Hayes.

Sadly, Susanna's execution drew a 'prodigious concourse of people'. Similar spectacle had been witnessed during the execution of Anne Williams at Gloucester earlier in 1753, and Anne Sowerby suffered such a punishment at York in 1767. Nine years into the reign of the *third* George, this barbaric form of punishment was still the way husband-killers were sentenced to die, for the *Gentleman's Magazine* reported another burning as occurring on 22 July 1769: 'Susannah Lett was drawn on a hurdle to *Pennendon* heath near Maidstone, and fix'd to a stake with an iron chain round her middle, and her body burnt to ashes for the murder of her husband.'

The punishment for petty treason: this is Anne Williams being executed in Gloucester. (As originally depicted in The Newgate Calendar Volume 2, *Andrew Knapp and William Baldwin, 1825.)*

TRAVELLING IN TERROR: FOOTPADS AND HIGHWAYMEN

The future King William IV was accustomed to relate how his great-grandfather King George II, while walking alone in Kensington Gardens, was robbed by a single highwayman. This audacious fellow, pleading great distress and with great deference to his majesty, relieved him of his purse, watch and buckles.

A view of the Italian Garden, Kensington Gardens; it was in this vicinity that King George II was held up by a trespasser who had the audacity to rob his majesty.

Despite the mythology of 'gentlemen of the road', clearly (as we have seen with Turpin) romantic figures like this who held up travellers on the highway were few and far between; most were desperate men. Robbery on the highway must have seemed attractive to many during these poverty-racked times; but equally anyone who set out to commit such a crime knew they were likely to be put in a position where they might have to kill.

A footpad might be distinguished from his brethren the highwayman by the fact that he was not mounted, and therefore perceived less dashing. The footbridge in the King's Road, Chelsea, which spanned the stream running from the Serpentine to the Thames, was at one time called Blandel Bridge: and this spot had a grim history of ambushes by footpads. In the early 18th century this part of London was naturally darker and more open; Blandel Bridge is said to have been about 12 or 14 feet wide, with a wall on either side of sufficient height to prevent passengers from falling into the narrow rivulet it spanned. This structure also went by the name of *Bloody* Bridge on account of the many murders committed by criminals in its vicinity. It appears to have borne this appellation for decades, and by the 18th century it proved just as effective a place for a robbery as it had in the 1500s.

For example, at about 9pm on 20 August 1742 this grimly-named place bore witness to the savage murder of Mr Smith, keeper of the Five Bells alehouse. Smith appeared to have been killed by two soldiers in a field nearby; this was suggested by a large stab wound in his breast that bore the look of an injury inflicted by a bayonet. Furthermore, one of his two dogs had torn the attacker's uniform, for a tattered red flap of cloth and a soldier's hat were found nearby. Two soldiers (one with ripped clothes, the other minus his hat) were seen going over Putney Bridge later that night. Poignantly, the two dogs – one with a stab wound – would not suffer anyone to come near their dead master's body until Smith's maid was brought to entice them away.

The periodicals and newspapers of the time were full of reports like this. In this year the *London Magazine* also reported the death of a carpenter called Cofield on 9 August, who had died after being stabbed nine times on Blackheath, between the Green Man and the Half Way House, by 'some footpads'. Company approaching, they had no time to rob him. North of the river, on 23 August 1742 an Islington brewer's servant fought a furious struggle with a footpad on the 'Causeway between the Turk's Head, and the Back-Door of Sadler's Wells', and saw him off despite suffering several stab wounds. It was written of this area: 'Scarce a night pass'd without some one being robb'd, wounded or murder'd, between the Turk's Head, and the road leading to Goswell-street.' Around this time, the keeper of the Turk's Head, one Coster, and his son were taken on suspicion of murdering a certain John Lack in this area of Islington on 16 August; Lack, 'who held a place in the Armoury of the Tower upwards of 40 years', was found dead by the New River, having been stabbed in the chest and neck, and 'under his right ear'. Both the Costers were acquitted of Lack's murder, being able to present witnesses who swore both the accused had gone to bed by nine o'clock on the night Mr Lack was slain.

Parts of London were infested with footpads, but Bloody Bridge seems to have been a persistent magnet for bandits. On 12 August 1748 four gentlemen drew swords when their coach was attacked, and managed to send two robbers fleeing. Another crime reported in the *Gentleman's Monthly Intelligencer* is a typical example of the brutality employed by these types of thieves. At about 9 o' clock on 17 September 1753 Mr Crouch, cook to the Earl of Harrington, was stopped by two footpads at the gravel pits near Bloody Bridge as he made his way to town from Petersham. They pulled him off his horse and a violent tussle ensued, the two bandits firing their pistols at Crouch. He, for his part, drew a large knife from his pocket and stabbed one of his attackers so violently that blood splashed all over him. Perhaps weakened by the pistol fire, Crouch was overpowered and the knife wrestled from him, and as he lay on the ground he was stabbed several times so that the robbers 'almost ripped his belly up'. The villains took his watch and money and then dealt him a good kicking, jumping up and down on his body for good measure.

The remarkable thing is that Crouch lived at all beyond this, but he initially survived and was taken to St George's Hospital, where his wounds were dressed. He then returned to his home in Green Street, Grosvenor Square, London. The following day Crouch died, and two soldiers were subsequently taken into custody for the murder and robbery.

Although it is not stated in the periodical, it seems the three wounds inflicted by Crouch on one of his attackers identified the culprits. At any rate, on 10 December John Hambleton was convicted at the Old Bailey for the murder and robbery, and three days later executed at Tyburn. He died a Roman Catholic, denying the murder to the last, and afterwards his body was delivered to surgeons for dissection. Of the second culprit, a man named Lattie, it is assumed he died from the stab wounds inflicted by Crouch after being thrown in Newgate, for we learn ''tis thought he cannot recover'.

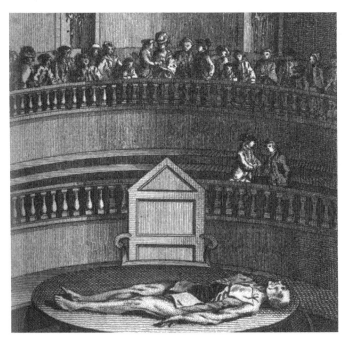

A convicted murderer's body, publicly anatomised within Surgeon's Hall, Old Bailey. (From William Jackson's New & Complete Calendar *Volume 6, 1795.)*

Perhaps these footpads thought the risk worth it; crimes on the highway – even murder – frequently went unsolved, as another instance in 1753 typically illustrates. William Maude of Sunderland went missing on 24 January, and very soon it was being supposed that he 'was assassinated upon the high road'. Maude's horse was found wandering on its own by a farmer not far from South Shields, and for four days the length of the road was searched to find Maude's corpse. In an attempt to get the criminals to turn on one another, the authorities promised a pardon and £50 to anyone (the murderer excepted) who might identify his accomplices. Crouch's widow offered 50 guineas, and another 50 guineas were promised by the Hon. Henry Vane and George Bowes, Esqs, the MPs for the county of Durham.

Maude's body was found several weeks later, apparently dragged from the roadside southwest of Cleadon. He had suffered a serious wound in and above his right eye, and an almighty black bruise on his torso indicated he had suffered a blow that knocked him off his steed. His whip was still in his hand. The slain man, it seems, was very highly regarded: yet despite everything a coroner was ultimately forced to return a verdict of 'Wilful murder by persons to them unknown' on 23 March 1753. Although 'several suspicious vagrants' were taken up on suspicion of the murder, it appears the crime went unsolved.

To this day, it is a curious fact that while footpads are generally perceived as having been common, vulgar robbers, highwaymen retain an allure of daring-do, romanticism and dashing audacity: despite there being little to distinguish between them when it comes down to it. The important distinction appears to have been the *horse* – which made the highwayman faster, sexier and to all intents and purposes appear more successful. A mounted robber was also far more capable of targeting a moving vehicle, while a footpad might have to settle for a pedestrian – again making the highwayman's accomplishments seem grander. Regarding highwaymen, perhaps the strangest story of the era concerns the Right Reverend Dr Philip Twysden, Bishop of Raphoe in Ireland, who died at his house in Jermyn Street in the St James's area of London. The bishop expired on 4 November 1752, two days after having been shot and wounded in mysterious circumstances on Hounslow Heath. Although it was put out he had died after becoming suddenly ill with 'an inflammation of the bowels' while traversing the Heath, it was – and is – suspected that he had been out undertaking robbery when he was shot in the body by someone he attempted to hold up. Why the bishop was out on dangerous Hounslow Heath at such an unsociable hour when he 'fell ill' was not adequately explained, and it appears there *might* have been some suppression of evidence when reports of his death appeared in the newspapers.

The lure of becoming a 'gentleman of the road' is neatly exampled in a case from the Cambridgeshire/Hertfordshire border. A grim cautionary tale was noted by the Cambridge antiquarian William Cole (d.1782). He explained that the region was within living memory the haunt of a highwayman: the brigand was the son of Mrs Gatward, who owned the Red Lion Inn that stood on Royston's

High Street. It was supposed that Gatward, under his mother's supervision, had been employed to tether the horses of visitors seeking refreshment at the inn, and some of those who rested there may have been highwaymen. This association might have engendered in young Gatward a desire for the romantic life of an outlaw, and for a while he terrorized the countryside between Royston and Cambridge. His luck couldn't hold out forever, however, and ultimately Gatward found himself before the judge at the Cambridge Assizes. In about 1753, Cole recorded, Gatward was sentenced to death for robbing the mail coach and after his execution he was hung in chains, his corpse suspended from a gibbet near the scene of his crimes along the Great Road. (He was probably displayed at Caxton Gibbet, where a replica of the gibbet post stands beside the ancient Ermine Street, the A1198).

Cole wrote of passing by this way, where he 'saw him hanging in a scarlet coat'. After three months the gibbet collapsed in high wind, and Gatward's corpse crashed to the ground. With ghoulish curiosity, a man named Lord approached the body to 'open the breast' and see what state it was in. He found it to be quite dry and during this Lord took a brass button from Gatward's waistcoat.

Apart from seeing the corpse swinging in the gibbet cage, William Cole wrote that he had actually met Gatward in 1752 when the young man had purchased two coach horses from him.

A later replica replaced the collapsed gibbet at Caxton, Cambridgeshire.

'THE INHUMAN VILLAIN'... THROWING ONE'S LIFE AWAY IN MONMOUTHSHIRE

On Sunday 25 November 1753 one Jonas Levi, a Jewish traveller, was found 'barbarously murdered' between Abergavenny and Crickhowell in Monmouthshire. A box he carried had been plundered of its valuable contents, and a belt had been 'girt and buckled' exceedingly tightly around his neck before his head had been struck so violently that his brains had been dashed out. Parts of the man's skull were scattered across the road, and two large stakes wrenched from the hedge nearby had clearly been used to commit the murder. The box was left by the body, almost empty but for a teaspoon, part of another teaspoon and some hardware. The value of the stolen plate and money was estimated to be around £100. Levi's trouser pockets were also turned inside out.

The coroner held an inquest where the slain man's body was found, and the Jewish community residing in Bristol raised a collection of £20 to be paid by the clerk of the synagogue to anyone who could provide information leading to the arrest of the murderer.

The *Gentleman's Monthly Intelligencer* reported that the culprit was quickly apprehended: 'Towards the end of the month we were informed, the inhuman villain was taken and committed.' The discovery of the killer - a joiner from Crickhowell in Powys called William Price - was occasioned not by the promise of reward, but by Price's own reckless stupidity in showing off his stolen wares. He audaciously carried in his pockets several watches, and wore at his knees and on his shoes genteel silver buckles - 'ornaments unsuitable to him' – while at the same time making extravagant gifts of gold rings, stone girdle-buckles and snuff boxes to several lady acquaintances in Brecon. In Monmouth Gaol he made this voluntary confession:

'Nov. 20, I was going from my mother's house to Brecon, I met Jonas Levi a Jew within two fields of *Crickhowel*, there I turned back and followed him to the place where I took a stake and laid it down; I was then before him, and then turn'd back, and met him, and with that stake I knock'd him down and haul'd him to the wood where he was found; I threw the first stake away, and was in such confusion that I could not find it again, but took another stake and struck him again, and no other blows, neither was there any body else with me; nobody knows anything of it but myself till this moment, and there I robbed the box of all that was therein of any value; after I killed him, I robbed him of a guinea in gold and two shillings and six pence in silver; as witness my hand, William Price.'

An interesting aspect of this case is that it illustrates the 'suicide mission' that many criminals embarked upon when their greed was excited; it is almost as if Price expected to get caught and therefore proceeded to live his life in as cavalier a manner as he could, making (it appears) little attempt to avoid detection and confessing freely when captured. Criminals such as Price appear to have been very much aware that, in committing such a murder, they were also throwing their own life away: yet circumstance prompted this scenario to play itself out uncountable times throughout the 18th century. What this says about the state of society could be debated endlessly; at any rate, Price was convicted of murder on 20 March 1754 at Monmouth Assizes and executed the following day. His body was delivered to surgeons for dissection.

A curious (and somewhat eerie) aspect of this case is that after he had been sentenced to death, Price provided the same bizarre part-explanation for his crime as John Davy had done a few years earlier in Exeter. Price told the court that he encountered 'a tall man' while traversing a field near the crime scene, who swore that if Price did not assist him in robbing a man coming with a box, it would be the death of him. This mysterious figure pointed towards Jonas Levi, at that time making his way up the road. Price, out of fear, consented to commit the killing because of this. The implication is that Price believed (or wanted the court to believe) he had encountered the Devil immediately prior to the murder.

THE MYSTERY OF HOPCROFT'S HOLT

At some point on the night of Friday 13 January 1754 a barbaric and mysterious crime was perpetrated at Hopcroft's Holt, a lone house at a crossroads near Steeple Aston in Oxfordshire. For many years the place had been run as a public house by one John Spurritt (or Spurrier) and his wife; as such, it had become a commonly known place to virtually all who travelled along the Banbury road. However, of late – the pair being elderly – they had begun to turn away business and did not keep a full-time servant.

They did occasionally employ a man and a woman, but on the day in question these two had gone home by 5 o'clock in the evening. The following Saturday morning they both turned up for work again, but found the old couple would not answer their knocks on the kitchen door; so after a while they went to a seldom used back door. Finding it upon the latch they entered the premises and ventured upstairs to their employer's bedchamber.

The bed was un-slept in, although from the looks of it several boxes in the room had been broken open and rifled. The pair, now thoroughly worried, dashed downstairs again and into the kitchen: here, a scene of horror greeted them.

Old Mr Spurritt lay dead on the kitchen floor, which was awash with blood. Near his body was a green ash club, about three quarters of a yard long, with which he appeared to have been dashed six times on the head. Any one of the injuries dealt him would have been severe enough to cause his death, but he appeared to have tried to defend himself anyhow - for one of his fingers (the third of his left hand) was almost smashed off. Mrs Spurritt lay in the chimney corner, mortally wounded from similar treatment.

A mug and a candlestick near Mr Spurritt's body indicated they had been attacked while in the act of preparing to retire for the evening at about 8 o'clock.

Poor Mrs Spurritt languished for three days, her forehead brutally bruised and one of her arms broken, before expiring; she lay speechless throughout, and was unable to impart any information about the attackers. A quantity of money appeared stolen, but it was difficult to ascertain how much.

The *Oxford Journal* reported at the time that 'there are several persons suspected'. However, two months later no-one had been charged, despite the offer of a £50 reward for information by the Duke of Marlborough. And – like so many similar cases throughout the century – the murderer of old Mr and Mrs Spurritt went unidentified: one can only wonder if they committed any other acts this heinous, or if they went to the gallows in Oxfordshire or some other county for another crime.

'*A CRIME ALMOST UNHEARD OF IN THIS COUNTRY*'

In 1754, Nicola Cockburn (the daughter of Alexander Cockburn of *Ormistonhall*) earned her place in the annals of Edinburgh's most notorious criminals.

On 18 March that year she contrived the death of her husband, a labourer named James Kidd, or Kiddie, to whom she had been married some 17 years. The pair lived at Newton, near Dalkeith, and Nicola stirred a quantity of arsenic into her husband's broth at dinner, by which method he died in tortured agony between nine and ten o'clock that evening.

This killing passed without suspicion, and so encouraged the now-widowed Ms Cockburn to commit another. A few days afterwards she went to Ormiston, where her own father lay ill. He died soon after her arrival, and so Nicola stayed on – ostensibly to help her stepmother, Susan Craig. On 3 April, while her father's body still lay unburied, Nicola mixed a quantity of arsenic into a pottage (i.e. thick soup) and presented the dish to her stepmother that morning. Susan Craig partook, and not long afterwards she was affected with excessive sickness and violent vomiting; in her torment, Susan confided her belief to visiting neighbours that she had been poisoned. Nicola Cockburn, she declared, had been spotted taking something out of her pocket prior to serving up the stew.

The remains of the contaminated pottage had been thrown below the chimney. The neighbours confronted Nicola, but she defended herself by saying she had put nothing in the pottage but a pickle sugar. When the pottage dish was found, it contained a residue whiter than any sugar – and so Nicola changed her story, claiming she had, in fact, stirred in a pickle *powder*. Expanding on her explanation, she elaborated this was what she had also fed her husband two or three weeks earlier. Around this time Susan Craig vomited up an almighty quantity of whitish substance, which the suspicious neighbours collected as evidence. Next they forced Nicola Cockburn before a Justice of the Peace called Robert Dundas, Esq, at Ormiston-hall, in order that she might explain herself.

Dundas had Nicola's house in Newton searched, and a great quantity of arsenic was found: and so, upon these corroborating proofs she was incarcerated in Edinburgh's Tolbooth. Her stepmother died in excruciating agony at about five in the afternoon on 3 April 1754.

A view of Edinburgh's Tolbooth. By A. Nasmyth, from an 1834 collection of illustrations for the Waverley *novels.*

Nicola Cockburn came on trial at Edinburgh on 12 August 1754, charged with the two murders. Her trial lasted one day, after which the jury unanimously found her guilty. Lord Justice Clerk next addressed those present with a very moving speech, commenting on the almost-unheard of nature of the crimes, and thanking the diligence and effort of Mr Dundas in providing enough proofs to convict the evil woman. He also urged greater vigilance among chemists and surgeons when they sold white arsenic.

Nicola Cockburn was sentenced to be fed naught but bread and water till 18 September, whence she would be taken from gaol and publicly hanged in the Grass-market of Edinburgh, before her body be delivered over to surgeons for dissection. On the day of justice, she confessed to killing her husband and stepmother, and acknowledged the justice of her sentence – but what lay behind her crimes remains something of a mystery. The news-sheets of the time do not even hint at a motive, despite the crime causing a minor sensation in Scotland and the north of England.

A WIFE'S ANTIPATHY TOWARDS HER HUSBAND

In July 1754 some of the news-sheets reported a wife's horrific revenge against her errant husband. The crime happened at 'a town called Blackwater' (probably meaning the Blackwater Estuary, at Maldon in Essex, since the news came from Braintree), when a farmer's wife, through some discontent with her husband, declared she would be revenged upon him.

Early in the morning, while he went about his business, the woman cut her infant daughter's throat with a case-knife while the child was in the cradle; she then picked up their other daughter, a girl of about four, and hung her by the body upon a meat hook in the parlour. Lastly, she grabbed her ten year old son and attempted to slit his throat, but he - being a stout lad - managed to struggle out of his mother's grip and alarm the neighbourhood with cries of 'Murder!'

The woman was immediately seized, and put in the hands of a constable while the parish officers sent for the coroner. Upon her own confession, she was committed to Chelmsford Gaol on 8 July. The eldest daughter was gently taken down from the meat hook seriously injured, and she expired soon afterwards of her injuries. It was reported: 'The woman does not appear to be disordered in her senses.'

Although the reports did not name the woman, it is possible they refer to Frances Cheek, who assize records show was hanged on 12 August 1754 for the murder of her daughter, Hester, after being convicted at Chelmsford.

'PRESSING' SEAMEN

The act of 'pressing' private seamen into naval service for the government was something of a gentle euphemism: for in fact 'pressing' was but one step away from abduction, and naturally resisted by those of a seafaring background who desired to avoid being taken into the British navy.

Throughout 1755 the government vessel *Winchelsea* was anchored at Liverpool with the specific order to board vessels and 'press' seamen who had arrived in England from the colonies. Typically, the *Whitehall Evening Post* reported in late June the arrival in Liverpool of a number of such targets: 'The wind blowing very fresh westerly, hindered the *Winchelsea*'s boats from boarding the *Achilles* and the *Ryder*; however, Capt. Drake being determined to board the *Jenny*, slipt her cables, gave her *chace*, and boarding her sword in hand, he press'd 17 stout seamen, who had confined their officers, but were hindered from escaping by the *Winchelsea*'s shot, which carried away her braces, and disabled them in their rigging.'

Not all attempts to impress seamen were this successful, however. Two weeks earlier, the *Upton* had docked at Liverpool after crossing the Atlantic from Maryland. This was just the sort of vessel the *Winchelsea* preyed upon, and her officers sent a barge down the River Mersey to forcibly recruit the *Upton*'s hands.

The seamen aboard the *Upton* had no intention of being forced into service, however. They confined their captain and officers (this often seems to have been the first move by those resisting being 'pressed') and refused the government men in the barge any admittance to the *Upton*. In fact, they threatened to sink the barge if it came any closer.

This was no idle threat. Seeing the barge sheer off a little, the men of the *Upton* boarded their yawl (a type of smaller two-masted sailing craft) and rowed up to the government barge; they yelled that they would open fire unless the government barge sailed away entirely.

It was not, of course, within the barge's remit to be so weak. And so a bloody battle was joined, with the barge and the yawl trading fire with each other while heaving on the waters of the estuary. According to the *Whitehall Evening Post* in mid-June 1755, 'Several on both sides are mortally wounded; the commanding officer of the barge received a shot in his cheek.' However, the government barge won the day, for the seamen on the yawl somehow overturned their vessel while attempting to board the barge armed with their swords. In the melee, the men from the *Upton* all plunged into the water, and in the end fifteen of them were hauled onto the barge and taken back to the *Winchelsea*, 'choosing to be press'd rather than downed'.

On 1 June 1755 three boats from the *Winchelsea* attempted to board the *Tarlton*, lately arrived at Liverpool from Barbados; however, musket fire was poured at the government boats, and on this occasion they withdrew, 'not caring for a second engagement with desperate men'.

THE TOLL-KEEPER'S MURDER

On 23 October 1755 a calculated and cold-blooded murder was reported. 'On Friday last' William Collet, the keeper of the turnpike at St John's Bridge in Lechlade, Gloucestershire, was roused from his bed by someone in the road calling out to him. One of the unpleasant duties of manning a turnpike was that it frequently meant having to interrupt one's sleep during the night, in order to open the toll gate to allow travellers to continue their journey. And since a toll had to exchange hands for the gate to be opened, it naturally made toll-house keepers unpopular, and turnpikes positively despised.

Thus was Collet roused between the hours of twelve and two in the morning, to answer the calls of the person out in the road. However, as soon as he had unlocked his door, in order to open the gate, he was shot through the body by someone who fired at him in the darkness.

Collet was fatally injured, the slug entering his breast and exiting his body through the middle part of his back. Upon a coroner's inquisition, a verdict of 'Wilful murder by a person unknown' was returned.

This crime seems to have gone unsolved, and the culprit unidentified; but it appears as though Mr Collet was lured from his bed simply to be shot – although what the motives of the assassin might have been are, quite naturally, impossible to guess.

THE DEVIL WHISPERED TO HIM...

Edward Morgan's crime in Glamorganshire is remarkable for its impulsiveness and brutality. The Welshman had been invited to the Llanfabon farmstead home of his cousin (some reports say uncle) Rees Morgan, so that he might spend the Christmas holiday with Rees' family in 1756. Following the first day's festivities, Morgan retired to a bedroom where there also slept a young apprentice. Here, in his own words, the Devil whispered to Morgan, ordering him to get up and murder everyone in the house.

Acting on this impulse, he immediately attacked the apprentice; however, Morgan was unarmed at this stage and so the lad was able to fight him off and escape, afterwards concealing himself in a safe place. Morgan then sharpened a knife and stealthily entered his cousin's bedchamber, cutting the throats of both Rees Morgan and his wife. He then proceeded to the bedroom of their daughter and cut her throat also. Seizing a firebrand, he torched the barn and all the corn, then a beast-house with 12 cattle in it, the outhouses, and finally the farmstead itself after plundering it of some valuables. Whatever the Devil's involvement *truly* was, it seems that behind it all – as usual – robbery was the motive.

We learn from the *Newgate Calendar* that: 'It was at first conjectured that the unfortunate people had perished in the conflagration. Their murdered bodies, it is too true, were consumed to ashes; but the manner of their death was proved partly by what the concealed apprentice overheard, but chiefly from the murderer's own confession. Morgan was executed at Glamorgan, on the 6th of April, 1757.'

Morgan behaved very penitently at the place of execution, again confessing the three murders. He was afterwards hung in chains on '*Cardiffe* Heath'.

Morgan sets the place on fire after slaughtering the inhabitants. (This depiction features in The Newgate Calendar Volume 2, *Andrew Knapp and William Baldwin, 1825.)*

THE SHUDEHILL FIGHT

The years between 1753 and 1757 saw general discontent over the scarcity and dearness of food in Manchester. The town at this time was a steadily expanding hub for the production of pure cotton fabrics, and rapidly growing in importance. But innovation and a burgeoning population naturally brought its own problems.

Shudehill, the old road leading to Christ Church and the Irwell, had already seen direct action by the mob on 7 June 1757, when a crowd of people waylaid the provisions being brought to Shudehill market and seized them. The resulting operation to protect the town almost gave Manchester the appearance of being in a state of insurrection and siege. Harvest time brought no alleviation to the sufferings of the poor, and on 15 November 1757 a mob of about 900 destroyed the corn mills at Clayton before marching to Shudehill.

Mr Bailey, the High Sheriff, ordered a detachment of soldiers to intercept the marchers, and this they did, the two parties confronting each other at about 11 o'clock. Great diplomacy was practised in an attempt to get the mob to disperse without violence; however, their number had been swollen by trouble-causers who insinuated the soldiery – being mainly elderly veterans, who were outnumbered 10 to one – would not dare to fire. The crowd immediately began to pelt the soldiers with stones, with such ferocity that their corporal was killed and another nine injured. In response to this the soldiers fired a volley of shots into the mob, killing three and wounding fifteen; these were taken to the infirmary. Among those shot was 'a fine young man' who was the son of Mr Newton: he had taken no part in the battle but had climbed a tree to watch the fighting – and there suffered a gunshot wound when the firing started. He later died of his wounds.

This scattered the mob, but they regrouped later and converged on Bramhall and Hatfield's mills within half-a-mile of the town. These they plundered and destroyed, next burning the haystacks, houses and outbuildings. They then marched back into Manchester where they attempted to storm the dungeon at Salford Bridge in order to release an imprisoned rioter. In order to prevent another violent disturbance the constables simply released the man, and after this the affair seems to have petered out. By this time a force of regular soldiery had also arrived to back up the invalids.

An 1839 map of Manchester: the scene of the battle.

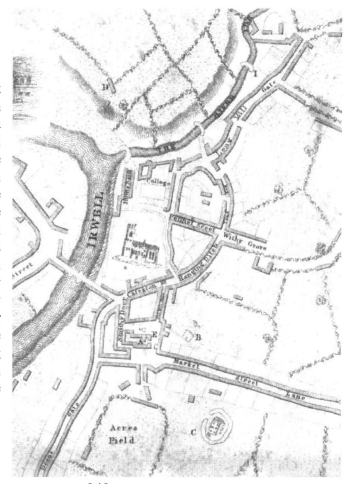

A subsequent coroner's inquest in December brought in a verdict of 'wilful murder' against the person who had thrown the missile at the corporal; it appears he went unidentified. In an effort to be seen as even-handed, an attempt was made by the authorities to try one of the veterans - Mr James Greatraeux the younger - for shooting young John Newton in the tree, but this came to naught.

OAKHAM'S HEDGE MURDERS

On 17 March 1758 Anne Woods enlisted the services of a man named Robert Broome to trim a hedge on ground not far from her house at Hambleton-on-the-Hill (Upper Hambleton), a picturesquely sited village near (where is now) Rutland Water outside Oakham. Both were 'poor aged cottagers', and Broome's employment aroused the competitive jealousy of a neighbour, John Swanson, who believed such work to be his right locally.

Swanson's reaction was extreme. He grabbed a hatchet, and marched to the hedge with the intention of confronting Ms Woods – however, before he had got three parts of the way he met her returning home, and with no prompting whatsoever simply struck her down with a hedge-stake. He then continued to the hedge, where he attacked old Mr Broome at his work, striking him down with the hatchet.

Hambleton near Oakham, where a barbaric double murder occurred.

Swanson then attacked Broome's body like a maniac, chopping his victim's neck until the head came away, before smashing open his rib cage and tearing out the man's heart. These two trophies he wrapped up in a piece of old rag. Swanson then returned to his first victim, Ms Woods, pulling down her stays and likewise cruelly removing her heart, which he wrapped up with the other grisly body parts. He then returned home and hid the blood-soaked rag with its horrendous contents in a chest under his bed.

The officers of the parish quickly suspected Swanson of this atrocity and went to his house to arrest him that evening. When they charged him with the crime, he stood dumb for three minutes before confessing fully and directing the officers to the parts beneath his bed. He was secured immediately and committed to Oakham Gaol. The *Annual Register* remarks of Swanson: 'It appears by all the circumstances of this murder that the man was mad, and ought to have been confined long before.'

John Swanson was arraigned at Oakham Assizes later that year. He refused to plead, and no sense could be gotten out of him whatsoever, despite his being warned of the consequence of such a course. In the end, the parish minister and the gaoler both testified that Swanson had provided manifold proofs of insanity: and so the judge ordered Swanson to be taken back to prison until he could be assessed by a physician to establish whether he was fit enough to stand trial.

In the end, following an evaluation of his condition, it was decided proceedings should continue as normal. Swanson was subsequently arraigned again on Saturday 10 March 1759 and sentenced to death. He was executed the following Monday and his body taken to Stamford in Lincolnshire for dissection by surgeons.

'HIS WIFE NOW LIES A-DYING'

On Friday 15 September 1758 a man named John Grindrod, or Grindred, a wool-comber who lived in Salford (at this time a growing town neighbouring Manchester) was taken into custody on suspicion of having poisoned his two children. During an examination at the Coroner's Inquest, it was given in evidence that Grindrod had purchased arsenic and induced the children to eat it in treacle mixed with brimstone. When they both died, an obvious suspicion had led to an autopsy on the children's bodies, whereby it became clear they had, indeed, been poisoned to death. Worse, the inquest also heard how Grindrod's 'wife now lays a-dying', having also partaken of the deadly treat.

Grindrod was confined to Lancaster Castle, his trial to be heard at the next assizes the following year. This duly occurred in 1759, the *Manchester Mercury* (26 March 1759) briefly reporting that Grindrod was executed 'Saturday last' for three murders, his wife having died in the meantime. He declared upon the ladder that he did not doubt entering Heaven, for he alone knew he was guiltless of deliberately contaminating the treacle; this prompted the newspaper to comment on his 'wretched stupidity' in denying the crime. Afterwards, Grindrod's body was brought to Manchester to be hung in chains, and it was gibbeted at Cross Lane on the road to Pendleton.

The grim fortification of Lancaster Castle, where Grindrod was imprisoned.

Grindrod's swinging corpse long remained an object of dread to the credulous. William Harrison Ainsworth's poem *Old Grindrod's Ghost* drew upon the fear of this ghastly exhibit, in part noting:

> *Chains round his middle, and chains round his neck;*
> *And chains round his ankles were hung;*
> *And there in all weathers, in sunshine and rain;*
> *Old Grindrod, the murderer, swung...*

'TO DIE IS NATURAL AND NECESSARY': THE TALE OF EUGENE ARAM

Seldom was there a robber and murderer such as Eugene Aram, whose crime attracted the attention of novelists and poets, due in part to the extraordinary circumstances surrounding the case and the cultivated mind of the man himself.

Aram was an unlikely person to be implicated in a potential murder. Born at Ramsgill, Yorkshire, in 1704, he received a good education and later took a position as a clerk in 'a counting-house' in the capital. He subsequently returned to his native county, however, where he set up a school and entered into a rather unhappy marriage with a woman called Anne Spence in 1731. Settling in Knaresborough, North Yorkshire, he devoted himself to archaic studies, and by great application he obtained an extensive knowledge of the Greek, Hebrew and Latin languages and literature.

In 1744, when Aram was about 40, he once more travelled to London, completely deserting his wife Anne and taking a position as an usher in a school in Piccadilly. Here, he worked laboriously and further enhanced his reputation as a learned man by amassing a considerable knowledge of Chaldee and Arabic, all with the aim of applying his great store of knowledge to a lexicon. During subsequent engagements at other schools he studied Celtic and also acquired a great wealth of information concerning botany. By 1758, Eugene Aram was employed as an usher at a school in Kings Lynn, Norfolk, and his life in Yorkshire was long behind him.

By this time, however, there had for many years been an uncomfortable rumour that Aram and another man named Richard Houseman (a flax-dresser) were involved in the defrauding of a number of people back in 1744. Furthermore, some also linked Aram and Houseman to the subsequent disappearance of a shoemaker called Daniel Clark, a close friend of Aram's who had vanished without trace from Knaresborough around the time of the fraud and was never seen again. Aram had shortly thereafter deserted his wife and embarked on his afore-mentioned journey of knowledge.

Eugene Aram when a young man. (As originally depicted in James Caulfield's Portraits, Memoirs & Characters of Remarkable Persons Volumes 3-4*, 1820.)*

At the time of his mysterious disappearance, fourteen years earlier, Daniel Clark had been recently married. It was later suggested that the three principal actors in this drama – Eugene Aram, Richard Houseman and Daniel Clark – had in 1744 entered into a conspiracy to borrow as much valuable property as possible, as if for Clark's wedding…the plan being to then simply divide the spoils among themselves like common plunderers. Their fraud was designed to work in this way. Clark, under cover of having received a fortune from his new wife, had 'borrowed' plate and other expensive wares from good-natured friends and acquaintances in order (he said) to present a good first appearance in the married state. In this Clark had succeeded, managing to obtain things of great value, such as linen and woollen drapery goods, silver tankards and silver mugs, emerald and diamond-encrusted jewellery, rings, watches and snuff-boxes. Afterwards (it was later suggested) the three had met at Eugene Aram's house to divide the wealth three ways.

Daniel Clark had vanished sometime around 8 February 1744. His intimacy with Aram and Houseman excited suspicion that they were involved in his disappearance, and a subsequent investigation found some of the appropriated valuables on Houseman's property, with another portion being discovered buried in Aram's garden; however, no plate was found, and the authorities concluded that Daniel Clark must have absconded with the greater part of the haul.

Thus the affair remained in abeyance, although the fact that nothing was heard of Clark *ever again* led some to believe that murder had been committed. Among these was Eugene Aram's own wife, who began to voice these concerns upon her husband's subsequent desertion of her. Rejected and abandoned when Eugene left for London, she intimated on several occasions her belief that her absconded husband and Houseman were guilty of Clark's murder. When word of this was carried to Aram, he allegedly told Houseman (as the latter later testified) that, 'he would shoot her, and put her out of the way'.

After 14 years of stagnation in the case of the missing shoemaker, there came a dramatic development. Houseman was brought before an inquest in 1758 and informed that a skeleton had lately been discovered on 1 August by some workmen digging for limestone at Thistle Hill near St Robert's Cave, outside Knaresborough, and it was believed to be Clark's. Houseman, taking up one of the bones, made the curious comment, 'This is no more Dan Clark's bone than it is mine', and when asked how he could know such a thing with certainty, Houseman began to become quite evasive. Eventually he broke down and confessed that Clark's *actual* body might be found by further excavation *within* St Robert's Cave: for – quite remarkably – the skeleton dug up by the workmen was nothing to do with the Clark case, it being a different skeleton from a different era discovered quite by accident.

Houseman, having now implicated himself, went on to declare he was innocent of the murder itself. This crime was Eugene Aram's work alone, he stated, and based on this testimony Houseman was admitted in evidence against Aram. His solemn declaration also named a certain Henry Terry as Aram's accomplice in the killing.

Houseman gave a graphic deposition of what had happened on that day 14 years before:

'That Daniel Clark was murdered by Eugene Aram, late of Knaresborough, schoolmaster, and as he believes, on Friday, the 8th of February, 1744-5; for that Eugene Aram and Daniel Clark were together at Aram's house early that morning, and that he (Houseman) left the house, and went up the street a little before, and they called to him, desiring he would go a little way with them, and he accordingly went along with them to a place called St. Robert's Cave, near Grimbald Bridge, where Aram and Clark stopped, and there he saw Aram strike him several times over the breast and head, and saw him fall as if he was dead, upon which he came away and left them. But whether Aram used any weapon or not to kill Clark he could not tell, nor does he know what he did with the body afterwards, but believes that Aram left it at the mouth of the cave; for that, seeing Aram do this, lest he might share the same fate, he made the best of his way from him, and got to the bridge-end, where, looking back, he saw Aram coming from the cave-side (which is in a private rock adjoining the river), and could discern a bundle in his hand, but did not know what it was. Upon this he hasted away to the town, without either joining Aram, or seeing him again until the next day, and from that time to this he never had any private discourse with him.' Subsequently, however, Houseman would contradict this; he also declared that he was sure Clark's body was buried in St Robert's Cave, and expressed the desire that it might remain there till Aram was taken.

Upon Houseman's disclosure, a further search was made and the remains of a second body – that of the missing Daniel Clark – were found.

On 19 August 1758 Aram was arrested at the school in Kings Lynn where he worked as an usher, and brought back north to face imprisonment and trial at York Castle.

Eugene Aram proved quite the intellectual. While Houseman's testimony was somewhat contradictory, Aram's was consistently eloquent and educated. His first statement admitted the fraud, and also implicated the aforementioned Henry Terry (a Knaresborough alehouse keeper) in this. He admitted St Robert's Cave had been a sufficiently remote locale for the four plotters to beat the plate flat without the noise arousing suspicion, and this they had completed by about four o' clock on the morning of 8 February 1744. Aram declared that, to the best of his knowledge, Dan Clark had intended to flee: and this circumstance had dictated that the latter hide in the cave throughout the next day. In the early hours of 9 February the three others had returned to the cave, where Houseman and Terry alone had entered to (as Aram supposed) complete flattening the plate. Aram himself had remained outside the cave to keep watch. An hour or so later,

Houseman and Terry re-emerged, and told Aram that Daniel Clark had fled. Returning to Knaresborough, the remaining trio stashed their stolen goods away in Houseman's warehouse. In short, Aram implied – without directly accusing anyone – that he had acted as look-out while Houseman and Terry had killed and buried Clark in the cave unbeknown to him.

After Aram had signed his written version of what happened that fateful night, he was committed to York Castle, where he and Houseman remained incarcerated until the following assizes. Henry Terry was also committed to the castle, but legal problems ensured the case did not come to trial until the Lammas assizes the following year.

Eugene Aram, Richard Houseman and Henry Terry went on trial on 3 August 1759. The court heard that while finding the first skeleton had been a curious accident not related to the case in any way, it had had the strange effect of bringing the whole matter to light. In the opinion of Mr Locock, the surgeon who examined the remains, it did appear that the *second* skeleton could be no other than Clark's, and the skull was displayed in court. On the left side it exhibited a fracture that had clearly been made by blunt force trauma; the injury could not have happened post-mortem, either by natural decay or the excavator's spade-end.

Eugene Aram at the time of his trial. (As depicted in The Criminal Recorder, or Biographical Sketches of Notorious Public Characters *Volume 1, 1815.)*

While Eugene Aram declared he had seen no murder committed, Houseman claimed to have actually seen Aram do the deed with his own eyes: thus the weight of circumstance was not in Aram's favour. Nonetheless, when he delivered his own defence it came in the form of a masterly and educated rendition from a manuscript he himself had written – and it held the court spellbound. Aram cast doubt upon his own ability to commit such a crime, citing his educated and studious disposition, and also a chronic complaint that had enfeebled him and which made it physically impossible for him to kill a full-grown man. A large part of his defence rested on the impossibility of proving conclusively that the bones found within St Robert's Cave were Clark's, and circumstantially this was correct. He argued that the sex of the bones was indistinguishable; that prehistoric remains were frequently unearthed; and that there was no *proof* the injury occasioned to the skull was caused by a deed of violence. But why would such an educated man go to such great lengths to deny there *was* a connection, unless he wished to subvert the supposition? And why would he wish to do that? Surely, the only reason to deny any connection so absolutely would be because he was a guilty man…

Perjurers were a persistent problem, Aram continued, implying that Houseman was a liar and that innocents had previously been condemned on the words of such people, as was well known.[1]

Furthermore, Aram declared, the complete disappearance of a person was no evidence of death.

Aram's continual dismissal of any link between the skeleton and Clark's disappearance, however well argued, perhaps – contradictorily – doomed him. Maybe his own arrogance also condemned him: his belief in his own intelligence

---

[1] *Here it is worth briefly digressing. Aram may have been referring to the notorious case of Stephen MacDaniel (or MacDonald), John Berry and Mary Jones. The* Criminal Recorder *Volume 1 (1815) aptly described this trio, who operated with three other men named Egan, Salmon and Blee, as 'a new species of murderers', their method being to recruit young men to carry out thefts and robberies - before they deliberately betrayed their luckless new accomplices to the authorities. This practice condemned at least four of their hired accomplices to the gallows upon false pretences, and very likely the gang claimed many more victims in this manner in order solely that they might gain the rewards offered by the authorities for identifying a thief. A typical victim was Joshua Kidden, who was tried at the Old Bailey in January 1754 for robbing Mary Jones, who was a widow, on the highway on 7th of that month. Of course, it later transpired Mary was part of the gang and the whole thing was staged by Berry, MacDaniel and the others simply for the rewards that were handed out; but the by-product of this was that unwitting dupes like Kidden ended up being hanged. The metropolis and its immediate environment offered the gang unlimited opportunities to sacrifice people in this manner without anyone being able to put two and two together, although in the end Blee betrayed the rest in a final ironic twist to the saga. It proved legally impossible to try MacDaniel, Berry, Egan and Salmon for murder (what became of Mary Jones is unclear, but she appears to have been discharged), and in the end an Old Bailey court was only able to convict them of perjury and criminal conspiracy. They were each sentenced to seven years in Newgate, but also ordered to be pilloried. On 8 March 1756 Egan and Salmon were set on the pillory in Smithfield, where they were violently treated by the public, who pelted them with stones, dead dogs and cats, and potatoes before half strangling them. Egan was struck so violently on the head with a stone that he died immediately while trapped in the pillory, and such was the Londoner's hatred of these men that it was thought best to forgo the pillory and simply imprison them. All three are reported to have died in Newgate.*

was such that he genuinely thought he could cast doubt upon the whole case. He was wrong, for the jury brought in a verdict of 'Guilty' and Aram was sentenced to death. Houseman, having turned king's, could not be executed and Terry was acquitted, no evidence appearing against him.

The schoolmaster accepted the death sentence with his usual stoicism, and – in the end – admitted his sentence was deserved in the presence of two clergymen who visited him in gaol the following morning. When one of them asked Aram why he had done it, Aram replied that he suspected Dan Clark of having 'unlawful commerce' (i.e. criminal associations or a sexual relationship) with his wife, and that at the time slaying Clark had seemed the correct thing to do. Since then, however, he had regretted it. During this conversation, Aram implied that Houseman's level of guilt in the matter was far greater than what the court had decided: for he had at the very least assisted in helping Aram drag Clark's body into the cave, where they stripped and buried it. Houseman may even have known of Aram's intention to kill Clark, and helped plan it; Aram also declared that it was Houseman who continually pressed him to shoot his abandoned wife, for this was not an act he would have considered himself - as Houseman had implied during the trial.

Aram promised to make a full confession on the day of his execution, but in this he was prevented by a horrid attempt upon his own life. When the jailer came to remove the irons that restrained him, Aram could not rise and claimed to be very weak; it was found that *somehow* he had obtained a razor and cut one of his arms in two places. It made no difference; the wound was bound, and - in a weakened condition - Aram, aged about 54 at the time, was conducted to the Tyburn (gallows) without Micklegate Bar on that same day, 6 August 1759. When asked if he had anything to say, Aram replied simply, 'No' before being launched into oblivion. His body was later taken into Knaresborough Forest and hung in chains from a gibbet post.

On the table in Aram's cell was found a suicide note he had written, declaring:

'What am I better than my fathers? To die is natural and necessary. Perfectly sensible of this, I fear no more to die than I did to be born; but the manner of it, in my opinion, should be something decent and manly... Certainly, nobody has a better right to dispose of a man's life than himself...'

Aram's body remained suspended in full public view for many years. As it disintegrated, it is said his widow Anne gathered up and buried the fragments that fell. A local physician, Dr Hutchinson, one night stole the skull, and this was subsequently placed in the Museum of the Royal College of Surgeons. This remarkable relic still survives, and is kept in King's Lynn Museum.

In the aftermath of the trial, Houseman incurred the full force of public dislike aimed at informers. A mob, thirsting for his blood, chased him through Knaresborough on his return. He was never afterwards seen in the daytime, and soon moved away from the town. He is said to have attempted several times to hang himself. At last he returned to die in 1777, and his body was secretly removed to Marton for burial lest tumult break out in Knaresborough.

It is a little known fact that Aram was rumoured to have committed other murders. When the entire affair originally came to light following the discovery of the first skeleton at St Robert's Cave, the very first person questioned was Aram's wife Anne, who had frequently been heard to utter that she had it in her power to hang both her absconded husband and others about the town. Mrs Anne Aram suggested that her husband, Houseman and Clark had sold some of their stolen wares to a travelling Jew and his manservant, who they had murdered after the transaction simply to recover the stolen articles following payment. Dan Clark had been dispatched shortly afterwards but buried in a different spot to the other two victims. Sometimes it is speculated that the *first* set of human remains that was found – upon which a 'murder by persons unknown' verdict was also returned – concerned one of these other victims.

At the time this raised the intriguing possibility that more remains lay interred in the vicinity of St Robert's Cave, as yet undiscovered…

And this was not entirely without foundation. In fact, in 1833 the *Hull Packet* reported that the full skeleton of an old man had been found by workmen in a gravel pit at Hay-a-Park. The remains seemed to be 'the relics of an aged man' who 'had been deposited there by the hand of an assassin'. Then, in 1846 *another* skeleton was found in the vicinity, at Low Bridge, two feet under the ground and with stones laid upon its head: according to the *Bradford Observer*: 'It is supposed to have been the doings of some ruthless assassin in a by-gone age'.

Could that 'ruthless assassin' have been Eugene Aram, or one of his cronies?

'A MOST CRUEL MURDER'

An instance of the enraged, mindless brutality inflicted on those attempting to enforce the law was recorded in 1759. On 13 April that year a 'most cruel murder' was committed at Halesowen near Birmingham. Two bailiffs, named John Walker and Nathaniel Gower, were in possession of the appropriated goods of one Joseph Darby, which had been confiscated 'on a distress for rent'.

At about nine in the evening, Darby's two sons – Joseph Jnr and Thomas - came into the bailiff's premises 'near Hales Owen' armed with a broom, hook and a bludgeon. They immediately attacked the two bailiffs: Gower somehow escaped, but Walker was left at the mercy of the two thugs, who beat and stabbed him until he was nearly dead. They then stripped him and dragged him out of the house, where the barbarity continued: naked, Walker was lashed with a wagon-whip until he was almost cut to pieces.

Gower, in the meantime, made his way to Halesowen, where he raised some men to come to Walker's relief. They found the unfortunate man 'in a close near the said house, weltering in his own blood', and gently carried him into Halesowen, where he died. The following morning Darby's house was searched, and he, his wife and two sons were secured. One of the apprehenders narrowly escaped being fatally injured when the old man struck at him with an axe.

All four so held were committed to Shrewsbury Gaol by the Reverend Mr Durant. Old Darby was jointly charged with the murder as well as his sons, since he had stood by and encouraged this scene of villainy; their guilt was never in doubt, since, quite apart from the evidence of Gower, the deceased's coat, waistcoat and breeches were discovered in the Darby household, bloodied from the attack.

The four members of the Darby family were tried at Shrewsbury Assizes later that autumn. The father and two sons were condemned to death and executed two days later; the sons being hung in chains near Halesowen and Joseph Darby's body being given to surgeons for dissection. Joseph's wife was acquitted of any involvement in the murder.

As an aside to this barbaric killing, there were – conversely – still cases where bailiffs thoroughly exceeded their authority. In May 1755, for instance, the *Whitehall Evening Post* reported: 'A few days since one John Roseveer, of the parish of Littlepetherick in Cornwall, was murdered by two or three bailiffs, who beat him to death on his endeavouring to avoid their arresting him.'

THE ASSASSINATION OF MR RICHARD MATTHEWS

The last sensational murder committed during the reign of the second George concerned a German, Francis Davies Stirn.

Stirn was the son of a Lutheran minister in the principality of Hesse-Kassel. His upbringing in Germany appears to have been good: a grammar school education was followed by his removal to the college at Bremen, and then the University of *Hintelin*. Stirn was at this time being supported by his brother, but following the plundering of Hesse-Kassel by French soldiers it became necessary – through lack of money – for the young Francis to be sent to London, where the German family had English friends.

Stirn duly came to the British capital in 1758, where his benefactors, the Crawfords, procured him the position of usher at an academy in Hatton Garden, Holborn. This proved unsuited to the young German's inflated opinion of himself, however, and we learn that around this time he considered enlisting in the military. We also learn that Francis was possessed of an impetuous temper – for his friends dissuaded him from this course of action in the belief that he would not be able to submit to the authority of his superiors in the army. It appears that Francis subsequently alienated these friends, for they refused to help him financially in his next plan: which was to go to one of the English universities.

Thus thwarted, Stirn now became acquainted with a surgeon called Mr Richard Matthews, who persuaded him that the German's benefactor, Mr Crawford, was not treating him as he deserved. Thus, the gulf between Stirn and the latter began to grow wider.

It is the bizarre nature of human beings that, for some reason, Matthews saw greater potential in the German than anyone else, and asked him to come to his house as a lodger. The terms were that Francis would teach Matthews' wife and daughter to play music, and generally instruct the family in the European classics. Mr Crawford, hearing of this, approached Matthews and subtly told him what a bad idea this was, since the German was almost ungovernable; Matthews merely told Stirn of the transaction in order to ensure that the German and Crawford further fell out, and he might get his own way!

Although Matthews did not know it at the time, his insistence upon having Stirn as a lodger would prove disastrous. Stirn duly moved in with his new family, but trouble erupted very quickly. It so happened that a child had left some bits of bread in Stirn's room while idly messing around in there, and when the German later found them he immediately thought someone in the household had placed them there as a slur upon his dependant situation. Inflamed with fury, Stirn actually had the audacity to barge into the Matthews' bedchamber, where Mrs Matthews was at that time abed; quickly dressing herself, and clearly frightened, she told Stirn that her husband would be home soon and he should discuss it with him. Luckily, at that moment Mr Matthews arrived home and with great tact he persuaded Stirn that the matter had been a total misunderstanding.

For a while things calmed down, but Stirn became increasingly unhappy with his dependency upon the Matthews family, as well as missing his own family in Germany. The atmosphere under their roof became intolerable and so Mr Matthews applied to a magistrate for advice on how to get rid of his arrogant, difficult guest; the magistrate advised Matthews to tell Stirn to get out in the presence of a constable, in case the German became aggressive.

When the time came Stirn at first refused to leave the premises, but his behaviour became increasingly erratic. After sulking in his room for some time he eventually stormed into the parlour, where Matthews, two friends and the constable sat talking. He insulted Matthews using the most cruel language, but then demanded a glass of wine so that they might depart as they had met: as good friends. Having drunk, Stirn made a veiled reference to what was coming when he asked Matthews if he would like to purchase his clothes and books, clearly indicating that he felt he had no need for them anymore. Matthews was cautious, and so the matter was dropped, with Stirn saying it mattered not for he had money enough and had been speaking to a person who would 'write both of their lives'. With this veiled threat he shook Matthews' hand and departed.

Stirn subsequently brought two pistols and sent a challenge to Mr Matthews, who declined to respond. Mr Crawford, Stirn's former benefactor, was in the meantime attempting to organize a reconciliation between all the respective parties involved when he actually bumped into Stirn in Cross Street. It was the early evening of 15 August 1760, and Stirn looked utterly miserable, saying, 'I am lost to God and man.' When Crawford offered him money to return to Germany, Stirn replied with tears in his eyes: 'My brother (back in Hesse-Kassel) will not receive me, after being turned into the street in so scandalous a manner.' The two apparently parted company at this point. Crawford, who seems to have been a very pious and charitable man, took himself off into nearby fields to walk and muse upon the problem.

Francis Davies Stirn knew that Matthews frequented the Pewter Platter in Cross Street, and so at 10 o'clock that night he made his way thither. In this he was accompanied by Crawford, who had returned from his musing to seek out the German in Owen's coffee-house and was desirous of preventing violence. As they walked, Crawford used all arguments to persuade Stirn from confronting Matthews, but – the German proving utterly obstinate – he swiftly departed at the door of the Pewter Platter, knowing what was likely to happen: for Stirn appeared quite intoxicated by this time.

And so it did. Stirn entered the Pewter Platter and found Matthews sat with some acquaintances. The German's behaviour was erratic, which should have forewarned Matthews what was coming, for he paced wildly about the room while trading comments with his former friend about the situation in the bedchamber pertaining to Matthew's wife. Matthews called Stirn 'a dirty fellow' and said he ought to go back to his own country; whereupon the German produced a piece of paper and held it out as though what was written on it were important. Matthews disregarded the extended arm and so Stirn burnt the note over a candle (it was possibly another challenge to a duel) before pacing about the room as before. In the end he ceased upbraiding his former friend and landlord, and then presented his two pistols: one weapon he fired without warning across the table at Matthews, hitting him in the chest and killing him stone dead on the spot, and the other he fired into his own breast. The second pistol either misfired or else Stirn's attempt was half-hearted, however, and the company in the place leapt upon Stirn and held him until he was arrested. The slaying occurred in the presence of Mr Crawford, who had forced himself to return to the Pewter Platter and so seen the murder committed before his very eyes. Matthews had died without a groan, his body simply starting when the shot hit him before toppling forward onto the table.

Stirn appeared to care not about his own fate, for he shouted, 'Shoot me! Shoot me! For I shall be hanged!' as he was being wrestled to the floor. He was quickly taken and lodged in Newgate pending his trial for shooting Mr Matthews and while awaiting his trial he fasted for a week in the hope he might starve himself to death. When he was brought to the bar of the Old Bailey he was so weak that a chair was procured for him, and he repeatedly passed out when the recorder was pronouncing the mandatory death sentence upon him. Nevertheless, Stirn's arrogance found in him strength enough to request that he might be drawn to the place of execution in a coach; he was told that this luxury could only be granted by the sheriff on the day.

That very night Stirn somehow managed to procure some opium (it was probably smuggled in by a sympathetic German minister who visited), and at nine o'clock at night the keeper of Newgate entered the court, which was still in session, and informed the sheriff that the German appeared to have taken poison, for he was at this very moment crippled with violent convulsions. An apothecary was sent for – the irony being that attempts were frequently made to revive prisoners in this situation only to execute them a few days later; however, it proved impossible to save Stirn. Despite being bled and having medicines forced down his throat he expired two hours later at about 11 o'clock on 15 September 1760. He was aged 25 at the time of his death.

The coroner being summoned, a verdict of 'Self Murder' was brought in and - in consequence of this - Stirn's body was later interred at a crossroads near Battle Bridge (King's Cross) with a stake hammered into his heart. He had been dissected first, pursuant to that part of his sentence, and what a gruesome spectacle this unhappy and tempestuous European must have presented when he was finally buried.

JOURNALISTIC MASS MURDERS

On 21 March 1752 it was reported that a horrific massacre had occurred 'a few days since' at a lonely house in Longparish, a hamlet east of Andover in Hampshire. A gentleman riding past this place between seven and eight at night heard the cry of 'Murder!' Alarmed, he hastened to the pub in the next village where he breathlessly explained what he had heard. It so happened that the owner of the house was there, and he was advised to round up as much assistance as he could before he returned home to see what the matter was. This he did, and, armed with a pistol, the posse went to the man's house.

When they arrived at the house they found the door secured, and so forced it open with a crowbar. The first person they encountered within was a 'gypsy woman' who raged like a wild animal and threatened to stab anyone who came near her; the gentleman who had first raised the alarm took a pistol out of his pocket and shot her through the head. She died instantly, dropping to the floor: the long knife she held slipped from her hand as she did so. Upon this the group proceeded and found 'three men gypsies', who had collected together most of the furniture in the house – having first murdered the owner's wife and two children. They were in the act of preparing to carry their plunder off when the posse discovered them, and, after some resistance, they were all secured.

It is unclear what to make of this story. The papers do not appear to have reported any further details. In the autumn two highwaymen named John Russelwood and John Billington were executed at Winchester gallows, principally for robbing Robert Bromfield, Gent, near Basingstoke. Russelwood in particular was a ruthless criminal, having been the ringleader of a plot to break out of gaol and kill the governor, as well as any others that opposed the escapees. However, there is no suggestion they were involved in the Long Parish murders.

The whole affair is an example of the unreliability of journalistic reporting during these times. Although the story was repeated and reported in other British newspapers, its authenticity is in doubt. Further suspicion is cast on this story because it was re-reported almost word-for-word in early October 1759 – only this time the bloodbath was said to have occurred in Wrotham, a village in Kent between Maidstone and Sevenoaks, with the added detail that a second gypsy died after being shot, as well as the woman.

Stories like this that were suspicious in nature were the bane of the 18th century's newspapers. In April 1789 it was widely reported that a confederacy of pirates and smugglers had been broken up in Dover following the arrest of one Captain Edgeley and two of his men, named Brett and Dixon. The three were taken on suspicion of robbing a whole wash of wet linen from a wrecked vessel, and one of them reportedly turned King's evidence – revealing an alarming operation that involved piracy and many murders. Among their outrages were: the keeping of a murdered corpse at Brett's home for ten days before the gang saw fit to get rid of it by throwing it in the water off Dover; coining dollars at a hideout in Birmingham; and scuttling a Dutch vessel from Amsterdam after slaughtering the entire crew and making off with its cargo of beeswax. It was even reported the beams of this ship could be seen above the waves off the coastline. However, the reports proved to be largely fiction, containing no more truth than the initial arrest of the three looters.

The interesting point is that such a criminal conspiracy was widely believed, and certainly plausible from the point of view of the newspapers - some of whom were supremely annoyed at a retraction they were forced to print when it began to appear the story was a falsehood.

Rumour was often reported as fact by less scrupulous periodicals, and even by the end of the century there were certain cases - widely publicised at the time, even by the most eminent of chroniclers - which a question mark of legitimacy now hangs over.

One such case concerns a brutal incident that supposedly occurred in Dereham, a town in the middle of the county of Norfolk. According to an undated chapbook entitled *The Bloody Tragedy*, one John Day had fallen into a debauched lifestyle, and returned to his parent's home one night in a drunken stupor. Using the vilest language, he threatened the aged couple and demanded money, but after a while they managed to pacify him and get him to go to bed, telling Day that if he still wished money the following morning then he would be given it.

However, John Day roused himself in the middle of the night and stealthily entered his parent's bedchamber, quietly slitting both of his parent's throats from ear to ear. His bloodlust appears to have gotten out of hand, for he 'quartered them in a most cruel manner' before making his way up into the loft. Here the maidservant slept, and Day leapt on her, raping her and then cutting her throat in the same manner as he had his parents. Afterwards, the wicked son rifled every room in the house for anything he might sell before setting the premises alight and slipping away.

The chapbook explains that in the general aftermath of the event John Day expressed public horror at the fire that wiped out his household, and denied he had been at home that evening. However, the truth came out when Day - his money spent - began to sell plate stolen from his parents: questions were raised as to how it escaped unscathed from the burning property, and following this the mass murderer was arrested and committed to gaol.

The following detail makes it clear the story *might* be a fabrication, for the pamphlet's author could not resist explaining how Day was tormented in his jail cell by the spiritual manifestations of his victims, who pointed bloodied accusatory fingers at him and told him that the judgement of the Almighty was upon him. Suffice to say that John Day accepted his fate and admitted he deserved death for his wicked lifestyle of gambling, Sabbath-breaking, drinking and lewd women.

This story, if anything, has a *17th century* feel to it. The tale bears all the melodrama and soap opera worthy of a play made for the stage. However, the Dereham massacre appears to have been touted as a 'real' event, and here the web of confusion that could befog so many reported crimes of the 18th century becomes vividly illustrated. William Jackson, of the Inner Temple, whose *New & Complete Newgate Calendar* was the first attempt to put the crimes of the era into some sort of readable format, considered the Dereham incident worthy of inclusion in his sixth volume as a *real event*. Jackson even recorded that Day was executed 'at Kennington Common about the middle of September 1792, and afterwards hung in chains near the bloody spot'. Kennington Common would have been nowhere near Norfolk, being in the capital, and it is inexplicable why Jackson thought the criminal was executed there. Fundamentally, the whole story illustrates the suspicious confusion that could sometimes engulf certain stories from the period: even as to whether they might be true historical events, half-truths, rumoured events - or complete fabrication.

For those who are interested, Part II of this work charts the years 1760-1799.

END.

INDEX

Printed in Great Britain
by Amazon